A Child's Journey

A CHILD'S
Forces that Shape

JOURNEY

the Lives of Our Young

JULIUS SEGAL, Ph.D.

and Herbert Yahraes

McGRAW-HILL BOOK COMPANY

New York   St. Louis   San Francisco   Düsseldorf
London   Mexico   Sydney   Toronto

The preparation of this book was made possible in part by a grant from the Maurice Falk Medical Fund. However, the statements of fact and expressions of opinion in this book are the sole responsibility of the authors.

Paperback edition, 1979

Library of Congress Cataloging in Publication Data

Segal, Julius, 1924–
A child's journey.

Bibliography: p.
Includes index.
1. Child development. 2. Child psychology. 3. Parent and child. I. Yahraes, Herbert C., joint author. II. Title.
HQ772.S39   301.43'14   77-17602
ISBN 0-07-056038-2

    567890   DODO   8987

This book was set in Caledonia with display lines in Modula Medium by University Graphics, Inc. It was printed and bound by R. R. Donnelley and Sons, Inc. The designer was Christopher Simon. The editors were Thomas Quinn, Cheryl Hanks, and Michael Hennelly. Frank Bellantoni supervised the production.

To the children

Contents

Preface

The subject of this book began to consume my interest one dawn over twenty-five years ago, when a white-coated obstetrician introduced me to a new human being—our daughter, Rebecca. As a new parent—and an only slightly less than new psychologist—I recall my sense of wonderment over the destiny of that infant.

What will she be like—tomorrow, next month, next year? What kind of personality will she have? Will she grow to be happy and well adjusted, or discontented and unable to cope? Has she already inherited what she will become from her parents and forebears? Or will her fate be shaped largely by the world outside her still tiny brain and body?

In the two and a half decades since Rebecca's birth, research aimed at answering such questions has flowered steadily. It has long seemed to me that no subject warranted the attention of a mental health writer more than the outcome of such studies, describing the psychological fate of our children—how they are shaped, their personalities made whole or broken, by the forces at work from the instant of conception.

For many years, therefore, I have written magazine articles dealing with one aspect or another of childhood, hoping all the while one day to tell a more complete story of the forces that shape a child's development. My aim was to produce neither a traditional textbook nor a "how-to" manual of child rearing, but a resource—grounded on research findings—for all of us who care about children and who want, therefore, to know more about why they develop as they do, and what we can and cannot do to shape the outcome of their journey.

The opportunity to do so did not emerge until five years ago, when two events converged in the persons of two dear friends. Norman Garmezy, professor of psychology at the University of Minnesota, began turning my long deferred goal into practical reality by serving as matchmaker between me and the McGraw-Hill Book Company, and his encouragement and wise counsel permeated the work thereafter. At the same time, Herbert Yahraes, a writer who has been my mentor and inspiration for over twenty-five years, decided to reduce his long-standing contractual commitments and devote a portion of his limited time and enormous talent to a collaborative effort.

The result is this book—the product of an exciting passage through the complex literature of child development, countless hours of interviews with authorities in the field, and the synthesizing ruminations that, throughout the years of this book's growth, swirled insistently in our heads.

Our intent is to convey the major outcomes and implications of broad areas of research rather than to identify the specific findings of individual studies. The descriptions of research found in this book, therefore, are often based on a variety of publications by a given investigator. For each investigator cited, all sources used are provided, by chapter, at the close of the book together with a few general references where relevant.

This book is meant to be an account both of exciting scientific efforts and their significance. For the richness of their research and their willingness to discuss it, therefore, we are grateful to the members of the child development research community—a creative network of scientists working tirelessly to uncover the facts about the child's world, and to translate them into practical action.

Thomas H. Quinn, our publisher, provided direction and guidance in rich measure, all of it with remarkable wisdom and patience throughout the years of this book's development.

The task of producing this book, enormous in its scope and complexity, could not have been completed without the financial support provided by the Maurice Falk Medical Fund—permitting the time required for research and writing. Philip B. Hallen, president of the fund, was a generous source of encouragement and assistance.

A pair of young and talented writers—Wray Herbert and Paul Sirovatka—helped in the preparation of Chapters 2 and 11. Joyce Wasserstein, Joyce Cooper, and Susan Clemmer served as research assistants at various periods, and the manuscript itself took shape through the skills and devotion of Harriet Schnapper and Sherry Prestwich.

In writing about the world of children, it was inevitable that the subject matter would evoke reminiscences of childhood and in a few places, such recollections are reported in the first person. Although the book is a product of collaborative effort, the episodes are reported as they were lived—as my own.

Ultimately, the inspiration to write a book such as this derives from personal experience with the subject matter. It is to our own families, therefore—to our wives, Zelda Segal and Dixie Yahraes, and to our children—that we are most indebted. For it is with them that each of us has shared the private events, the dramas of human development, that are the real subject matter of this book.

Julius Segal

Bethesda, Md.

Acknowledgments

Acknowledgments for permission to use excerpts from copyrighted material include:

Leroy F. Aarons, "Chicano Children Shortchanged by Schools, Study Finds," *The Washington Post*, February 5, 1974. Copyright © *The Washington Post*.

Dick Gregory, *nigger: An Autobiography*. Copyright © 1964 by Dick Gregory Enterprises, Inc. Reprinted by permission of the publishers, E. P. Dutton.

A. Kaplan (ed.): *Genetic Factors in Schizophrenia*, 1971. Courtesy of Charles C Thomas, Publisher, Springfield, Illinois.

Kenneth Keniston, "For Him, There is No Exit from the Cellar," *The New York Times*, Feb. 20, 1976. © 1976 by The New York Times Company. Reprinted by permission.

Gregory A. Kimble, Norman Garmezy, and Edward Zigler, *Principles of General Psychology*, Fourth Edition. Copyright © 1974 The Ronald Press Company, New York.

Michael Lewis and Leonard A. Rosenblum, *The Effect of the Infant on Its Caregiver*. Copyright © 1974, John Wiley & Sons, Inc. Reprinted by permission of John Wiley & Sons, Inc.

Margaret Mead, "The Once and Future Home," *The Washington Post*, July 4, 1976. Copyright © *The Washington Post*.

1

How Do They Get That Way?

Helen is a friendly, outgoing twelve-year-old for whom the world is a warm and exciting place. She is an average student and a fine swimmer, and is loved by her friends—a normal, happy human being.

Harold is a high school dropout with a growing police record. He is awash in anger and violence, scarred by insecurity and self-doubts that deny him peace. Harold is a delinquent.

Shirley is a frail three-year-old, silent and waxen, unable or unwilling to speak, incapable of relating at all to the world outside her own shell. She is a young schizophrenic.

How did these children get that way? What determines the course of a child's mental health? Is it accidents of heredity—the roulette wheel of genes and chromosomes—or the child-rearing strategies of parents? Is it the impact of friends, the quality of family life, the stresses of our society, or is a child, as psychologists strongly believed just a few decades ago, simply "born that way"? What is it that causes one child to be aggressive and another passive, withdrawn or friendly, depressed or optimistic, focused on goals and achievement or mired in self-deprecation and defeat? Moreover, why do some children, although beset by massive trauma, bend but never break, while others appear to crumble in the face of apparently far lesser stress?

This book is intended to provide the considerable light that behavioral science can now shed on the enigma of the child's unfolding world. It grew out of the conviction that parents, teachers, doctors, and all those who deal with children deserve to have distilled for them the maze of information—and misinformation—available about the forces at play in our children's development.

The effort was stimulated also by the awareness that simple and unequivocal answers to complex questions adults ask about their children's mental health do little service to either the parents or their children. Researchers have learned a great deal about the subject, but despite the glib pronouncements of those who offer quick "conclusions" for fun and profit, there are many questions to which answers from science continue to be either ambiguous or altogether unavailable. It will help us all, as guardians of our young, to know what we do *not* know for certain as well as what seems clear in the light of research.

For reasons of order and clarity, the organization of this book dictates that each of the major factors thought to affect the emotional life of the child be described individually, apart from the others. In the real world, however, no such independence exists among the factors. A child's development is likely to be shaped by a number of forces, all of them interacting in ways that either intensify or subdue the impact of any one of them. Genetic endowment, experiences with mother, sibling order, relationships with peers, social upheavals—no one of these exists altogether apart from the others. The reader should remember, therefore, that, although a particular factor is being scrutinized, it is only one of a number of interlocking forces operating simultaneously.

Research on the child's behavioral development is today a thriving scientific enterprise. In universities, medical schools, clinics, and hospitals across the land, hundreds of scientists set out each day to throw additional light on the ways a child evolves into a psychological entity—with a personality, attitudes, and behavior that stamp him or her as an individual.

Today's child development researchers include, for example, psychologists studying the impact of the mother on the newborn infant, psychiatrists analyzing the family relationships of mentally ill children, sociologists assessing the impact of poverty and racial discrimination, and geneticists tracking the effect of heredity on a child's psychological destiny. Their efforts are steadily unraveling the mysteries surrounding the psychological flowering of a child, the processes by which a spot of protoplasm ultimately becomes either a happy and productive youngster or a sick and defeated one.

No book, however weighty, could possibly encompass all the research designed to clarify how children become what they are. From this massive effort we have drawn largely on a relatively small number of illustrative studies, along with interviews with key investigators in the field.

In every age, men and women have recognized the special importance of the child's role in society. Whether through ancient tribal initiation rites or the pronouncements of contemporary child development theorists, each succeeding civilization has acknowledged that our children will carry after us the imprint of the world we create around them. The impulse to improve the world of the young has been present always, but paradoxically, the child has also been a chronic victim of our negligence and brutality. We have not yet linked our best instincts with comparable action.

This book is intended to help forge that link, not from theory or opinion, but from the findings of child development studies. The data reported here have been filtered through our own minds not only as mental health professionals but, equally important, as parents concerned about the fate of children. We have not been satisfied simply with reporting the findings reached by researchers; we have also mined them for their implications for all those who deal in any way with the young. We have sought to report not just the facts but also the messages they imply. Therefore, the book provides guidance and direction— based on the best evidence available—for protecting the mental health of our children.

The actions of our forebears toward their children, the next chapter makes clear, were often based on unfounded theories and misguided convictions—with results that were not always in the best interest either of the young or their parents. Today our fund of knowledge is considerably greater, but that knowledge alone serves little purpose. Knowing how children "get that way" is meaningful only if, as a result, we act more effectively as advocates of our young.

Searching for the Key
From Brain Cells to Society

"It's all a matter of the body's fluids. The baby's personality is in those juices right from the start."

"Totally blank, that's what they are. It's the environment that takes over with the first breath."

"They're all born in the grasp of Satan. Some will shake loose, some won't."

"It's Mom—she's the key. Either she sets her kids up, or she ruins them for life."

In broad paraphrase, those views of child development were voiced through the centuries by figures as diverse as Hippocrates, Locke, Calvin, and Freud. They are only four of a parade of philosophers, poets, physicians, clergymen, and armchair experts who have claimed to possess the key to understanding why children develop as they do.

Their impact has been enormous. In every age, attitudes toward children—and techniques of parenting—have been shaped by the underlying convictions of adults about "what makes kids tick" in the first place. Unfortunately, these convictions, more often than not, have lacked scientific foundation, and the resulting attempts to help the child frequently have been misguided or even perverse.

Few subjects have inspired such extreme viewpoints as the sources of a child's personality. Rarely have opinions reached for a middle ground; rather, views have been entrenched on one side or another of a

4

pseudoscientific debate—as if the mystery of child development could be solved with one convincing clue, or one blinding flash of adult insight. The enigmas of human development have not yielded to such simple solutions. The child's fate could not be explained in a single stroke, no matter how hard our forebears tried.

The Child's Nature or the World's Nurture

Underlying virtually all the theories and convictions about children has been a division of opinion on a basic issue: Is the child a product of heredity or environment? Even until quite recently, it was fashionable among psychologists to side with "nature" on the one hand, or "nurture" on the other, as the cause of psychological health or illness in children. Where one stressed only what the child brings into life, the other emphasized only the experiences that life brings.

The argument was not lost on the front lines of child rearing in homes across the land: "She's got the old man's genes," one grandmother might argue. "She can't go wrong." "He grew up in squalor," father might recall. "He never had a chance." The extremists on each side, both professors and parents, denied even an ancillary role to the opposition.

The nature-or-nurture argument has become *the* cliché of child psychology, and it is difficult, in retrospect, to imagine how hard the lines were drawn on the issue just a few decades ago. Advocates on either side of the debate came by their positions honestly, however, reflecting major currents of thought that have swirled among philosophers and child development theorists over the centuries.

Perhaps the original advocate for the importance of the child's physical nature in shaping mental health was Hippocrates. He suggested that every person is born with a unique proportioning of the "four bodily humours"—phlegm, blood, black bile, and yellow bile—which determined not only physical health but temperament. The variety of human personalities, Hippocrates explained, was the result of these four fluids. Some people, with more yellow bile than others, were "choleric"—easily angered—while others, with an excess of blood, were more "sanguine"—cheerful and buoyant. The humors were also regarded as the physiological basis of severe mental disorders: Depression, for example, was diagnosed as an extreme excess of black bile. Epilepsy, mania, paranoia, and many psychosomatic disorders were similarly diagnosed, signaling a medical, drug-oriented approach to emotional problems which is still important today.

It was not until the rediscovery in 1900 of Gregor Mendel's notes on the crossbreeding of pea plants that genetic research took strong hold. What the Austrian monk had called *elements* were soon relabeled *genes* and *chromosomes,* and it was then just a short but intricate biochemical step to our modern understanding of hereditary pedigree as one important key to child development.

Before Mendel, however, there were various notions about that part of a child's personality that is "given." It was commonly believed in the nineteenth century, though even medical researchers did not know precisely why, that children received not only their hair color and physical stature from their parents but also their parents' germs—so that syphilitic or insane parents would inevitably beget syphilitic and insane children. Parental values and ideas, whether criminal or scholarly, were similarly bequeathed. A corollary belief was that when a man and woman mate, their blood mixes forever, with the result that a child by a second marriage would inherit characteristics—skin color, disease, or morality—from the mother's first partner.

"The sins of the fathers," Ibsen wrote in his 1881 play *Ghosts,* "shall be visited upon the children"—a biblical notion that the dramatist derived also from considerable theory in the air at that time. Some doctors suggested that the child receives the entire emotional and mental history of both parents at conception, leaving virtually no room for individual personality development. From another quarter came the theory that it is the child's physical legacy—overall body build—that determines personality. In 1921, psychiatrist Ernst Kretschmer, for example, identified three body types which, he claimed, were directly related to personality and emotional disorder. The *pyknics*—short and stocky—tended to be moody and extroverted, and in extreme cases, this physique was associated with manic-depression. Likewise, the *leptosomes*—tall and gaunt—were invariably shy and introverted and, again in the extreme, schizophrenic. The *athletics* were what they are popularly portrayed to be even today—well proportioned both physically and emotionally.

As the field of biochemistry matured, there were naturally many notions about the relationship between body chemistry and personality. In 1928, biochemist Gilbert Rich, for example, searched for the key to temperamental extremes in the alkaline level of saliva and urine. Though his idea was too simplistic and unsupported by laboratory research, Rich was heading in what would prove to be a very important research direction. Roger Williams, in his biochemistry texts of three decades ago, came closer to our contemporary understanding when he suggested that both anatomy and physiology affect personality, but through very complex interaction of the endocrine system, nervous system, blood chemistry, and the neuromuscular and gastrointestinal network—all inherited equipment.

The extremist position on the role of heredity lives on, even today, in the theory of controversial psychologist Arthur Jensen that racial differences in intelligence are determined largely by heredity. As much as 80 percent of a child's intelligence is inherited, he estimated in 1969, through genes that may influence also the average endowment for intelligence among members of a given race. The bottom line of Jensen's views was read to be that blacks are intellectually inferior to whites. The ensuing controversy, discussed in Chapter 11, beclouded the scientific issues and disinterred the nature-nurture controversy.

It took many years before students of child development—medical researchers primarily—started distinguishing between the influences of genetic heritage and prenatal experiences. In the nineteenth century, there was a popular folk theory that the actual instant of conception—neither the parents' genetic legacy nor the child's social experiences, but that one unpredictable moment—was the key to the child's emotional future. If either parent, but particularly the mother, was irritable or exhausted, the infant might be born pathologically lethargic or apathetic. If the mother had a nasty thought at the instant of conception, she might give birth to an incurable pervert.

This idea was soon extended to the entire pregnancy: women were advised to avoid sex during pregnancy lest the child be born impotent, and to eschew everything from arguments to tobacco to whiskey. Though many of these notions have not held up under scientific scrutiny, others have survived. Childhood *in utero*—between the joining of the seeds and the delivery from the womb—is now recognized as a period not only of physical formation but of emotional formation as well. It was the thalidomide tragedy of the late 1950s, more than any other event, that focused professional attention on pregnancy itself, and researchers have since investigated everything from the mother's diet and social habits to her socioeconomic situation and mental state as possible factors affecting the child's personality.

Among the first to argue for the environment as the basis of child development was seventeenth-century philosopher John Locke. He insisted that each child comes into the world "tabula rasa," a blank slate to be filled by experience, by sensation. But Locke offered little in the way of evidence to back up his educational philosophy, and the environmentalists had to wait until 1859 and the publication of Charles

Darwin's *On the Origin of Species* for a scientific advocate. With the same intellect that he turned to fossils and fauna, Darwin watched his own son grow in the cradle and looked for analogues of the species' evolution in the actions and reactions of babies. Darwin suggested that the human child carries with it the biological history of the race, but at the same time struggles to adapt to society. The growing child is a flux of warring responses, with the "fittest" behaviors establishing themselves as part of the child's personality at various stages of development. A growing child, like an evolving species, Darwin suggested, adapts—or tries to adapt—to constant variations in the environment.

In the twentieth century, John B. Watson carried Locke's philosophical tenet to its extreme, proving its validity, he insisted, not through introspection but through rigorous experimentation. He stripped the child of its mystery, viewing it as a "lively squirming bit of flesh," and, building upon experimental psychologist E. L. Thorndike's theory of associationism, he insisted that personality is exclusively a result of conditioning—of administering the appropriate schedule of rewards and punishments. A certain measure of energy causes a certain physical response, he claimed, and child rearing—indeed, life—is that simple. Administer a given stimulus, he argued, and get a given response.

Care givers were everything to the strict environmentalist. "Parents do the emotional planting and the cultivating," insisted Watson. "At three years of age the child's whole emotional life plan has been laid down, his emotional disposition set. At that age the parents have already determined for him whether he is to grow into a happy person, wholesome and good-natured, whether he is to be a whining, complaining neurotic, an anger-driven, vindictive, overbearing slave driver, or one whose every move in life is definitely controlled by fear."

Watson frightened many young parents by his insistence that the newborn is nothing more than a bundle or unorganized reflexes—that all infants are the same at the start, and whatever they become later, is the result of what we do to them: "Give me a dozen healthy infants," Watson boasted, "and I'll guarantee to take any one at random and train him to become a doctor, a lawyer, artist, merchant. . . ." Psychologist B. F. Skinner, more than anyone else, has perpetuated and popularized the Watsonian spirit. In his utopian novel, *Walden Two*, he prescribed a system for "engineering" the behavior of children through an elaborate schedule of rewards, calling attention also to the natural reinforcements of the social environment. The real goal of science, Skinner insists, is to create the kind of environment for children which will, by its very nature, reinforce healthy behaviors.

But while Watson and Skinner were laying down the foundations of modern behaviorism, psychology was moving also from the pragmatic to the analytic—from an attention not to visible behaviors, but to hidden dynamics. Among the psychoanalysts—extraordinarily influential as child development theorists—there was evolving a view of the child containing a peculiar blend of allegiance to both innate and environmental forces.

The Couch in the Cradle

In 1900, Swedish essayist Ellen Key predicted that the twentieth century would be the "Century of the Child," and as if to prove her point, Sigmund Freud made his historic visit to Clark University four years later to shake up the academic community with his theory of infantile sexuality. The Viennese doctor thus forever marred the image of childhood innocence. The beginning years were suddenly thought to be filled with turbulent and complex sexual stirrings, and the modern era of "watch-your-step, mother" child rearing was underway.

It is difficult even today to estimate the influence of Freudian childhood theory. He certainly was not the first to suspect the importance of the infant's experiences, but he did call special attention to the mental life of the infant, and he underscored, more than anyone before, the significance of early emotional events. The bonds that tied children to parents had been so uncomplicated—love and obedience; now, however, with the "psychoanalytic revolution," parenting was suddenly a complex ordeal; simple slips could bring disastrous results.

Though the importance of the mother in a child's development had always been taken for granted, never had she been charged with such responsibility. The role of the mother, Freud insisted, is "unique, without parallel, established unalterably for a whole lifetime as the first and strongest love object, and the prototype of all later love relations. . . ." For many of his American professional contemporaries, Freud was too often clinical and poetic, too seldom scientific and statistical. He had no laboratory experiments to support his theory; instead he brought Ernest Jones along to the United States to demonstrate the "truth" of the Oedipal complex through a reading of *Hamlet*.

Freud was also accompanied to Massachusetts by a young student, Carl Gustav Jung, who would, in time, introduce his theory of the collective unconscious: The child, he would say, is influenced not only by early sexual experiences but also by the mythic residue from eons of history—by ancient psychic facts, or archetypes, that are his birthright.

But even more than Freud, Jung turned not to the data of science but to literature—to such sources as the Tibetan *Book of the Dead* and Joyce's *Ulysses*—in support of his notions.

The lack of objective data from the private consultation rooms of the earliest analysts did not inhibit the wide acceptance of their ideas. Slowly, however, the strictly Freudian notions were altered and embellished. Among Freud's modern interpreters and followers, there have been acknowledgments that not everything a child becomes is due to subterranean psychic forces. The child's natural equipment or the child's culture may also be at work.

Alfred Adler, more than any other of the psychoanalytic school, for example, stressed the importance of physique in the child's social and emotional development. Children who are born deformed, he pointed out, are constantly comparing themselves with the "normals" and trying to compensate for their physical handicaps. Their personalities are molded by their constant need to compensate, and the result is often the now well-known "inferiority complex." Family position can similarly cause such a complex, taught Adler, with siblings struggling to make up for their age and size, and developing emotional problems as a result.

Karen Horney also reinterpreted Freud, switching the emphasis from the child's instincts to society—to what she called *cultural contradictions.* Childhood insecurity is the root of later mental illness, according to Horney, and results when children grow up on the one hand hearing about ideals such as altruism and on the other hand seeing the reality—selfishness.

For psychoanalyst Otto Rank, neither unconscious psychic juices nor outside social forces were the critical factor in the child's psychological fate. Rank focused on birth itself—the trauma of being born into an impersonal universe—as the source of emotional problems in children. This single harsh experience more than the sweep of Oedipal feelings or cultural conflicts, he believed, molded the young personality.

It was analyst Harry Stack Sullivan who directed attention to the child's social relationships, suggesting that the young personality is affected profoundly by interactions not just with parents but also with siblings, peers, and all those "significant others" who move in and out of the child's life space. A child's self-concept and world view are a complex product of all the child's episodes with these others: how these others deal with the child determines whether his or her perceptions—and behaviors—will be distorted or normal. More important,

Sullivan taught that personality development is not irreversible, as Freud implied, nor is it confined to the first few years of life; deviant behaviors and misperceptions can be corrected by later social encounters.

Even among child experts bound together by the label "psychoanalyst," it is clear that child development theories varied widely. In one respect, however, they were similar: Though often profound, their insights sprang primarily from well-worn couches, not from the research laboratory.

The Leap from Theory to Practice

It has always been just a short step from theories of child development to instructional manuals on parenting. How parents have raised their children has depended heavily on the basic assumptions they adopted about childhood and, in fact, about human nature.

Modern parents, of course, do not turn directly to pediatric journals or psychoanalytic literature, any more than eighteenth-century parents turned to philosophical treatises in deciding how to deal with their young. What parents read are the "manuals" and magazine articles that address themselves to the techniques of parenting. With the publication of John Holt's classic, *The Care and Feeding of Children,* in 1894, and the Yale studies of child development by Arnold Gesell beginning a few decades later, parents—and particularly mothers—were transformed into technicians.

Parenting manuals are not unique to this century. The Rev. John Abbott's *Mother at Home,* published in 1833, was probably the first popular guide of this type, emphasizing, in typically Puritan tones, the child's tyrannical nature, and *Godey's Lady's Book*—a nineteenth-century woman's magazine—offered advice to mothers long before *Redbook.* What is unique today is the diversity and overwhelming number of child-rearing manuals from which modern parents can choose. It has been estimated that most bookstores today stock an average of 30 such manuals ranging from Dr. James Dobson's *Dare to Discipline,* which recommends pinching and other methods of inflicting pain, to Dr. Haim Ginott's *Between Parent and Child,* which stresses that parents must learn to communicate with rather than judge their children. There is still vast disagreement on the best methods of parenting, and they continue to spring, as they always have, from adult convictions about why children are as they are.

Calvinist parents, for example, believing that babies arrived in a stained and sinful state, felt that children could best be raised by austere and repressive measures. Early American settlers—influenced by Calvin's belief that children brought into the world with them the burden of original sin—saw no choice but to *defeat* the child, to bend the child's satanic will with hard work and constant and often severe punishment. It was less important to raise a mentally healthy child than it was to raise a saved child, and although a child could be chosen for salvation only by the grace of God, it was essential to *appear* saved. A chosen child was somber, even morose, while the clear signs of damnation were playfulness, cheeriness, and energy. As a result, the childhood vitality that might normally go into play was quickly turned by adults to labor. Directly out of the cradle, the child's work was rigorous and full time; seven-year-old Calvinists were hardened laborers, and even toddlers had assigned household chores.

Locke, by writing *Some Thoughts Concerning Education,* in the seventeenth century wiped out the concept of inborn depravity for generations of children to come. Childhood personality, he suggested, was constructed gradually as bits and pieces of the environment were encountered: "delight in discovery" became, for the first time, an important educational idea—an idea that has been carried into the Headstart programs of today, emphasizing early enrichment of the child's experiences.

Locke's work was not simply an elitist philosophical tract to be circulated among the cultured and academic. For years, in fact, his ideas were popularized through calendars—with a Locke quote for every month—that hung in many homes, so that they were quickly translated into the nuts and bolts of child rearing. But though he enlightened many parents, Locke was by no means soft on children: Speaking with one voice as physician and moralist, he prescribed punishment worthy of the most misguided Watsonian parent almost three centuries later. Put cold water on their little feet and make them wear thin-soled shoes, he advised, to prepare children for the cruelties and uncertainties of life.

As the Calvinist view was gradually relaxed during the eighteenth and nineteenth centuries, and damnation was no longer a foregone conclusion, parenting took on a new importance. It was the parent's responsibility now to keep the child from *learning* sin—an idea that acutely affected child rearing. Toilet training, for example, was viewed as a moral victory. Swaddling was commonly used to prevent masturbation and crying—both considered signs of Satan's presence—and if crying persisted, various substances were liberally administered, from sugar to alcohol and other drugs. Godfrey's Cordial—a potion laced with the opiate laudanum—was very popular, especially among the wealthy, as a tool for keeping annoying infants quiet and Satan in tow.

Probably one of the most influential parenting "manuals" was not a manual at all, but Jean-Jacques Rousseau's educational treatise in the form of a novel, *Emile,* published in the eighteenth century. It, too, was based on the author's own view of human development. In writing the narrative of Emile's upbringing, Rousseau produced one of the most radical documents of the time, for he proposed that parents cannot, regardless of method, improve on nature in raising children. The child is worthy of dignity, he insisted, not because he will someday contribute to adult society but simply because the child possesses a natural dignity. The child is a "noble savage," born with an intuitive sense of right and wrong: "God makes all things good," he stated, turning Calvin on his head. Only when man meddles with them do they become evil.

The implications of such a document for parenting were profound, for the essence of bringing up children was no longer to command obedience, but rather to indulge—to allow the games, the freedom, the innocence of growing children. Rousseau introduced the idea of child development as *unfoldment* or maturation—the idea, so familiar now, that children grow through a series of natural stages. Whereas Locke had viewed child development as passive and receptive, responding to the stimuli of the exterior world, Rousseau insisted that children actively engage their surroundings—organizing world data as their own personalities unfold. The role of the parent, Rousseau suggested, was simply not to interfere, and by not interfering, to offer the ideal milieu for growth.

While the importance of parenting has long been debated, an obsession with the mother's special contribution to the child's development has been largely a twentieth-century phenomenon. Unencumbered by scientific data, theorists have found little difficulty in "explaining" why the mother's role is so critical. Psychologist Paul Mobius, for example, suggested that attachment to children by mothers is natural, for it is a function of certain lobes of the brain—lobes which are larger in women than in men. For Freud, in contrast, the awesome infant-mother bond was forged between sucking mouth and milk-filled mammaries.

No better example exists of the translation of unsubstantiated theories into rigid practices than that made on the subject of breast-feeding. To nurse or not to nurse: That decision has been often based on the

presumed importance of the offered breast in the child's later psychological destiny.

Early in the seventeenth century, Moravian educational reformer and
theologian Johann Amos Comenius taught that nursing by mothers is
critical for a child's proper ethical development. A mother passes on her
morals through her milk, he insisted, and to depend on the milk of a
"wet nurse" hired for suckling was to risk infecting the infant with
lower-class morality. Despite such pronouncements, the practice of
engaging a wet nurse to satisfy a baby's feeding needs was fairly
common even in the early 1900s—an implicit acknowledgment among
many parents that the practical matter of nourishment is unrelated to
the ties that bind mother and child. It was not long afterward, however,
that the teachings of Freud would swing attention dramatically once
again to maternal breast-feeding as the fount of the child's psychological destiny.

For many mothers growing up in the Freudian tradition, breast-
feeding became virtually a test of maternal skill and power. Freud,
perhaps the leading celebrant of mother, warned parents that suckling
is not just a method of supplying nourishment to an infant. It is a sexual
experience: the infant—every infant, normal and abnormal—becomes
attached to the mother's breast as a sexual object, and subsequently to
the mother. Childhood behaviors, from thumb sucking to masturbation,
could be traced to an erotic attachment to the mother's breast.

But while mother was being canonized in one psychological quarter,
she was losing a large measure of her importance in others. To a strict
Watsonian it made no difference who administered the rewards and
punishments, as long as the schedule was rigorous and consistent; any
care giver—from father to cousin to neighbor—could "mother" the
child. Rousseau's notion of unfoldment was given modern voice by
Gesell who, while nodding to the role of the mother, never budged
from his belief that it is primarily germ plasm—the bearer of genetic
information—that directs the child's life. This notion was modified by
the ubiquitous Benjamin Spock, who has now told mothers to relax, to
trust their feelings, and to enjoy watching their children grow—a
welcome reprieve from the horrific warnings of Freud and Watson.

The impact of theory on practice continues unabated. Though they
are unaware of it, American parents continue to reflect in their child-
rearing approaches convictions as strong as those of Calvinists or
Freudians. The father who will batter his child tonight out of a belief
that the infant was "born bad" is a throwback to the most repressive
Colonial parent, and still functions without solid information about the
true nature of child development. And, the mother who is racked with

guilt over what she—and she alone—did to "make my son neurotic" might just now have stepped out of an anxiety-provoking but data-free psychoanalytic lecture of 1910.

Such parents—and millions more like them—need not continue facing their children in ignorance. We can turn increasingly now not to unfounded theories, personal biases, or arbitrary "how-to" manuals, but rather to the growing body of exciting and instructive scientific information being gathered by today's new breed of child development researchers.

Building a Science of the Child's World

Many childhood historians point to the publication of Rousseau's *Emile* in 1762 as the beginning of the formal discipline of child study. In writing a narrative of Emile's upbringing—of the child's passage through varied stages of development—Rousseau inspired the first really scientific observation of infants by the Swiss educator Johann Heinrich Pestalozzi and signaled the beginning of a new trend: Parent-as-scientist. Childhood psychology owes a great deal to Doddy Darwin, Polly Watson, and Jacqueline Piaget—children who obliged their fathers by growing up under their scientific gaze.

Freud, too, despite his heavy reliance on the subjective reports of patients, deserves credit for sparking a devotion to child research. Although he never actually engaged even in clinical work with the young before completing his theory of infant sexuality in 1905, that startling theory signaled the scientist's serious interest in children. Childhood had been worked over by philosophers and religious zealots, and embraced by social reformers and poets, but only in the twentieth century has there been a concentrated scientific effort to understand how children get the way they are. Finally, researchers turned to children themselves in an attempt to structure a science of childhood, with painstaking observations of their subjects—at birth, in the cradle, the playground, the school, the community.

The names of history's grand theorists—from Locke and Rousseau to Freud and Spock—are so familiar to us today in part because they offered dramatic and often emotional pronouncements about the child's nature or nurture, not conclusions based on hard data. If some of the earlier controversies have abated in the recent decades, it is because both the hereditarians and the environmentalists began turning to scientific analyses of the child's world and, in doing so, discovered that the answers lay somewhere toward the center of yesterday's extreme viewpoints. By studying children directly, investigators could actually test, rather than theorize about, the importance of genes or mothers or family dynamics. And they found, early on, that while some childhood behaviors may develop regardless of environment, others are clearly catalyzed by experience.

The science of the child's world, unlike the theories, did not come into existence by fiat, nor can it be dated. The large mass of data that is now being accumulated about childhood is the product not of a few armchair superstars, but of many people with the relatively unfamiliar names found throughout this book—Rosenthal, Parke, Chess and Thomas, Bell, Yarrow, Brazelton, Garmezy, Rutter, Kagan, Mercer, Fraiberg, Hartup—and many others who are their kindred in child development laboratories around the world.

We know now from piecing together the results of various studies that a child's emotional health is a complex product of many forces— the information contained in each unique genetic configuration, prenatal diet, infantile attachments, parental attitudes, familial dynamics, social pressures and more—the influences, in short, of both nature and nurture. It is clear today that even traditionally "social" diseases— childhood alcoholism, for example, or delinquency—grow also out of both hereditary and constitutional factors; it is equally clear that an apparently normal newborn baby can be transformed by sufficiently deleterious social forces into a hapless victim of mental illness. The relevant question is no longer whether a child's behavior has innate or environmental roots, but how the two are related, and how stable the behavior is—how resistant or responsive to outside influences.

We know today, too, that developmental threads are not isolated and distinct but rather dynamic and interacting to form a pattern. A mother's behavior toward her infant, for example, does not exist apart from a particular family context, and the family cannot be understood apart from the social and economic milieu in which it functions. A child's emotional well-being depends on the biochemistry of the brain as well as on the quality of mother-child relationship, on interactions with peers as well as on the values of political leaders, on physical constitution as well as on family stress.

The skein of childhood behavior is a many-stranded thing, and science has taken important and dramatic steps toward sorting out these strands. With the grandiose theories discarded, or at least held in abeyance, serious students of childhood have begun accumulating a body of solid information about our children's mental health—working not toward one grand answer, but toward a mosaic of many answers to one grand question: How do they get that way?

3

The Genetic Factor

Helping to shape the child from the moment of conception are the elements of heredity—the genes of the father carried in the wriggling sperm, the genes of the mother embodied in the waiting egg. The genetic blueprints packed into these microscopic cells have long been known to determine, among a myriad of other characteristics, the color of the child's eyes, the shape of the nose, the pigmentation of the skin, the curliness of the hair, and the limits on eventual height. Now, contrary to widespread beliefs of even a few years ago, research has shown that the genes also have a major influence on the emotional well-being and mental health of children, and of the adolescents and adults they will become.

That conclusion is based, in part, on follow-up studies of the psychological fate of children whose heredity appears clouded from the beginning. Peggy is one such child—a young girl of superior intelligence who had always been regarded as sensitive, and in the words of psychiatrist E. James Anthony, "given to taking life over seriously." All the same, she was fairly popular with her classmates.

"One day, on the playground at school, when Peggy was eight," Anthony reports, "she was asked by a boy to throw him a rock so that he could bat it with a stick. Before she could bring herself to realize that this was against the rules, she had done so, and immediately she was overcome with guilt and remorse. When they went into the classroom again, she felt as if everybody was staring at her and that the teacher was paying special attention to her."

All of a sudden, Peggy noticed, the boy involved in the situation went up to the teacher's desk, whispered to her and went out. The boy had simply asked permission to go to the boys' room, but Peggy was sure that he had told on her and had been sent to the office to make a full report. She became terror-stricken and broke into loud crying. The teacher was unable to comfort her. Peggy felt that she was trapped and was about to be terribly punished.

Her fears persisted at home, so Anthony admitted her to a hospital, where she thought he was simply trying to get her to confess. Gradually, however, her suspicions subsided, and within three months "she resumed her normal, pleasantly cooperative behavior and was even able to laugh at the silly ideas she once had had. She returned to school and continued to do very well."

Eighteen months later, Anthony saw her for an episode which, considered alone, appeared minor. Peggy was disturbed by some pimples on her skin, and she felt that some of the children might have been slipping in offensive additions to her diet. This crisis quickly subsided.

Peggy is helping to make medical history because—together with thousands of other children—she is participating in longitudinal studies to determine the fate of children of mentally ill parents. Peggy's mother has been hospitalized twice for schizophrenia of the paranoid type. Taken together, Anthony believes, the episodes in Peggy's life described here are quite likely to foreshadow serious mental illness. Many children with similar backgrounds, however, do not suffer serious mental health problems; like the children in numerous other such investigations in this country and abroad, therefore, Peggy will be followed well into adulthood in order to obtain accurate answers to such questions as:

• How important is the genetic factor in the major mental illnesses—schizophrenia and depression in all their forms?
• If a child has inherited a parent's predisposition to mental illness, what factors in the environment—including events before and around the time of birth—can trigger this predisposition and, along with it, lead to a breakdown?
• What environmental and genetic factors help protect a child who is at risk, so that he or she never develops a serious mental illness?

Until recently, knowledge of the events leading to serious mental illness was based on retrospective investigations—those that start with the sick person and attempt to find pertinent information about the case all the way back to birth and before. A far greater volume of accurate, pertinent, and useful information is likely to be turned up by longitudinal studies which seek to record the influences on a person's development as they take place, beginning in childhood or at least early adolescence.

Very few of the longitudinal studies have been under way long enough to have produced substantial results. Through other means, however, research has already contributed a large store of knowledge about the genetic factors involved in a child's psychological development. No insight into the origins of mental health problems of children is complete without that knowledge.

Schizophrenia: A Tragic Inheritance

A common way of estimating the strength of the hereditary factor in mental illness—or any other condition—is to look for that condition among the relatives of people manifesting it. In the case of schizophrenia, 15 investigators cited by National Institute of Mental Health (NIMH) psychologist David Rosenthal did so among the parents and siblings of known schizophrenics. They found rates of schizophrenia among parents of schizophrenic offspring running as high as 12 percent, in contrast to 1 percent in the general population. Among the brothers and sisters of the patients, the rates ran somewhat higher.

Six of the studies made it possible to compare two groups of families—those in which neither parent of the afflicted child had schizophrenia and those in which at least one parent had it. Where neither parent had been stricken, from 6 to 12 percent of the brothers and sisters of the schizophrenic child had schizophrenia, too. Where at least one parent was sick, this proportion was considerably higher—from 8 to 34 percent.

Identical twins provide another popular tool for investigating hereditary forces. Such twins have developed from a single egg in their mother's ovary, an egg that has split into two so that the twins have identical genes—and, as one consequence, look alike. If one identical twin develops schizophrenia, the co-twin often develops it, too. But fraternal twins, which arise from two separate eggs, are no more alike genetically than ordinary brothers and sisters.

Geneticists Irving I. Gottesman and James Shields studied 24 pairs of identical twins and 33 pairs of fraternal. In each pair of twins, at least one was schizophrenic. Among the identical pairs, 40 percent of the co-twins had the same disease. In the language of research, 40 percent of the pairs of identical twins, each with the identical genetic inheritance, were *concordant* for schizophrenia. Among the fraternal pairs, however, only 10 percent were concordant.

Two other geneticists, G. E. McClearn and J. C. DeFries, cite seven studies—compiled by L. L. Heston—of 358 pairs of identical twins. In each case, one member of the pair was known to be schizophrenic, and in 46 percent of the cases, the other member also had the disease or developed it later.

Clearly, heredity plays a major—but by no means the only—role in the development of this psychosis. To check results from the research on families and on twins, investigators in recent years have turned to adoption studies. These researchers have been particularly interested in ruling out the possibility that schizophrenia in the child with one or two schizophrenic parents might have been produced simply by exposure to severe family stress and bizarre parental behavior. In such research the investigator may start with schizophrenic adults who were adopted early in life, and then look for evidence of schizophrenia in the patients' natural and adopted relatives. Or the investigator may start with adults known to have had at least one schizophrenic parent and to have been adopted as children by presumably normal foster parents. Such studies are most often undertaken in the Scandinavian countries, where records of adoptions and of psychiatric histories are unusually reliable and complete.

The results of adoption studies again highlight the genetic factor. Even when the children of schizophrenic parents were raised by normal foster parents, a significantly greater proportion of them—as compared with children of nonschizophrenic parents—eventually became schizophrenic themselves. Yet the rate of schizophrenia among the foster parents of the children who became schizophrenic was no higher than among the foster parents of normal children.

For example, Seymour S. Kety, David Rosenthal, and their associates studied 150 blood relatives of adopted children who became schizophrenic and about the same number of blood relatives of adopted children who did not become schizophrenic. Thirteen of the first group were found to have schizophrenia, in contrast to only three of the second. The children with schizophrenia, then, had four times as many blood relatives with the same disorder as the nonschizophrenic children.

If one individual closely related to a schizophrenic patient eventually develops the illness, why don't more of the other close relatives do so as well? In particular, if there is a strong hereditary factor, why is the concordance rate for schizophrenia in identical twins not more than 40 or 50 percent?

One answer is that the identical twins who do not develop schizophrenia, even though they have a schizophrenic co-twin, may develop other mental abnormalities, presumably under the influence of the gene or genes for schizophrenia. From the seven studies noted earlier, for example, it would appear that, on the average, 46 percent of the co-twins of schizophrenic identical twins also developed schizophrenia. But these studies found, too, that another 41 percent of the co-twins had other mental abnormalities. Among these was *borderline schizophrenia,* a poorly defined state in which a person may appear fairly normal most of the time but have brief psychotic intervals. Ronald O. Rieder, a research psychiatrist at NIMH, gives an example. Every few months a young working woman who shared an apartment with another young woman became convinced that her friend was a lesbian and was trying to seduce her. So she stormed out of the apartment. In a few days she returned and asked how she could have been so crazy. Such brief episodes are referred to as "micropsychotic." Rieder's laboratory is trying to define borderline schizophrenia and determine how widespread it actually is. "It may be the most prevalent of the schizophrenic illnesses," he observes, "if it really is a schizophrenic illness."

Other abnormalities often found in the families of schizophrenics are *schizoid state* or *schizoid personality,* which may be manifested by seclusiveness, oversensitivity, antisocial activity, particularly among males, and other abnormal behavior. Frequently present also is evidence of *neurosis.* Less than 13 percent of the nonschizophrenic twins in the seven studies reported earlier were completely normal or had only a mild abnormality.

There is another reason that the identical twin of a schizophrenic may not break down: differences in environmental factors can make one twin more vulnerable to schizophrenia than the other, even though, biologically, both contain exactly the same hereditary material.

The importance of such environmental factors has been demonstrated in a study, carried out by NIMH researchers William Pollin, James R. Stabenau, and others, of schizophrenic twins and their identical but nonschizophrenic co-twins. The twins who eventually became schizophrenic, the investigators found, were usually the ones who had weighed less at birth. Because of their lower weight, the parents from the very beginning had perceived them as weaker and more vulnerable to all kinds of hazards than their co-twins. And because of the parental worry and the stress that resulted, the twins who became schizophrenic found it impossible to achieve a life of their own.

It is illuminating to note that several of these twins who developed schizophrenia had weighed *more* at birth than their co-twins. But each of these twins had developed an illness or suffered an accident in early childhood and consequently had become the weaker of the two and the primary object of parental concern.

Of the original 17 pairs of identical twins, 16 were followed up about eight years later—when they were 37 years old, on the average—by Robert Belmaker, Pollin, and others. By that time, one pair had become concordant for schizophrenia, three previously healthy co-twins showed "new psychopathology of a possibly schizophrenic nature," and 12 pairs remained discordant.

From very early in life, then, in most cases, the twin who would be stricken with grave mental illness was edged into a threatening view of the world. As he or she struggled with the problems of adolescence and of the years beyond, the stresses grew until they could no longer be borne. From this and similar findings, it appears that schizophrenic breakdown is most likely when the genetic predisposition is there, like a built-in time bomb ready to go off, and when life stresses conspire to weaken the fabric of the personality.

The Schizophrenic Quadruplets

Several decades ago, a highly unusual event took place in the United States—the birth of identical quadruplets all of whom were to develop schizophrenia. The chances of such an occurrence are 1 in 1.5 billion births. Until the arrival of the Genain quadruplets, no such case had ever been reported, and none is likely to be soon again. The Genains offered mental health scientists a unique opportunity to study the course of genetic and environmental factors in a single family.

The family's pseudonym was derived by Rosenthal from Greek words meaning "dire birth" or "dreadful gene." Rosenthal, who directs a continuing study of the family, also gave the quads pseudonyms having the same initials as his agency (National Institute of Mental Health—NIMH): *N*ora, *I*ris, *M*yra, and *H*ester. The city in which the family lived was called Envira, coined from *environment*.

The role of heredity seemed clear. The father had a paranoid personality and was an alcoholic, and there was a history of widely spread psychiatric disorders among his relatives.

The role of environment was even clearer. The mother was often harsh and demanding, and she played one child off against the other. The father was intrusive to the point that he would fondle his daughters' breasts and barge into the bathroom to watch the girls change sanitary pads. To make the quads keep to themselves, the parents literally fenced them in, forced them to march to school by themselves, forbade social activities. When some of them finished school and got jobs, they didn't know how to get along with fellow workers because they had never been permitted to mingle with people outside the family.

All the girls were of the highly introverted—or shut-in—personality type, which has been found to occur fairly commonly among children who later develop schizophrenia. There is evidence that both introversion and its opposite, extraversion, are influenced by hereditary factors. In Rosenthal's words: "The best evidence available suggests . . . that a disproportionate number of schizophrenics are drawn from the pool of introverts, but that only a small fraction of introversives ever become hospitalized schizophrenics."

Before the girls developed schizophrenia, during their early twenties, their behavior "was manifested primarily by marked underactivity, and then by speaking too little, speaking too softly, having feelings of sadness, avoiding socializing, and failing to be cooperative. . . . Although these are traits which may be found in any group of nonschizophrenic individuals, they may also be interpreted as accompaniments of a predominantly catatonic syndrome [characterized by immobility, muscular rigidity, and sometimes excitability] which the girls manifested" during a long period of examination and treatment at NIMH.

If any of the Genain daughters were to have escaped a breakdown, the betting among nonpsychiatric observers would have been on Nora. She was the first born of the quads, their natural leader, and apparently the strongest emotionally of them all. Yet Nora was the first to be hospitalized. As the favorite of her disturbed father, Rosenthal explains, she found it impossible to put any distance between them. Nora's crying spells and signs of nervousness when she was twenty, Myra explained, occurred "because he was giving her more attention than she wanted or needed. He expected her to ride home with him every day and come home for lunch with him." She was upset also because he forbade her to date or to socialize in any other way. "Nora was getting awfully confused and was trying to please father and work on the job also."

Myra, on the other hand, was relatively successful in dodging her father's attentions. And Myra, in spite of a breakdown, recovered and became the one quad to lead a reasonably normal adult life, including marriage and parenthood.

The contrasting histories of Nora and Myra support the theory that genetic inheritance and environmental stress act as a team in producing mental illness in children, and coloring its manifestations.

Organic or Parental Defects?

Where there is an inherited predisposition to schizophrenia, many kinds of stress apparently can act to pull the genetic trigger. They may include damage to the central nervous system from a variety of causes before or during birth—damage that may not be seriously impairing but that makes the child the object of concern, which in turn fills the child with foreboding and lessens his or her ability to cope with the problems of living. Also among the stresses that may lead to a schizophrenic break in a vulnerable youngster are the vicissitudes of family life.

William Goldfarb, a psychiatrist who has been studying groups of schizophrenic children since 1962, reports that such children can be divided into two general classes. The children in one class, which he calls *organic*, are considered to have brain damage, although this is so slight as to be detectable only by a close examination. (There are, of course, psychotic children who do have obvious damage, but they have been excluded from this study.) The children in the other class, called *nonorganic*, have no sign of even the slightest physiological defect.

Paul is an example of children in the organic group. Slow to develop, he did not begin walking until he was eighteen months old, and even after that he often fell and needed help to get up. He took to staring at his feet for long periods and then, following the birth of a brother when Paul was four, to having uncontrollable tantrums. He also began sucking his fingers for hours on end. His nursery school teachers described him as "completely unreachable."

Paul's parents are typical of those in Goldbarb's study whose children have organic deficiencies. The father, a self-deprecatory person though a successful businessman, unknowingly saw Paul as an image of his own weaknesses; the mother subconsciously viewed Paul's problems as a punishment for her sexual experience before marriage. Responding to different motivations in the same way, both parents pressed the boy to do better.

As Goldfarb explains it, Paul from the start had a limited capacity for finding meaning in what he saw and heard, so his environment was more than normally complex and puzzling. The complexity was increased by his parents' efforts to get him to respond. As a way of handling his panic, he came to avoid looking and listening altogether.

In spite of shortcomings, Paul's father and mother and the parents of the other children in the organic groups were found to be more nearly adequate than the parents of the nonorganic schizophrenic children— those without even the slightest neurological signs. The parents of these latter children may seem normal enough to the casual observer, but in Goldfarb's words they have a "paralyzing perplexity" about life and, in particular, about child rearing. They have offered rewards and punishments inconsistently, if at all. They have failed to let their children know where and when they are free to act, and where and when they are not. For example, one boy threw a tantrum and wrecked a neighborhood store while his perplexed mother just stood and watched. The same boy's father indulged in table tricks. For instance, pointing to a glass of milk, he would order his son to "pass the catsup." When the boy seemed confused, the father insisted on instant obedience.

The "parental perplexity" displayed in that case was found to be considerably more marked among the mothers of the nonorganic children than among the other mothers. "There can be little doubt," Goldfarb says, "that schizophrenic children with evidences of physiological aberration come from the more adequate families, whereas schizophrenic children displaying no evidence of intrinsic physiological aberration come from the least adequate families." Evidently, an organic child doesn't need so much family stress to occasion a break as does a child without physiological complications.

Heredity in Childhood Depression

Recently a girl we'll call Beth was referred for treatment to a child psychiatrist. The girl was becoming progressively withdrawn, her mood was depressed, her sleep disturbed, and her appetite failing. She hardly ever played or had any other kind of social life. She was six.

In a flat and lifeless voice, another child, Charlie, told a psychiatrist of his loss of interest in everyone and everything, and of his inability to find pleasure in life or even to concentrate. The task of living had become a downhill struggle, had lost all meaning and purpose. Despairing of any change, Charlie had swallowed the contents of a full bottle of medicine but had survived. He was fourteen.

Beth and Charlie are examples of the countless children now known to be suffering from serious depression, a condition that was thought until a few years ago to be confined to adults. Like schizophrenia, depression appears to be a product of both a genetic disposition and environmental stress. But the hereditary element in depressive illness seems stronger than in the other major psychosis.

Researchers at NIMH—child psychiatrists Donald H. McKnew, Jr., Leon Cytryn, and others—demonstrated recently that children and even grandchildren of people with a psychotic depression—or a *primary affective disorder,* the preferred term among mental health professionals—ought to be considered greater than average risks to develop the same condition.

These researchers are studying all the children and grandchildren of people who have been hospitalized at NIMH because of a severe depression. The children range in age from four to fifteen years. Their examination includes a psychiatric interview in which, among other clues, a history of depressive signs—such as sadness, hopelessness, despair, and suicidal thoughts—is noted; the child's self-esteem is evaluated; and fantasy material is elicited through such means as having the children tell their dreams, make up stories, and interpret pictures.

While one psychiatrist interviews the child, two others watch through a one-way mirror—a device that enables investigators in the next room to look into the room where the interview is taking place but remain unseen. None of the three researchers knows the child's background. Following the interview, all three rate the child independently on two psychiatric rating scales, or checklists.

Among the 25 children studied thus far, more than half have been rated as overtly depressed. These include 64 percent of the girls and 46 percent of the boys—a high prevalence indeed. Earlier investigators reported much lower prevalence rates, but the NIMH group suggests that the discrepancy arises because often the investigators did not study the children directly and, when they did, failed to take into account the unique features of childhood depression.

None of the children in this study was judged to be psychotic. In fact, the investigation confirmed earlier findings that in childhood depression it is rare to find severely depressed mood and behavior. Usually the children's fantasies were the most disturbed, and their mood and behavior the least.

Some examples of children who were rated as depressed:

During the interview, this boy was sad, tense, and fidgety. He spoke in a low voice and was unspontaneous. He feels inferior, talks of being sad and lonely. He draws a plane and says, "It will kill people on the beach."

This girl has a sleep disturbance. She talks in a tense, low voice—a monotone—and often looks sad. She says she feels ugly, dislikes her nose, and has had suicidal thoughts; she jokes about jumping out of a window. In one of her dreams she left the house and couldn't find it; in another, she ran away and injured her foot.

This girl is soft-spoken and relaxed and shows only occasional sadness. She stays alone a lot, she says, and cries sometimes when criticized. In one series of dreams, a girl died, a boy ran away from his stepfather, and King Arthur's kingdom was destroyed. In another series, dogs chased her in a maze; she was caught by a man with a gun, hurt her leg, and couldn't get up.

In terms that would be applied to adult patients, most of the children could be said to suffer from a *primary depressive* (or affective) *disorder;* that is, they did not show signs of other types of emotional or mental disorder. In this respect, these young relatives of depressed patients differ from adult relatives who are afflicted; the adults show a wide range of psychopathology—the so-called depressive spectrum.

Most of the depression in this study was classed as *unipolar,* meaning that the strongest symptoms were of depression alone, and not also of mania or of an elated restless state, hypomania, falling short of it. Where depression and mania occur together, the illness is classed as *bipolar* (meaning two opposite conditions), or as manic-depressive psychosis. Such a person generally has moods that swing from abnormally high to abnormally low.

Twin studies, too, point to a powerful genetic element in major depressive illness. If one identical or *monozygotic* twin has a psychotic depression, the chance that the other twin has already been or will be stricken is very high. Some investigations show it to be 60 percent; others, as high as 90 percent; a few, even higher. These rates are much higher than those for fraternal or *dizygotic* twins (who have developed from two separately fertilized eggs rather than one), as would be expected if there were a genetic factor. Since investigations usually find the concordance rate to be less than 100 percent, environmental factors, too, almost certainly play a role.

In the research described earlier in this section, the investigators started with depressed adults and then looked for depression among their children and grandchildren. Cytryn and McKnew have also taken the opposite approach: They have started with children under treatment for depressive illness and then checked upon their parents. They find three types of childhood depression: *chronic depressive reaction of childhood,* typically suffered by children whose early life has been afflicted by separation from a loved one, or a succession of loved ones, who have a history of poor adjustment, and who often have an emotionally disturbed mother; *acute depressive reaction,* a child's response to a great loss, such as a parent's death or departure; and *masked depressive reaction,* evidenced by hyperactivity, temper tantrums, truancy, and other behavior problems.

Only the first of these types—chronic depressive reaction—appears to have a strong genetic base. Cytryn and McKnew offer the following example, that of a girl we'll call Anna:

... a seven-year-old girl born out of wedlock, [Anna] was referred on an emergency basis because of severe depression. She had had insomnia, anorexia, weight loss, and screaming episodes for several months. She told the pediatric resident that she wanted to kill herself; according to the mother she had made suicidal threats repeatedly, claiming that she was "a bad girl" and that nobody loved her. Ten months prior to this episode she had been seen in the Psychiatric Crisis Clinic because of persistent insomnia.

The girl's mother was an immature, helpless woman; she had a tendency toward frequent depressions and was overwhelmed by family responsibilities. She shared with her daughter a passive, helpless attitude toward life as well as poor self-esteem. There is some evidence that the mother had been neglected as a child by her own mother and was exposed to frequent violence in her surroundings. She was hospitalized once with what seems to have been an agitated depression. During our contacts with her she had at least one serious depressive episode, during which she made suicidal threats. She had left home twice for several months, once when the patient was one and one-half years old and again when she was four. Her only marriage was stormy, and at the time of our contact the parents were separated, after the child's stepfather had beaten the child severely. . . .

According to the child's mother the paternal grandmother had been one of the most significant persons in the patient's life. This relationship, however, was abruptly interrupted when at one year of age the child was transferred to the care of a maternal aunt.

As the patient grew up she became shy and retiring, usually withdrawing from stressful situations. At the age of three she would punish herself (whenever she thought she had transgressed) by quitting her play or favorite toy and sitting quietly in the corner until she was told to resume her activities. . . .

After her discharge . . . the patient again became depressed and developed abdominal cramps and diarrhea. When the mother again separated from the stepfather, these symptoms rapidly disappeared. . . .

Anna was typical of the other children with chronic depressive reaction—and unlike those with different types of depression—in three important ways: She had a chronically depressed parent; beginning in infancy, she had been several times separated from persons important to her; and there had been no single, clear-cut, precipitating incident.

The second type of depression Cytryn and McKnew found in children from six to twelve years old they named *acute depressive reaction.* Beatrice is an example:

[This] six-year-old girl, was referred by the pediatric clinic because of progressive withdrawal, depressed affect, sleep disturbance, lack of appetite, school failure, and separation anxiety sufficient to interfere with all social activities. These symptoms appeared after the rape of her 17-year-old sister three months prior to the referral. Before this incident the sister had served as a mother substitute to the patient because of the mother's relative unavailability due to full-time work. After the incident the sister became withdrawn, preoccupied, and less attentive to the patient. Prior to the present illness the patient had never exhibited signs of depression and had a reasonably good social and scholastic record but was described by relatives and friends as stubborn and negativistic. There was no history of depression in other family members. . . .

At the time of admission to the hospital her mood was markedly depressed, as evidenced by a sad and tearful facial expression, slowness of movement, monotone voice, and verbal expressions indicating hopelessness and despair. On the ward her clinical picture changed within several days. She became outgoing and started to eat and sleep regularly, her mood brightened, and she was sociable, active, and alert. . . .

According to the mother's report, she maintained her gains and behaved during the follow-up period of two years very much as she did before the onset of the presenting complaints.

In the children with acute depressive reaction, the investigators were always able to find a precipitating cause. As in Beatrice's case, this was usually the loss of someone to whom the child felt close. Occasionally the loved one had died; more often he or she had simply become less involved—with a consequent reduction of love and care—for such reasons as a new baby, a remarriage, a move out of town, or personal difficulties.

By far the most common type of childhood depression encountered by these investigators would not appear to the casual observer—or to many mental health professionals, either—as depression at all. Cytryn and McKnew call it *masked depressive reaction* and offer Claude's case as typical:

[Claude] was a 12-year-old boy who was referred to us by school authorities because of his disruptive behavior. He had a long history of school difficulties that included hyperactivity, aggressive behavior, poor scholastic performance, and marginal social adjustment.

The home situation had always been very unstable. The mother was unavailable to the children due to full-time work; at one time she was investigated for child abuse. The father was a chronic alcoholic who frequently beat the patient and assumed no responsibility for the family. There was no history of overt depressive illness in the family.

In the interview situation the patient was in a very depressed mood and was apathetic and sad throughout. He described himself as dumb, as the laughing stock of his schoolmates, and expressed the belief that everyone was picking on him. On the fantasy level the boy showed a strong preoccupation with themes of annihilation, violence, explosions, and death, invariably with a bad outcome for the main figures in those fantasies. It was also evident . . . that he viewed himself as inadequate and helpless. . . .

The follow-up period of one and one-half years was very stormy. The boy continued to have serious school difficulties, leading finally to his suspension from school and admission to a residential school for delinquent boys.

Cytryn and McKnew suggest that the child's aggressive and delinquent behavior was an attempt to escape from his basically depressed state. "Although such a defense is self-destructive," they observe, "it helps to ward off the unbearable feeling of despair."

Children with a masked depressive reaction may show numerous forms of emotional disorder, including hyperactivity, aggressive behavior, psychosomatic illness, concern with imaginary ailments, and delinquency. Periodically, though, they may look or act depressed, and their underlying depressive state can be diagnosed through tests designed to bring their fantasies to the surface.

As in adults, not all downswings in children's moods should be considered clinically significant. Ordinary signs of depression in children, particularly sadness in response to environmental trauma, are very common. Usually they do not last long and, in the words of Cytryn and McKnew, "do not interfere substantially with the child's thinking, functioning, and physical health." The trouble is considered to be depressive illness when it has lasted at least several months "and is associated with severe impairment of the child's scholastic and social adjustment and with disturbances of food intake and sleep. In more serious cases the child's thinking is affected by feelings of despair and hopelessness, general retardation, and, in the severe form, by suicidal thoughts."

In chronic depressive reaction, the first type described, no single incident appears to precipitate the illness. However, Cytryn and

McKnew find that the afflicted children generally do have a chronically depressed parent. In contrast, neither acute depressive reaction nor masked depression—the other two types of childhood depression identified by the investigators—appears to be heavily influenced by the genetic force.

Heredity versus Parent-Child Relations: A Comparison

Research has shown that the manifestation of such an inherited characteristic as vulnerability to psychosis or other psychopathology depends in part on a person's environment. The relationship between parent and child has been found to be particularly important. But is it more or less important than heredity?

To answer this question, David Rosenthal and five colleagues examined 258 young men and women who fell into the following groups:

- The so-called index adoptees: persons who had a schizophrenic or manic-depressive parent and had been adopted early
- Control adoptees, whose biological parents had no known psychiatric illness
- Cross-foster subjects: persons whose parents were free of schizophrenic or manic-depressive disorders but who had been adopted and reared by foster parents, one of whom did have such a disorder
- Nonadoptees: persons who had a schizophrenic or manic-depressive parent and were reared in the parental home for at least their first 15 years

The persons with a psychotic biological parent turned out to be those with the severest psychopathology. This was true whether they had been raised by their biological parents, one of whom was psychotic, or by nonpsychotic foster parents. Moreover, the association between parent-child relations and child psychopathology was found to be weak in both those groups.

But among those young people whose biological parents had not been psychotic, the association between parent-child relations on the one hand and child psychopathology on the other was much stronger— 50 percent so.

When the groups were combined on the basis of whether the subjects had been reared by a psychotic or a nonpsychotic parent, and then compared, no significant difference was found in the subjects' degree of psychopathology.

Further, the quality of the parent-child relationship among the subjects with a psychotic parent was just about the same as that of the parent-child relationship among the controls.

In sum, when children have a mentally sick parent and may, therefore, be genetically tainted, heredity seems more potent than environment as a cause of illness. In such cases the quality of the parent-child relationship, and by inference the quality of the parenting, seems to make little difference. Note, though, that this study was based on Danish government records of the subjects and their parents and on extensive interviews with the subjects. Unlike some of the longitudinal studies now being conducted, there had been no attempt at intervention.

On the other hand, in those children not at genetic risk to mental illness, the quality of the parent-child relationship apparently has an appreciable effect on mental health. Cytryn and McKnew, whose findings as to three types of childhood depression were summarized earlier, report that many of the children they studied had

suffered rejection and depreciation by their parents or loved ones either all during their lives or at least over a period of many years. Such rejection may take the form of blunt statements, stressing the child's worthlessness or inadequacy, or it may be expressed more subtly through attitudes and actions that indicate a lack of respect, involvement, or caring. In some cases the parent has subjected the child to a constant barrage of criticism and humiliation. In other cases there is no frank rejection or depreciation, but rather a void in the parent-child relationship. The parents may or may not be consciously aware of their behavior. . . .

Depreciation of the child can be shown through over-protection as well as through rejection; both attitudes convey the same basic message of the child's inadequacy and worthlessness. How much of the child's subsequent depressive outlook is caused by identification with this negative view of himself and how much is caused by a sense of alienation from important love objects is often hard to determine.

Among those children who may have inherited a predisposition to schizophrenia or manic-depressive illness, the Danish studies suggest, the quality of the parent-child relationship is much less important than the genetic factor in determining whether or not the child will become psychotic. But when hereditary factors are apparently not involved, the quality of the parent-child relationship seems to strongly influence the likelihood that the child will or will not have good mental health. Among children suffering from depression, only one form of which appears to be genetic, the cause is often parental depreciation—whether this is expressed through criticism, lack of interest, or overprotection.

Neurotic Traits and Drinking Problems

A Research Task Force established by the National Institute of Mental Health reported recently that the psychoneuroses are "probably the most prevalent of all mental disorders" but that researchers have tended to pay little attention to them. Presumably this is because such conditions—for example, feelings of guilt and anxiety, or compulsions and phobias—are usually more difficult to define and categorize than the more dramatic and devastating symptoms of the psychoses. Nevertheless, psychoneuroses may indeed burden afflicted persons with lifelong misery and, at the very least, lessen both the joy of living and the effectiveness of their careers.

In several twin studies examined by Rosenthal, the concordance rates for psychoneurosis in identical twins ranged from 25 to 100 percent. Taken together, the studies found that the concordance rate among identical twins was 53 percent and among fraternal twins, 40 percent. The small difference, Rosenthal points out, "leaves little doubt about the importance of environmental factors in the development of clinical neurosis." These studies started with persons who had been diagnosed as neurotic.

Rosenthal also cites a study of normal twins ("normal" in the sense that they had not been diagnosed otherwise), from twelve to fifteen years old, among children in South London during the early 1950s. Two major results emerged. Less than one-fifth of the children had no significant neurotic traits; and the degree of concordance was far higher among the identical twins than among the others. The findings "suggest that neurotic traits are almost universal among children aged 12 to 15, that such traits are heritable with respect to both type and degree, and that they are . . . probably polygenically conditioned [that is, involve many genes]."

Other twin studies have shown that neuroses occur more frequently in the families of schizophrenics than would be expected by chance. Heredity probably plays a role in the development of psychoneurosis, Rosenthal concludes, but little can yet be said about the genetic factors involved.

The same cannot be said about a problem area of increasing prominence among children: alcoholism. The most abused drug in the world, and one that is becoming increasingly popular among youngsters of high school age and even younger, is alcohol. Estimates of the number of alcoholics in this country run as high as 10 million, and the number is likely to increase in the light of recent data: Nearly 25 percent of adolescents 13 years old or younger drink frequently enough and in large enough quantities to be classed as at least moderate drinkers.

McClearn and DeFries review several investigations which, taken together, suggest that alcoholism not only runs in families—a common observation—but also has a heritable base. Early in the 1950s a Swedish investigator, Curt Amårk, studying large samples of alcoholics, found that persons with an alcoholic father had a 26 percent risk of becoming alcoholic themselves; those with an alcoholic brother, 21 percent. Persons with an alcoholic mother or sister were at very small risk. So were controls without an alcoholic parent or sibling.

Though family factors, rather than genetic ones, might have accounted for the results of the Swedish study, they appear to have been ruled out in several other investigations. In a study headed by D. W. Goodwin, the subjects were 55 men in Denmark who had an alcoholic parent but had been adopted by nonrelatives during the first few weeks of life. They were compared with young men who did not have an alcoholic parent but had also been adopted. In both groups the average age was thirty. Of the men who had been born to an alcoholic parent but had been raised by adoptive parents, 18 percent at some point had become alcoholic, too; of the other men, only 5 percent. This finding seems particularly telling because, although the proportion of alcoholics distinguished the two groups, the proportion of heavy drinkers did not.

McClearn and DeFries call attention also to a United States study by Marc Schuckit and others of 150 persons with an alcoholic half-sibling. Twenty-eight of the subjects eventually became alcoholic themselves. Of these, 65 percent had a biological parent who was alcoholic. Of the subjects who did not become alcoholic, only 20 percent had an alcoholic parent.

Had the environment played an important role in those developments? Apparently not. Of the subjects who became alcoholic, 35 percent had lived with an alcoholic parent or foster parent; of those who did not become alcoholic, 25 percent. The difference could well have occurred by chance.

Again, about 50 percent of the subjects had "shared their childhood"—living in the same families and going to the same schools— with the half-sibling who became alcoholic. However, only 6 percent of the subjects who did not have an alcoholic biological parent became alcoholic, in contrast to 25 percent of those who did. This finding "suggests the relatively greater importance of biological parentage than of shared childhood with a half-sibling who became alcoholic."

In the etiology of alcoholism, McClearn and DeFries conclude that all the comparisons in this study "suggest a preponderant role of heredity."

Antisocial Behavior and Criminality

Six studies of criminality summarized by Eliot Slater and Valerie Cowie showed that if one identical twin became a criminal, the probability that the other one would also engage in crime ranged between 50 and 100 percent. Among fraternal twins, the same probability ranged only from zero to 53 percent.

McClearn and DeFries also report a study by R. R. Crowe in Iowa of 41 women who had been convicted of crime and sent to prison. Fifty-two of their children had been adopted when they were less than eighteen months old, and these were the subjects of the investigation. They ranged in age at the time of the study from fifteen to forty-five years. The control group comprised 52 adopted persons matched with the others as to age, sex, race, and age at the time of adoption.

Among the adopted children of the criminal offenders, eight had been arrested a total of 18 times at the time of the study. Among the controls, two persons had been arrested, each once. Seven of the first group were convicted, as compared with one of the controls.

These findings suggest that heredity plays a role in criminal behavior, but McClearn and DeFries point out that the possibility of environmental factors cannot be dismissed. For instance, the adoptive parents may have known of the mothers' criminal records, and this knowledge may have influenced their attitudes toward the children. But the results, when viewed along with those from the twin studies, are "highly suggestive."

If criminal behavior can be influenced by the genes, just what is it that a parent with criminal tendencies, whether he or she is aware of them or not, may pass on to the offspring? To illustrate that heredity's role in criminality is borne by no single genotype, or genetic makeup, Rosenthal names a few of the *secondary* factors that may be involved:

• Abnormalities of the brain waves, as shown by the electroencephalograph, or EEG. Numerous studies "indicate a higher incidence of

EEG abnormalities and borderline abnormalities in juvenile delinquents and adult criminals. . . ." How could such abnormalities predis-
pose to criminality? Possibly because they are "associated with poor
impulse control and bad judgment."

• Low intelligence. "A large number of criminals have low IQs.
Heredity contributes significantly to intellectual level, but educational
and cultural deprivation also produces low IQ test scores in individuals
who may otherwise be normally gifted."

• Body build, or somatotype: "Criminals seem to be predominantly
mesomorphic." A mesomorph "is well-muscled, athletic, strong, tough,
and durable. Temperamentally, he is aggressive and less fearful than
others." Rosenthal cites a 1956 finding that about 60 percent of almost
500 delinquents were mesomorphs. This rate was double that of a
control group.

The *primary* factors involved in the genetic transmission of a disposition to criminal behavior must include whatever contributes to the type
of personality known as psychopathic, sociopathic, or—the term preferred by the American Psychiatric Association (APA)—antisocial. As
defined by the APA, *antisocial personality* is "a personality disorder
characterized by a basic lack of socialization and by behavior patterns
that bring the individual repeatedly into conflict with society. People
with this disorder are incapable of significant loyalty to individuals,
groups, or social values and are grossly selfish, callous, irresponsible,
impulsive, and unable to feel guilt or to learn from experience and
punishment. Frustration tolerance is low. Such individuals tend to
blame others or offer plausible rationalizations for their behavior."

Little is known about the heritability of antisocial personality
because, Rosenthal explains, "its study has been limited by the constant confounding of hereditary and environmental variables."

Rosenthal emphasizes also that "in all likelihood, many if not most
crimes are committed by individuals in whom the role of heredity is
minor, nonspecific, or perhaps irrelevant." He states:

For a long time in the United States, the crime rate has increased steadily
and sharply. From a genetic point of view, one might assume that criminal
psychopaths have a high fertility rate which contributes an accelerated
frequency of the pathological genes into the general population. However,
there is no good evidence of such an elevated fertility, and in fact, there is
good reason to believe that their fertility rate is *below* that of the general
population. If true, the low fertility rate and the increasing crime rate

provide additional testimony to the overriding importance of environmental factors in "crime."

Still, breeders of animals know—and geneticists have demonstrated—that brute aggressive behavior in animals can be inherited. Among humans, aggression is admittedly colored by experience, and is expressed, therefore, not only in specific criminal acts but, for example, in the driving ambition of the executive or the skill of the football hero. Nevertheless, as McClearn and DeFries conclude, "There is no reason to believe that heritable differences in aggressive behavior do not exist in man."

Until recently there was a widespread belief that an unusual amount of crime, particularly violent crime, is committed by men who have an extra Y chromosome. A normal male is designated, on the basis of his two sex chromosomes, XY. The men once thought to have a predisposition to violent crime because of a chromosomal abnormality are XYY.

The XYY syndrome came to public attention when a few men charged with heinous crimes were found to carry the abnormality or were said to carry it. The most notorious case was that of the young man who murdered eight nurses in Chicago. After his reported abnormality had been widely publicized, investigation showed that he carried a perfectly normal chromosomal complement. But the notion continued that a single Y might contribute to aggressiveness in males and that a second one might double the contribution.

Scientific and public interest in the XYY anomaly was heightened not only by journalistic accounts but also by scientific reports that were concerned with only one or a few cases, or did not adequately compare the behavior of XYY's with that of XY's, or in some other way fell short of thoroughness. The studies did apparently demonstrate that XYY's tended to be unusually tall and that more of them had been convicted of crime than would be expected on the basis of their numbers in the population. Studies of infants indicated that an XYY occurred once in every 600 to 1,000 male births.

In 1976 the first findings of an unusually large and more nearly definitive study clarified the picture. The investigation was conducted by a team of 12 scientists, headed by the American psychologists Herman A. Witkin and Sarnoff A. Mednick and by the Danish psychiatrist Fini Schulsinger. The team started with a subject pool of about 31,500—all the male Danish citizens born to women who lived in Copenhagen during the years 1944–1947, inclusive. This was reduced to 4,139, chiefly by ruling out all men shorter than 6 feet, 1½ inches.

Chromosomal studies showed that 12 of the 4,139 men were XYY's— a prevalence rate of about 3 per 1,000. Five of the twelve, or 41.6 percent, had been convicted of one or more criminal offenses. Among the XY's—men with the normal complement of sex chromosomes—the criminal rate was 9.3 percent. Thus, a significantly larger proportion of XYY's had been convicted of crime.

However, no evidence was found that the XYY's were especially aggressive. Crimes of violence occurred no more frequently among them than among the controls. The higher crime rate simply reflected a higher rate of property offenses. Most of the XYY's received mild penalties, evidence that their crimes were not regarded as particularly serious. The most severe sentence by far was a prison term of less than a year—imposed on one subject.

Why the higher crime rate among the XYY's? Lower intelligence, the investigators believe. On measures of intellectual functioning, the XYY's as a group rated significantly lower than the XY's, although some individuals were within the normal range. Moreover, the criminals among the XY's were significantly less intelligent than the noncriminals.

"Intellectual impairment," the research team points out, "may contribute to antisocial behavior. It seems plausible also that when individuals with impaired intellectual functioning commit crimes, they are more likely to be apprehended than are criminals of normal intelligence." For example, one XYY committed burglaries while the owners were on the premises.

Do the findings mean that the Y chromosome is directly involved in intellectual functioning? Probably not. More likely, according to the researchers, the intellectual deficit is simply a manifestation of altered development resulting from the abnormal organization of genetic material.

What about the idea that XYY's somehow get into more trouble because they are generally very tall? Not confirmed. And among the XY's, there was a *negative* relationship between height and criminality; that is, the noncriminals were significantly taller than the criminals.

The socioeconomic status of the parents was investigated also. Among parents of noncriminals it was significantly higher than among the parents of criminals. But among the XYY's in general, it was not significantly different from that of the XY's.

This study also turned up 16 men with an extra X chromosome instead of an extra Y. In general, these XXY's were much the same as the XYY's. Whether the extra sex chromosome is an X or a Y seems to make little difference.

Genetic Counseling

Since genes play a prominent role in predisposing children to a wide range of suffering, how can parents learn about and weigh the chance of producing a child at risk to a serious mental disorder? The answer is genetic counseling, widely available at medical centers.

For example, psychiatrist-geneticist Elliot Gershon of NIMH is sometimes asked by a couple, one of whom is a manic-depressive, the chances that any child of theirs will develop the same disorder. If the family tree of one of the inquirers is free of major depressive illness, he answers, "About 10 percent." He also tells them that because of lithium and other medicines, the disorder is much less of a liability than it used to be. It is unusual, he reports, for a couple not to marry, or not to have children, simply because one of them has manic-depressive illness. Gershon tells them, too, that their children will also be at greater risk than other children to the less serious forms of depression. There are medicines effective against these forms, too.

Suppose that one of the partners is a schizophrenic and that the question concerns the probability of having a child who will likewise develop schizophrenia. In that case the risk is again about 10 percent, provided that the other parent is neither a schizophrenic nor related to one. But if two schizophrenics produce children, the probability that they will develop the disease runs from 30 to 50 percent. And some investigators find evidence that the risk of developing some type of mental disorder reaches as high as 75 or 80 percent.

Even so, the risk that a child will develop *some* type of mental disorder or personality quirk is less when one parent has a schizophrenic rather than a depressive psychosis. But a nongenetic factor must also be considered. Schizophrenia, in particular the chronic type, interferes with family relationships to a much greater extent. In fact, chronic schizophrenia is almost certain to block a couple from having a normal family life. The same is not always the case when depression is present. "There is a certain warmth within the families of people with mood disorders," Gershon testifies, "that is not found in schizophrenic families." Moreover, the drugs now available for treating schizophrenia are considerably less effective than those for depression.

Again, suppose that a young adult says to a genetic counselor, "My sister is a schizophrenic—what's the risk that my children will be?" The answer will be, "Not very high." The children at risk will be nieces or nephews of a schizophrenic, and the chance that they, too, will develop schizophrenia is about 2.5 percent. In other words, if the person asking the question—assuming that he or she is normal and has a normal mate—goes ahead and has 40 children, one of them very likely will develop schizophrenia. The problem, of course, is that there is no way of predicting whether this child will be the first, the fifth, or the fortieth. As noted earlier, the risk in the general population is about 1 in 100.

An increasing number of conditions likely to make for abnormality can be detected through amniocentesis—a technique for analyzing the fluid surrounding the embryo in the womb. Where the analysis predicts a grave abnormality such as the form of mental retardation known as Down's syndrome, or mongolism, the parents can request an abortion. Some day it should be possible to correct some of the diagnosed defects while the child is still in the fetal stage.

In the case of mental illness, however, there is as yet no way to tell whether or not the unborn child carries a predisposition to a grave disorder—simply because scientists, in spite of gigantic advances during the last 25 years, have not yet certainly identified biochemical abnormalities that either contribute to psychosis or serve as a clear indication of vulnerability.

Exciting work goes forward, however, on the *neurotransmitters,* chemicals that carry the electrical messages from nerve cell to nerve cell. After the transmitter has done its work, it must be cleared away fast. In one case, part of the clearing away is done by the enzyme known as *monoamine oxidase,* or MAO. And in identical twins, one of whom has schizophrenia, the MAO level in the blood platelets—tiny elements that help form blood clots—has been found to be lower than normal. It is also lower in people with manic-depressive psychosis. The problem is that MAO levels are also low in apparently healthy relatives of psychotics.

More recent work has focused on another enzyme, *cathecol-O-methyl transferase,* or COMT. This enzyme, too, works to break down neurotransmitters. People with psychotic depression have more COMT activity; most of their normal relatives apparently do not.

Thus it appears that we may be able, perhaps soon, to detect even in the womb children vulnerable to psychosis. But what do we do about the possibility that these same children also carry genes for greatness?

4

Born That Way

A Child's Physical and Emotional Constitution

"I've tried everything, but nothing seems to work. Why can't I get my son to study more? Now take the boy next door. . . ."

The words are those of an unhappy and confused mother. The object of her concern is Mark, a friendly, outgoing twelve-year-old boy for whom the real world is too exciting to spend much time on books. Mark is only an average student. But he is a leader among his friends, an expert photographer, and a fine athlete. Moreover, he is a happy human being.

His mother isn't. She is anguished and intense, searching for a formula to change her child's personality.

Mark's mother is a member of a generation of parents who have come to believe they can reshape their children—make them energetic or relaxed, sociable or studious, sensitive or thick-skinned—if only an expert would give them the key, tell them what strings to pull to produce the desired changes. Encouraged by the advice of child-rearing commentators—in the press, on TV, and in the backyard—parents have come to expect miracles of themselves, and of their children.

How *can* a parent go about changing a child?

She, or he, can't—at least not in the spectacular ways so many parents aim for. Despite what some experts say, there is still no scientific support for believing that parents can dramatically reshape their children simply by applying child-rearing formulas. Indeed, the weight of recent research suggests that the child's makeup is largely constitutional, or something that the child is born with, something inherent in his or her body and mind. Some aspects of a child's constitution may have been shaped by heredity; others by the mother's physical and emotional state while carrying the child; still others, by events at the time of birth. An especially important constitutional factor is a child's basic temperament, which, like intelligence, is a psychological trait; it is probably best defined as behavioral style. In interaction with the environment, it determines personality. The range over which temperament and other elements of the child's makeup can be changed is narrower in most cases than many parents suppose.

This does not mean that home environment and training count for nothing. As much of this book makes clear, children's lives are certainly colored by the attitudes and values they learn at home—by the examples we set them in our own lives. The Marilyn Monroe who went inexorably to her doom was, at least in part, a product of a nightmarish childhood. Similarly, the nobility of Helen Keller's life is the result, to some degree, of wise handling by a kindly nurse.

But examples like these should not delude us into assuming that any change—even the subtlest kind—can be induced in every child. The child's destiny will ultimately be influenced not only by the parents but also by peers, teachers, the culture—and, much more so than we have until now believed, by constitutional makeup. For the fact is that the child's future has been determined in part before he or she is brought from the womb.

In detailed tests of hundreds of newborns at the Albert Einstein College of Medicine, Wagner H. Bridger found that babies are individualists, both in their physical makeup and in their behavior. Observing the responses of infants to a variety of stimuli—to loud noises, for example, or to gentle rocking—he discovered that the reaction of any given baby to a particular stimulus might be just the opposite of that of another. And whatever the response—whether a sharp rise in heart rate or increased irritability—it appeared to be constant for that baby from the beginning.

Other investigators have also noted a remarkable constancy as the child develops, not only in physiological characteristics but also in such matters as mood and responsiveness to people, in attention span and persistence, in adaptability to new situations, and in the pacing of eating and sleeping schedules. The phrase "born that way," long out of vogue among child development experts, may be considerably more relevant than many have thought possible.

Types of Children: Easy, Difficult, Otherwise

Most parents know that children may show strong temperamental differences among themselves, almost from the start. For example, some children respond positively to new situations, adapt quickly to new foods and people, are generally cheerful, and display highly regular patterns of eating, sleeping, and eliminating. They enjoy learning new games and taking part in new activities, including school. At the opposite extreme are children who are highly irregular, who withdraw or protest vigorously when exposed to new situations, whether pertaining to food, clothing, people, or places, and who, when frustrated, tend to react violently, with a tantrum.

Alexander Thomas and Stella Chess, who since 1956 have been studying temperament in children and its relationship to mental health, term the children at one extreme *easy* and at the other extreme *difficult*. They have also identified a third group: *children who are slow to warm up*. Such youngsters tend at first to withdraw from new situations, with little or no fussing, and to adapt to them slowly. As babies they are likely to respond to a new food by letting it dribble out of their mouths; in nursery school, they remain on the sidelines several weeks; in kindergarten, when pushed to take part in some new activity, they struggle quietly to escape. Such differences in temperament are established by the time a baby is from two to three months old.

Thanks to the findings of Thomas and Chess, who are psychiatry professors at the New York University School of Medicine, and to those of investigators who have replicated their work or applied their results, science has substantiated what observant parents have always known—that children have constitutional differences. Science has also demonstrated the truth of the corollary—that children with different temperaments ought to be handled differently. But many parents have failed to act upon this corollary because, as Thomas sees it, they have been intimidated by child-care authorities.

Since a child's response to parental handling will vary with the child's temperament, no one rule can be applied to every child—a finding that helps to explain the swings of the pendulum in child guidance. During the 1930s and before, the prevailing wisdom emphasized strict rules of feeding and discipline. When it became clear that not all children thrived equally well under this regimen, the pendulum began swinging to the opposite extreme. During the next few decades, the authoritative word was *permissiveness.* Now the pendulum has begun to swing back. Hopefully it will not make a full return, and hopefully parents will realize the need to deal differently with different offspring.

The way that parents and others respond to a child's temperament can help determine whether his or her behavior will be deviant or normal. Of course, there are many patterns of normal behavior, and of course, as Thomas and Chess point out, temperament is only one attribute of the growing child. Important as it is, for a rounded picture of the child and an explanation of problem behavior, temperament has to be considered in relation to the child's abilities and motivation, and to the play on all these of the forces in her or his environment.

In their major research project, Thomas and Chess have been observing the temperament and behavior of 136 persons, members of some 80 families, from early infancy into adolescence. Most of the subjects come from middle-class or upper-middle-class families, in which the fathers are usually professional men or business executives. These children have been compared with a sample of children from Puerto Rican working-class families.

Extensive information about each child and his or her family was obtained through parental interviews, direct observation, teachers' reports, and batteries of psychological tests. Nine separate characteristics of temperament were found: (1) level of activity, (2) rhythmicity or regularity of biological functions, including activity, sleep, eating, and elimination, (3) approach or withdrawal, based on the child's initial reaction to any new stimulus, (4) adaptability, (5) intensity of reaction, (6) threshold of responsiveness, or level of stimulation necessary to evoke a response, (7) quality of mood, or the amount of pleasant behavior as contrasted with unpleasant, (8) distractibility, and (9) attention span and persistence.

Statistical analysis showed that two-thirds of the children could be described by one or another of three different combinations of traits— those characterizing the *easy,* the *difficult,* and the *slow-to-warm-up* children. In the rest of the children, the traits were too mixed for a general description. The easiest children represented 40 percent of the total; the difficult children 10 percent; the slow-to-warm-up children 15 percent. Some children, too, were very easy to distract.

Of all the youngsters under study, 30 percent developed behavior problems, sometime between infancy and adolescence, considered serious enough to warrant psychiatric attention. Most problems were mild but there were marked differences among the groups: As might be expected, easiest children were the most likely to come through unscathed; only 18 percent developed serious problems. In contrast, 70 percent of the difficult children needed psychiatric aid. Of the slow-to-warm-up children, about 40 percent were judged to require help.

The investigators found themselves facing several questions: How can basic temperamental differences be explained? Why did some children develop behavior problems, though most did not? Can temperament be modified?

The Origins of a Child's Temperament

Thomas and Chess could find no explanations for the striking differences in temperament, either in the developmental histories of the children or in the characteristics of the parents, including their ideas about child rearing. The parents of the children who fell into any one of the three groups could not be distinguished from all the rest of the parents. However, evidence for several likely explanations has now been found by other investigators, building upon the New York team's work, and is included in a new Thomas-Chess account of research in the whole field of temperament.

A Norwegian investigator, Anna Marie Torgersen, used the techniques of the American team to study twins at two months of age, which is about the time a baby's behavior becomes stabilized, and again at nine months. Each time she found that the identical twins, the ones with the same genes, were likely to resemble their co-twins in temperament much more closely than were the nonidentical twins. There seemed to be a genetic component for all the nine traits identified by the New York team. Moreover, the curves showing the distribution of temperament traits in the Norwegian children turned out to be similar in the main to those of the New York City group. This was so in spite of some marked differences in child-rearing principles.

Evidence for heredity's role in temperament is strengthened by a finding reported in the first book-length account of the work by Thomas, Chess, and their collaborator until his death, pediatrician Herbert G. Birch. In general, children of the Puerto Rican working-class sample showed no dramatic differences in temperament from the other children, even though their parents had different ideas about child raising.

> The middle class native-born families . . . had high educational and career expectations for their children, emphasized early accomplishment of self-care activities, particularly feeding and dressing, structured feeding and sleep schedules and were greatly concerned over any evidence of deviant behavior, even in early infancy. The Puerto Rican parents, by contrast, had more modest goals for their children, did not press for early self-care achievement, were very permissive with sleep and feeding schedules in the preschool years and tolerated behavioral deviations with the formulation "he's a baby and he'll outgrow it."

A genetic influence, Thomas and Chess point out, "in no way implies fixed predetermination and immutability of temperament. . . ." A person's characteristics "are always the final product of the continuously evolving interaction between genetic and environmental factors. Depending on the nature of this interaction, an infant's separate temperamental characteristics may be reinforced, modified, or changed as he grows older."

Other factors than genetic appear to be at work also, at least in families at the lower socioeconomic levels. Psychologists Arnold J. Sameroff and Melvin Zax at the University of Rochester found four characteristics prominent among mothers of children with difficult temperament at four months of age. These mothers tended to have a high level of anxiety as measured late in pregnancy; they were more likely to be black than white; they were of low social class; and they were more likely than others to have a large number of children. Sameroff also found that babies born of mothers who were judged late in pregnancy to be emotionally disturbed "were less adaptable, more intense, and more negative in mood"—characteristics of the difficult child—than the babies of other mothers. Of all the maternal factors related to the development of difficult temperament, anxiety was the strongest, with social class and race close behind.

Abnormalities of behavior have often been attributed to complications during the mother's pregnancy and the delivery. Research leading to such findings has been retrospective; that is, it started with the disturbed child or adult and then sought information about early events in his or her life. More likely to be trustworthy is longitudinal research, for it starts with the child at birth, or some time later, and seeks to record possibly influential experiences as they occur.

Sameroff has reviewed a number of longitudinal studies of children who experienced complications of pregnancy and delivery and finds little evidence of a direct relationship between such complications and later abnormal behavior. One study, for example, followed the 670 children who in the course of a year had been born on the island of Kauai, Hawaii. The results "seem to indicate that perinatal complications were consistently related to later physical and psychological development only when combined with and supported by persistently poor environmental circumstances." In other words, birth trauma was likely to lead to poor development only when coupled with a family's low socioeconomic status and an accompanying lack of child-rearing ability. The various studies, Sameroff sums up, "have yet to produce a single predictive variable more potent than the familial and socioeconomic characteristics of the caretaking environment." At one extreme, "supportive, compensatory and normalizing environments appear to be able to eliminate the effects of early complications"; at the other extreme, "caretaking by deprived, stressed, or poorly educated parents tends to exacerbate early difficulties."

To explain what happens, Sameroff and a colleague, M. J. Chandler, have proposed a "transactional model of development." This scheme holds that a child's characteristics interact with the parents' to produce "an individualized ongoing miniature social system." Stated another way, what's going on is not simply the shaping of the child by the parents, but also the shaping of the parents by the child. There is an example of this in the Thomas-Chess-Birch study of children with a variety of temperaments. The mothers of the *difficult* children tended to become either anxious or hostile.

Sameroff believes that the transactional model can help explain even child abuse, a subject discussed in Chapter 8. "It appears," he says, "that certain children ... tend to elicit abusive behavior from their parents." As Sameroff puts it, a difficult child can convert "a formerly normal mother into an abnormal one."

Difficult children were much more likely than the others to need psychiatric help. But where parents could understand and make allowances for their child's constitutional style of behavior, the outcome was good.

Sameroff has also found that the children rated as having a difficult temperament at the age of four months are those most likely to score lowest on an intelligence test at thirty months. Why? The investigator finds an answer in the way mother and baby were getting along—as shown in intensive home observations—when the latter was a year old.

"Mothers of children with difficult temperaments," he reports, "tended to stay away from them more, to look at them less, to socialize and play with them less." It was the other mothers—who stayed close to their babies and socialized a great deal with them—whose children tended to score higher on the IQ test.

"The child's temperament at four months of age," this investigator believes, "influences how the mother is going to treat him in the future. The mother of a child with a difficult temperament becomes turned off to that child in some way and as a consequence does not provide the stimulation and caretaking that would lead to the child's competent performance at thirty months of age."

Such elements as maternal anxiety and race, Thomas and Chess believe, were not at play in *their* sample of parents because of its high socioeconomic level and "the presumably smaller percentage of unwanted pregnancies and severe psychopathology in the mothers." Perhaps temperament is fashioned in part by chemical and physiological influences on the developing brain before birth. Perhaps, too, temperament is influenced by the characteristics and behavior of the parents during the first two or three months of the baby's life. It is during this period that the child's style of behavior emerges and then remains fixed, at least for some time. No definitive study of this possibility has been done. A third possibility—that temperament is influenced by brain damage before birth or during the birth process—has been tested in one study, with negative results. The most to be gleaned at present from research is that temperament is constitutional, with heredity probably playing an important role, and that a pregnant woman who is markedly anxious or psychiatrically disturbed may be more likely to bear a temperamentally difficult child.

"The findings of our longitudinal studies and the reports of other workers ... ," Thomas and Chess conclude, "indicate that temperamental characteristics play significant roles in the genesis and evolution of behavior disorders in children. It is clearly necessary for the clinician to give as much attention to temperamental factors as to environmental and psychodynamic influences in diagnosis and treatment."

English psychiatrist Michael Rutter and his collaborators have used interview measure techniques based on the Thomas-Chess approach and found that the children who shared certain features were the ones most likely to have a psychiatric disorder during the four-year period of the study. These features included low regularity in physiological functions, negative mood, low variability in emotional expression, and low fastidiousness. When at least two of these adverse temperamental features were present, the psychiatric risk was tripled.

Half of the reason why temperamental adversity put the child at increased risk was to be found in the transactional effect with parental criticism. Children with adverse temperamental features were twice as likely as other children to be the target of parental criticism. Thus, in discordant and quarrelsome homes, the child's temperament protected him or put him at risk by virtue of its influence on parent-child interaction. Even when there was marked disharmony in the home, the temperamentally easy child tended to escape much of the flak.

Obviously, temperamental differences in children deserve more attention by parents than they have often been given. The result could be to forestall the onset of behavioral problems in the young.

How Behavior Problems Evolve

Trouble most often arose in the families studied by Thomas and Chess because parents did not know how to handle a difficult, a slow-to-warm-up, or an easily distractible child. Trouble continued because the parents were either unable to accept or unwilling to follow professional advice.

Some examples:

• Nancy was one of the difficult children, and her parents, responding negatively to her behavior, made demands she could not always meet. By the time she entered elementary school, she was displaying fear of the dark and engaging in fits of explosive anger. Her trouble was diagnosed as a neurotic behavior disorder. But during the fourth and fifth grades, she gave evidence of musical and dramatic talent and won praise from her teachers and the parents of schoolmates. Her own parents, then, changing their attitudes, began to show pride in her. She was a bright and happy adolescent.

• Norman was a pleasant and intelligent child but highly distractible—given to quick shifts of attention and apparent forgetfulness. His father, a hard-driving professional man, viewed the boy's distractibility as a mark of irresponsibility and lack of character, and told him so. Brushed aside was the mother's explanation that the boy was normal enough but temperamentally unable to work as his father did. Efforts by Norman to stick to his studies for long, uninterrupted periods led to tension and numerous tics. At seventeen, he had dropped out of two colleges in a year and had become depressed. "My father doesn't respect me," he told a psychiatrist, "and, let's face it, why should he?"

• David as a child was active, cheerful, friendly—one of the easy children. But at seventeen he was fat and apathetic, and in spite of his high IQ, sliding down the academic hill. His parents were in almost constant discord but agreed upon and kept emphasizing a single point: David's school problems, since he was so intelligent, must be caused by poor teaching. He gradually adopted the same attitude.

Such cases suggest that no one factor is necessarily important in the development of behavior problems. With David, the easy child, for example, temperament traits that marked his early years and seemed to indicate a happy future disappeared when his parents, in almost paranoid style, began attributing his school difficulties to his teachers. Nancy's experience—she was the girl who began displaying show business talent—makes the same point, though the outcome this time is happy: The emergence of new factors in either the child or the environment can decisively influence the course of development. Environmental factors can also have the opposite effect; they can intensify a given characteristic. Norman's distractibility, for instance, was only worsened by his father's attitude. This case exemplifies the potentially tragic outcome of rejecting a child's temperamental style instead of helping him or her cope with it.

Of 42 cases with a behavior disorder in childhood, about one-half had recovered by adolescence, and about one-third had grown worse. In the main, the parents of those who recovered had followed psychiatric advice and reduced stress on the child—stress created by expectations that did not harmonize with the child's temperament. With some exceptions, the other parents had not.

So far, adolescence has brought five new cases. They are marked by depression, hostility, rebelliousness, or antisocial behavior, and are more severe than those that arose earlier.

Thomas and Chess view the development of temperament—and, indeed, of intellectual competence and other psychological patterns— as "a constantly evolving and changing process of organism-environment interaction." As in Nancy's case, temperament may remain consistent, but the interaction between temperament and environment may change. As with Norman, distortion may occur in the way temperament is expressed. ("The acceptance of his father's derogatory and hypercritical value judgment on himself led to increasing drifting, shifting quickly from one vague plan to another, grasping at straws—all in all a caricature of his temperamental characteristics of distractibility and short attention span.") Or, as with David, the victim of his parents' paranoia, temperament may undergo a marked change, which may or may not endure.

Adapting to a Child's Nature

Since a child's temperament and the parents' reaction to it can greatly influence his or her life—and theirs as well—what should parents do? In general, psychiatrists Thomas and Chess suggest, they should try to make their demands and expectations consonant with the child's temperamental characteristics. Otherwise, the highly active child who is punished each time he or she breaks the rules may decide there is no point in even trying to observe them. The highly distractible child may be viewed as lazy, disobedient, or lacking in willpower and may be subjected, therefore, to excessive pressure and punitive attitudes.

With easy children, that advice can usually be followed without undue trouble, though even they are not always immune to behavior problems. Such children adapt fairly readily to almost any child-rearing program. The trouble is most likely to come with the difficult children, the slow-to-warm-up children, and children who can be easily distracted. Children who are very persistent and who have either a very high or very low level of activity may also develop problems if demands and expectations are excessive for their temperamental style.

The mother and father of one difficult boy displayed unusual tolerance and consistency. As the investigators recount, the parents took the boy's stormy adjustment periods calmly, waited out his negative moods without becoming angry, and dealt good-humoredly with the battles between him and the family's younger children. Though permissive, the parents set safety limits, and they consistently explained the rights of his peers. Consequently, by the time the boy entered nursery school he was functioning well—except for the usual difficulties triggered by new situations. The parents came to understand that the youngster's behavior was simply the expression of his characteristics. Because of this constructive approach, troublesome behavior did not become symptomatic of a behavior disorder, as it did with most other such youngsters.

Slow-to-warm-up children should be allowed to adapt to their surroundings at their own speed. Pressure to move quickly into new situations may only strengthen their tendency to withdraw. They do, though, need to be encouraged to try new experiences; as evidence, consider the story of a youngster named Bobby. Starting in babyhood, whenever Bobby rejected new food, his parents crossed it off his diet list. Also, because he shied away from the kids on the playground, they kept him home. At ten he was a loner, and he subsisted mainly on hamburgers, applesauce, and medium-boiled eggs.

Youngsters who rank low in persistence and high in distractibility should be encouraged to function up to their abilities. Persistent and nondistractible children should be warned well ahead of time when they will be required—in the interest of the family's schedule, or the school's—to drop what they are doing. Children with difficult temperaments need to be handled with an exceptional amount of patience and firmness and understanding if they are ever to learn appropriate behavior.

The investigators have nicely summed up the practical implications of their findings. "A child who stands at the periphery of the group in nursery school," they remind us, "may be anxious and insecure, but he may also be expressing his normal temperamental tendency to warm up slowly. An infant with irregular sleep cycles who cries loudly at night may possibly be responding to a hostile, rejecting mother, but he may also be expressing his temperamental irregularity. A six-year-old who explodes with anger at his teacher's commands may be aggressive and oppositional, but he may also be showing the frustration reactions typical of a very persistent child when he is asked to terminate an activity in which he is deeply absorbed. A mother's guilt and anxiety may be the result of a deep-seated neurosis, but they may also be the result of her problems and confusion in handling an infant with a temperamental pattern that characterizes a very difficult child."

Such findings should relieve many a parent—and many a teacher as well. No matter how great the teacher's competency, the investigators say, he or she "will not be able to make a high-activity child sit quietly or a distractible child concentrate for long periods of time." Moreover, pediatricians, nurses, and mental health professionals also need to take temperament into account; otherwise, judgments of children's behavior may be wrong.

These authorities offer a warning: "Negative mood, withdrawal tendencies, high motor activity, marked distractibility, extreme persistence, etc., may be normal for a particular youngster but may still interfere with desirable peer relations, school and play activities and academic achievement. A parent or teacher may also tolerate or even be pleased with a child's behavior, such as the quiet, peaceful withdrawal tendencies of the slow-to-warm-up child, and yet this behavior may interfere with the child's development of constructive social experiences. In such instances, when a child's temperament may have undesirable consequences if allowed unrestricted expression, appropriate guidance and structuring is necessary. Thus, the distractible, nonpersistent child cannot sit and concentrate on homework for long periods of time. But he can be told he must return to his work after each short break. The slow-to-warm-up child may not be able to become an active part of a peer group immediately, but complete withdrawal should not be tolerated or encouraged. . . ." Each case must be studied individually.

The investigators have a hopeful word for families where an unhealthy, pathogenic parent-child relationship has continued into adolescence. Where this happened in the study, some of the youngsters improved or recovered, while others became worse. One significant difference was found between the two groups—"the ability of the youngster to shift the center of his activities, interests and emotional commitments from the home and the parents to extra-familial individuals and groups." When the adolescent could do this, the situation improved; otherwise, it got worse. But Thomas and Chess do not yet know why one youngster could achieve an identity outside the home and another could not, or even whether the separate identity was the cause of the improvement or the effect.

Behavior problems in children can often be tracked to pathology in a parent or in the family as a unit. But even when such pathology exists, Thomas and Chess advise that its "long and expensive treatment . . . with all the uncertainties as to outcome, should not be undertaken if simpler measures can be effective." They approvingly quote Anna Freud, "who refused to believe 'that mothers need to change their personalities before they can change the handling of their child.'"

During their years as researchers and clinicians, Thomas and Chess have been particularly impressed by one finding—"the breadth and scope of individual differences in behavior of even the youngest infants." This seems to be true throughout nature. They point out that Bryan Clarke, the biologist, has recently reviewed the evidence showing that "most natural populations of plants and animals are genetically heterogeneous, to an extent not previously appreciated." Moreover, Clarke emphasizes, "There is strong evidence that the diversity of forms exists because natural selection favors it; that is, because the variants themselves affect the survival and reproduction of the individuals carrying them."

Clarke quotes Sir Thomas Browne, seventeenth-century physician: "It is the common wonder of all men, how among so many millions of faces, there should be none alike: now contrary, I wonder as much how there should be any." The differences acknowledged by Browne exist in the psychological "faces" of children as well as in the physical. Moreover, it appears that they may arise as a result of parental characteristics displayed not only during the infant's first weeks and months of life, but even while the child is still germinating in the womb.

Some Longtime Effects of Not Being Wanted

The unwanted child may not suffer from a constitutional defect in the usual sense, but he or she may well come into the world at greater risk than other children of encountering circumstances deleterious to mental health and quality of life.

Examining this proposition, several investigators have considered what is probably the worst case—that of the child who was so unwanted that the mother sought an abortion.

In one of these studies, 220 children born to Czechoslovak women whose requests for abortion had been twice denied were compared with a similar number of controls. The children were all about nine years old at the time of the study, and they were judged on the basis of behavioral data, academic achievement, and evaluations given by parents, teachers, and classmates.

The study, reported at the 1975 American Psychological Association by psychologist Henry P. David, was conducted by the Transnational Family Research Institute in Bethesda, Maryland, and David's associates, Zdenek Dytrych, Zdenek Metajcek, and Vratislav Schuller, of Prague, and Herbert L. Friedman, of Geneva.

The investigators hypothesized that children born to women who had been refused abortions would be raised in a less accepting atmosphere than those whose mothers had not attempted to terminate the pregnancy, and that boys would suffer more than girls because of negative attitudes toward males on the part of the reluctantly impregnated mothers.

They found that children born as a result of unwanted pregnancies did, in fact, have difficulties adjusting socially, apparently because of a defensive reaction to stress and frustration. Adjustment problems were particularly noticeable among boys, in whom the most common pattern was aggressive, assertive behavior. Although the pattern may not result in an overt psychiatric disorder in grade-school children, the investigators suggest it may lead to difficulties at puberty and during adolescence.

The children were also evaluated for physical development and medical history; the two groups were generally similar in these characteristics. Acute illness and hospitalization were more common among the children of unwanted pregnancies, however, again particularly among the boys.

Another study of unwanted children, this time in Sweden, makes the point even more clearly. The investigators were Hans Forssman, a psychiatrist, and Inga Thuwe, a social worker, of the psychiatric department of Göteborg University. Their subjects, whom they followed from birth to the age of twenty-one, were 120 children born of women who had been refused a therapeutic abortion. (The grounds for such an abortion included the following: Childbirth would endanger the mother's health; the pregnancy resulted from a felony, such as rape or incest; the child might inherit mental illness, mental deficiency, or a severe physical illness or deformity.) One-third of the original sample of women who had been refused permission for an abortion had one anyway.

As controls, in each case, the investigators usually took the next child of the same sex born in the same hospital. Of the unwanted children, 27 percent were born out of wedlock; of the controls, 8 percent. There was no significant difference between groups in the social class of the fathers—or of the mothers if the child was illegitimate—most of whom were at the middle and lowest of three levels.

Of the unwanted children:

• Sixty percent—more than twice the proportion of the controls—were judged to have had an insecure childhood.
• Twenty-eight percent—almost twice the proportion of the controls—received psychiatric help.
• Eighteen percent were registered with the child welfare board for delinquency, as against 8 percent of the controls.
• Significantly more received some form of public assistance between the ages of sixteen and twenty-one.
• Also, as a group, the unwanted children got significantly less education.

Conclude the investigators: "The very fact a woman applies for legal abortion means that the prospective child runs a risk of having to surmount greater social and mental handicaps than its peers, even when the grounds for the application are so slight that it is refused." They say, too: "Provisions for therapeutic abortion in the law should not only aim to prevent the private tragedy; they should also aim to improve mental hygiene in a wider sense."

It appears that the quality of a child's life may be shaped in part by the degree to which its existence was welcomed by parents in the first place. From other studies, it is equally clear that the quality of the mother's life can be determined by the kind of child, however welcome, that is born to her.

How Parents Are Shaped by Their Children

Developmental psychologist Richard Q. Bell points to a fascinating trend in research on parent-child relationships—and even to some extent a reversal of long-accepted findings.

Until very recently, it was generally accepted that parents, particularly mothers, molded the child—that a youngster's characteristics were shaped mainly by parental influence (with some help, to be sure, from hereditary and constitutional factors). Investigators never considered that the influence might also run the other way—that the child might act upon the mother and the father, might even be responsible for the kind of parental treatment the child received.

"The literature is replete with examples of how certain maternal behaviors affect specific infant functions," point out Michael Lewis and Leonard A. Rosenblum in a book on this subject. "This emphasis needs to be corrected, lest we conclude that the infant is a passive organism constantly being affected but having no effect, constantly being altered but producing no change itself."

For example, many studies over many years have found a relationship between restrictiveness on the part of the parents and dependency on the part of the child. A child who was hemmed in too much by the parents, it was thought, became the child who lacked the freedom to explore and to test his or her capabilities. Consequently, this child failed to develop the skills needed for acting independently.

Bell suspects that very often the relationship runs in the contrary direction: that parents, instead of acting restrictively, *react* restrictively. They keep telling children what to do, keep trying to manage their lives for them, because the children are dependent in the first place. He cites research indicating that if a child is persuaded to act dependently and is then brought into interaction with the parents, the parents will act restrictively.

In one such experiment, the investigator told parents and child to handle a task jointly in order to demonstrate how they worked together. But first the child was told privately that he or she would be working on a difficult task with the parents and that it would be quite all right to ask them for help. Then when parents and child began working together, the child acted dependently, since asking for help had been encouraged. Under those circumstances, even parents who did not normally interfere too much became bossy and restrictive—kept telling the child what to do.

In the second phase of the experiment, the children were told not to ask for help. This time the task was easier. The child seemed to be handling the job all right, so the parents were less inclined to interfere.

By altering the nature of the child's behavior, Bell points out, the investigator can get either effect. If the child is dependent, the parents are more restrictive; if the child is independent, the parents are less restrictive. In the psychological laboratory, then, the child's behavior can alter the parents' behavior—toward greater or less restrictiveness.

More striking examples, because they occur in real life, are provided by research on constitutional differences. One young mother, for instance, had looked forward enthusiastically to the birth of her child. But the baby cried a great deal, demanded an unusual amount of attention, failed to be comforted when held, and smiled only belatedly. The mother's feeling of love and attachment rapidly waned. In fact, she told investigators that she wanted nothing more to do with the baby. Later the infant was found to have come into the world with a damaged brain.

Reporting on studies by other researchers of crying in normal infants, Bell notes that "in the first month or so there is a period during which the mother is in essence at the mercy of the crying of her infant." By the third month, however, "crying is well within what seems to be the tolerance levels of most parents." Still, there are exceptions. The findings of one study showed that in some cases "there was evidence of a breakdown in the caregiving system . . . and something of a vicious cycle developed. Apparently, some infants exceeded their mothers' limits. The mothers' efforts to cope with the crying were inadequate. The infant responded by crying even more, and the mother withdrew even more."

The interaction between mother and infant is also affected by the baby's pattern of wakefulness and restlessness. Different babies have significantly different patterns, and evoke contrasting reactions—calm or frustrated—by parents.

Constitutional differences may even account for many cases of battered children. Note the section in Chapter 8 called "Children Who 'Ask For It.'" Early investigators concluded that the parents of battered children were simply taking out their frustrations on the kids. Many of these parents, however, thought it was they who were being abused. "This could readily be dismissed as a parental defense mechanism," says Bell, "except that it is quite typical to find that other children in the family of an abused child are not abused. . . . Constant fussing, strange and highly irritating crying, or other exasperating behaviors" were often described as characteristic of the one child in the family who was subject to abuse. Moreover, some of these children continued to be abused in a succession of foster homes where no other child had been abused. One survey "indicated that deviance in the child was at least as substantial a factor in explaining the incidents as was deviance in the parents, and the stressful circumstances under which they lived."

Moreover, as noted later in this chapter, psychologist Mary F. Waldrop and colleagues studied children with numerous minor physical defects—too small to be noticed except by someone looking for them— and found a connection between such defects and hyperactive behavior. The mothers of such children "tended to be less supportive and more restrictive than mothers of children with few or no defects." A hyperactive child, the investigators suggest, "might be so demanding and disruptive when frustrated that a parent would feel inclined to invoke punitive and restrictive responses; the punished child could react with hostility and thus stimulate further aggressive parent behavior. Thus, the frequently observed relation between aggressive behavior in children and parental aggression . . . could be due, at least in part, to congenital characteristics of the child."

But the majority of children with constitutional problems suffer psychological rather than physical damage. Recall the case of Nancy, a "difficult" child, described earlier in this chapter. Her parents responded to Nancy's vexing behavior by setting unreasonably high standards. Nancy in turn developed an emotional disorder. The story ended happily because Nancy's teachers eventually discovered that the girl had unusual talents. It is painful to think what her life might have been had her talents been only ordinary. Clearly, from this case and many others, a child's characteristics can vastly affect parental behavior.

These characteristics of course can affect the mother—and the father—for the better as well as for the worse. Even in early infancy Bell finds there is a congenital contributor to smiling and other positive emotional expressions. Babies who possess this factor are in a better position than others to help the parent-infant system get off on the right track. The babies seem to be saying: "Isn't it great to be together!" Such a baby's smiles and noncrying vocalizations, Bell reports, "both stimulate enjoyable social interaction and serve as attachment mechanisms, binding the parent and infant." It is not yet known whether this factor is genetic in origin or caused by environmental forces, perhaps operating before the baby is born.

The baby's capacity for eye-to-eye contact with the mother has also been found to be a key factor in the development of the mother's attachment to the infant. The forerunner of this capacity is the infant's state of visual alertness. And newborn babies differ in how often they spontaneously become alert and in how quickly they respond with alertness to the mother's care.

Infants differ greatly not only in behavior but also in size and shape. J. M. Tanner, of the British Institute of Child Health points out in the Lewis-Rosenblum book that such variation among new babies is just as great, relatively, as it is among school children and adults. Variation in physiological maturity is large, too, "amounting to about 3 to 4 weeks of development among babies all of exactly 40 weeks' gestational age." Tanner adds that the effects of such variations on the caregiver have not been studied scientifically, but "it would be strange if they were negligible."

Developmental psychologist Marian Radke-Yarrow and her associates used a nursery school to study the effects of children's behavior upon adults. Two motherly appearing women experienced in teaching young children were observed as they conducted groups of youngsters who were from 3½ to 5½ years old.

During half of the play periods, the women played a highly nurturant role; that is, they displayed a high frequency of interest, praise, help, and affection. As an example, a child caught a fish in a play pond, and the adult exclaimed, "What a big fish you caught!" In the other play periods the women played the opposite role, and the nurturant behaviors were virtually absent. For instance, a child held up a crayon drawing, and the adult said, "You can do better than that, Marilyn."

Within a given role, the women were instructed to treat each child the same way, and they tried to obey. It soon became clear, however, that different types of children were being treated differently. One example was the adults' response to attention-seeking behavior, such as clowning and bids for help or approval. Such behavior is generally characterized as dependency. Dependent children, it developed, received more than their share of attention when the adults were nurturant. But when the adults were low in nurturance, dependent children met a different fate. For instance, bids for help were rejected 70 percent of the time.

"Do children's dependent qualities," the investigators ask, "intensify nurturance from the warm parent or parent surrogate, and similarly do they magnify nonnurturance from cold parental figures?"

It is tempting to answer yes, but the returns are not yet in. However, the nonnurturant adults also rejected the child when he or she was *not* manifesting dependency. "It was," the investigators comment, "as if the adults were acting according to the child's reputation."

Animal studies, too, highlight the extent to which infants influence mothers. In the research of psychologist Harry F. Harlow, who has used infant monkeys and their mothers to derive important truths about their human analogues, monkey mothers who had been traumatized as infants grew to be neglectful and abusive toward their own babies.

Harlow and his team found in many abused infant monkeys, however, a persistence of the infant's love for the mother—and a capacity to alter thereby her behavior. Those infant monkeys who were fortunate enough to survive their battering persisted, somewhat miraculously, in their intense efforts to make and maintain contact with the maternal body "whether or not the mother scraped them away or engaged in maternal mayhem."

Moreover, Harlow reports, after they had continuously coaxed the mother monkey into accepting prolonged contact, some of the comfort, softness, and warmth appeared to "rub off on the hard heart and head of the unnatural mother." After the maternal contact had been achieved over a period of time, mothers tended to undergo a gradual but progressive rehabilitation; formerly abusive, they now succumbed to the infantile affection offered them. The mothers who yielded were substantially cured by the therapeutic interventions of their young. They were, in Harlow's words, "impressively more normal in the treatment of subsequent infants of their own."

In the human world, too, a mother cannot help but be affected by her baby. The two will match up best, therefore, if she recognizes early what kind of infant she has and acts accordingly.

Anneliese F. Korner, of Stanford, reports in the Lewis-Rosenblum book that "an extraordinary degree of flexibility is required for mothers to respond appropriately to the cues of different infants as they are at birth and as they grow and change."

Korner notes some pitfalls: "A mother's conviction that even very young babies require a good deal of stimulation may severely hamper an excitable baby's success in achieving any kind of homeostasis. A mother's fear of 'spoiling' her infant may make her refrain from soothing efforts which he requires to settle down. Or a mother who . . . may wish for a cuddly newborn to whom she can give a lot of contact comfort, may react in disappointment if she happens to have an active, uncuddly baby who resists physical restraint."

Clearly, the relationship between mother and child depends vastly both on the baby's temperamental qualities and on the mother's ability to recognize them and guide her behavior accordingly.

Psychological Effects of Physical Illness and Injury

Though physical illness is not usually considered constitutional, some children actually are, or seem to be, more predisposed to physical illness of one kind or another than other children. And in any child a physical illness may bring with it a host of psychological troubles.

The intimate interaction between the body and the mind is increasingly recognized by doctors and nonprofessionals alike, but somehow we are less prone to recognize it in the case of children than in adults.

Encouraged by an army of child experts in recent decades, we have become inclined to look only for psychological dynamics to explain every item in a child's behavioral repertoire. If a child is hostile, depressed, anxious, apathetic, hyperactive, fearful, or even psychotic, it *must* be something in his or her environment or upbringing, parents believe, that caused the condition. We act as if our children are comprised only of psyches, without brains or bodies that contribute to personality and behavior.

Perhaps it is because of children's difficulty or inability to communicate many of their internal physiological feelings that their mental health is often thought to be unaffected by their physical condition. Nevertheless, just as in adults, their physical and mental worlds are inextricably related.

Last fall, a brilliant high school sophomore, whom we shall call Mark Barnes, began to show signs of emotional problems serious enough to begin seeing a child psychiatrist regularly. He became chronically anxious and downcast, began staying in bed too late to make classes, dropped his social life, stopped eating, and belligerently thwarted his friends at every turn. Six months later he was back on top of his class— and the world.

Was it the therapy that turned Mark around?

Not so. What caused his symptoms was actually a physical illness rather than psychological "hang-ups." The psychotherapy Mark received was irrelevant, and actually delayed his recovery. He regained his health only after getting off the couch and securing appropriate medical treatment.

It was a chance meeting between Mark's parents and his childhood pediatrician that led to Mark's recovery. The pediatrician ordered blood tests, and his suspicions were confirmed. The young patient was suffering the emotional fallout typical in severe cases of mononucleosis ("mono") found so frequently among high school and college students.

Mark's case highlights a problem in diagnosis—and subsequent treatment—that is badly underestimated. Too many doctors and their patients overlook the fact that mental health problems can spring from physical as well as psychological causes. Not every dramatic change of mood need have an emotional basis.

Parents especially have been unduly persuaded that every aspect of their children's behavior is filled with psychodynamic meanings. No Freudian stone has been left unturned, and we have come to regard our young as bundles of complexes and conflicts, as if their bodies are only along in life for the ride.

The sources of our emotional distress cannot always be neatly categorized. Each of us—children as well as adults—is a wondrous mix of physical and psychological forces, of neurons and hormones as well as memories and attitudes. Neither life nor emotions—which are part of life—can be explained in simple terms.

This much is certain: When the child's normal physiological processes are disrupted or when physical illness erodes the child's well-being, mental health is likely to suffer.

As in adults, the physical illnesses and injuries of children bring with them changes that significantly affect the victim's emotional well-being. Pain, weakness, fatigue, alterations in daily routine and emotional climate—all of these, for example, challenge the patient's resources for coping with life. For the child, physician Charles R. Shaw and child psychiatrist Alexander Lucas point out, such experiences are especially troubling and frightening, since they are new and the child has not yet learned that they are likely to pass.

Anna Freud identified four potential sources of maladjustment introduced into the lives of children as a result of physical disease:

- The emotional climate between the sick child and his parents is altered. Unexpected handling or unexpected indulgences may leave the child feeling helpless and bewildered, yet later, when circumstances change, the emotional "gains" are difficult to give up.
- Nursing care—in which, for example, the child is fed, cleaned,

and helped with excretory activities—appears to the child as a loss of control in areas where control has only recently been won. The result is a pull toward earlier and more passive levels of development. The child may then lapse into a state of helpless infancy or, instead, become obstinate and uncontrollable.

• Restricted movement and diet may lead to body tics or to recurrent rages or temper tantrums.

• If they are required, surgical procedures elevate the child's level of anxiety by conjuring up thoughts of being attacked, overwhelmed, or castrated, or by suggesting that repressed fantasies are somehow becoming real.

Whatever the particular source of maladjustment, Freud believes that children have a choice of two major ways of reacting to the awareness that their bodies are disabled. They can either seek extra love and attention from the mother or other caretaker, or they can withdraw from the world about them and concentrate instead on their bodily needs.

Psychologist F. E. James has identified five major categories of psychological problems posed by the stressful experience of illness:

• Behavior disorders—among them, night terrors, sleepwalking, fear of the dark or of hidden dangers, hypochondria, and excessive irritability

• Disturbances in interpersonal relationships—for example, withdrawal from social contacts, frequent outbursts of temper, shyness and timidity, and a peaking in demands made on the mother

• Habit disorders such as bed-wetting, nail biting, or rejection of food

• Conduct disorders—for example, stealing—intended to draw attention and concern

• School learning problems

Even minor illnesses can carry considerable emotional repercussions for the child. Shaw and Lucas find that following an illness, regardless of severity, children often revert to earlier behaviors such as those just listed. New symptoms are known to develop as well, frequently taking the form of mood swings, changes in the child's relationship with parents and siblings, loss of self-confidence, or temper tantrums.

While regression and anxiety are the most common reactions in both children and adults, other responses occur. Believing that illness has been inflicted on them because they did something wrong, many youngsters feel guilty and view the disease—and the death they may fear it is leading to—as their due punishment. Helplessness and lowered self-esteem are common. At the same time children become angry and resent the disruptions in their usual routines. They may resort to self-indulgence or, especially if their movement is restricted mechanically, there may be an increase in aggressiveness, restlessness, and irritability. Nevertheless, Shaw and Lucas declare that most children recover from the emotional effects of an illness, whether it is prolonged and serious or short and mild.

Physical handicaps, whether the result of accident, illness, or a congenital condition, also can cripple a child emotionally. Psychiatrist Ednita Bernabeau points out, for instance, that crippled youngsters usually adopt an air of superficial cheerfulness, optimism, cooperation, and nonaggressiveness. But this frequently gives way to crying spells, stubbornness, temper tantrums, and semblances of revenge and revolt. Such outbursts are understandable because their affliction propels them into an internal world wrought with fears—of death and suffocation, fragmentation, separation from others, castration, loss of love, punishment, and their own aggressiveness. It is common for these children to carry a good deal of guilt as well. This stems not only from the belief that their condition is a punishment but also from their wishes that it had struck someone else and from their desire for revenge so that normal people can see what it is like to be crippled.

Psychologist Stephen Richardson of the Association for the Aid of Crippled Children adds that a handicap tends to be "blunting" because the child is usually excluded from the activities of his or her peers, lacks social experience, and has fewer friendships.

Psychiatrists U. P. Seidel, O. F. D. Chadwick, and Michael Rutter have found that a child with a mild handicap is likely to develop more psychiatric problems than one with a more severe disability. This may be so because, able to participate normally in many activities, the child finds it hard to accept that some activities are simply beyond his or her capability. The child with a severe incapacity more readily accepts that he or she cannot behave entirely like a nonhandicapped person. Indeed, the taste of normality that the partially disabled child experiences can be a source of unrelenting frustration.

Plainly, physical illness and disability may considerably affect a child's mental health. Though the impact may be temporary in some cases, the relationship between emotional and physical well-being ought to be better recognized by parents and physicians alike.

Hidden Physiological Factors

Some children have exhibited clear psychological disturbances and been treated for years by mental health professionals to no avail. Consider the following case report, based on one written by the boy's mother:

Paul was born prematurely, weighing 5 pounds and 2 ounces, and meal times, throughout his life, have triggered behavioral symptoms. In infancy, he regurgitated food. In adolescence, he had stomach cramps. As an adult, he is selective and critical.

A dual personality appeared to be developing. He was toilet trained and spoke in full sentences at nine months old, rode a bicycle before he was two years old, was exceptionally curious and eager to learn, and could be taken anywhere. But he would nap unusually long and at times fall asleep while playing. Though an active, bright child who knew right from wrong, he would suddenly become rebellious and very difficult to control. At times he was a miniature adult and at other times an uncontrollable, rebellious child.

Because I insisted that something must be wrong, Paul was admitted to a children's hospital and extensive tests were taken. The decision was that he was healthy and that I was just an overconcerned parent.

His teachers, too, recognized that Paul was exceptionally bright but that he seemed bored and disinterested. He was underachieving, particularly on tests. He received ten awards for his ability to play the piano. Yet when he was to play the next time, for an award for which he had worked hard for ten years, his memory suddenly failed.

I took him to a clinical psychologist, who found that Paul scored at the average level on the tests one day and at a very high level on another day. The psychologist reported that the boy needed help to cope with the inner conflict that confused him and made him feel insecure.

Paul proceeded on to college determined to develop his potential. Again his instructors were puzzled by the discrepancy between his daily performance and his lack of achievement on tests—and by the A performance that would mysteriously drop to the D level. Tormented by fear and guilt, Paul overextended himself to the fatigue point. Finally, worried about the money being spent on tuition and self-driven to prove himself, he left school and went to work.

Though quickly advanced, his erratic behavior under pressure eventually cost him the job. He returned home defeated, guilty, and difficult to live with. His behavior seemed irrational and hysterical—almost violent. But after several weeks of rest and of eating whenever he wished, the other personality emerged. He had no difficulty finding an equally good job. However, the pattern did not change. . . .

One time at a party, towards the end of the evening, he suddenly felt the need for help and demanded to be taken to a hospital. Belligerent and irrational on arrival, he was given a sedative. When the effects of this wore off, he demanded food. Soon after, very apologetic, he insisted on being released because he felt perfectly well.

One day not long after, while watching television, Paul suddenly started to pace up and down the room. He began to perspire and to complain of feeling cold. He lay on the couch shivering as though he had a high fever. He lapsed into what appeared to be a semi-conscious stage. He moaned something about pain but didn't respond when asked where he felt it. He begged to be helped; he asked for something to eat. By the time the doctor arrived, Paul appeared to be perfectly well. The demand for food made the doctor suspect hypoglycemia. The 8-hour glucose test confirmed the diagnosis.

Understanding the nature of Paul's illness and how to manage it was the beginning of physical and mental recovery. Thereafter there were to be no more such crises.

Behavioral abnormalities secondary to episodes of *hypoglycemia*—an abnormally low level of sugar in the blood—are common. New York University pediatricians Harry Bakwin and Ruth Morris Bakwin explain that hypoglycemia causes a change in the brain's functioning. Young children show this change in their irritable and fretful behavior, older children in their confusion, negativism, and violent outbursts. Other symptoms include emotional lability, depression, weakness, daytime drowsiness, nighttime insomnia, anxiety, inability to concentrate on or comprehend a problem, and restlessness.

Physician Charles K. Gorman of the University of Toronto notes that sudden, violent activity in a quiet and withdrawn child when excited ever so slightly is a sign of this condition. Involuntary twitching is typical, as is impairment of ability to execute coordinated movement. Prolonged hypoglycemia can result in brain damage, ranging from mild to severe.

Undetected thyroid disorders can lead to severe problems, too. An example is *hypothyroidism*, which results from too low a level of the thyroid hormone. For more than half a century, researchers and clinicians have emphasized the inevitability of mental retardation due to hypothyroidism in children born with this condition unless there is adequate treatment, which entails the administration of the hormone in graduated doses.

In 1972, University of Pittsburgh pediatricians Alan H. Klein, Stephanie Meltzer, and Fredric M. Kenny studied children born with hypothyroidism in an attempt to discern a critical period in which to begin therapy. They compared four groups of these children in terms of when their therapy began: A—before three months of age, B—between three and five months of age, C—between five and seven months, and D—after seven months. Three years later intelligence tests indicated that the later therapy is initiated, the lower is the range of IQ scores. (The range in Group A was 64–107; in B, 36–96; in C, 34–97; and in D, 25–80.)

Hypothyroidism can be either congenital or acquired. Pediatricians David Smith, Robert Blizzard, and Lawson Wilkins, at the Johns Hopkins University School of Medicine, found that its most serious deleterious effect tends to occur during the period between fetal life and two years of age. When the defect is acquired after this critical stage, it does not seriously affect mental attainment.

Mental dysfunction as the result of hypothyroidism manifests itself in various ways, including *perseveration* (an identical response to varying questions), *periphrasis* (the use of a longer phrasing in place of a shorter form of expression), and *aphasia* (loss or impairment of the ability to use language). Accompanying these are lethargy, feeding problems, unwanted weight gains, and other symptoms. Once treatment is instituted, additional disturbances—such as rebelliousness, extreme assertiveness, obstinacy—may appear for a time until the body has adapted to the hormone.

The opposite condition, know as *hyperthyroidism* or *thyrotoxicosis*, occurs when the level of the thyroid hormone is too high rather than too low. From a study of 70 children with this condition, Krishna Saxena, a Harvard Medical School pediatrician, and his colleagues identify common symptoms. These include nervousness, restlessness, difficulties with school work, crying spells, temper tantrums, irritability, lack of concentration, staring, and hyperkinesis. Other investigators have found that anxiety and emotional instability are also common and that affected children are easily excitable, quarrelsome, and hostile. They may have suicidal tendencies, fainting spells, and a morbid concern about health, and they may be clumsy in their use of the fine muscles and prone to enuresis. Unfortunately, thyrotoxicosis is sometimes not diagnosed as such because of its presumed rarity.

Yet another physical disorder that is frequently overlooked in attempts to explain children's behavioral symptoms is iron deficiency anemia, a blood condition resulting from the depletion of the body's iron stores. Anemic children often suffer from fatigue, weakness, inability to concentrate, irritability, and loss of appetite; they may display conduct disorders in school and show disturbances in attention and perception. Among children with the deficiency there is also a high incidence of breath holders.

Psychiatrist Sidney L. Werkman and his associates, examining the behavioral correlates of iron deficiency anemia, found that affected children are less mature, more easily frightened, and more passive. They have more behavioral difficulties, cry more often, throw more tantrums, fight more, have more sleeping disturbances, are more often enuretic, and display more habits like finger sucking and nail biting. A poor home environment may be involved as well, but the impact of the child's physiology is difficult to deny.

Minor Physical Deviations and Problem Behavior

John's head is a little bigger around than normal. His eyes are slightly farther apart than usual, and each has a fold of skin covering the inside corner, where upper and lower lids join at the nose. This, called the epicanthus fold, gives him a faintly Oriental look. The little fingers of his hands curve slightly inward, toward the other fingers, and the gaps between his first and second toes are somewhat greater than in most children.

John is a restless, boisterous, attention-demanding child. During babyhood, his mother was forever keeping him from getting into things. In first grade he suddenly shoots from his seat several times a day and runs around the room. On the playground, when permitted to join in a group activity, he usually breaks it up fast.

Several things can be said about this boy. First, he has some minor physical abnormalities, which have gone unnoticed by his parents, the family doctor, and the boy himself. Most other children have such abnormalities, but John, with five, has two or three more than usual. Second, he is hyperactive, which almost certainly means that—unless he can be successfully treated—he is destined for trouble both in school and in his relations with other children.

Thanks to a growing body of research, something else can be said: John's minor physical deviations, known also as *anomalies* or *stigmata*, are somehow linked to his hyperactivity. Indeed, if we had known when John was born what we know now, the slight physical deviations could have been used to *predict* the behavior deviations, and possibly something could have been done to prevent or ameliorate the hyperactive behavior.

Physical abnormalities like John's are congenital, or present at birth. Although hundreds have been recognized, only 18 have been used to any extent in research. These include head circumference, larger or smaller than normal; very fine hair that won't comb down; a larger than usual distance between tear ducts; low-set ears; lack of ear lobes; high-steepled palate; curved fifth finger; only one crease across the palm horizontally; third toe longer than or equal in length to second toe; and two middle toes partially webbed.

Such anomalies have long been associated with Down's syndrome, or mongolism. Through the work of psychiatrist William Goldfarb and pediatrician Anne Botstein, they have been related to childhood schizophrenia as well. Goldfarb examined three groups of children: those with schizophrenia, those with behavior disorders, and controls. He found that the schizophrenic children had the largest number of minor abnormalities, and the control group the smallest.

Mary F. Waldrop and her associates at the National Institute of Mental Health studied a number of presumably normal 2½-year-olds who were attending a research nursery school. The greater the number of minor physical anomalies (from a list of 18), it was discovered, the more likely it was that the child was hyperactive, aggressive, and hard to manage. It was the number of such anomalies, not the presence of any particular one, that was related to problem behavior.

When the study was repeated with another sample of children similar results emerged. Again, boys with more than the average number of anomalies were found to be characterized by frenetic, impulsive, poorly controlled behavior. Not so this time with the girls. Those girls with high anomaly scores did indeed have a behavior problem, but it was one of overcontrol. Instead of darting about, these girls tended to withdraw. They also tended to be inhibited, stubborn, fearful, and perseverative.

To help explain this inconsistency, the investigators noted that attempts to classify behavior disorders had usually found two groups of children. The first comprised the aggressive and rebellious children; the second, the anxious, neurotic, and inhibited. And girls were more likely to be found among the latter. "Since minor physical anomalies appear to be associated with a major problem that is characteristic of boys," Waldrop and her colleagues pointed out, ". . . it is reasonable to expect an association of anomalies with the most salient problem of girls—that is, with inhibition."

Testing that idea, the NIMH team studied some 90 elementary school girls, in grades from kindergarten through sixth. About half had been selected by their teachers as being among the most inhibited, inattentive, fearful, and socially inept in their classes. These were called the inhibited group. The others—called the outgoing group—

had been selected for being outgoing, attentive, spontaneous, and socially at ease.

When the anomaly scores of the two groups were compared, the inhibited girls were found to have—as had been expected—a significantly higher number of anomalies than the others. They also had significantly lower IQs and significantly lower ratings of coordination.

Why should girls differ from boys in the type of behavior associated with minor physical abnormalities? The investigators answer that "the fundamental hormonal and central nervous system structures involved in the control of motor and expressive behavior may differ for males and females. A genetic or teratogenetic [anomaly-forming] agent operating during pregnancy could have a different effect because of basic differences in the nature of the target systems. Consistent with this possibility is the fact that there are known sex differences in vulnerability to complications of pregnancy and delivery."

Another possibility is the age-old difference—at least until day before yesterday—in the behaviors considered appropriate for males and females. Waldrop points out that boys in the main have been encouraged to engage in strongly assertive, if not actually aggressive, behaviors; girls have been discouraged from doing so. Possibly girls with a number of minor anomalies are inclined when very young to be impulsive and frenetic, as Waldrop in her first sample found them to be. But because of socialization standards, perhaps girls have been punished for such behavior and rewarded for the opposite type. So by age three some girls may have learned to overcompensate for their tendencies to be impulsive, thereby becoming inhibited. Acting, perhaps, as a counter to this behavior modification hypothesis is the fact that males are more vulnerable not only to hyperactivity—by ratios as large as 8 to 1 in some studies—but also to some other neurological and behavioral problems, including learning disorders and psychosis.

"Inhibited girls," Waldrop and her associates add, "may have as many problems and be as distressed as hyperactive boys but fail to get comparable attention, because they are not as disturbing and disruptive to either the classroom or to the home."

The NIMH investigators have also studied a sample of children who had been referred to an Easter Seal Treatment Center Nursery School because of congenital deficiencies in speech or hearing or both. The hypothesis was that in a sample of children selected for congenital deficiencies, there would be a higher incidence of minor physical abnormalities. This was borne out. In the case of boys, the number of anomalies ranged from 3 to 12; in girls, from 4 to 11. The teachers characterized at least 75 percent of these children as hyperactive.

What causes minor physical anomalies? Research has turned up a number of clues. Study of fetuses aborted at different stages of development shows that such anomalies are formed during the first three months of pregnancy. Moreover, some of them are found in the children of mothers who took certain drugs very early in pregnancy in an unsuccessful attempt to induce abortion. Further, child psychiatrist Judith L. Rapoport, pediatrician Patricia O. Quinn and colleagues at the Georgetown University have found that a high anomaly score is often associated with a history of obstetrical complications in the mother, including bleeding and toxemia. Finally, a high score is often associated with a history of hyperactivity in the father.

From such findings it may be inferred that some untoward event—an insult, in medical terms—early in pregnancy can lead to both a physical and a behavioral abnormality or, in the latter case, at least to a predisposition to one. The untoward event might be engineered by genetic factors, or by constitutional elements in the mother, or by external factors—such as a chemical or a virus—acting upon the mother.

A recent discovery by Rapoport and her associates points to yet another possible factor. These investigators have found that a certain enzyme involved in producing a compound of major importance to the proper functioning of the nervous system seems to be associated with higher-than-average numbers of physical imperfections.

The enzyme is dopamine-Beta-hydroxylase (DBH). It is the final enzyme used by the body to manufacture norepinephrine. Norepinephrine in turn is one of the major *neurotransmitters*, compounds essential for transmitting messages from nerve cell to nerve cell. Differences between individuals in basic levels of DBH seem in large part to be genetically controlled. But changes in the enzyme's activity, as measured by the amount of DBH found at various times in the blood plasma, may reflect changes in nervous system activity.

The investigators found that in a group of hyperactive boys referred to a clinic, the higher a boy's stigmata score, the greater the likelihood that his hyperactivity and problem-behavior scores would be high, too. Also, the higher his stigmata score, the greater the probability that the amount of DBH in his blood plasma would be high.

The significance? No one can yet say. Possibly there is none. Or possibly the finding may be an indication of the importance of biochemical systems in influencing behavior.

Case histories and classroom studies demonstrate that children who have more of the slight physical imperfections than usual are unpopular with their peers. Apparently the imperfections by themselves have nothing to do with this unhappy state; unless looked for carefully, they are not noticeable. Rapoport and her associates showed color photographs of 72 children to nurses and teachers and asked them to rate each child on the basis of attractiveness. No relation was found between this rating and a child's anomaly score. Unpopularity appears to be based not on appearance but on temperament and behavior.

It should be emphasized that the research findings presented in this section apply to groups of children but not to every individual in each group. For example, Rapoport found three siblings who were apparently normal and happy although they had a number of minor anomalies. At the opposite extreme, three hyperactive siblings had low stigmata scores. The findings do demonstrate, nevertheless, that early warning systems to detect many of the children *likely* to develop serious problems can now be established. In addition to Down's syndrome, hyperactivity, and childhood schizophrenia, these problems include severe learning disability, borderline psychosis, and autism. No link between anomalies and either neurosis or physical illness has been found.

The impact on mental health of the child's physical and emotional constitution clearly can be considerable. At the same time, as subsequent chapters portray, the environment into which our children are born and in which they grow carries potent effects as well. These effects can now be more accurately defined than ever before, and an understanding of them should profoundly shape our relationship with the young.

Mothers
Saints or Sinners?

The judge rapped for silence. He wore a pure white robe, and with his beard and pipe and stern but knowing look, he was the popular image of a psychoanalyst. Before him was an elaborate nameplate: JUDGE SIGMUND FREUD.

The jury filed in—a panel of experts on child development that included psychiatrists, psychologists, sociologists, social workers, and syndicated counseling columnists.

In the prisoner's dock sat a young mother, her eyes heavy with torment. She faced a vast courtroom strangely occupied only by infants and young children.

The clerk arose to read the charges: "Sometimes loses temper with son. . . . shouts. . . . On one or two occasions has been known to slap her child in anger. . . . Once slammed the door on her screaming three-year-old when he refused to go to sleep. . . ."

"How do you plead?" asked Judge Freud.

"Guilty," whispered the prisoner. And then, in a crescendo of sobs born of remorse and self-hate, she screams again and again: "GUILTY. . . . GUILTY. . . . G-U-I-L-T-Y!"

At this moment in the courtroom drama, the "prisoner" awoke from her dream, bathed in the cold sweat of a nightmare.

The dreamer is the mother of three youngsters, and she needed no help in interpreting her nightmare. It neatly summarized the conflict of guilt and doubt that pervaded her waking life as a mother—the very same kind that shrouds so many hours in the lives of countless of her contemporaries. Like so many other mothers, she is an unintended victim of the age of psychology and its parade of experts in child development, from Sigmund Freud himself to the overzealous school counselor. They have taught us that parental attitudes and behavior can be important factors in shaping the child's personality. True—to a degree. But the message has been overstated by many professionals and overlearned by eager parents.

Faced with years of admonitions about the do's and do not's of child rearing, the anxious mother lives, in the opinion of child expert Fritz Redl, "as though a psychiatrist just flew by the window." Such a mother is quite convinced that somehow she is to blame for all of her child's shortcomings. Worse yet, she is certain that her very next parental sin will spell eternal psychological damnation for the child—a life of maladjustment, neurosis, or worse.

In the past, the mother has been a special target, for example, in explaining schizophrenia in children and the adults they become. The literature of psychoanalysis in particular is filled with reference to the "schizophrenogenic" mother—a mother who gives rise to that devastating psychosis in children unlucky enough to grow in her environment. Such mothers have been tagged as "cold and castrating" in their relationships with their young, unable to provide unambiguous signals of love to the growing child. Now, however, the emphasis has slowly turned from the mother as the lone culprit to the emotional environment of the home and, as the basic underlying cause, to a genetic defect leading to neurological impairment that renders the child vulnerable in the first place.

Similar data, taking mothers off the hook on which they have long been impaled, have emerged from studies of other child disorders as well, from autism to hyperactivity. Despite new research information, however, it is still the mother who is often regarded as the sole architect of a disturbed child's emotional miseries. A few years ago, there was no evidence to help reverse the resulting guilt of many conscientious mothers. Today, however, we know better. Mothers simply do not deserve all the blame—or all the credit—for what their children become. As is evident from material throughout this book, the mother does not stand alone, bestriding her child like some giant psychological colossus. Rather, she is one of a complex web of factors—father, school, friends, the baby's nature itself.

Nevertheless, the mother's special relationship and influence cannot be swept aside. The work of many investigators has helped us now to sharpen our understanding of her actual role, and what she may—or may not—contribute to the mental health of her children.

The Origins of Attachment

The intimate relationship between mother and child has been celebrated since the beginning of time by scribes, poets, and philosophers. Thackeray said it well: "Mother is the name for God in the lips and hearts of little children."

Contemporary behavioral scientists have continued to view the mother-child relationship as a significant element in a child's evolution. "During the early months of life," explains child psychiatrist John Bowlby, a pioneer investigator in the field, "the infant is learning to discriminate a particular figure, usually his mother, and is developing a strong liking to be in her company. After about six months, he shows his preference in unmistakable fashion. . . . Throughout the latter half of his first year and during the whole of his second and third, he is closely attached to his mother figure, which means that he is content in her company and distressed in her absence." According to psychology text authors, Gregory A. Kimble, Norman Garmezy, and Edward Zigler, of all the processes that influence a child, probably none is more important to later development than this attachment.

In defining *attachment,* these psychologists point out that the child's desire for closeness to other people is one of the most striking characteristics of infancy—a basic fact of infant life. "He is pleased when this proximity results in physical contact and/or attention, and is unhappy when the proximity is reduced or denied him." In real life terms, attachment embraces all those things children do as they strive to stay in touch—physically or at least psychologically. As every mother knows, during the first year of life, the most prominent of such behaviors is crying, whose meaning is described in detail in the next section.

What's back of attachment? Is there something inherent in the mother, something built in biologically or genetically, which the young infant senses and to which it responds? Or, does the mother become the object of the baby's attachment because it is she who provides the stimulation for the infant's senses and who responds to the child's attempts to master the world? Or, is it perhaps just that the mother is usually the one who is there?

In the attempt to make psychological sense out of the process by which an infant attaches itself emotionally to the mother, a bewildering array of theories has emerged. Three stand out.

It was Sigmund Freud, the patron saint of all those who point to mother as the key figure in human development, who developed a *psychoanalytic theory* to explain the infant-mother attachment process. The baby, according to Freud, brings into the world a degree of psychological energy (Freud called it *libido*), and the baby focuses this energy on the object which, in a social sense, is nearest to him or her. For Freud, the baby's psychic energy can be directed and focused or pulled back when necessary, almost as if the baby had psychological antennae used to probe the environment and find the right object for attaching the energy with which he or she comes into the world.

For Freud, the psychic energy is already in place when the baby is born. The libido and the energy it radiates exist by predisposition in the newborn and extend toward the mother because it is she who satisfies the baby's oral needs. The child incorporates the mother and through the sucking process makes the mother part of himself or herself.

In contrast to Freud's ideas, there is *social learning theory*. This sees the mother in the role of responding—at first consistently and then intermittently—to the baby's needs as the baby expresses them. Thus the young child is reinforced or rewarded for crying, or for whatever other behavior elicits the mother's attention. Psychologists have found in experimental work that intermittent reinforcement strengthens the desired behavior—which in this case would be attachment—more than constant reinforcement.

The third major theory argues that attachment behavior promoted the survival of the species through the ages and thus became a genetic characteristic. Prominent proponents of this theory have been child psychiatrist Bowlby, in England, and, more recently, psychologist Mary D. Salter Ainsworth, of the University of Virginia. Together with associates Silvia M. Bell and Donelda J. Stayton, Ainsworth explains:

From what is known of ground-living nonhuman primates and present-day human communities of hunters and gatherers, it is believed that in the original environment of evolutionary adaptedness mother and infant, usually with companions, moved about frequently through open country where predators presented an ever-possible danger. In a wide variety of mammalian species that currently occupy such environments, the victims of predation tend to be limited to the very young, the very old, and those disabled through illness or injury. Under such circumstances it is of obvious survival advantage for an infant who has somehow lost proximity to his mother to emit a vocal signal perceptible across a distance; it is equally of advantage for his mother to respond to such a signal promptly. Since a vocal signal might also attract a predator, it is of advantage also that it be terminated promptly once infant and mother are together again, but at the same time it seems adaptive for an infant to continue and perhaps intensify his signals should his mother not respond quickly. Nevertheless it is advantageous for an infant to learn to reserve crying for the more alarming situations he encounters.

In other words, when babies are out of contact with their mothers or distressed for other reasons, Ainsworth believes they have a built-in command to cry and to behave as though the situation were a matter of life or death. This is so even though the conditions that usually obtain in the Western world today do not require such behavior.

Whatever one's theoretical orientation, it is clear enough that the attachment between baby and mother is there. It cannot be argued away.

Differences in Attachment Behavior: When Baby Cries

Ainsworth and her associates have been analyzing mother-infant relationships in the home for a decade. Supplementing these observations, they have also devised a laboratory situation to which baby and mother are introduced when the child is about a year old. The investigators wished to see how the child would explore an unfamiliar environment and react to a stranger outside the home. Moreover, how would the child respond to brief separations from the mother and behave when she returned?

They found striking differences in the responses and could, in fact, distinguish three main groups of babies:

• Babies who were *secure* in their attachment to their mothers. These children comprised the largest group. They responded to the mother's return by seeking to be close. Most of them wanted to be picked up; they resisted attempts to put them down quickly.

• Babies who behaved much the same way as the first group, except that they not only sought contact but also angrily resisted it. These were labeled *ambivalent.*

• Babies who either ignored the mother completely upon her return or who, though sometimes seeking closeness, also kept looking, turning, or moving away from her. These were called *avoidant*. The mothers of the babies in this group either disliked physical contact with their children or were indifferent to it. Compared to other mothers, they tended either to rebuff the child who sought contact or to make the contact so disturbing or painful that the babies did not enjoy it.

Ainsworth believes that the babies in the second and third groups "are anxious in the attachment relationships" and that "early patterns of interaction . . . tend to have their own momentum." But she points out that many later experiences, including interactions with the mother and other figures, "undoubtedly have an effect—for better or for worse."

Of the mothers studied intensively in their homes (the families are white and middle class), many responded promptly when their babies cried, but many others did not. Some of these deliberately failed to respond because they held the belief—still very common—that to respond would be to spoil. But the researchers' findings suggest otherwise: Babies who fuss and cry a good deal after the first few months and are considered "spoiled children" are the very ones whose cries have not been responded to for a long time or have been ignored completely.

From other aspects of mother-infant interaction in the first year, these investigators conclude that the mother's responsiveness, instead of spoiling the child, promotes desirable behavior. They report:

Infants whose mothers have given them relatively much tender and affectionate holding in the earliest months of life are content with surprisingly little physical contact by the end of the first year; although they enjoy being held, when put down they are happy to move off into independent exploratory play. In contrast, those held for relatively brief periods during the early months tend to be ambivalent about contact by the end of the first year; they do not respond positively when held, but yet protest when put down and do not turn readily to independent activity.

Additional findings:

• Babies who show no distress when, at home, the mother leaves the room briefly, "tend to have mothers who have been responsive to crying and other signals, while those who more frequently cry when she leaves and do not want to let her out of sight tend to have mothers who have been unresponsive."

- Infant obedience is not fostered by such disciplinary practices as "frequent commands and physical interventions intended to restrict and modify a baby's behavior."
- Babies who do what the mother commands and who can be controlled across a distance are those whose signals—such as crying, gesture, facial expression—have been answered "promptly and sensitively."

"In short," the investigators say, "those infants in our sample who are fussy, demanding, and difficult to control are those whose mothers have been unresponsive to signals and generally insensitive or interfering in their efforts to mold their babies to their routines, wishes, and expectations. . . . infants whose mothers are responsive to their signals have less occasion to cry—not only in the first few months but throughout infancy . . . a mother who is responsive to the signals implicit in a wide range of her baby's behavior creates an atmosphere in which he can signal through varied means less urgent than crying."

Unfortunately, mothers have received conflicting advice on this subject—whether or not to pay attention to crying—from a source as authoritative as the *Infant Care* pamphlets prepared by the U.S. Children's Bureau. Bell and Ainsworth reviewed these publications and found that, between 1920 and 1940, "mothers were admonished not to pick up a baby between feedings, lest the baby learn 'that crying will get him what he wants, sufficient to make a spoiled, fussy baby, and a household tyrant whose continual demands make a slave of the mother.'" More recently the Bureau has encouraged mothers to follow their natural impulse to respond to crying.

Won't constant attention to the baby's crying and other signals interfere with the development of independence?

Not so, the investigators reply. Crying is "one manifestation of an emergent communication system." Through it and other signals, and the responses, the baby learns to affect the behavior of people in his or her environment. Far from interfering with the development of competence, maternal responsiveness actually encourages it.

The researchers, who conducted their studies at Johns Hopkins University, have also found an example of what they call a *virtuous spiral*: "Mothers who are tender and careful in their physical handling of the baby in the early months seem to engender in him a tendency to respond positively to close bodily contact. This in turn tends to evoke an affectionate response in the mother, which may contribute all the more to the baby's enjoyment of contact."

Such tender and affectionate behavior, it might be thought, would make the baby reluctant to leave the mother in order to explore the world. But Ainsworth and her associates have found just the opposite to be true. The child who has a secure attachment with the mother also has a secure base—the mother—for exploratory operations.

Why Attachments Flourish—or Fail

Evidence that maternal attachment begins very early, perhaps during a particularly sensitive or critical period soon after birth, as in some animals, may be seen in cases where hospitals have mistakenly given the mother somebody else's baby. In some such incidents, mothers have become so attached to a stranger's child that they hesitate to give it up even for their own.

Are there ways for encouraging or strengthening attachment? The research answer is yes. For example, work by pediatricians Marshall H. Klaus, John H. Kennel, and their associates at the School of Medicine, Case Western Reserve University, suggests that a modification of hospital practices immediately after a baby is born may significantly strengthen the bond between mother and child.

In this study, 14 women giving birth for the first time were allowed an unusual amount of physical contact with their infants. The mothers—mainly lower class and black—were given their babies for an hour shortly after birth, and then for five hours each afternoon for the three following days before they went home. These 16 hours of contact were in addition to the routine contact permitted all mothers of normal infants. For controls, the investigators selected 14 women whose backgrounds were similar to those of the others; they were given their babies for only the brief periods customary in many maternity wards.

A month later, each mother's behavior was assessed by means of a standardized interview, observation of how she acted while the baby was being examined, and a time-lapse moving picture of her bottle-feeding the baby.

The findings were as follows: Since their return from the hospital, the mothers who had been given the extra contact with their infants had been more reluctant to leave home and trust the baby to someone else; usually they stood and watched while their babies were being examined; they tried more often to soothe the baby when it cried; they fondled the baby more and engaged in more eye-to-eye contact. Similar differences were found at one year, two years, and five years. Moreover, at two years, the mothers who had had the extended contact used twice as many questions in talking with their children and fewer commands.

Considering the many factors that influence maternal behavior—including the mother's experiences as a child and adult—the investigators find it surprising that just 16 extra hours during the first few days had such persistent effects. The findings suggest "a special attachment period in the human mother somewhat similar to that described in animals. . . ." (For example, separation of a cow or a ewe from her infant after birth "for a period as short as one to four hours often results in distinctly aberrant mothering behavior, such as failure of the mother to care for the young. . . .")

Kennell makes a telling point. "In a number of studies," he reports, "infants who had been premature constitute a disproportionately high number of both battered children (23 to 31 percent) and those with the 'failure to thrive' syndrome (25 to 41 percent). Significantly, prematurity and low birthweight often lead to prolonged mother-infant separation." In other words, prolonged separation from the mother after birth, *and even the relatively short separation periods enforced by most hospital nurseries*, may have a deleterious effect upon mother-child relations.

This investigator suggests that the human mother may have a unique period soon after delivery—he calls it "a maternal sensitive period"—when she is most ready to interact with her baby and become attached to it. He reviews research on the subject and concludes: "It is impressive that close contact during the first minutes, hours and days after birth appears to enhance maternal attachment in five separate studies and significantly increases maternal breastfeeding in five out of six investigations."

Since disorders in maternal attachment may lead to the baby's failure to thrive (FTT), a condition marked by an inability to gain weight and to develop normally, and to other psychological disturbances as well, it is important that the attachment disorders be understood. Giulio J. Barbero, of the University of Missouri Medical Center, has found a number of disturbing events in the mother's life that help explain them. He groups these potentially causative circumstances as follows:

• Past events, which include early deprivations—such as loss of parent figures—early in the mother's life; illness during childhood; and the death of, or illness in, the mother's earlier children.
• Events during pregnancy, including protracted illness and the deaths or severe illness of key family figures.
• Events around the time of the FTT child's birth, such as birth complications, prematurity, acute illness of mother or infant, congenital defects, and disruptions caused by doctors or hospitals.

• Current life events, including marital strain, financial crisis, medical or physical illness, and abuse of alcohol or other drugs.

One situation with a presumably potent effect on the mother-infant attachment occurs when the baby is premature and must remain behind for a while in the nursery for prematures. In answer to a questionnaire about parental visiting and related practices in such a nursery, one hospital—among the earliest to relax its rules—gave this moving reply: "In May of 1965, we had a three-month-old baby, who had been with us for three months, expire from a heart condition. At no time had we considered the feelings of the parents who had visited every single day, standing at the observation window. When the baby died, the mother asked to hold him. Crying, she rocked him and explained this was the first time she had ever touched him. From that time on, all mothers of prematures are allowed to scrub and gown and to touch their baby in the incubator, regardless of the baby's condition."

Such relaxation of rules is now common—and should one day be universal.

Do we know just what happens to the attachment phenomenon when the mother leaves the hospital but her baby must remain?

"Separation of a mother from her premature infant for as short a time as three weeks in the immediate postpartum period," answers psychiatrist P. Herbert Leiderman, "can lead to lowered feelings of maternal competency and decreased maternal attachment, sometimes continuing for as long as one month following their reunion."

Leiderman, who was reporting on research at Stanford University Medical Center, then gave the results of a two-year follow-up study. Twelve months after the separation, it was found to have had little continuing influence on maternal attitude and behavior. And 15 months after the infant returned, it was found to have had little continuing effect on the infant's behavior. Nevertheless, as reported in Chapter 8, it is the premature baby who frequently turns out to be the abused baby.

Babies without the Human Connection

Instances of failure to thrive may be severe, and the effects threatening to the life of the child. Selma Fraiberg—who directs a center devoted to infant health at the University of Michigan—tells of Billy, a healthy baby at birth, who five months later weighed only a little over 14 pounds and had gained no weight during the preceding three months. His mother, Kathie, explained that he vomited after each feeding. Since no medical reason for his trouble could be found, the pediatrician referred him to Fraiberg and her associates. Billy, said this physician, was a failure-to-thrive baby.

Although above the median in motor and mental development, the boy seldom approached his mother and never engaged her in eye-to-eye contact. He did not like to be cuddled, Kathie said, and turned away from her when she held him. Instead of embracing him, however, Fraiberg noticed that the mother, and the father, too, were holding him so that he faced away from them. Clearly, the boy and his parents were out of synchrony: smiling on the part of the mother, for example, could not be noticed and responded to by the child, and vice versa. "There was no spontaneity, joy, or mutual gazing in their interaction."

During home visits by a psychotherapist, a distressing story emerged. The parents had left their hometown. Kathie, only seventeen, missed it and was overwhelmed by motherhood. "An unfinished adolescent, she had become a parent while still in need of a mother." The boy's father, Bill, had only a part-time job, which brought in $12 a week.

Kathie fed Billy by setting the bottle on the floor. The five-month-old crept urgently toward it, succeeded in grasping it after several attempts, and finally got the nipple into his mouth and gorged himself. Kathie remarked that Billy liked to have his bottle alone, on the floor.

When the therapist expressed her strong concern for both the mother and the child, "Kathie responded by revealing that Billy's after-meal vomiting completely unnerved her." She then picked up Billy, rushed to the bathroom, and suspended him head down over the sink. He promptly vomited.

The human connection between Billy and his parents had never been made. For many babies, the results are even more severe. Pediatrician Barbero, whose work was described earlier, tells of a boy so stricken that he originally was believed to have cerebral palsy. Another child specialist, Harvard pediatrician T. Berry Brazelton, describes infants who simply withdraw from all interaction with the mother.

Can the deterioration be reversed? Yes, but reversal often requires the heroic efforts of expertly trained and dedicated clinicians. Fraiberg and her staff therapist, for example, concentrated on Billy's feeding problem by giving the mother direct advice and simultaneously using every opportunity to promote the mother-baby attachment.

The therapist soon discovered that as she responded to Kathie's needs and feelings, Kathie began to attend to Billy's needs. An acknowledgement of

Kathie's distress at Billy's turning away from her was followed by renewed attempts to hold her child. Billy's nascent overtures to his mother were carefully pointed out. Kathie seized onto every bit of evidence that Billy liked her.

When Kathie had become able to regularly feed Billy in her arms, she and the therapist worked out "a definite, written feeding plan which gave Kathie a sense of control." Moreover, after demonstrations by the therapist, Kathie learned to burp the baby in a way that aided digestion and did not induce vomiting. And she was gradually persuaded to add solid foods.

Billy quickly gained two and a half pounds, and the medical emergency—after two months of treatment—was over. But Billy was still considered very much at risk psychologically. He still avoided eye-to-eye contact with Kathie, and Kathie "tended to be mechanical and erratic" in her mothering. "Her ambivalence was dramatically expressed when in the midst of an unusually successful feeding, she suddenly began to tease Billy by competing with him for his bottle. In this 'harmless game,' Kathie seemed to behave as a sibling."

Encouraged to describe her childhood, Kathie revealed that she considered herself the unwanted middle child.

She could barely control her rage when she spoke of her younger sister, Essie. We began to suspect that there was a ghost in Billy's nursery, and that the name of this ghost was "Essie." Essie had been the first intruder in Kathie's life, an intruder who deprived her of maternal affection and, at least in symbolic terms, of food. . . .

Kathie remembered inventing games in which she wreaked revenge on her intruding sister. These suggested the teasing game she played with Billy. She recalled greatly resenting her young sister's following her around the house, and the young child's avid gazing at her.

Forbidden as a child to express her feelings toward her sister, Kathie now found that she could do so to the therapist. Gradually she was able to separate her feelings about her sister from her feelings about her son. As she unburdened herself of anger toward Essie, she was able "to reach out to Billy, to hold him close, and to nurture him."

It should be emphasized that clinical interventions such as the skilled and concentrated efforts of Fraiberg and her associates are available to only a small fraction of our children. There are not enough professionals available to supply the "bonds that nourish." That task lies with parents.

Brazelton tells of the gains made by totally withdrawn, failure-to-thrive infants who learn to make the human connection. When care-takers learn the natural rhythms of such children and overcome the babies' wariness by repeated rewarding contact, the infants begin to interact and become responsive. This may take two weeks, but even a day or so after responsiveness is established, the FTT baby starts to gain weight.

The point is, Brazelton and other pediatricians emphasize, that if failure-to-thrive infants are to develop the physical mechanisms for gaining weight, they must first be served with rewarding emotional experiences.

Brazelton has used a split-screen technique to videotape simultane-ously an interacting mother and infant during the first four months of life. The result is a remarkable choreography of two human beings responding instinctively and sensitively to each other.

While interacting with a person, all parts of the infant's body move in cyclical patterns, outward to the person (attention) then back to his body (non-attention). This ebb and flow of attention occurs several times per minute. . . .

As the infant who is interacting . . . approaches the peak of his attention cycle, he slowly reaches out and coos, his eyes dilate and both arms jerk forward, his head moves backward, and his face brightens. He then appears to reach a limit and begins to turn away. This begins a cycle of non-attention in which the infant seems to recover or readjust. His eyes shift from his mother's face to a point beyond her and his hand grasps his shirt, "place-holding" as he overtly tries to maintain this non-attention despite her continuing clues. Several seconds later, he slowly returns his gaze toward his mother, lets go of his shirt and smiles faintly as he begins a new attention cycle. When in synchrony, his mother increases her behaviors (in frequency and in intensity) as he approaches the peak of his attention cycle, then decreases her behaviors as he shifts to non-attention.

Unless the mother is sensitive to this cyclical pattern, Brazelton says, she may overload her baby's capacity for prolonged attention. The baby's response to such overloading is to show only brief periods of attention and prolonged periods of nonattention.

A pediatrician in Brazelton's group wondered at what point in life an infant came to expect interaction. So he asked mothers of three-week-old babies, following a period of normal interaction, to maintain a still face for three minutes. After a brief attempt at interaction, he found, "the infant becomes aware that his normal expectancy is not being fulfilled. He responds with brief attempts to elicit a response, followed by 'waiting' periods. The extent and urgency of the attempt to elicit response is especially impressive. After repeated attempts to get his mother back on track, however, he withdraws and seems to expect no response."

In failure-to-thrive babies, such withdrawal is seen by Brazelton in the extreme as a "wariness and aversion." It is as if the baby, unsuccessful in attempts to establish human contact, has given up the ghost. The world has become suspect, and life itself too unrewarding to pursue. Without help in establishing human bonds, such babies will remain unable to take the next step in human development: separation from mother, and development of an individual indentity.

The Child's Separation from the Mother

In a sense, the mother-child attachment is permanent. As Freud emphasized, in the words of one of his followers, "a lifelong, albeit diminishing, emotional dependence on the mother is a universal truth of human experience."

But of course the child does break away from the very early, very close interlocking relationship with the mother and does become an individual. And the way the two of them manage this breaking-away, which begins when the child is about five months old, or slightly earlier, may well have a permanent effect on the child's emotional and mental well-being.

These are the views of the internationally known children's psychoanalyst, Margaret S. Mahler, who, with her colleagues, has probably studied what she terms the *separation-individuation phase* of child development more closely than any other authority.

The research on separation grew out of Mahler's earlier work with psychotic children and their mothers. Discussing it, she recalls an experiment by another investigator, in which chick embryos and newly hatched chicks were pricked with a pin. The chicks that had hatched showed only infinitesimal damage but those still in the shell developed major anatomical defects.

"The lesson is applicable to the child's psychological development," Mahler observes. "There is a natural timetable for the maturation and development of the controlling, steering, integrating part of the personality, the ego. The earlier in life that this timetable is interrupted, the more detrimental to the total personality." From her previous research, the investigator believes that in childhood schizophrenia the timetable has been interrupted very early, either before or not long after the beginning of the separation-individuation process.

Because of disturbed or insensitive mothers, some of the children who later developed schizophrenia had suffered numerous and severe frustrations and emotional trauma during the first few months of life. At one extreme there was the depressed mother who could show no sign of affection for her daughter. At the other extreme there was the smothering and overwhelmingly affectionate mother who constantly overstimulated her son and showed no comprehension of his need to experience life at his own pace.

But Mahler found just as many cases of childhood psychosis in which the mother had been of at least average competence and devotion. In some of these cases the child had shown such an extreme vulnerability—had behaved so abnormally almost from birth—that not even the most favorable environmental situation, the investigator is convinced, could have prevented psychosis. In such cases, she says the vulnerability is apparently innate.

Whether the disposition to childhood schizophrenia is innate or acquired, Mahler believes that the core of the problem is the same: an inability on the part of the child to use the mother as a "beacon of orientation." She points out that an infant's mental apparatus is too underdeveloped to organize and act upon the stimuli received both from within and without; hence, the infant's survival depends upon the mother. The newborn's psychological development also depends upon her. Even after the baby has passed the completely helpless stage, he or she looks to the mother for guidance and strength in a world that can be terrifyingly—as well as enticingly—strange.

In the mental illness described as *autism,* Mahler therorizes that the baby's personality development has failed to move beyond (or else has regressed to) the "normal autistic phase" of development. During this phase, lasting from birth until sometime in the second month, the infant seems completely unaware of any distinction between itself and the surrounding world. The most conspicuous symptom of the autistic child, says Mahler, is the apparently complete failure to perceive the mother as a living being who represents the outside world and serves as a beacon and guide. Mothers say: "I never could reach my baby. . . ." "He never greeted me when I entered, he never cried or even noticed when I left the room. . . ." "She never made any personal appeal for help at any time." Such a child seeks refuge in an "autistic shell," the investigator believes, because reality—and even the mother—has been experienced as an intolerable source of irritations to be defended against by withdrawing into an utterly constricted, deanimated world.

In another type of child psychosis she describes as *symbiotic*, Mahler thinks the trouble arises at a later stage and results from an imbalance between the rates at which the child is maturing physically and emotionally.

As the investigator explains it, a maturational spurt puts the normal toddler, in the second year, in the position of relatively advanced physical independence. But in some cases the emotional development seems to lag far behind. Physically, in such a case, the child is able to move away from the mother, but not emotionally. So the child is bewildered and panicky. Minor frustrations common to the early part of the separation-individuation phase bring extreme reactions. The child may give up walking for months because of a fall.

Typically, a break with reality is triggered by some event—such as enrollment in nursery school, the birth of a sibling, hospitalization— that makes the child fear loss of or separation from the mother and throws him or her into a panic that cannot be handled. In hallucinations, the victim seems to be trying to restore the delusion of an earlier period that the child and the mother are one. Since constant panic is unbearable, the child retreats into "secondary autism" and cuts off contact with the world. Though the child's behavior is then like that seen in autism, says Mahler, successful treatment depends upon realizing that the personality has developed further, to a stage in the process by which a child separates from the mother.

To sum up, the first few weeks of life are seen by Mahler as comprising the "normal autistic phase." Then, beginning about the second month and continuing into the fifth, comes the "symbiotic phase." The boundaries between infant and mother still tend to merge, but the baby seems to be dimly aware—particularly when being fed, changed, or otherwise actively cared for—that its needs are being met by something external.

By the fifth or sixth month, the infant seems to recognize that the object through which gratifications are provided and discomfort relieved is the mother. When her face is near, the baby tries to touch and investigate it; the baby watches her play peek-a-boo and then plays it, too. This is the beginning of "the separation-individuation phase." The research on it—with more than 40 normal children and their mothers—was undertaken both to check Mahler's ideas about its critical importance and to help establish—as an aid to mental health workers—the normal course of events during that period. The families were middle class and the parents, in the main, college graduates.

The research was carried out at the Masters Children's Center, New York City, an organization for the study and treatment of disturbed children and the study of normal children. Several days a week a number of young mothers spent a morning or an afternoon in the old brownstone house serving as the Center's headquarters. Their children played or slept. The mothers cared for them as usual, talked to one another, or read. All the while, the mothers and children were being closely observed, and the mothers knew it. The young women who served as playroom teachers were trained observers as well and slipped out periodically to dictate a report on the activities of a mother and her child. Other observers, out of sight, took notes. Mothers were interviewed weekly, and long, informal visits were made to the homes. The babies were tested periodically, and moving pictures made of mother-child interaction.

This intensive study of early childhood began when the children were about five months old and continued through their third year. Separation-individuation was found to require four major steps, or subphases:

- *Differentiation.* Beginning at about the fifth month, this subphase is marked not only by explorations of the mother's face and mouth and hair but also by a turning to the outside world for pleasure and stimulation. The baby begins to creep, climb, and stand up. During this period the children at the Center showed a distinct preference for playing at their mother's feet.
- *Practicing.* This period, which overlaps the preceding one, begins as early as the tenth month and as late as the twelfth. During it, the child delights in trying out his or her new skills, particularly the ability to get around alone. The infant's dominant mood during this practicing period is elation. Sometimes the baby slips into the toddler room, which is equipped with toys and apparatus for the older children. But in the midst of the investigations the child stops as if suddenly aware that something is wrong and goes back rapidly to the mother for "emotional refueling," only to venture forth again a little later.
- *Rapprochement.* At 18 months, or a little earlier or later, children gradually become more subdued and even a little troubled. They begin to realize that they must cope with the world as individuals who are very small, relatively helpless, separate, and lonely. In the playroom, they are no longer either relatively unaware of their mother or unmind-

ful of frustrations. Children during this third stage of the separation-individuation process are continually concerned with their mothers' whereabouts. Some mothers cannot accept the child's demandingness, cannot understand why a toddler who is obviously more capable and independent than during the practicing period a few months before, must now insist upon her sharing every aspect of the child's life.

As the investigator explains it, children need the mother's active emotional support at this time in order to prevent serious injury to their self-esteem. They have had inklings that they are not really the omnipotent beings they had fancied. If they can count on backing from the mother, they come gradually to accept this fact and to pour their energy into normal psychological development.

"The less emotionally available the mother has become," Mahler says, "the more insistently and even desperately the toddler attempts to woo her." If emotional supplies are not forthcoming, children seek substitutes in eating and sucking. They also turn to such aggressive behavior as throwing things and hitting people. All this may drain so much of the energy available for development, Mahler theorizes, as to hamper psychological growth.

One sign of an unusual degree of conflict in toddlers, the investigator believes, is a more than average amount of "shadowing"—that is, keeping the mother in sight even in the midst of play, and at other times following her around. Another sign is an exaggerated use of the game of darting away in order to provoke the mother into pursuing them and scooping them up. A third danger signal is severe and protracted "separation anxiety" when the mother leaves the room.

"One cannot emphasize too strongly the importance of the optimal emotional availability of the mother during this subphase," declare Mahler and two associates (Fred Pine and Anni Bergman) in a recent book. Nevertheless, these investigators also learned that "the emotional growth of the mother in her parenthood, her emotional willingness to let go of the toddler—to give them, as the mother bird does, a gentle push, an encouragement toward independence—is enormously helpful. It may even be a sine qua non of normal (healthy) individuation."

• *The Final Phase*. The fourth subphase of separation-individuation occupies approximately the child's third year. It is a complex stage during which children develop the ability to retain mental representations of themselves and their mothers as distinctly separate individuals. When the mother is absent, they can picture her as being away from them and also as returning to them; her continual physical presence becomes less imperative.

As an indication that this stage has begun, children make their way to the toddler room for prolonged periods and accept the nursery teacher as a partial substitute for the mother. Children show an increasing interest both in their playmates and in adults other than the mother. They are mildly or moderately negativistic, showing resistance quite often to the demands of adults—a characteristic, remarks Mahler, that seems essential for the development of a sense of identity. They begin to develop an awareness of time. Along with it they show an increased ability to endure separation and delays. Concepts like "later" and "tomorrow"—generally first associated with the activities of the mother—come to be used as well as understood.

Crises arise in this period, Mahler notes, when the mother cannot accept the child's negativistic behavior and the display of *primary process* type of thinking, manifested in primitive, illogical talk and actions, and seen at its most extreme in schizophrenics. This kind of thinking is common among youngsters during the period, says Mahler, but even some apparently normal mothers are unable to deal with it calmly and help the child progress to the rational *secondary process*. One mother, for example, found fault with her youngster for eating well at Grandma's but poorly at home. Angered, the child told her, "I eat you up. Then I spit you out. Then I put you in the garbage pail." The mother was hurt, angry, and disturbed. She and the youngster bickered for an hour. Finally, the girl said, "Then I put you back together again." It would have been more conducive to emotional health, Mahler observes, had the mother said at the very beginning something like: "Now you know you are just being angry at Mommie. Maybe I shouldn't have said anything about how well you eat at Grandma's. Anyway, you know very well that nobody eats people and puts them in garbage pails."

Bridging the communicative gap between the child's world and the adult's, says the investigator, requires the deciphering of the child's primary-process language and actions, playing along with them, and gradually offering more logical expressions and more realistic solutions to the child's problems. Fortunately, most mothers do this.

The types of behavior characteristic of one subphase are not limited to it. In other periods, though, either they are seen less frequently or they are less important to the particular developmental tasks with which the children are dealing.

Nor does every child follow the pattern most characteristic of a particular stage. For some children in the rapprochement period, the need to assert separateness overshadows the need to establish close-ness. While one child seeks out the mother with every new toy or activity in order to engage her attention and participation, another may be primarily engaged in making sure that this very thing does not happen, particularly if the mother has been overprotective and intrusive.

The research has documented what most mothers know—that differ-ent children do not proceed through a given development stage either at the same rate or in the same way. And it has uncovered evidence that the mothers themselves influence the pattern.

Two sisters, Ann and Susan, are offered as particularly good illustra-tions of the strength of the maternal influence during the separation-individuation phase.

When Ann was nine months old, she was often observed sitting at her mother's feet, looking up at her and patiently begging for attention. She got very little of it and in consequence, the investigators say, had little psychic energy for investing in the activities normal to the next, or practicing, subphase. She would make only brief forays from her mother; her "love affair with the world" was subdued and of unusually short duration. Throughout the final subphase, Ann was an unhappy little girl who could not easily endure physical separation from her mother, did not get along well with other adults and children, yet showed little joy when the mother returned after brief, everyday sepa-rations. In one camera-recorded scene, she has a tantrum when her mother starts to leave the room; the child insists on going along but then gives up and just stands there, suffering. Finally she regresses by retiring to the play area for the youngest babies. She turns her back on the other people and is clearly hurt and angry.

Like a few of the other children in the study, Ann was described as already vulnerable—already in trouble. The investigators believe that these vulnerable children, unless further environmental experience amply compensates, may well develop emotional problems rooted in the unmet needs and unaccomplished tasks of the separation-indivi-duation phase.

With Susan, Ann's younger sister, the mother had mellowed even though she was the same somewhat aloof, self-centered person. At the research center, every so often she would put the baby down and bury herself in the newspaper. But Susan was a more outward-going and determined baby than Ann, and when she wanted her mother's atten-tion, she knew how to go about getting it. In one scene, she tugs at her mother's dress, beseeches her with her eyes, and finally starts to pull herself up to her mother's knees. The viewer can almost hear the mother say, "Oh, the heck with it," as she puts the paper aside and lovingly picks up the baby. In a later subphase, Susan looks distressed when her mother leaves the room but, unlike her sister, soon turns happily to playing with the other adults and children. She is joyful when her mother comes back. A child who has a good relationship with her mother, Mahler emphasizes, shows relatively little separation anxiety.

The difference between Ann's experiences and Susan's, the investigators suggest, may have had a genetic basis, since the younger girl was able to command the mother's attention and draw upon and be secure in her love while the other was not. But they believe that Ann's progress through this critical period would have been less stormy with a mother more attuned to the child's emotional needs.

"The research has clearly established," Mahler reports, "that the emotional availability of the mother is necessary for the optimal unfolding of the child's innate potentialities." This is so, she explains, because the child, throughout the process of separating from the mother, is emotionally so dependent upon her. If the child is left markedly uncertain about the mother's emotional availability, signs of potential trouble are seen.

Mahler adds that the research also points to the sturdiness and adaptive capacity of the normal toddler. "Even against considerable odds," she remarks, "he is usually able to extract from his mother the necessary emotional supplies." It naturally follows that for the process to take place, mother—or an adequate substitute—must be present.

When Mother Is Absent

The mother has traditionally been the mainstay of the nuclear family. But more and more she has been absenting herself from the typical American home, and her role as caretaker of children—as measured timewise, at least—seems waning. Statistics tell part of the story:

- Over half of American mothers with school-age children are working outside the home, two-thirds of them at full-time jobs.
- In families with children under six, one mother in three is holding an outside job.

The vast majority of these women work solely for financial reasons, others to satisfy an inner need for self-fulfillment. Despite many psychological sanctions of the women's liberation movement, many career-minded mothers often feel guilty about the time spent away from their children. "I would love to stay at home with my baby," says a young teacher, "but I can't possibly be as interesting a person without my career."

Virtually all mothers are working mothers, in the sense that taking care of the home and the family is work—and work that traditionally has been considered of the utmost importance to the welfare of not only the family but of society as well. Of concern here, however, is the effect upon the family, and particularly the child, of mothers who take jobs outside the family.

After reviewing the research relevant to that question, Helen L. Bee suggests that the mother's indispensability has been overdramatized, in part because the research findings have been misinterpreted.

One team of investigators has suggested, for example, that children of mothers who work may be more dependent, have more problems establishing their sexual identity, and perhaps tend to be more delinquent. But, says Bee, the research results leading to that suggestion can also be interpreted "as showing that these three conditions occur primarily when there is family instability" or unstable alternative care. For instance, other investigators have found that "when the mothers in *unstable* families work, the sons are more likley to be delinquent, but when the mothers in stable families from the same general kind of background and environment work," the delinquency rate among their sons does not rise. In other words, the crucial factor seems to be, in part at least, the stability of the family.

Other research suggests that the mother's *satisfaction* with her role is just as important as family stability (and indeed may be an integral part of it). In this work, Marian Radke-Yarrow, of the National Institute of Mental Health, and her associates studied 100 mothers from social classes that ranged between upper middle and upper working. About half of these mothers had gone at least part way through high school; the others, at least part way through college.

Some findings:

• Mothers who wanted to work but did not, out of a feeling of "duty," showed the greatest problems in child rearing. They described "more difficulties in the area of control, less emotional satisfaction in relationships with their children, and less confidence in their functioning as mothers." They were rated significantly less adequate in their mothering.

• Among the working mothers, those who wished to work and those who did not showed few differences in child-rearing practices. The investigators think this was because the mothers who worked even though they preferred to remain in the home were helping to achieve certain valued family goals, such as cultural and educational advantages. So their situation was hardly one of great frustration.

There is at least a suggestion here that if a mother is happy in what she is doing, then it does not really matter—from the standpoint of how well she brings up her children—whether she chooses to be a homemaker or a worker outside the home.

Also important is the stability of the care provided for the children of working mothers. Researchers in one project cited by Bee found that the children with substitute care were "the ones showing greater dependency, greater attention seeking, and more anxiety about being separated from the mother." But children with *stable* substitute care "did not show these anxious dependent behaviors; in fact, they were more assertive than were mother-reared children."

Still another investigator compared children who had received stable substitute care with children who had been reared at home. The group getting substitute care had attended the same day-care center for 1½ years, starting when the children were about a year old. The investigators wondered if the relationship of the child to the mother would turn out to be different in one group from that in the other. The answer was *no.*

On the basis of these studies, Bee comments, "it looks very much as if stable, adequate substitute care is functionally equivalent to (or even better than) having good home rearing. . . . Inadequate or unstable care, however, may have potentially disruptive effects, probably particularly for very young children."

Does the age of the child at the time the mother goes out to work make a difference? Studies of children raised in kibbutzim—collective settlements in Israel where settlement children, beginning during their first few weeks, are reared together—suggest that the answer is *probably not.* This assumes, of course, that the care is adequate and stable. Otherwise, says Bee, there may be potentially disruptive effects, particularly on very young children.

Are there long-term effects? What little work has been done on this question suggests that there may be one. College students whose mothers were working or had worked were found to have broader views of male and female roles. These students "saw women as more competent and capable than is usual or saw men as warmer and more affectionate than is usual." However, this study did not take into account the possibility that in the families of the working mothers the views of appropriate roles for men and women had been from the start less stereotyped than usual.

Bee sums up the available evidence on the effects of maternal employment as follows: "When the mother is satisfied with her role and adequate alternative care is arranged, the separation of the mother from her child that accompanies maternal employment has no demonstrable negative effect. Indeed, in some cases positive effects are noted. . . . When the children of working mothers have developmental difficulties, they seem to be associated more with family instability or inadequate care [when the mother is gone] than with working per se."

Two points in that quotation should be emphasized: the mother's satisfaction and, probably even more important, the provision of *adequate alternative care*.

Some years ago, the Harvard psychologist, Jerome Kagan, warned that taking children away from their homes during the critical early years might well interfere with their emotional development. He was not alone in this belief.

Now, however, as the result of a five-year study under his direction, Kagan has reversed his position. The study compared infants who had been placed in a day-care center administered by Kagan and his colleagues seven hours a day, five days a week, with children who had remained home. The children were thoroughly tested a number of times, beginning at 3½ months of age and extending to 29 months. The tests included measures of language development, attention span, and relationships to other children. Between the day-care group and the home group, no substantial differences were found.

Kagan emphasizes, however, that the Harvard-operated center cared for the children under close-to-ideal conditions—conditions not likely to be found in many other centers. Poor centers, he still believes, can be harmful to young children. And he estimates that at least 15 to 20 percent of the country's centers may be poor.

Social critic Nicholas von Hoffman is considerably more militant. Writing in the *Washington Post* two days after Christmas, 1976, he said: "If Jesus had been sent to a day care center shortly after Mary had recovered her strength enough to go back to work as an account executive in an advertising agency or as a lawyer, her Son might not have become the symbol and ideal of love, both human and divine, which He has been for our civilization for 20 centuries."

Further on, he wrote:

The clamor for day care centers from some, but by no means all, women's organizations is . . . not for the benefit of the child, but only the mother and father who don't want to or can't take care of their offspring. However, since there is no data anywhere suggesting the institutional rearing of infants and small children is better than or even as good as a good home, feminist groups might be wiser urging women who don't want to take care of their children just not to have them. . . .

The least we can do . . . is debate the significance of what we're drifting into here. There are other ways to handle these problems. Many have been suggested but scarcely given a serious hearing, such as according wives and mothers Social Security protection even if they don't work outside the home; universal child allotments; and perhaps the novel idea of one job (decently paid) per every two parents, perhaps jointly held by the wife-husband-father together. Call it a shared employment program. . . .

Von Hoffman concludes: "Certainly we need the role models of women Supreme Court Justices and women in other power, prestige positions, but the role of Mother in the Holy Family isn't without honor either."

Clinical views on the relationship between the mother's presence during the early years and the prevention of mental or emotional disorder in the child later on have been changing.

During the 1950s, psychiatrist Peter H. Wolff points out, a prevailing clinical view "held that absence of a single caretaking adult during the first year is a sufficient condition for psychopathology and social deviance in later life, and that the cause of abnormal outcome is the failure of social attachment during a critical stage of mental development." However, "The view was revised after controlled observations on children who had been raised in 'good' institutional settings indicated that the behavioral effects of different social rearing conditions are extremely variable, and depend not only on the degree but also the kind of deviation from the 'natural' mother-infant relation. . . ."

Even so, noted anthropologist Margaret Mead has made a point that bears repeating. Every child deserves to have someone around, she says, "who knows what happened yesterday." Yet too may children get shunted among caretakers who seem hardly aware, many of them, of what's happening today, let alone of how what's happening today affects the child tomorrow and tomorrow and tomorrow.

Even mothers who elect to stay at home don't necessarily spend time with their children. Mothers may be present in the flesh but psychologically absent.

Sociologist Sarane Boocock of Rutgers University has reported that some mothers devote as little as 15 minutes a day to actual communication with their preschoolers. Precise information of this kind, she acknowledges, is difficult to obtain since few parents willingly admit to neglecting their children. Nonetheless, from her own interviews with 250 children in several United States cities, and from reading their diaries and listening to their group conversations, Boocock finds that "many of the old-fashioned things have disappeared." Few children eat dinner regularly with their parents, she reports, "and few spend as much as two hours a day with adults other than teachers. While a few children go shopping with their mothers, almost none do errands or chores or contribute in any other way that matters."

The richness—or poverty—of the mother's interaction with her child, it now appears, may be foreshadowed by attitudes that are present early in their relationship.

How a Mother Views Her Child—and Herself

One investigator provides evidence that the way a mother views her infant—that is, what concept she has of the newborn child—is closely associated with the likelihood that the baby will or won't develop an emotional disorder.

In 1963, child psychiatrist Elsie Broussard of the University of Pittsburgh undertook a longitudinal study of some 300 firstborn, biologically healthy infants and their mothers to verify an intriguing hypothesis: that a mother's perception of her baby during the first month of life would be related to the baby's emotional health later on. As a measuring stick, Broussard designed the Neonatal Perception Inventory, the score on which represents the discrepancy between the mother's perception of the average infant and of her own infant. When the babies were one month old, the mothers rated 61 percent of them as better than average. These were considered by the investigator to be at low risk for the development of emotional disorder. The other 39 percent, who were rated by the mothers as not better than average, were considered at high risk.

When the children were 4½ years old, 120 of them were evaluated by child psychiatrists who were unaware of the original ratings. The high-risk children (designated as such because their mothers had not rated them better than average) were found to have significantly more emotional disorder as preschoolers than the low-risk children. Again, some years later, 104 of the children were evaluated by psychiatrists who were unaware of the previous findings. This time, too, a significant association was found between the ratings at one month and the extent of emotional disorder between the ages of ten and eleven years.

A mother's perception of her newborn child, says Broussard, seems to reflect her self-esteem, which in mothers of high-risk children is low.

These women are depressed, lack confidence in themselves as mothers, are less able to assess and fulfill their children's needs, and have difficulty in perceiving danger to the child.

This investigator also concludes: "The woman whose early experience has not supported the development of a healthy self-esteem. . . . seems to view the infant produced by herself as defective as she feels. . . . The mirroring of the mother's perception of what she has created and her inability to gratify the child's needs seem to foster the development of another generation with emotional difficulty."

Ten years after undertaking her first study, Broussard began another—to learn if an intervention program could prevent the development of emotional trouble in high-risk children. This time, 205 infants were considered at low risk when they were one month old and 76 at high risk. Intervention was offered to half of the mothers in the high-risk-infant group, and 17 accepted.

Intervention includes interviews with the child's parents or with the mother alone, design of a program to meet the needs of the infant and the parents, weekly or biweekly home visits, and biweekly group meetings of the mothers, along with their children. This mother-infant group, Broussard reports, "has evolved as an extended family system." It has also provided the mothers "with a multitude of 'mirrors,' each slightly different from the other and which reflected back to the individual mother a perception of herself slightly different from her own. . . . As she feels herself valued and respected and her child valued and respected, she can then begin to modify her self-perception and her perception of the child."

Evaluation of 84 infants at one year of age showed that the low-risk children had significantly better scores on a number of behaviors considered important. The average scores of the intervention group were closer, though not significantly so, to those of the low-risk group, who were developing well, than were those of the group to whom no intervention had been offered.

Seventy-five of the children were again evaluated when they were 2½ years old. Though the data analysis is incomplete, clinical impressions indicate that the intervention group was continuing to progress toward optimal development.

Since "the mother's perception of the infant during the first month of life was associated with the child's later development," Broussard concludes, " . . . it is highly desirable to develop programs which will have an impact on that perception." And since the early maternal perception can change during the first month of life, mothers need support and guidance during the time immediately after birth—"yet this is exactly the time when the present system of care does not provide professional support for new parents."

Broussard points to her own earlier work in providing guidance, by way of a special closed-circuit television program, during the mothers' hospital stay after the birth of their babies. Among those mothers receiving such guidance, there was a significant increase in the number who had a positive perception of their infants at one month. This was not true among the mothers who had not received the guidance. The findings indicate to Broussard "that an intervention program which could modify the mother's perception of her newborn in a positive manner prior to one month of age could have a significant impact on the subsequent development of the child."

The "Jewish" Mother

For at least two generations, the "Jewish" mother—anxious, over-bearing, upward striving, zealous for her children's welfare—has been the subject of microscopic scrutiny, among others by psychiatrists, stand-up comedians, and novelists. Hide behind any analyst's over-stuffed chair, and you will hear a stream of associations that ultimately lay the roots of neuroses—from guilt to hypochondria, from shyness to colitis—at the breast of such a mother. Comedian George Jessel's routine concerned a mother who wouldn't let go, who sought to extract every drop of loyalty and commitment that flowed in the veins of her harrassed son; and the mother of Philip Roth's Portnoy was the ulti-mate caricature of every harrassing "finish-what's-on-your-plate," "after-all-I-did-for-you," "do-as-I-say-or-I'll-put-my-head-in-the-oven" mother who ever stalked her brood. The result has been a mother figure that we have come to indict as the crowning example of parents who produce psychopathology in their children.

How does that popularly accepted judgment stand up? How bad for the mental health of our children actually *is* the "Jewish" mother—or the Italian, Irish, German, black, or Plains, Georgia, mother—who chronically looms and hovers over her brood?

To answer the question, it helps to examine the child-rearing behav-ior of a "school" of mothers whose approach contrasts sharply with that of the Jewish matriarch. Such a group is comprised of young women who were the dropouts and hippies of the 1960s, now in their early middle years and mothers themselves. A group of them—and their children—have been described in a book, *The Children of the Coun-terculture,* by John Rothchild and Susan Berns Wolf. The authors visited diverse groups of communities made up of such "families," among them urban and rural communes, and institutes of the new religions such as Lamas and Hare Krishnas.

Rothchild and Wolf wondered how life was turning out in the communes, especially for the children. Just what were the new parental answers—from those who had boldly insisted that they had all the answers? How were the children of the 1960s—those in the new communities, at any rate—now rearing their own children, far removed from the values of the middle class populated by so many Jewish mothers?

Until their journey into deep counterculture territory, Rothchild writes, he and Susan were part of a group which concluded that Americans strangle their children with rules and regimens and expectations, "that a new generation should be raised more on Abbie Hoffman, less on Dr. Spock."

Their convictions were badly shaken. What they found were communities in which virtually all children were neglected and abused, victims of treatment that would be judged cruel and inhumane by most parents. The authors were struck by the boredom, apathy and melancholy of the children, many of whom showed signs of emotional disturbance and psychological disorganization. Getting through the day seemed to be the only goal set for the young.

In most of the rural communes described by Rothchild and Wolf, the parents seem bent on keeping the children out of their way, even if it means denying them everything. Themselves still children, they continue to seek gratification without sacrifice, as if it were actually possible to deal with the young without fully accepting their presence in our lives. Without schools, toys, stimulation, or direction, the children would try to amuse themselves by pulling the covers off their mothers when they were in bed with a new man.

Nowhere in this new utopia could one find a sense of commitment to the children. For instance, adults in one of the groups observed by these investigators hardly notice their young, even rejecting them from their devotions. Members of another group studied by Rothchild and Wolf send them away to their own grim and often merciless religious schools. Rothchild describes a school in Dallas to which children as young as 5 are sent: "I couldn't get over the spareness and cruelty of the place, the straw mats on the floor. . . . the boy who still had chicken pox lying with his head on the linoleum and orange peels scattered around him like the garbage from a zoo animal: the way the teacher made the sick boy get up and come to class. . . ."

The children of the counterculture observed in this study are growing up in a world of forlorn-looking trailers, shacks, and abandoned cars, an unstructured and aimless world, without the benefit of parental guidance or an unfolding sense of purpose. In some communes the children do not get enough food. In a scene out of Dickens, an eighteen-month-old baby struggles to get to the oatmeal pot before the cereal is eaten by others, and the authors report one episode in which a group of mothers lock themselves in the kitchen to get some special treat before the children can get at it. More than any other, that event emerges as symbolic of the emptiness of commitment, the vacuum of caring that afflicts this particular portion of the new generation of mothers—as it does to a lesser degree so many contemporary mothers and fathers in more stable communities across the country.

It is this very characteristic of caring and commitment that has been overlooked by modern psychopathologists in all the psychological biopsies of the heart of the Jewish mother. Whether at the kitchen table arguing about how much food is enough, at the bookladen dining-room table harrassing her child to finish his homework, at the piano urging her budding Rubinstein to practice, or in the front hallway at dawn tearfully and angrily greeting her son suddenly turned "bum", these were mothers who cared—and weren't afraid to show it. These "mommas" were full time, committed, protecting, hovering, skin-close, truly loving. They left no doubt about their investment as parents, and while they may have thereby spawned some neuroses, more often than not their children were strengthened. The errors of these parents lay almost exclusively in their chronic hovering and concern—errors that may very well induce painful, guilt-coated anxiety in some children, but not the anger, emptiness, and despair that so often haunt children denied the nurturance of human contact and the lifelong benefits of early affectional bonds. The Jewish mother surely produced a few ripe candidates for therapy, but she did not nurture a cohort of angry criminals or flat schizoid personalities, empty shells incapable of recognizing or giving love.

"Whatever tendencies Jewish mothers and fathers have to be 'superprotective,' and whatever that may do in creating unusual anxieties in their children," child mental health authority Selma Fraiberg says, "these are at worst diseases of moral conflict, which are after all curable. In contrast, there is *nothing* one can do to overcome the diseases of non-attachment created when there is no bond to begin with."

Moreover, as Fraiberg reminds us, "neurotic" reactions to the overprotective mother can often lead to some very successful adaptations.

Among the products of her commitment and caring are not only couch-riding Portnoys, but the Leonard Bernsteins and John F. Kennedys of the world. She has produced the builders and leaders of civilization, not the assassins and destroyers.

If the self-oriented, neglecting, and rejecting mother were restricted to members of the "dropped-out" generation, our concern might be minimal. Unfortunately, however, the behavior seen in parents of counterculture children is not encapsulated in communes. Nor, to move elsewhere, is it restricted to ghetto parents engulfed by poverty and deprivation. Fraiberg bears witness. "After thirty years of experience in the field, I am seeing for the first time in the past decade forms of neglect in educated, middle-class parents which cannot be differentiated from our slum population. These parents may not recognize it, but their children are clearly neglected. Often both parents are working or are in school, and their young are peddled around to various neighbors, to tenement centers, or casual and haphazard child care arrangements. Or, they are dumped off at the 'Y,' in the kiddie park, anywhere. These children suffer some of the same problems that we used to see only in the slum children—the psychopathic behavior, the 'acting out,' the disorders of conscience."

Cornell University social psychologist Urie Bronfenbrenner also observes that the incidence of family pathology is spreading swiftly among all sectors of United States society, and ". . . the middle-class family of today is approaching the level of social disorganization that characterized the low-income family of the early 1960's." It is clear that millions of children are being seeded today by parents for whom children are a tangential and essentially intrusive aspect of their lives. "We have become," says anthropologist Margaret Mead, "a society of people who neglect our children, are afraid of our children, find children a surplus instead of the raison d'être of living."

It is just this view of children as the ultimate reason for our existence that epitomizes the "Jewish" mother. Such mothers are remnants of a generation of parents who would *die* for their children—protect them and love them with a love more fierce than the love of life itself. Although they have been satirized as neurotic, these women are actually demonstrating a degree of emotional maturation often found lacking among contemporary parents. In the view of psychologist David Bakan, the maturing personality experiences a transformation of lust into love, and of that love into love of children, and the love of children into the willingness to conscientiously protect them and care for them. In similar terms, Erik Erikson described the individual grown into mature adulthood as the product of a process called *generativity.* According to Erikson, "Generativity . . . is primarily the concern in establishing and guiding the next generation. . . . a gradual expansion of ego-interests and . . . a libidinal investment in that which is being generated." In the view of Erikson, "some young parents suffer, it seems, from the retardation of the ability to develop this stage." These parents, he contends, are "in the lack of some faith, some 'belief in the species,' which would make a child appear to be a welcome trust of the community."

In the long perspective of historian Lloyd deMause, such faith and belief may finally be emerging in the hearts and minds of contemporary parents. Mankind, deMause contends, has begun to reach for a new era in the upbringing of its young, leaving the murderous and abusive modes—described in Chapter 8—behind. He calls it the helping mode, an attitude which involves "an enormous amount of time, energy, and discussion on the part of both parents. . . . continually responding to the child, playing with it, tolerating its regressions, being its servant rather than the other way around. . . ."

"Few parents," deMause admits, "have yet consistently attempted this kind of child care." The exception may well be the "Jewish" mother. For many an even highly dedicated mother, however, the task is made more challenging and more difficult by forces outside herself. The mother does not stand alone in her influence. It is clear that the child is affected by a world far greater than simply the mother's. Included, but long overlooked, is her partner in parenthood.

Fathers
The Hidden Force

"Mommy, if the doctor brings the baby in his bag, and if Santa Claus brings us toys; if God will punish me when I am bad; and if money grows on trees; why do we need Daddy?"

That child's question, reported by psychologist Dee Appley, has long had its echoes in the adult's view of the father's role as well. Most parents have focused their concern on the mother's role in the destiny of children rather than on father's. "Parenting" has been equated largely with "mothering," with the father seen merely as an economically useful but psychologically unimportant appendage to the structure of the family. He may "bring home the bacon," but he contributes little nourishment to the child's emotional life. In an official World Health Organization report of 1951, pioneer child development expert John Bowlby observed that the father is of no direct importance to the young child, but is only of indirect value as economic support and in his emotional support of mother. And, anthropologist Margaret Mead has referred to the father as "a biological necessity, but a social accident."

The relative disregard of the father as a force in child development is all the more surprising given the demonstrable staying power of the father figure across time and cultures. Anthropological studies graphically reveal the ubiquitous role of the father. His special, enduring place emerges even among the most remote peoples. Among the Tallensi in the African Sudan, for example, any child born to a married woman is the property of the husband, another addition to his portfolio of family heirs. Even a child born of adultery is quickly absorbed into a legal, child-father relationship—not by the biological father, who keeps his distance, but by the woman's husband. It is he who displays unabashed paternal feelings, although he knows he is not the true father; he also receives all of the credit and responsibility given to fathers in that society.

From such field studies, Polish-born British anthropologist Bronislaw K. Malinowski concluded that societies everywhere somehow make provision for the psychological state we call fatherhood. This he regarded as the "principle of legitimacy," a regulation ensuring that "no child should be brought into the world without a man assuming the role of . . . guardian and protector, the male link between the child and the rest of the community."

Why, then, has the dynamic role of the father as parent been so clouded from view?

The answer may well have its roots in the lack of attention given fathers by researchers studying child development. The psychological literature can hardly be accused of masculine bias; it is heavily skewed in the direction of the mother. "In the area of parental influences on personality," report psychologists Kimble, Garmezy, and Zigler, "the father remains a relatively neglected object of study."

The bias of developmental psychologists toward the mother is everywhere embedded in the research literature. Helen L. Bee points out, for example, that one of the repeated conclusions drawn from early studies of orphaned children in institutions is that they suffer from "maternal deprivation," the springboard of later retardation and emotional difficulties. But, she asks, what about *paternal* deprivation? Children in institutions obviously lack father figures; in fact, since virtually all caretakers in such institutions are female, the loss of father is actually greater than that of mother. Yet, the impact of "fatherlessness" in child facilities and elsewhere continues to be analyzed only rarely in the mental health literature.

However small their number, studies dealing with the father show his impact—for better or worse—to have been sorely underestimated. His sole purpose, they make clear, is not simply to work and earn—to pay the rent, the doctor bills, and ultimately, the college tuition fees. There is convincing evidence that the father's inadequacy or absence can erode the child's emotional well-being and that his wholesome, committed presence can help promote the mental health of his children.

Especially as we shift toward a more balanced family arrangement, with fathers and mothers sharing more equally in the child-rearing role, it becomes of more than passing academic interest to understand—and act on—the potential effect of fathers on their children.

Fathers of Maladjusted Children

Despite the relative paucity of available research data, it appears that the father's personality and behavior, no less than the mother's, can carry important mental health consequences for the child. A number of studies convey this important message.

In one investigation, conducted over 17 years ago by Rutgers psychologist Donald R. Peterson and his colleagues, the parents of two groups of children were studied—one group composed of children who were well adjusted, the other made up of children suffering a range of emotional difficulties. The investigators examined the psychological makeup of the parents. They were surprised to discover that the personalities and attitudes of the fathers were closely related to whether or not the child was maladjusted—as much so as mothers' traits and attitudes.

The fathers of the children who had psychological problems were themselves less well adjusted, less sociable, and less democratic than fathers of the well-adjusted children. Moreover, the actual problems of the children appeared to reflect specific qualities of the father's personality. Weak and ineffectual men tended to be the fathers of children who suffered from hyperaggressive behavior, for example, while men who tended to be dictatorial and unconcerned about their young had children given to shyness and feelings of inferiority.

Peterson's study was published in 1959. More recently, in her 1971 Ph.D. dissertation at the University of Virginia, Margaret Sells Emanuelson reported similar data. Emanuelson drew a sample of 120 emotionally disturbed children from the Virginia Treatment Center, a hospital for children with emotional and behavioral disorders. The mothers and fathers of these children—a total of 194—served as the parent sample for the study. The children, ranging in age from six to fifteen years of age, had all been evaluated during a two-year period for possible admission to the hospital.

The investigator used two tests—the Minnesota Multiphasic Personality Inventory for measuring parental personality factors, and the

Virginia Treatment Center Behavioral Questionnaire for measuring behavioral disorders in the children. Contrary to theoretical assumptions of the past, the test data showed that it was the father's personality that was more closely related than the mother's to the personality pattern of the child. In the language of the statistician, the fathers' personality patterns had more "predictive ability" than the mothers.' Evidently the personality traits and child-rearing tactics of the father may be more important for the child than many mother-obsessed researchers have thought possible.

One such characteristic is the style the father uses to fulfill his role as an authority figure in the family. Traditional psychoanalytic theory has held that the father is instinctively viewed by the child as the symbol of society's authority. He is the forbidding vehicle by which children incorporate the prohibitions and values of the larger world. But if he abuses his natural power, as many fathers attempt to do, what are the results? How do children fare, for example, whose fathers exploit their natural authority role to the limit?

The evidence, according to University of California psychologist David B. Lynn, is that an unloving, punitive, and authoritarian father tends to rear dependent, anxious, withdrawn, dejected children, whose self-esteem is chronically low. Studies of fathers whose children suffer behavioral problems such as school phobia or bed-wetting often reveal patterns of rejection, disinterest, harsh punishment, and psychological distance. Even some young infants, it seems, can be sensitive to the presence of an overbearing and threatening father; they appear, for example, to be the frequent victims of disrupted and disturbed sleep.

The attitudes and behaviors of fathers differ, of course, from one social and economic group to another. "Whatever his ideals," psychiatrist C. Christian Beels reminds us, "a man will be one kind of father if he has no prospect of steady work, another if he is preoccupied with keeping his job and still another if he is mainly occupied with how to style his leisure and affluence." Still, results to date suggest strongly that the presence in a child's life of a disturbed and disturbing father— no matter what his class or culture—may leave hard-to-heal scars on the child's developing personality.

Often in research, the impact of a given force can be understood best by studying not what happens when it is operating, but rather when it is removed. That approach has been used liberally in the case of fathers. His importance has been deduced not so much by analyzing what occurs when he permeates the household as by observing what penalties children suffer when he is missing from the family picture.

Children without Fathers

Tommy, now ten years old, is regarded by all who know him as a "difficult" child. He would rather fight than play with his friends, and he seems bent on evoking anger rather than approval from his teachers. He has been known to steal, lies chronically, and is disruptive in class. Tommy appears angry and troubled most of the time.

Although Tommy now enjoys the loving presence of two parents, he spent over half his lifetime without a father. He is a second-generation victim of the tragic war in Vietnam. Tommy's father, a navy pilot, was shot down over North Vietnam and held captive for five years. During the period of American involvement in Indochina, Tommy—and the children of over 300 other American POWs—became the subjects of a natural experiment on the impact of fathers' absence on children's development. From clinical observations, these children appeared to be suffering more than the normal share of behavioral problems— rebelliousness, exceptional shyness, nail biting, fear of the dark, frequent temper tantrums and nightmares, and proneness to crying.

Through the efforts of a group of San Diego investigators, clinical hunches are being translated into more substantial research data. Detailed studies of the psychological fallout for children of their fathers' incarceration have been conducted by a team of researchers at the U.S. Navy's Center for Prisoner of War Studies. These studies are unique. The length of time spent in captivity by their subjects—the POWs returned from Vietnam—is the longest of any previous group studied; some were incarcerated for as long as eight years, and their average time in captivity was five years. Moreover, the research is the first attempt to study the families of POWs over an extended period of time rather than to seek more tenuous retrospective data after the fact.

The army, navy, and marine families studied by the San Diego group resembled many American nuclear families. The average age of the returnees was thirty years, and one-third had college degrees. Their wives were between twenty and forty-nine, and the families averaged two children each. The majority of the children were between eight and fifteen just before their fathers' repatriation from long captivity.

In one longitudinal analysis, Barbara B. Dahl and Hamilton I. McCubbin gathered data during the first year after the return of the POWs. The researchers drew their children from a sample of 50 families, randomly selected. The subjects were 55 boys and 44 girls, ranging in age from five to seventeen years. They lived in cities throughout the United States, the majority of them in California, Virginia, and Florida.

They had been without their fathers for an average of over five years. Each child completed the California Test of Personality, measuring both personal and social adjustment. Testing took place in the family's home, where the mother and father were interviewed as well.

As a group, the children scored significantly lower than the norm in both these areas of adjustment, social and personal. Based on their test scores, they appeared relatively lacking in a sense of personal freedom and more likely to be given to withdrawal; they were more likely to harbor antisocial tendencies and to find obstacles in adjusting to family, school, and community.

The investigators have since compared children whose fathers returned with those whose fathers did not. Both groups diverged from the norms in both personal and social adjustment, and the differences between the two groups were only slight—suggesting, at least, that the father's return does not quickly undo the impact of his prolonged absence.

The finding that the children as a whole scored below the norm in their adjustment to school dovetails with observations made by French social workers. In their assessment of prisoner-of-war families of the Indochina War, they found both behavioral and academic difficulties among the children long after the repatriation of their fathers. The problems were so great that the French established special education programs specifically designed to assist these children.

The results of the U.S. Navy studies may, of course, not hold up over time; many of the children may overcome whatever penalties they suffered by their fathers' absences. The researchers conducting the studies are quick to admit, too, that their results may be confounded by factors other than the father's direct influence—factors ranging from the trauma of wartime to the prevailing anxiety of many of the mothers. Moreover, it must be admitted that the absence of husband and father was not a totally negative experience for some of the families; in those torn by discipline problems or constant friction, for example, the separation was experienced with relief rather than stress.

Similar methodological and mitigating factors intrude in interpreting the results of father-absence studies in other contexts—for example, when separation, divorce, or death rather than wartime crises destroys the family unit. Nevertheless, without being altogether conclusive, the overall data do suggest strongly that the father's absence from the family can often have a significantly deleterious effect on the child.

Prominent among such effects are the scars left on the child's developing sense of identity. From studies to date, it appears that children who grow up in fatherless families have trouble achieving a secure sense of their role in society. The outcome for boys is often either antisocial behavior or overly feminine traits and attitudes, and for girls chronic difficulties in their relationships with members of the opposite sex.

Father Absence and the Identity Problems of Sons

Over 25 years ago, pioneer delinquency researchers Sheldon and Eleanor Glueck reported that more than 40 percent of a group of adolescent delinquent boys they were studying came from homes in which the father was absent; the comparable proportion in a matched group of nondelinquents was less than 25 percent. The theme of the Gluecks' findings has been struck repeatedly: A significant number of boys who grow up in homes where there is no father appear unable to learn appropriate ways to handle their aggression. They tend to "act out" their hostile feelings, apparently without much concern for the consequences, instead of realizing them in fantasies as most children tend to do.

Why?

Explanations for the finding vary.

Without a model of self-control usually supplied by the father, some contend, boys from father-absent homes suffer a lag in the development of restraint and, therefore, display an unbridled impulse for immediate gratification.

Other investigators suggest instead that it is the father's traditional force of moral authority that is lacking. University of Rhode Island psychologist Henry B. Biller, who has made extensive studies of the father's role, finds that authoritative fathers who guide rather than force their children to understand right from wrong appear to nurture a healthy moral sense.

The most prevailing explanation, however, is that the male child growing up without a father is threatened ultimately by his mother's enveloping presence. Many researchers have concluded that the exaggerated toughness, aggressiveness, and delinquency typical of various gang members, for example, are an expression of rebellion against the feminizing influence of overprotective mothers. Delinquent behavior, in their view, is a manifestation of a young boy's continuing search for masculine identity—a flight from becoming submissive to mother and overly dependent on her influence. Only by the overt expression of aggression can he shake loose from his mother and demonstrate his budding masculinity. Such children seem to behave out of a conviction that hostile acts toward others are the earmark of manhood.

The results of numerous studies have connected the absence of fathers with the angry, antisocial, or outright delinquent behavior of their sons. Researchers have taken diverse paths to make the point. Aron W. Siegman, for example, studied the responses of medical students to a questionnaire, and found that those who had lived without a father for at least one of their first four years admitted to a greater degree of antisocial behavior in childhood than those who had enjoyed a father's continuous presence. Robert E. Anderson took quite a different path, studying the earlier histories of boys committed to a training school. He found among them, too, an atypically high incidence of children who had experienced father absence.

Such results may admittedly be confounded by other conditions existing in homes without fathers—among them, for example, poverty, dissension, or uncaring mothers. Yet it is noteworthy that data linking the father's absence with delinquency emerge from studies not only of American populations but also of people the world over.

In their 1963 cross-cultural analysis, Margaret K. Bacon and her collaborators reported a striking relationship between the availability of the father and the amount of crime among juveniles in 48 different societies. They found that an early lack of opportunity for young boys to form an identification with their fathers was associated later with the higher frequency of theft, assault, rape, murder, and other crimes.

If exaggerated masculinity and delinquent behavior do, in fact, arise from an overly feminine environment in early childhood, we should find plentiful evidence in segments of our own society where fathers are especially scarce.

And we do. In the woman-dominated culture of the black lower-class family, for example, the rate of father absence increases from the national norm of one-tenth to almost one-half in some regions, and it is here especially that young males often display aggression and violence virtually as a badge of their identity. Their attempts to prove their masculinity have been seen as one reason for the high rate of juvenile delinquency among blacks in lower-class neighborhoods.

From their study of the subject, John H. Rohrer and Munro S. Edmonson concluded that the black juvenile gang member rejects femininity in every form, finding it not only in women and in effeminate men, but "in laws and morals and religion, in schools and occupational striving." The "subculture of violence" which sociologist Marvin Wolfgang has found to be so prevalent in the black ghetto arises also in communities of homes in which the adult male is often absent. Could it be that in such homes a boy identifies early with women, and then is forced later on to go overboard to prove his masculinity? The data available lend support to this hypothesis.

In contrast to boys who express their identity crises through hyper-masculine behavior, others appear to develop as if guided by the old, pragmatic motto: "If you can't lick 'em, join 'em." Growing up in homes without fathers, such boys—like their delinquent counterparts—also do not succeed in shaking loose from their mothers' overbearing influence. But instead of reacting with aggressiveness and delinquency, they emerge with personalities strongly tinged by their mothers' feminine traits and attitudes. They appear to be victims of having gone without a masculine model with whom they could identify—an especially critical limitation in the first few years of life, when the child is developing his sexual identity. Instead of interests, attitudes, and behaviors appropriate to their sex, many father-absent boys seem to absorb the ways of the mothers who have so pervaded their early years.

Data supporting this theory emerged as a result of the separation of many fathers from their families during World War II. That crisis spawned a number of studies in which middle-class children from father-absent homes were compared with those from homes in which father was present.

In a widely cited 1946 project, for example, psychologist George R. Bach found that preschool boys separated from their fathers during their early years were less aggressive, more dependent, and harbored weaker masculine self-concepts and game preferences than their peers whose fathers were available. In a similar vein, psychologist Robert R. Sears and his collaborators conducted an experiment involving doll play. They showed that boys whose early years were spent without the benefit of fathers engaged in play patterns more characteristic of preschool girls; moreover, such boys expressed aggression primarily through verbal rather than physical means—as young girls typically do.

An even more extensive study was conducted by psychologist Lois M. Stolz and a team of researchers of children born during the war. The subjects were 19 families of married veterans—either students or faculty members—returning to Stanford University in California. These families included children who were born during the war while their fathers were absent and who did not meet them until at least a year later. A control group consisted of families in which no children had been separated from the fathers. The two groups of families were matched in age and sex of children.

The investigators conducted a series of intensive interviews with the fathers and mothers and observed the children in social settings with peers and adults, as well as in various play situations. The resulting data revealed a number of graphic differences between the two groups. The war-separated children showed more serious behavior problems, fears, and tensions than the control children; in the company of other children, they were less skillful in establishing or maintaining relationships. Significantly, the children born during the father's absence were closer to their mothers than to their fathers, and they were more dependent than the other children on adults, particularly female teachers. The fathers themselves complained that much of their sons' behavior was unmasculine.

From these studies—and many more like them—researchers have conluded that boys separated from their fathers may have a relatively difficult time in establishing their masculine image. Support for such findings emerges also from investigations conducted in widely divergent cultures—from the Philippines to Kenya. Based on their far-ranging studies, for example, psychologist Roger V. Burton and anthropologist John W. M. Whiting reported in 1961 that in societies where the father is excluded from close interaction with his infant son, and where the newborn's early contacts are entirely with mother or other females, the child later encounters a serious problem in establishing his sexual identity. Eventually he must shift from his early psychological alliance with the mother to one that fixes his masculine role in society. To accomplish this, the boy must endure complex and dramatic initiation rituals designed to erase once and for all his feminine identification and to ease his entry, albeit late, into the world of men.

Whiting made a special study of the *couvade,* a custom that involves the mimicking of the female role for varying periods by fathers after the birth of a child. Wherever the custom has been kept, it was found the couvade has introduced a serious gap in the relationship between father and son during the earliest phases of the child's development. Having assumed a feminine role, the couvade father is, in effect, an absent father.

Whiting and his collaborators wondered about the impact of the couvade on the child's development. They found that the longer and more severe the practice—that is, the more sustained the father's absence from fathering the developing infant—the more confused the male child's sex identity tends to be, and the stronger the later puberty initiation rites devised to reverse the sense of feminine identification flowering in the male child.

To lend support to the theory that the couvade was associated with a feminine orientation in male children, a Harvard husband-wife team, Robert L. and Ruth H. Munroe, studied practitioners of the couvade among the Black Carib population of British Honduras, now Belize. They found that those males who practiced the couvade intensively had spent in their own childhoods an average of more than half of their first three years without a male adult in the home; in contrast, those who practiced a weaker form of the couvade had averaged only eight months without benefit of masculine figures. It would appear from the results that the degree to which a man engaged in the couvade ritual reflected the degree to which he experienced paternal deprivation many years earlier.

There are hints of similar patterns in our own culture. Although Americans do not practice the couvade, some do experience "sympathy pains" during their wives' pregnancies. In a sample of white American males Ruth H. Munroe found 40 percent reporting dramatic symptoms suggesting strong identification with their wives when they had been pregnant—for example, nausea, vomiting, food craving. The men with symptoms tended to respond more like females on a number of measures—on the way they completed a drawing, for example, on their preferences in TV programs, and on their attitudes toward children.

In many cases, it turned out, the fathers of these men had been gone from home, permanently or for long periods, while their sons were young. The men with pregnancy symptoms had experienced a significantly greater loss in this respect than the others.

Further evidence of the subtle ramifications of father absence is contained in the findings emerging from a Harvard Ph.D. dissertation by Lyn Carlsmith, who analyzed the cognitive skills of college males. Her data were the responses on college entrance tests of around three thousand students. Normally, girls score higher on the verbal section of such tests than do boys; boys, in turn, do better on the mathematics section. She found that those boys whose fathers had been absent for an appreciable length of time during their earliest years scored in a typically feminine pattern—that is, higher on the verbal subscales; in contrast, the scores of those boys whose fathers were at home more nearly fitted the male norm. Moreover, the longer the father had been absent, or the younger the child at the time of his absence, the stronger the tendency for the students to score in a feminine pattern. Apparently, the effects of paternal absence may intrude even on such relatively subtle aspects of personality as cognitive style.

Not all students of the subject see the fatherless family as a mental health risk. Elizabeth Herzog and Hylan Lewis are two of them. In comprehensive reviews of the relevant research literature, they find at least as many studies that show no effect of father absence as those that do. They conclude that "father absence is only one among an interacting complex of factors which mediate and condition its impact on a growing child."

Few researchers in the field would contest the matter. Nevertheless, it would be foolhardy to assume that father absence—or any other individual factor shown to be related to the child's well-being—is of secondary importance simply because it is correlated in real life with other factors. To protect children's mental health, we must by all means view them in their total life contexts; no single one of the interrelated factors that can affect children may be dismissed. The father is clearly one of them—and not only for boys but for girls, too.

The Romantic Problems of Fatherless Girls

Although most of the research on the father's impact deals with boys, it appears that the father can be a potent force in shaping the mental health of daughters as well. The behavior of girls without fathers, however, in contrast to that of boys, shows few differences during the preschool years; these emerge gradually and are more clearly present at adolescence. Moreover, it is not the female child's interests and activities that are so much disrupted as her patterns of behavior in relating to the opposite sex.

The annals of psychiatric lore are filled with case histories of women whose lives have been marked by romantic and marital upheavals. Beginning at adolescence, many of these women have seemed chronically unable to establish satisfactory relationships with boys and, later in life, to form meaningful attachments to men.

Rita is a twenty-seven-year-old staff assistant to a congressman, dramatically successful in her career but agonizingly troubled in her relationships with men. Rita's father—chronically alcoholic and promiscuous—was a shadowy figure at best during her earliest years. Her memories of him now are of a violent and abusive man, but most of all, she remembers a household empty of a father. The living rooms, kitchens, and backyards of her friends, it seems to her now, echoed with the voices of men who lent security and joy to the lives around them. Her world, in contrast, was strangely without a masculine presence.

Two marriages have already ended for Rita in divorce. They have left no trail of bitterness or anger—only a vacuum of caring and commitment that she seems destined always to carry with her. "I guess," she says ruefully, "I cannot really trust a man. I don't really know how much of myself I can commit to a relationsip. Sex for me is a passive, flat experience, and so are all the other experiences we share. The thought of bringing up a child with a man fills me with horror. He could never be depended on for anything." Nothing so accurately symbolizes the tortured interaction between Rita and the men in her life than the hysterectomy she elected to undergo in the prime of youthful womanhood. No male, she made certain, will ever enter her life with any impact.

Clinical records like Rita's highlight in human terms a theme embedded in existing research data. A study by psychologist E. Mavis Hetherington, for example, showed persuasively that adolescent girls growing up without fathers tend to display difficulties in their heterosexual behavior—either shyness and discomfort around males and anxiety about sex, or, in contrast, promiscuousness and inappropriately assertive behavior with male peers and adults. The first pattern appeared to be more prevalent among girls whose fathers were removed by death, the second for those whose fathers either deserted or were divorced. The investigators found no comparable results in the interactions of such girls with other females. The findings strongly suggest that some girls without fathers sorely miss the opportunity to acquire the social skills necessary for building appropriate heterosexual relationships—a deficiency that becomes significant with the advent of puberty.

For many girls absence of the father breeds not suspicion and anxiety about males, but a grandiose, unrealistic idealization of what a man is really like. Without the experience of a male in early life, without the opportunity to learn about him as a human being—his imperfections as well as his glories—young girls grow to maturity seeking, but never finding, the "man in shining armor." Such girls may nurture an exalted image of the father for whom they are constantly searching—an image against which all men are doomed to fall short.

The young girl with an absent or only dimly present father never really has a fair chance to observe a meaningful male-female relationship. He may not be aware of it in his day-to-day interactions around the house, but the father is actually providing a learning situation which shapes his daughter's skills in relating to males. "A girl learns how to be a woman and how to get along with women primarily from her mother," writes Benjamin Spock. "But she learns from her father in early childhood how to get along with the other half of the human race." It is from him that she gets used to some obvious, but important things—the low voice, for example, the rougher, more daring kinds of play that fathers are apt to go in for, how to take kidding, how to flirt. "These may not sound like important steps in development," says Spock, "but that's because we take them for granted."

A daughter's overall normal personality development may also be subjected to risk when the early paternal presence is lacking. In a 1973 study, Kathleen D. Fish and Biller used an extensive family background questionnaire to survey college girls' perceptions of their relationships with their fathers during childhood. Those girls who perceived their fathers as having been very nurturant scored high on a personal adjustment scale, as did those who saw their fathers as having been positively involved with them. In contrast, girls who remembered their fathers as highly rejecting scored extremely low on the adjustment measure.

As a result of their comprehensive review of the father-daughter literature, Biller and Anthony Davids concluded that the father's participation in a secure and consistent relationship with his daughter—emotionally warm, stable, and democratic—seems to provide a highly significant ingredient for her psychological well-being. "It appears," they conclude, "that the more a father participates in constructive interplay with his daughter, the more adequate will be her sex-role and personality development."

The conclusion may seem bland, but its ramifications are not. In words shorn of the language of social science, the evidence says simply this: The chances for a girl to grow up to be a woman secure in her womanhood are brighter if, years earlier, a father has lit her way.

Can Fathers Be Good "Mothers"?

Consider the arrangement of a real-life Washington, D.C., couple, now married two years. From Monday through Wednesday, the psychiatrist-father is on duty at the local community mental health center. On Thursdays and Fridays, the mother, who is an attorney, practices law. On their respective days "off," each shares the responsibilities of homemaking and parenting—shopping, house cleaning, and the care and feeding of their son, now seven months old.

This family's pattern, while admittedly extreme, is hardly unique. An increasing number of couples find themselves with their traditional roles comfortably reversed. The desire of many women for equal opportunity in the job market is being balanced among males by a desire to engage in child rearing. In Sweden, some families have arranged their lives in a way that permits the wife to work and support the family, while the husband (called "househusband") remains at home to keep house and raise children.

In the past, close female relatives were likely to take the mother's place during her absence. Today, however, members of the extended family no longer so readily absorb motherless children. In typical families, members are widely dispersed; moreover, many relatives themselves work, leaving little time or energy to spare even for their own children, let alone those of others.

According to Helen Bee, the result of the trend is that approximately 15 percent of all American children under fourteen whose mothers work either full or part time are cared for by their fathers. Interest in the father's influence naturally shifts, therefore, from the impact of his absence to that of his growing presence in the American household.

The emergence of father as a part-time mother figure is not readily accepted by everyone. "If fathers were meant to be mothers, God would have given them breasts," thundered one hard-liner on sex roles recently. How valid is this "masculine" protest? How well can fathers actually fulfill the role traditionally reserved for mothers?

Child development experts have long assumed that there is something special about a mother's connection with her infant. Freud, for example, saw their relationship as the bedrock of all later human transactions of love. Because only mothers can breast-feed their young—and so much of the early parent-child contact is built around feeding—we have imagined all of the baby's sources for warmth, affection, and psychological nourishment to be focused at the milk-engorged breasts. Moreover, as long as mother has taken the lead in filling the child-care role, she naturally has spent more time than others with her children. For both biological and cultural reasons, then, the mother has been seen as having a special relationship with her infant that the father could not possibly build.

Granted that only mothers can offer the breast, and granted, too, that the child care traditionally assumed by mothers has brought them into greater contact with their young, the question persists: Is the capacity to feel "maternal" emotions and to behave in "motherly" ways restricted only to females?

Evidence from diverse studies suggests that it is not—that fathers can develop the kinds of strong bonds with infants traditionally reserved for mothers. Contrary to long-held assumptions, the "mothering instinct" is not embedded in the bodies and souls of females alone. Instead, maternal behavior can evidently be produced by male and female alike.

One dramatic indication emerged from Harry Harlow's studies of infant female monkeys deprived of a mother figure in their midst. Harlow showed that motherless monkeys grow to be inadequate mothers themselves. Without an opportunity to learn how to be a mother, no maternal "instinct" survived. The business of mothering, it would seem, is learned through the kinds of observations and experiences that, theoretically, are equally available to both sexes.

Human studies also provide evidence that at least some aspects of maternal behavior are learned rather than instinctual. Some of these studies were described in Chapter 5. In another, a team of Stanford University investigators headed by Aimée Leifer studied the attachment behavior of mothers of prematures, who were separated from their infants for up to two months while the newborns were in incubators; they compared these women with a group of mothers of full-term infants, who were separated from their babies only sporadically during the first several days. The full-term mothers showed evidence of greater attachment. They smiled at their infants more and held the babies close to their body more often. They were also more confident about their ability to care for the infants than the mothers of the prematures.

Moreover, even among the mothers of prematures, there was a noteworthy difference. Those who had been given an opportunity to hold their infants while in the incubator and to share in some of the caretaking tasks were more confident about their mothering skills than those who had been able only to look at their infants during hospital confinement.

The full-term mother's stronger bond with her infant suggests that such attachment may simply require sufficient early physical contact with the infant. Fathers generally do not have such an opportunity, and it is logical to assume that with it, they, too, could learn to be "maternal." In fact, recent studies by psychologist Ross D. Parke and his associates seem to demonstrate the truth of these assumptions.

In the first of these studies, mother, father, and baby were observed for ten minutes sometime between 6 and 48 hours after the delivery. Among the behaviors that were sampled were holding the baby, looking, smiling, vocalizing, kissing, touching, imitating, exploring, feeding, and handing the infant over to the other parent. Fathers, it turned out, were just as involved with their child as mothers and did not differ from them in the majority of measures. "In fact, fathers tended to hold the infant more than mothers and rock the infant in their arms more than mothers. But these fathers were middle class and well educated; all but one had been present at the birth of their baby, and more than half had attended classes in the Lamaze method of childbirth."

So the investigators next studied lower-class fathers who had not attended childbirth classes and had not been present during delivery. They were observed both while they were alone with their baby and while the mother, too, was present. The results were the same. The father not only was very much interested in the baby but also actively involved himself with the child whether or not the mother was present.

Moreover, Parke and his associates have found, fathers are fully as nurturant as mothers, a finding based on the extent to which the parents touched, looked at, vocalized to, and kissed their offspring. In the second study, when all the babies were bottle-fed, fathers were more likely to feed than mothers when both parents were present, but fed less than mothers when alone with the baby. When each parent was alone with the infant, the mother spent more time in feeding the baby and in related caretaking activities such as wiping the child's face.

To Parke and psychologist Douglas B. Sawin, these differences "suggest some role differentiation between mothers and fathers in the feeding context during the first three days of infant life." Considering the way most prospective fathers have been brought up, this slight difference in the time devoted to caretaking is hardly to be wondered at. There is more reason for surprise to find that fathers after the birth of a child are just as nurturant as mothers. Moreover, these investigators found that though the father may spend less time overall, "he is as sensitive as the mother to infant cues in the feeding context." Conclude the investigators:

The next task is to provide cultural supports for these potential activities— by modifying hospital visiting arrangements, providing paternity leaves, making available training classes so that fathers will have the opportunity to both learn and practice caretaking skills. In turn, fathers will be more likely not only to share these responsibilities, but execute these tasks effectively and view these behaviors as role consistent. By providing this type of support, fathers will no longer be viewed as a mere "biological necessity" but be recognized as playing an important, influential and continuing role in the development of the infant.

Parke says also: "There is a lot of learning that goes on between the mother and infant in the hospital—from which the father is excluded, and in which he must be included so he'll not only have the interest and a feeling of owning the baby, but also the kinds of skills that the mother develops."

University of Wisconsin researchers Michael and Jamie Lamb believe that fathers should be instated as significant figures in the lives of their infants. If fathers could be assured that they, too, had a major part to play in the socialization of their children from the start, "this would significantly reduce the incidence of marital conflict engendered by a baby's birth . . . [and] one might predict that an enthusiastic commitment to fatherhood would both expand the amount and improve the quality of father-infant interaction."

And what of the infant? Will newborns become attached to a male caretaker? For Biller, the evidence is clear. The newborn exhibits no consistent preference for one specific parent, he states. Just who it is that holds, feeds, and stimulates the baby is less important than whether these needs are met. It is the primary providers of such comforts—male or female—to whom initial attachments are made. Reviewing the relevant research, Lamb concludes that "the infant's social world is far more complex than most have assumed, and that, from the earliest age, the baby is likely to be influenced and reciprocally to influence . . . at least both its parents and probably other relatives and friends as well."

For the child, there is safety in numbers. Margaret Mead believes that a growing portfolio of attachments provides the newborn with an increased security it would not have if it were dependent for emotional nurturance on only one adult. There is survival value for the child in not "going for broke" with the mother alone.

In the late 1950s, Harlow showed clearly that the infant monkey attaches itself not to the animal or object that gives milk but to the source of "contact comfort." Ingeniously devised "mothers" made of soft cloth became the objects of the infant monkeys' love, not the impersonal, mechanical milk-feeding machines equally available to them.

The human infant, too, is likely to build its primary bonds with the person who holds, cuddles, and strokes. Working at the University of Denver, researchers Leslie J. Cohen and Joseph J. Campos have shown that newborns can receive a clear message of love from males as well as females. With sufficient exposure to the father, the infant comes to recognize the male voice, the "feel" of being held by him, and the pleasure of playing with him. The child begins naturally to associate the father with feeding, warmth, soothing contact, and the removal of pain.

A dramatic demonstration of the reciprocal feelings of attachment possible between infant and father was made by psychologists Gary Mitchell, William K. Redican, and Jody Gomber at the University of California in Davis. Mitchell became interested in the father's role after becoming a father for the third time. His doctorate had brought him into

Harlow's University of Wisconsin primate laboratory, devoted to the effects of mothering on infant primate development. It was clear to him that a study of fathering was long overdue. Perhaps fathers, when given the chance, he reasoned, could be as successful as mothers at raising emotionally healthy infants.

In their California studies of paternalism, the researchers used rhesus monkeys despite good reason to worry about the safety of the infant animals. The male rhesus generally shows little affection for newborns—indifference at best, but more usually, outright hostility. There have been reports of infanticide by adult males.

Nevertheless, with safeguards in place to protect the animal, Redican decided to remove an infant rhesus from its mother and test the capacity of a male "father" to rear the child.

In a detailed account appearing in *Psychology Today*, the investigators have described the behavior of one pair. The infant, named Pierre, was removed from his small, protective cage, and his father, named Mellow, was allowed to approach. The animals touched, then independently explored the cage. After a few minutes, Mellow groomed Pierre until the infant returned the gesture. For the next six minutes Pierre clung to Mellow, climbed on his back and head, and leaned over backwards, holding onto Mellow's ears. Mellow withstood these infantile liberties, albeit with some anxiety. Then he began to threaten Pierre; several times his open mouth hovered over the infant's head. The investigators stood by nervously. When Pierre screeched, Mellow pushed him away. The infant fled up the side of the cage and watched Mellow pacing the floor. Later Pierre climbed down again and huddled in the corner and began sucking his penis, a behavior typical of animals whose social development has been distorted. Within seconds, Mellow sat down beside Pierre and began grooming him. During the entire seven months of rearing, when Pierre assumed a depressed posture, Mellow would typically begin to groom him—an important part of their physical interaction—and on occasion, Pierre reciprocated.

At the start, Pierre initiated physical contact more often than Mellow and broke it off less often. Later, however, Mellow began to look at Pierre more often—one index of social attachment in monkeys. Ultimately, the attachment between the two grew firm and intense. At the end of seven months, when they were separated for two days, Mellow went into a rage. He bit himself so severely in the leg that he cut a number of blood vessels, and would have died without prompt treatment. Pierre, in turn, regressed to mournful penis sucking, and his calls of distress were unmistakable.

When reunited, Mellow and Pierre immediately clung to each other. Pierre seemed to be a healthy little monkey, physically and socially. He continued to show entirely normal development and Mellow continued to act as an exemplary father.

When the investigators paired adult males with infant females, they found similar, if less intense, attachment.

For the investigators the implications of their study are clear: "If adult male rhesus monkeys, characterized as indifferent or even hostile to infants in the wild, can become intimately attached to them in the laboratory," they ask, "what might this augur for man?" The researchers see their data as helping refute the argument that, because of innate factors, males cannot form close attachments with infants. "Human males," they feel, "are a rich resource which can be tapped during this period of changing social and sex roles."

Countless fathers do not require evidence from primate or child development laboratories to validate the tender feelings to their young that spring from within. Yet attempts by fathers to act on impulses of warmth and protectiveness toward their young are not always easily realized in our society. An emotional wall, which may be impenetrable, often surrounds the mother-child relationship. Because the attachment between wife and new infant is so immediate and so strong, fathers often begin to view themselves as superfluous.

In the view of Baltimore psychiatrist Leo Bartemeier, many men feel that to intrude upon the mother-child attachment would be unmanly; in their own childhoods, they saw only women dealing with children. Taught to stifle their warmest impulses and to view physical contact as appropriate only if tinged with either aggression or sex, men often avoid the "nonmasculine" responsibility of cuddling and comforting their children. For many, affection for children can only be expressed through material gifts. Bartemeier clarifies the issue confronting many fathers:

Loving almost means being soft. . . . A loving and gentle father is consciously or unconsciously looked upon as a psychological failure in the sense that he isn't really a he-man. A great many family tragedies in which children fail to develop normally and grow up to be either lazy bullies or aggressive, conceited, sterile members of society have developed as a result of the fact that the father either did not dare to be soft and gentle or that his softness and gentleness were mistaken for femininity and weakness.

All things being equal, Harvard child development authority Burton L. White believes, mothers will probably do better at the task of child rearing than others. "But," he adds, "if anyone could do as good a job as a mother in providing beneficial early childhood experiences, I would guess that it would be the father." Most of the factors involved in being a child rearer in the first three years, White contends, do not seem to be sex linked. "Designing a home that is safe and interesting for a child does not seem to require male or female genes. Nor does responding naturally to a child's overtures and providing assistance when needed. In general, as you look beyond the superficial and into the actual details of the provision of early educational opportunities, I see nothing that a mother does (except breast feeding) that a father could not do. . . ."

As a matter of fact, in a growing number of families in this country, the father *is* doing everything except providing the breast because he is the only parent in the house.

Fathers Alone

In nearly half a million American households, the family consists of father and his dependent children. The reasons vary—widowhood, nonmarriage, adoption, separation, or divorce. The number of such single fathers seems bound to rise. Between 1965 and 1972, for example, the number of households headed by separated or divorced fathers jumped 71 percent, while the number headed by separated or divorced mothers rose 58 percent. Moreover, an increasing number of children of divorce are being awarded to the custody of their fathers rather than mothers. The result is that many men are today being challenged with the full-time responsibility of "bringing up baby."

In an attempt to describe the life-style of single-parent fathers, child development authority Dennis K. Orthner and his associates conducted lengthy interviews with 20 such fathers in the Greensboro, North Carolina, area. The fathers range from twenty-five to sixty-four years. Nine each have one or two children; two have three. The children range from eighteen months to seventeen years. Fifteen of the fathers are separated or divorced; three are widowers; two never married. Their average income exceeds $18,000.

The fathers were satisfied with their lives and in no hurry to marry again. Over two-thirds viewed cohabitation as unacceptable for themselves because as parents they felt the need to be sexually discreet. All but two sometimes took their children along on dates.

Common problems mentioned by the fathers are lack of patience and time for their children, making decisions alone, and having to be away from their children more than they want to be. The fathers generally felt they demanded more independence in their children than other parents might. . . .

Since becoming single parents, these fathers became much more appreciative of the responsibilities of being the primary parent. In particular, they had become less discipline-oriented, more concerned about the adequacy of day care, more interested in education and more protective of their children. . . .

Almost all the fathers reported that child-care problems had not interfered with their regular work. One, though, lost his job because of interruptions to see teachers, doctors, and the like.

Three-fourths of the fathers had no help with housework. Of the others, only one had a full-time housekeeper.

The investigators offer a general conclusion: "These fathers feel quite capable and successful in their ability to be the primary parent of their children. The confidence they express and the satisfaction they seem to derive in fatherhood is very difficult to deny."

Orthner and his associates believe that in areas where strains are indicated, solutions could be found if some of the following recommendations were considered: day-care facilities offering extended services in the evenings, child-care facilities located in shopping centers, the organization of baby-sitting cooperatives, transportation of children to and from day-care centers, classes in single-parenthood, and "big sister" as a counterpart to "big brother" organizations.

Psychiatric social worker Helen A. Mendes, who also interviewed single fathers—32 of them, in southern California—came up with some different findings, possibly because only 14 of her sample were members of the middle class. These fathers were raising from one to six children, ranging from three to seventeen years old.

Commonly, fathers hired caretakers, found them unsatisfactory, and then entered their children in nurseries, child-care centers, or the like, which were considered more satisfactory, presumably because the personnel were trained.

Of the 32 fathers, all but 4 regularly cleaned, shopped, prepared the meals, and managed their homes. A frequent complaint was that "they were *required* to cook every day." As they tried to manage the various tasks of caring for the home and the children, more than half of the fathers admitted to feeling stressed.

Mendes quotes J. Louis Despert, whose work on divorce has become a classic:

... when the mother has left the home, the father has a considerable task. Distressed as he may very well be, he can take it for granted that the young child feels far worse.... The child needs his father's immediate and convincing expression of his own love and reliability. Daddy is still here, and Daddy is staying, Daddy will not leave him.

Apparently the area most crucial to the children's welfare, Mendes sums up, "was the quality of the emotional relationships between the fathers and their children." Yet the fathers lacked information about normal childhood development and, with one exception, "found books useless in answering the many questions they had about the normalcy of their children's behaviors." Mendes concludes that this concern about normal child development "reflects the socialization of males in our society—that is, males are generally not expected to care for children and, consequently, this aspect of their family life education is usually neglected."

Although at times against odds, fathers undoubtedly can perform a key and sometimes the only nurturing role. Many do so successfully. The reluctance of others to do so is unfortunately blocked not so much by circumstances or culture as by a glaring lack of internal motivation.

The Involved Father

The quality of sheer impenetrable selfishness in the human breast (in my breast) is a never-failing source of wonderment. I do not want to be disturbed, challenged, troubled. Huge regions of myself belong only to me.... Trying to act fairly to children, each of whom is temperamentally different from myself and from each other, each of whom is at a different stage of perception and aspiration, is far more baffling than anything Harvard prepared me for.

That statement, written by Professor Michael Novak of Columbia University, exposes honestly and directly a conflict in the hearts of many contemporary fathers. It is the conflict between the "outside" world of work and the "inside" world of paternal tasks and feelings.

For many fathers, the conflict has been resolved in favor of a world altogether irrelevant to their children. The masculine role of family provider has been a signal for many men to abdicate virtually any involvement in the duties and challenges of parenthood. For some, an addiction to work appears often to provide a guilt-free rationalization for their lack of commitment to the responsibilities of child rearing; the task of "making a living" is used as a convenient excuse by such fathers to sidestep the considerable responsibilities toward children inherent in paternity. The worlds of business, academics, or government, difficult and challenging as they may often be, are seen by many of them as considerably more rewarding than PTA, homework, Little League, or quiet hours with a child.

In an article titled "Life without Father," syndicated columnist Ellen Goodman mourns the resulting loss of meaningful, regular contact between fathers and children. Even in cases where divorce does not end a fragile marriage, Goodman insists that fathering as a career for husbands is "a vanishing devotion." She cites one recent study of middle-class men showing that, on the average, a father spends 20 minutes a day with his one-year-old baby, but only 38 seconds actually interacting in any meaningful way with the child.

Goodman believes that such fathers have become "emotionally irrelevant" in the lives of their children. Most of the children in the country, she contends, are "fatherless" to a remarkable degree. While there is a core of men who have always developed a rich and deep attachment with their children and there is a new core of men who seek to share far more than 38 seconds of time with their young, many others, says Goodman, "deal with their children as if they were merely warts on the surface of their lives, and simply excise them at will." She describes such children as the progeny of invisible fathers, or "transparents."

Are these children of uncommitted fathers at a disadvantage?

The evidence is meager, but it suggests that they are. The father's involvement—or lack of it—does seem to make a difference. When his role remains shadowy or insubstantial, the result can be a gap in the child's emotional resources.

When, for example, a boy enjoys frequent opportunities to observe a competent, confident adult male operate in a variety of situations, it seems to accelerate his maturation. Bronfenbrenner showed that the amount of time adolescent boys spend with their fathers is reflected in the degree of leadership and responsibility they display in school. And from their study, psychologist Paul H. Mussen and his colleagues concluded that the motivation to achieve is more likely among adolescent boys enjoying warm relationships with their fathers than among those who are without them.

Mark W. Reuter and Biller designed a family questionnaire to assess the perceptions of college males of their relationships with their fathers and the amount of time the fathers spent at home. They then analyzed the association between the degree of paternal nurturance and availability on one hand, and the students' personality adjustment scores on the other.

The investigators found that those boys who remembered their fathers as highly nurturant and at least moderately available scored high in personality adjustment; the same was true for those whose fathers were only moderately nurturant but very much available. In contrast, those students who reported their fathers as having been home much of the time but giving them little attention perceived themselves as undependable and insecure; so, too, did boys whose fathers were remembered as highly nurturant but seldom available to them.

Reviewing these findings, Biller and Davids conjecture that the father who is warm and supportive may enjoy a more adequate overall personality adjustment than other types of fathers, and boys who have adequate opportunities to observe such a man can, therefore, begin to imitate his behavior and thus develop positive personality characteristics themselves. In contrast, it may be that the relatively detached father is an inadequate and insecure person and that as a poor model, his consistent presence is a detriment to the boy's personality development. The boy with a cold, unloving father may be better off, in other words, if his father is not too available. This speculation is consistent with evidence—supplied, among others, by Biller—suggesting that boys whose fathers are absent often show better personality adjustment than boys with the "advantage" of passive, ineffective fathers.

It is not materialistic success that children evidently seek of their fathers but rather a quality of attention and commitment—and availability. Morris Gershwin, father of the composer George Gershwin, was a man who specialized in business failures. His sons once counted 28 flats in which they lived while moving about to be near their father's latest business. Morris tried his hand at restaurants, Russian and Turkish baths, bookmaking, bakeries, a cigar store, and a pool hall. The development of his sons undoubtedly reflected more of *who* he was than *what* he amounted to.

Here are the recollections of one confident and successful teenager about the generous paternal commitment of her father. "He had a big effect on me because he was a very gentle person and he was always interested in what I had to say. *Anything* was important and he was willing to sit and listen to me and to talk with me. I was a person to be listened to, not a thing to keep quiet. He never said he couldn't talk to me because he was too busy. He would always stop what he was doing and help me."

That kind of involvement may be a vanishing art among contemporary fathers, and from the available evidence it would seem that it is their children who are the losers.

Will Another Man Do?

A child's need for a committed male parent has been generously documented not only through the kinds of research described here but also through mountains of clinical case history files. The question remains: Must it be the child's biological father who fills these needs— or can substitute male figures do the job? The evidence is that they can. In fact, given the right conditions, substitute fathers can often deliver the "emotional goods" to their young more effectively than can their natural fathers.

A recently completed study by a research team at Western Behavioral Sciences Institute in La Jolla, California, shows clearly that stepfathers are as competent as natural fathers in their role as parents and, more important, that stepchildren are as happy as children who live with their natural fathers.

The study, headed by anthropologist Paul J. Bohannan, was based on a random sample of over 1,700 respondents in San Diego County. Nine percent of the households, it turned out, were headed by stepfathers; national samplings reveal the number to be between 3 and 4 percent. Through a combination of interviews and questionnaires, Bohannan and his team collected a portrait of the roles and attitudes not only of the stepfathers and their children but also of the mothers and their original husbands.

Contrary to common opinion, the researchers found, children brought up in a home with a stepfather view themselves as being just as happy as those reared by both natural parents. They also turn out to be as successful and as achieving. The children in the study reported getting along with their stepfathers, and the mothers agreed.

The stepfathers rated themselves poorly, however, despite the generally high marks given them by both their stepchildren and their wives. They see themselves and their children as less successful and happy, for example, even though the children and mothers did not feel that way. "They simply don't believe they're doing that good a job," Bohannan reports, "and they thereby perpetuate a negative image of themselves." In contrast, natural fathers rated themselves as significantly better fathers, and their children as significantly happier when living with them. Despite the fact that they don't believe it, however, there is every evidence that substitute fathers can be as effective as natural fathers, and that their stepchildren can be content.

The importance of providing adequate father substitutes for the child without a male parent was demonstrated in the study by Anderson described earlier. He found that a history of paternal absence was much more frequent among boys committed to a training school, but he discovered also that among the nondelinquents who had experienced father absence, there was earlier a much higher rate of father substitution—stepfathers or other father surrogates—than was the case for the delinquent group.

It appears clear that it is the cast of family characters who make up the child's world at home—more so than their actual biological relationship—that counts for the child. Bohannan's results clearly demonstrate not only that the original father's absence can be overcome but also that his presence may actually upset the family balance. Even when the stepfather acts at times in ways that may not be in the child's best mental health interests, the impact is not significant as long as the child's original father does not become a "fly in the family ointment." If the natural father attempts to intrude and capture the child's attention, the result is often tension and confusion.

Bohannan organized a series of seminars among the stepfathers in his study and discovered that the existing problems did not center around the stepfather household but rather around the absent natural father. "The natural father plays the role of the joker in a game in which jokers are wild. That does not mean that he is a bad guy, but only that he is usually not in the communications network of the household. . . . Sometimes the natural fathers begin to think that their children's stepfathers are raising 'their' children in a way different from the way they themselves would do it. The children, they fear, will become like 'him' instead of 'me.' From time to time, they are likely to get a little bit desperate and perhaps do something that the stepfather family experiences as capricious. Then the animosity that often exists subliminally between the natural father and the mother can get out of hand. The stepfather takes the mother's side—and suddenly there is an explosive situation."

Bohannan's findings are important because many persons believe unequivocally that children involved in divorce and remarriage must inevitably pay a heavy price in mental health. Conventional wisdom has held that children experiencing parental divorce and remarriage invariably endure psychological trauma that can affect them for the duration of their lives. As will be shown later, this can be true, of course. But the presence in a child's life of an adequate substitute father, left free to fulfill his paternal role, can go a long way in shoring up a child's psychological resources.

The Father-Mother Team

"I want my child to grow up with a sense of who he is and a sense of being very, very secure, surrounded by a lot of people around that love the child and give it the kinds of support that maybe I alone cannot provide for it. That's what's really essential, not the fact that the father is there or not."

That is the statement of one of the growing number of mothers who are rearing their children without the benefit of a father figure in the home. For many, the adventure is clearly a success. For many others, however, the struggle is difficult. So it is, too, in homes where fathers alone are attempting to rear their young.

Do children profit most from the presence of both members of the parental team?

The evidence is that they do. It suggests that each parent makes a unique contribution to the child's development, playing separate and complementary roles.

At the Children's Hospital Medical Center in Boston, for example, Michael W. Yogman found that, as early as four weeks, it is obvious that infants are able to differentiate among mother, father, and stranger. In Yogman's study, the babies were seated comfortably in infant seats, and their mothers, their fathers, and strangers came in, sat directly in front of the children, and began to talk and play. The sessions were video-taped, and the infants' responses were analyzed in minute detail. Sixteen sessions involving six infants ranging in age from ten days to six months were analyzed.

Typically, mother and infant would play reciprocal vocal games, with the mother echoing the infant's sounds. The infant's movements tended to be smooth and rounded, moving its limbs softly toward and then away from the mother, who appeared to incorporate the gestures in similar responses of her own. In contrast, the vocal interactions between infant and father were typically short and intense, and the babies' movements were more abrupt, often bouncing up and down.

When in the company of their fathers, it was clear that the infants were responding naturally to stimulation quite different from that offered by their mothers. Fathers characteristically touched their children in short bursts, mainly tapping various parts of the tiny body, and they were given to exaggerated facial expressions, as if stimulating the baby for play. A newborn, it seems, learns at the very start how to respond in unique ways to each parent's style.

Lamb's research with somewhat older infants—ranging from seven to thirteen months old—showed that "the two parents played with their babies in different ways, and held them for different reasons. Mothers more often engaged in conventional games, such as pat-a-cake, and in games invoking stimulation of the children with toys. Fathers, on the other hand, were more likely to engage in vigorous, physically stimulating games, or in unusual and unpredictable types of play—the types of play, in fact, which the infants most enjoyed."

The findings showed a dramatic difference in the reasons for holding the babies. Mothers most often held them either for caretaking or to restrict exploration; "fathers were far more likely to hold the babies just to play with them, or because the babies wanted to be held."

The results indicated that

infants are attached to both parents, and that the relationships they experience with their fathers and mothers differ in quality, involve different sorts of interaction, and consequently, that fathers, like mothers, have the potential for a significant and differential impact on the psychological and social development of their infants from early in infancy.

Similar findings emerge from animal studies. When Mitchell, Redican, and Gomber paired their infant rhesus monkeys with fathers and mothers, they were able to show that paternal behavior is not simply maternal behavior adopted by the adult male. The two are somewhat different.

Over a seven-month period, infants paired with their mothers grew progressively independent, and the physical contact between them decreased. In contrast, the father's attachment to the infant apparently increases over time. Pierre and Mellow, for example, maintained a steady level of physical contact for a time, and then their episodes of physical contact grew longer as the pair lived together. There is a suggestion that while the intensity of attachment between the adult male and the infant increases over time, the mother-infant attachment decreases.

The complementary nature of the mother-father team was demonstrated in a study of military families by psychologist Frank A. Pederson. He found that psychologically healthy mothers are able to counteract the effects of father absence. Some of the boys, ages eleven to fifteen, were emotionally maladjusted; others were well adjusted; all had experienced relatively long periods of father absence. But among the maladjusted boys, the mothers themselves were significantly more disturbed than the other mothers.

In Bohannan's stepfather study, a number of fathers—mainly stepfathers but also natural ones—were found to be highly autocratic. Their children described them as controlling and punitive. These children— typically around fourteen years old—often responded by avoiding their fathers as much as possible, finding their social involvement outside their families among their peers. They turned out to be always among the troublemakers at school, apparently having incorporated the antisocial power-wielding style which their stepfathers modeled. They did poorly in their studies, were prone to delinquency, and were generally unhappy. The study revealed, however, that the children of autocratic stepfathers showed fewer of these problems than the children of similarly autocratic natural fathers.

Why?

University of Southern California sociologist Carlfred B. Broderick maintains that the reason lies in the behavior of the *other* member of the mother-father team. In the stepfather families, the mother was much more likely to intervene between the child and the male parental figure, to compensate for father's behavior to a greater degree than in natural parent families. "The fact that stepchildren, taken as a group, did as well as natural children in school, among their friends and in their own self-esteem," says Broderick, "seems to bear witness to the effectiveness of these mothers' compensatory efforts."

Broderick recalls the process clearly from his own childhood. When his stepfather threatened to bully him or beat him, his mother would step in as a zealous advocate of her child. "Hey, wait a minute," she would say, "you can't do that. That's my boy."

Such data portray how the mothers and fathers, acting as a team, can structure the emotional climate of the child in the family. Indeed, it is the family as a dynamic unit of interacting forces that provides one of the major bases for the child's journey toward either mental health or illness.

The Child in the Family

"In the whole range of human problems I've dealt with in my 12 years in the Senate—hunger, housing, labor, Indian education, migrant workers, children, aging—I keep getting back to one thing: the strength of the family. It's such a simple point, it should have been obvious."

Those are the words of then Senator Walter F. Mondale, spoken in 1976 as he sought the Vice-Presidency of the United States. Mondale's view of the world, gained from the pragmatic perspective of politics and social legislation, is well supported by the conclusions of researchers in child development. It is in the environment of the family that the psychological destiny of a child is, in large measure, determined.

A newborn may be plunged into a household warmed by an abiding love between parents, or torn from the beginning by strife and hate; burdened by the mental illness of mother or father—or both—or blessedly free of the grinding strains that anxiety, depression, and paranoia bring; without competition from other children, or already filled with siblings who have long since begun to leave their mark on the household; supported by an extended family available to help meet the child's needs, or isolated and bereft of outside human contact.

It is in this complex system of constantly interacting family members that the child is embedded. The quality of that system leaves its mark— for better or worse—from the very beginning.

Birth Order: Does It Make Any Difference?

Hundreds of studies over the years have reported a relationship between birth order—meaning the ordinal position a child occupies in relation to his brothers and sisters—and a variety of characteristics. Most commonly these characteristics have been intelligence and achievement. But research can be found that relates birth order to sharpness of eyesight, artistic creativity, marital adjustment, schizophrenia, tolerance of pain and frustration, conformity, juvenile delinquency, and other characteristics. Many of the studies are now known to be of dubious scientific merit, a factor that helps explain why the results of one investigation have sometimes contradicted those of another.

The most extensive work on the whole question of birth-order effects has been done by Brian Sutton-Smith of Teachers College, Columbia University, and B. G. Rosenberg of Bowling Green State University in Ohio. They reviewed the research of several hundred other investigators in this field, conducted studies of their own, and published the results as a book in 1970. A number of the studies cited concern the attitudes of parents toward firstborn compared to other children.

In addition to the parental attention that firstborns command, these children might be assumed to differ from their siblings because the parents know less about child rearing and may harbor unrealistic expectations of their first baby. Bruce Cushna's study of middle-class children from sixteen to nineteen months old found that mothers of firstborn children expected far more from them than mothers of later born and, while the babies were given a variety of tests, encouraged and helped them more.

In another study by J. K. Lasko, firstborn and second born were observed in their homes, along with their mothers, at frequent intervals, starting when they were a year old and ending when they were nine. During the first two years, the firstborn children received much more attention than their younger siblings would get when their turns came. This was not true later on. In fact, the investigator reported that by the age of three or four, firstborns were treated less warmly than their younger siblings would be at the same age. Even so, the mothers continued to make more attempts to push the firstborns than their siblings. It seems to be a general finding that parents continue for years to expect more of their first child than of the others. This is true, even though experience with first children has taught parents that their expectations for them in infancy and early childhood were unrealistic.

Presumably, these expectations lead to the greater level of anxiety that researchers have found in the firstborn.

Seeking to explain what happens to the first child, some investigators emphasize the parental pressure on the child to achieve. Others emphasize that the firstborn turns naturally to the parents for attention and love, is rewarded by them for doing so, and thus learns to reach out to them—and, later, to others—through the years.

By expecting higher levels of achievement from her firstborn, paying more attention to him or her as an infant, and giving rewards and imposing demands, Sutton-Smith and Rosenberg point out that the mother gradually shapes the child. "There is scattered evidence that firstborns are more conservative," these investigators report—as might be expected if they modeled themselves on their parents. There is also some support for the view that firstborn children have a tenderer conscience, presumably because they have taken in or adopted adult values at an early age.

What about the only child—who, of course, is both the firstborn and the last born? Evidence has been found that such children are both more dependent and more achieving than the firstborn and that they think more highly of themselves than do other children. Further, unlike the firstborn, they rate "relatively high on aggression and low on anxiety." But they see themselves as "more powerless in relation to parents than do children with siblings."

One investigator cited by Sutton-Smith and Rosenberg reports that only boys are favored by the mother much more than only girls. Other studies find that the only boy is more feminine and the only girl more masculine and that both have a greater tendency to sex deviations "consonant with these tendencies."

As for middle-born children, Sutton-Smith and Rosenberg suggest that they are more likely than the others to be neglected. More often than the others, they use negative means—such as whining and quarreling—of getting attention. Further, they are the "most changeable . . . are less often given affectionate nicknames by parents . . . and are least popular."

Studies of birth order as related to popularity have led to contradictory results. In one of the latest, dealing with 1,750 grade-school children in Riverside, California, the investigators—Norman Miller and Geoffrey Maruyama—had a hunch that last-born children should be the most popular with their peers and that firstborn children should be the least popular. Middle-born children should fall somewhere in between.

The reasoning went like this: It seems to be true everywhere that the older the children, the more status they are accorded and the more power they exercise. Consequently, the later-born children, if they are to receive anything like a fair share of the good things that are part of family life, have to develop interpersonal skills to a greater extent than the firstborn found necessary. Among such skills are powers of negotiation, accommodation, and tolerance. The development of these skills should facilitate relations with peers and increase popularity.

The children were individually asked to choose the person they would most like to have on their ball team, the one they would most like to sit next to in class, and the one they would pick to be their partner in doing school work.

The results confirmed the hypothesis. Last-born children were chosen significantly more often than others as ballplayers and seatmates. Middle-born children followed in popularity. Least popular were the firstborns. The answer to the question about work partners showed no significant differences among the three groups, presumably because "work choices predominantly tap differences in achievement rather than differences in interpersonal skills."

Teachers' ratings were confirmatory: the children considered to be more sociable and friendly and less demanding and jealous turned out to be, in general, the later borns. The differences appeared by kindergarten and persisted throughout the grade-school years.

A prominent skeptic of the importance of birth order, social psychologist Carmi Schooler, calls attention to a study of 600 finalists for National Merit Scholarships. Intellectually, they ranked in the highest one-half of 1 percent of all Americans. And more of them had been firstborn than could be explained by chance alone. The answer, which may apply to numerous other findings of a connection between birth order and intelligence, is simple: There had been more firstborns to begin with. If the finalists were 17 when they took their test in 1964, they had come into the world during a year when 43 percent of all the new babies had been first ones. The percentages the year before and the year after had also been high. Schooler believes birth order may have been important in other times and places, particularly where primogeniture was the rule. But "not here, not now!"

It stands to reason that a child's ordinal position in the family often does make *some* difference. The last born of 10 children—or 6 children, or even 3—comes into at least a slightly different atmosphere than the firstborn. And the son (or daughter) who finally arrives after a succession of daughters (or sons) is likely to get more attention than some of his or her predecessors. But the differences are hard to measure, and those attributable to birth order alone are very difficult to separate from those caused by heredity and constitution and by the resulting differences in parent-child and sibling-sibling interactions. Part of the responsibility—and fun—of being a parent is to note the differences among children, for whatever reasons, and shape one's parenting accordingly.

The timing and the order of entry of a child into the family may have some impact. But it is likely to be subtle and less consequential by far than the impact of the basic parental attitudes, values, and behaviors that are palpable to the child in the family environment, no matter what his or her place in the hierarchy of siblings.

The Impact of Family Stress

It has long been assumed that conflict between parents imposes an emotional burden on the children whom they have created. Because the young child is so heavily dependent for a sense of well-being on the quality of interactions with parents, signals of stress between mother and father are logically thought to have a tangible impact.

At the Family Therapy Center of the Philadelphia Child Guidance Clinic, family therapy expert Salvador Minuchin and his associates have been investigating the role of family conflict in the physical ills of children, diabetes among them. No one has suggested that stress in the family—or elsewhere—can, of itself, produce such physical ailments as diabetes. As psychologist Bernice Rosman, researcher director at the clinic, puts it: "The sick child admittedly has a predisposing physiological vulnerability. A diabetic child has diabetes, and will inevitably manifest its symptoms. What happens, however, is that some children, already diabetic, cannot be managed medically. They are resistant to treatment. And for them, we suspected that stress in the family is a factor."

Minuchin and his associates have observed repeated cases of children whose psychosomatic problems were especially severe and who were typically unresponsive to treatment. They began working in 1966 with a small group of severe, or "brittle," juvenile diabetics, children incapacitated by their disease. These children had been hospitalized on the average of every three to four weeks because of *ketoacidosis*—a serious disturbance in the blood's acid-base metabolism. Exhaustive study had failed to uncover any organic cause for such recurrent crises. Moreover, when the children were removed to a hospital or children's residential facility, away from home and family, their bouts with ketoacidosis ceased. When they returned home, however, the pattern inevitably resumed. Individual psychiatric therapy failed to change the pattern of hospitalization.

In one typical case, a diabetic eight-year-old girl, whose daily insulin dosage was about 30 units, was given over 500 units of supplemental insulin over a 24-hour period, and still required hospital admission. At that time, her blood glucose was 890 mg percent (the normal upper limit is 180), and her diabetic acidosis acute. Yet a single, standard dose of insulin in the hospital proved readily effective.

Such episodes led to the hypothesis that bouts of ketoacidosis, and the subsequent resistance of the child to standard treatment, were being triggered by the family environment.

Perhaps these diabetic children were reacting in a special way to conflicts within the home. If so, how were they different from other children who, while also diabetics, were free of disabling attacks of acidosis?

To answer, Minuchin and his associates contrasted the stress reactions of the "psychosomatic" diabetics with those of two other groups of diabetic children. One of these groups was composed of youngsters showing symptoms of behavior disorders; the other, children without psychological difficulties—that is, "normal" diabetics.

The biochemical mechanism responsible for the onset of diabetic acidosis is widely considered to be the release of free fatty acids (FFA) in the blood. The level of FFA is also considered an index of emotional arousal or stress. Typically, within 5 to 15 minutes of exposure to stress, this level rises. Minuchin's study involved, therefore, an arrangement to test changes in the FFA levels of the vulnerable children at the very time that stressful events in the family were unfolding.

The children in each of the three diabetic groups, along with their parents, were subjected to study in a setting designed to evoke and intensify conflict and tension within the family. To establish a baseline, a half hour was spent settling the parents in an interview room, while the child took a place in an observation room behind a one-way mirror. From that vantage point, the child could see and hear the parents, but not take part in the conversation. The psychiatrist told the parents to discuss a family problem and then, having sowed the seeds of discord, left the room. Half an hour later he returned and heated up the conflict by allying himself with one spouse against the other. The child was then brought into the interview room and asked to help the parents resolve the now boiling discord. After half an hour, the family adjourned to another room for a "recovery period."

Throughout the whole experience, which was videotaped, the parents and child were each equipped with a *heparin lock*. This is a specially designed needle to allow blood samples to be drawn from the arm without disturbing the subject and without the risk of clotting. The samples were drawn every 15 minutes by laboratory personnel, placed behind a screen.

The free fatty acid levels in the blood were later measured, and the results correlated with clinical appraisals of the families' videotaped transactions. Thus the investigators were able to define the relationship between the patterns of family behavior, on the one hand, and the emotional arousal patterns of the diabetic children on the other.

The results clearly marked the seriously ill diabetic child—the "psychosomatic" diabetic—as different from the others. At each point in the experiment—while watching the parents become involved in conflict, seeing it exacerbated by the psychiatrist, and becoming immersed in the conflict themselves—the "psychosomatic" children experienced a significantly greater "turn on" of stress as measured by the free fatty acid levels in their blood. This was particularly true when they themselves participated in the transaction. Moreoever, the FFA levels continued to rise even after the conflict had subsided, while the children and their parents were unwinding in a natural setting.

In the next part of the experiment, the investigators observed family members—including one or two siblings of the diabetic child—interacting with one another as they attempted to answer a series of questions and to perform a task in concert. Minuchin and his coworkers were able to identify some distinct aspects of their relationships.

To begin with, the "psychosomatic" diabetic appears to be inextricably and pathologically *enmeshed* in the family's currents of conflict. Also, family members intrude on each other's thoughts, feelings, and communications. One member, for instance, may relay messages from another member to a third, thus blocking direct communication. Further, executive hierarchies in such families are confused. Children may join one parent in criticizing the other, and often the children take inappropriately parental roles toward one another. Parents work at cross-purposes in relating to the children. Frequently one parent enlists a child's support in struggles with the other.

In such families, too, members exhibit an undue degree of *overprotectiveness and concern* for one another's welfare. A sneeze sets off a flurry of hankerchief offers, and queries and complaints about fatigue may punctuate the flow of conversation. The parents' overprotectiveness retards the children's development of autonomy and competence.

The "psychosomatic" diabetic child was typically also a member of a family marked by *extreme rigidity* and committed to maintaining the status quo. Such families experience great difficulty in periods when change and growth are necessary—for example, during adolescence. The families operate like a closed system. When events that require change occur, members insist on retaining accustomed methods of interaction; issues that threaten change are not allowed to surface. Consequently, these families live in a chronic state of submerged stress.

The sick child often serves as a pressure valve or a detour route. When the family's low threshold for conflict is approached, this child simply displays symptoms, thus allowing family members to avoid conflict via a show of concern. For the sick child, the investigators believe, this display of symptoms and the consequent avoidance of family conflict may act as a major reinforcement or reward.

Also characteristic of the families was an *inability or unwillingness to resolve problems.* Often a strong religious or ethical code buttresses the pattern. As a result, problems are left unresolved, to threaten again and again and continually activate the family's "avoidance circuits."

Often one spouse is the avoider. The other may bring up areas of difficulty, but the avoider always manages to turn away from the kind of confrontation that would lead to the acknowledgment and settlement of conflict. A man, for example, may simply leave the house when his wife tries to discuss a problem.

Embedded in the records of the experimental conflict situation, Minuchin and his team found characteristic patterns of behavior that clearly affect the "psychosomatically" sick child's ability to "turn off" psychologically—and physiologically—after the stress has passed.

Three patterns of involvement seem to severely limit or handicap "turnoff" and, Minuchin concludes, are therefore related to psychosomatic illness of the type studied. They may, in fact, be common as well to all families in which children become the target of adult conflict and stress.

The first, which Minuchin calls *triangulation,* involves a splitting of the spouses. The child is openly pressed to ally with one parent against the other. Statements such as "Wouldn't you rather do it my way?" are used in the attempt to force the child to take sides. He or she cannot voice an opinion without siding with one parent.

In the second pattern, which Minuchin calls *parent-child coalition,* a split between husband and wife tends to lead the child to a stable coalition with one parent against the other. One wife, for example, was unable to express her rage over her husband's refusal to protect her from his mother's attacks. The sick son became heavily involved as his mother's protector and spokesman for her complaints. He urged his father to protect her from her mother-in-law. Although the father tried to persuade his son to reject the mother's "childish" demands, the boy doggedly maintained his enmeshed "adult" stance.

In the third type of pattern, called *detouring,* the spouses submerge their conflicts by either "protecting" or blaming their sick child, who is now defined as the only family problem.

Detouring may often occur, of course, in the transactions of even effectively functioning families. In Minuchin's view, however, normal families do shift to other transactional modes—do confront conflicts and negotiate settlements. The rigid families with "psychosomatic" diabetic children are more likely to engage in self-defeating maneuvers exclusively, virtually as a way of life.

Minuchin found dramatic evidence that the parents of such children are using them to absorb the stresses induced by the adults' conflicts. Analyses of the blood samples of parents and children showed that when the children were brought from behind the one-way mirror into the presence of their squabbling parents, the youngsters' free fatty acid levels rose dramatically as they became enmeshed in their parents' tensions. At the same time, the parents' FFA levels were dramatically reduced. In today's vernacular, the adults had "laid it on" their children.

How, then, do seriously ill "psychosomatic" diabetic children get that way?

Minuchin sums up the findings: First, the child is physiologically vulnerable; that is, a specific organic dysfunction is present. Second, the child's family is characterized by enmeshment, overprotectiveness, rigidity, and lack of conflict resolution. Third, the sick child plays an important role in the family's pattern of avoiding conflict—a role that serves to reinforce his or her symptoms. Little wonder that the acutely ill diabetic children fared better when removed from the family scene!

Family Communications and the Child's Mental Health

According to one influential theory, the root of the disordered thinking in severe mental illness can be found in the disordered ways that some parents—those with a child who becomes schizophrenic—communicate with each other, their children, and others. The theory was developed by Lyman C. Wynne and his associates while he was head of the Adult Psychiatry Branch of the National Institute of Mental Health.

"Early in our work with families with at least one schizophrenic member," the group recalls, "we noticed that the therapist's experience was singularly different from that with families in which other kinds of mental disorder were present." In describing it, the therapists use such words as *maddening, bewildering,* and *exhausting.*

"One may from time to time become disconcertingly aware of something utterly crazy going on during the session," they observe, "while the family continues to behave as though this were not so. . . . The 'something utterly crazy' may include the practically simultaneous presence of gross and apparently quite explicit contradictions, which are simply not heard as such." For example:

In a session which was not unusual for this family, the mother of Mary, who was severely schizophrenic and much of the time demurely paranoid, openly dismissed the therapists as lunatics. Her manner was almost disarmingly affectionate, thus both augmenting and obscuring the murderous character of the assault: They were obviously harmless, well-meaning, and even amiable lunatics, but to take them at all seriously was patently absurd. Both the therapists in this group were men, and the mother had frequently made it clear . . . that men were inherently unreliable and abandonment by them was inevitable. Thus the fact that they were also childlike, ineffectual, and stupid was perhaps less than tragically consequential. It was within the framework of this position, and in the immediate context of the comments about the lunacy of the therapists, that the mother angrily reproached her daughter for "not really wanting to get well," since otherwise she would trust the doctors and confide in them.

The father of this family spent a great deal of time delivering weighty and protracted homilies to his wife and daughter. The tone of his remarks was generally kindly and detached, condescending and moralistic. His decidedly pompous air neatly complemented his wife's uniformly depreciating fondness. . . . He dealt with his daughter's intense distrust by gently lecturing her on the need to rely on others: While it was clear, he said, that untrustworthy persons existed, the majority were decent enough human beings, and her distrust was "just a part of her illness" which she should try to put out of mind. . . . He often interrupted his wife, scolding her for having interrupted Mary. He would sometimes sternly reprimand her for failing sincerely to acknowledge the fact that Mary was seriously ill, but otherwise seldom failed to refer to this as anything but "her little nervous trouble."

Whenever the therapists tried to bring the contradictions into view, the parents simply denied that they had said anything of the kind.

The Wynne group then set to work to pinpoint certain features of parental communications that could be quickly scored through the use of appropriate manuals. The investigators reasoned that deviant communication patterns were likely to impair a growing child's ability to attend to and understand parental advice, to learn what is expected of him and her, to think clearly, and to develop normal relations with others.

The material used in analyzing communications was a transcript of what the parents said. In some cases, the transcript covered excerpts from family therapy sessions, in others, responses to various tests.

Whatever the material used for the analysis, the investigators were interested mainly not in what a parent said but in how he or she said it. In fact, they early learned that only the style of communications, not the content, distinguished the parents of schizophrenics from other parents.

One major stylistic feature was found to be how the speaker handles the task of sticking to the subject at hand. Communication begins with the efforts of people to focus their attention on an idea, feeling, or perception advanced by one or more of them. If this phase is aborted or confused, the investigators point out, the rest of the communication process is bound to be disturbed. And if parents show confusion in this phase, it is easy to understand that a growing child's capacity to attend to an idea or a feeling and to think purposefully might well be impaired.

For example, in one family, the mother's characteristic response to the therapist was to agree with a yes and then to add further comments in a loosely connected manner, while the original point was disqualified or contradicted and thus obscured and lost. She was impervious to the ideas and feelings of others. The husband, instead of helping to establish a sustained focus of attention, jumped around after her.

On the basis simply of the parental patterns, the investigator predicted that their disturbed daughter would have developed little capacity to trust her own feelings or judgment. She would have a vague, confused, amorphous way of thinking about what she could actually do or what she could think about herself and her roles. Her thought processes and her emotions would be more poorly organized than those of either parent. She would be schizophrenic, with evidence of disturbance since childhood.

The clinical picture bore out the prediction. As a child the girl had been shy, apathetic, and withdrawn, and she had become increasingly so during preadolescence and adolescence. She had been extremely dependent upon her mother and nervous about doing anything without her mother's consent. At seventeen she had a schizophrenic episode. Subsequently, she had been classified as an amorphous schizophrenic of mild severity, with characteristic vague and poorly directed thinking, a flattened, apathetic emotional tone, and poor relationships with others.

In their research, the investigators noted many other types of attentional problems. In one, attention is given to partially defined perceptions or thoughts, but then vaguely drifts. No overall final point is established or pinned down. Asked to tell a story suggested by a picture of a boy and a violin, a man remarks that the boy hasn't the hands for playing, that he himself played very well when he was four. Expressions of doubt of one's own perceptions, even when they are straightforward, are included in this pattern. One parent, looking at a Rorschach card that is almost always seen as a bat, said: "That looks like a bat. The more I look at it, the less it seems like that, I guess. I'm not sure about that bat anymore."

Negation of this sort leaves listeners with no real interpretation. They are asked in effect to see something in their memories and then, when it has been visualized, to discard it. As the process continues, eventually they become perplexed or apathetic.

Other common types of attentional problems occur when the speaker fails to explain confusing remarks or to reach closure—a settlement or rounding out of the subject under discussion. The listener is left feeling that no particular meaning or emotion has been expressed.

A second main feature used to differentiate families is the general emotional relationship among family members. In normal families, the investigators explain, this is marked by *mutuality*. The members come to recognize one another's identities and potentialities and to respond—and expect the other members to respond—accordingly. As individuals grow and as situations change, the expectations of members of such a family change, too.

Among families with a young adult schizophrenic, however, the relationship is usually characterized by *pseudomutuality*. This is an attempt to deny, or ward off recognition of, any change or other experience perceived as threatening. Divergence is seen as leading to disruption of the family relationship and therefore as something that must be avoided. But if it is avoided, growth of the relationship is impossible.

The investigators found a number of mechanisms for maintaining pseudomutuality. One was a "desperate preoccupation with harmony."

One mother insisted again and again (and her husband agreed): "We are all peaceful. I like peace even if I have to kill someone to get it." And then, speaking of her schizophrenic child: "A more normal, happy kid would be hard to find. I was pleased with my child! I was pleased with my husband! I was pleased with life. I have *always* been pleased!"

Another mechanism serving pseudomutuality is "a bland, indiscriminate, but determined approval" of a person's activities and interests. This was sometimes verbalized as respect for self-determination and freedom. One set of parents kept telling their youngster, who later became schizophrenic, "We only want you to do what you want to do." The investigators comment: "The open recognition of differences then becomes literally impossible, except by a truly violent, disruptive move, which the schizophrenic break seems to represent."

Such mechanisms, the investigators believe, help keep the potential schizophrenic from learning to discriminate or value who or where he or she is, except in terms of a blurred place in the family. "For a child who grows up and develops his perceptual capacities in a setting in which obvious contradictions are regarded as non-existent, it seems reasonable to suppose that he may well come to regard his senses and emotional responses as a tenuous and unreliable guide. . . . Models of thinking, perceiving, and communicating built up in such a way render unavailable to the person the capacity to attach clear meanings to his own intrapsychic states, such as anger at the mother, or disappointment. Instead, he may have a vague uneasiness, sometimes merging into panic."

A psychologist member of the team, Margaret Thaler Singer, scored particularly well in the "blind" matching of parents and patients. In doing so, she first studied the transcripts of the parents' psychological tests, which had been administered by other psychologists. Knowing nothing about the patients except their sex and approximate age, she deduced from the parents' transcripts not only the offsprings' type of illness but also its severity. Of 20 patients who had been clinically diagnosed as frankly schizophrenic, she was right in 17 cases; of the group of 9 borderline patients, 7; of the group of 6 neurotic patients, 4. These results were statistically significant at a high level, a probability of less than 1 in 1,000 that they could have happened by chance.

Later, in a particularly notable example of what might strike a non-professional as legerdemain, Wynne's research team studied samples of communications from the parents of 280 families. In 122 of these families, an offspring was schizophrenic. In the other families the offspring included nonschizophrenic psychiatric patients, medical patients, and normal, healthy individuals. The families had been examined in widely separated medical centers—in Bethesda, Maryland, by Wynne's group and in Houston, San Francisco, and Japan by collaborators. The communication samples were the parents' tape-recorded responses to the Rorschach and other tests.

Working only from these samples, the investigators diagnosed the condition of the offspring in from 85 to 95 percent of the families. The results could have occurred by chance not more than 1 time in 100.

Did it make a difference if only one parent instead of both showed a disordered form of thinking? Yes. Whenever one parent was judged to be fairly clear minded and to have, therefore, a counteracting influence on the other, the patient—their son or daughter—was never frankly schizophrenic. Where both parents showed communication deviancies, so the problems generated by one parent's defect were aggravated by the other parent's, the patient was distinctly schizophrenic.

The adults in such a family are in an easy position compared to that of the children. Adults are trained to be alert to certain deviancies, and they can try to produce some order and clarity for themselves by making allowances for other people's statements. Children, on the other hand, have to depend heavily on parents for learning how to understand things. Styles of communicating that prove frustrating to a therapist or a researcher may have devastating effects upon a child. The investigators think the child is likely to grow up with unusual difficulties in trusting not only his or her own perceptions and judgments but also those reported by others.

Wynne's team emphasizes that its results are not incompatible with the evidence, discussed in Chapter 3, that inherited biological factors play an important role in schizophrenia. Where the parents showed serious communication disorders, the hereditarily vulnerable child would be more likely than others to become psychotic.

Could it be that the disturbance in the child actually caused, rather than resulted from, the parental disturbance? The investigators think not. They report that the parents' disturbed forms of thinking seem to be highly stable and to be manifest in any situation.

Nevertheless, the findings of Wynne and his associates, though indeed impressive, cannot be considered the last word because of that very question: Was it the parents' abnormal communication style that made for schizophrenia in the child, or was it schizophrenia in the child that made for abnormal communication style in the parents?

Among the investigators who have tackled the problem are social psychologist Elliot G. Mishler and sociologist Nancy E. Waxler, members of the Harvard Medical School faculty. Like Wynne and others, they have found "consistent differences in patterns of interaction between the families of schizophrenic patients and other types of families." But when they tried to find out who was influencing whom, they got ambiguous answers.

In the Mishler-Waxler investigation, the interaction of parents and their schizophrenic child was compared with the interaction of the same parents with one of their normal children of the same sex as the psychotic child and close to the same age. The interactions were also compared with those of parents of normal children.

The study began with family members answering—independently— a 38-item questionnaire. A typical item follows:

Mrs. Thomas is concerned about her 19-year-old son who she feels is always making plans that he does not carry out. For instance, he may decide in the evening to look for a job the next day, but when morning comes she cannot get him out of bed. Do you think Mrs. Thomas should try to pressure him or should she let him carry out his plans in his own way?

Next, the investigators told the parents and one child which items they had disagreed on and asked them to try to reach a consensus. On another day the same procedure was followed with the parents and the other child. The discussions were recorded and analyzed.

Upshot: The differences found could be explained by supposing that children were schizophrenic because their parents interacted with them differently. But they could be explained equally well by supposing that the parents interacted with them differently because the children were schizophrenic.

Trying to throw more light on the problem, Waxler then experimented with artificial families comprising a father and a mother and an adolescent child not their own. Some of the fathers and mothers were parents of a schizophrenic child. Each family worked together on a task developed to measure a person's ability to solve abstract problems. In some trials, the child in an artificial family was schizophrenic; in the others, normal. Before and after the family tests, each individual worked alone on the same problem.

Result: Schizophrenic children showed significant improvement after they had worked on the problem with normal parents; in fact, their performance rose to the same level as normal children's. (Waxler explains that if a child initially shows little skill, normal parents work to have him or her improve; but if a child shows competence from the beginning, they do not.) That was the most consistent finding. The investigator uncovered "little evidence that shows disruptive effects of schizophrenic parents on a normal child and only minor evidence that the presence of a schizophrenic child disrupts cognitive performance of normal parents."

Joan Huser Liem, a Harvard Medical School psychologist, followed up Waxler's research by using a word game to study communications in 11 families with a schizophrenic son and 11 with a normal son. The sons ranged in age from seventeen to twenty-five years.

The game involved describing to a tape recorder a common object (for example, a lamp) or concept (for example, a teacher) in such a way that a listener could quickly identify what had been described. The father and mother in each case worked together in one room to make the tape; the son, in another. Then parents responded to tapes made by their own son and tapes made by the sons—normal and schizophrenic—of strangers. Sons responded to tapes made by their own parents and by the parents of strangers, normal and schizophrenic.

The descriptions and responses were scored as *appropriate, overly general,* or *irrelevant.* Using a system that had been developed by Wynne and Singer, the researcher also looked for instances of peculiar language and logic and for "closure problems," which included incomplete sentences, loose associations, and negations.

Liem had hypothesized that schizophrenics and their parents would show significantly more disordered communications than normal sons and their parents. This turned out to be true for the sons but not for the parents.

Other findings:

- The sons who communicated least appropriately generally had parents who also communicated least appropriately. So, again, a relationship was found between the communications of parents and those of offspring.
- Normal and schizophrenic sons did not differ significantly in the ways they responded to their own parents and the parents of others.
- All parents made fewer misidentifications in responding to normal young men than in responding to schizophrenics.

"The communication disorder of schizophrenic sons," Liem observes, "had an immediate, observable, negative effect not only on the parents of schizophrenic sons but on all parents who heard and attempted to respond to them. Disorder was not observed in the communications of parents of schizophrenic sons nor were their communications found to adversely affect sons who heard and responded to them."

What about the findings—by the Wynne group and others—that parents of schizophrenics do have a communication disorder? Liem suggests that they may have picked it up as a way of responding to their sick child.

Then why didn't the parents studied by Liem display peculiarities? Perhaps, Liem answers, her families belong to a special subgroup— maybe one "in which undetected organic deficits account for the thought disorders of the child."

Thus, the question of which comes first in schizophrenia, the presence of disordered communications in the family or the presence in that family of a schizophrenic child, remains unsolved. Probably a final answer can be reached only through the longitudinal studies referred to later in this chapter. Meanwhile, studies on communication disorders, whether or not the findings are ultimately accepted, have at the very least led to investigations that will broaden our knowledge of the causes and manifestations of schizophrenia and clarify the role of parents in their children's mental illness.

The Effect of Different Kinds of Parental Control

For most parents, communications with children are often affected by the parents' roles as guides and disciplinarians. One of the questions most asked by parents—addressing neighbors, friends, pediatricians, or clinical psychologists—is, in effect: "How can I best exert control over my child's behavior?"

Considerable research effort has been given to the same question, and some fairly clear-cut answers have emerged.

Reviewing the consequences of different kinds of parental control, psychologist Wesley C. Becker a dozen years ago divided disciplinary techniques into *love-oriented* and *power-assertive*. Love-oriented methods include praising and reasoning with the child and also such negative approaches as withdrawing love and separating the child temporarily from the parent. Power-assertive methods typically include physical punishment.

Many research findings strongly suggest that when the disciplinary methods are love-oriented, children are more likely to feel responsible for their actions, to be cooperative in their relations with others, and to have, appropriately, feelings of guilt. On the other hand, when the parent is simply asserting power, the child is more likely to become noncooperative and aggressive. There is some evidence that these latter characteristics may disappear with time; one group of investigators, for instance, found that crime rates were lowest where both parents had been "consistently punitive [power-assertive] during the early years."

Becker himself and his associates confirmed findings that aggression by boys in school was directly related to physical punishment, and little use of reasoning, by their mothers. "In general," says Becker, reporting on a number of studies, "these results suggest a positive relation between power-assertion and child aggression. . . ."

Other investigators classified children's moral judgments according to whether these were based on an internal standard "or merely the fear of detection and punishment." Mothers of boys with internal standards "were less likely to use force, threat of force, deprivation, or direct commands (power-assertive techniques) in disciplining them, and . . . were more likely to stress how the child's misbehavior hurt the parent."

Becker summarizes: "These various studies suggest that internalized reactions to transgression in the form of guilt or acceptance of self-responsibility for misdeeds are far more likely to occur when the parent is warm and uses techniques of discipline which utilize the love relations to the parent for their effects. The use of praise and reasoning appears to have the most predictable effects across studies, while love-withdrawing methods seem effective primarily when the parent is high in warmth."

A somewhat different view is offered by research psychologist Diana Baumrind, who for almost two decades has been investigating how various types of discipline affect children's behavior. Her current project is a longitudinal study that got under way in 1967. Its subjects are 134 white and 16 black children, originally enrolled in 13 nursery schools, and their families.

Baumrind finds three main types of parents, each with a different effect upon the child: *authoritarian,* which "values obedience as a virtue and believes in restricting the child's autonomy"; *permissive,* which aims "to give the child as much freedom as is consistent with the child's physical survival"; and *authoritative,* which "attempts to direct the child's activities in a rational, issue-oriented manner."

In this research, the authoritative parents seem to be proving the most effective, as judged by such qualities in their children as social responsibility, independence, orientation to succeed, and vigor.

All but two of the families in this study have used corporal punishment. In fact, the authoritative parents, "who were particularly effective, favored corporal punishment over other negative sanctions." By corporal punishment, Baumrind means nonbrutal physical punishment delivered in response to behavior the child knows is not acceptable. It differs from brutal and arbitrary physical punishment, which many researchers have shown to be associated with such undesirable behavior as withdrawal, dependence, and antisocial activity.

Psychologist Ross D. Parke, in a 1977 review of research on the effects of punishment, points out that corporal punishment may achieve its effect "partly because it symbolizes the withdrawal of approval or affection." In that event, punishment should be a more potent controlling technique when used by a nurturant parent or teacher. He cites results from a 1957 study: "Mothers who were rated as warm and affectionate and who made relatively frequent use of physical punishment were more likely to report that they found spanking to be an effective means of discipline. In contrast, cold, hostile mothers who made frequent use of physical punishment were more likely to report that spanking was ineffective." A laboratory study 10 years later by Parke and an associate confirmed these findings.

Parke does not see the results of his research as support for physical punishment. Rather, he observes that "children *can* both understand and effectively utilize" a grown-up's explanations "to govern their behavior." He believes that "continued reliance on physical punishment as a control tactic is probably unjustified."

Baumrind, too, reviewed research on punishment and offered these general principles: Punishment is most effective when given as closely as possible to the undesirable behavior, when it is consistent and cannot be escaped, and when it is accompanied by an explanation that specifies both the unacceptable behavior and a more desirable one.

Such parental communications reflect rational and thoughtful approaches to the child's struggle to learn to live in society. Unfortunately, for many children, messages of this sort are not likely to be delivered—for these children are growing up in homes marked not by rationality but by severe emotional disturbance.

Children of Mentally Ill Parents

In countries around the world—the United States, Israel, England, Denmark, Sweden—investigators are trying to find out what happens over time to children with a high risk for mental illness. Prominent among such children are those born into disorganized families already marked by emotional illness.

The forerunner of today's long-range studies of high risk children is research conducted since 1962 by American psychologist Sarnoff A. Mednick, and Danish psychiatrist Fini Schulsinger. Their subjects are 200 young Danes who were selected—at an average age of fifteen—because their mothers were victims of schizophrenia and who, therefore, were regarded to be at high risk themselves for the disease. As controls the investigators used 100 Danes whose parents were free of psychopathology.

Like other investigators in the field, Mednick and Schulsinger have found a higher rate of either actual or borderline schizophrenia among their high-risk children. A ten-year follow-up disclosed that eight of the high-risk subjects had died, at least four by suicide. By means of a clinical interview, 13 of the survivors were classified as schizophrenic. In contrast, only one of the controls received the same diagnosis—and, it was later found, the mother of this person had been hospitalized for psychotic episodes before the longitudinal study began. The proportion of high-risk subjects free of mental disorders was less than half of that in the control group.

Mednick and Schulsinger have also identified those young people who strongly appear to show marked or incipient signs of mental disorder in early adulthood. Such persons in this investigation are predominantly males whose autonomic nervous systems seemed unusually responsive to stress when the study began; who had been separated from their parents early in life, mainly because of the mother's illness; and who had been involved in prenatal birth difficulties. Why these results apply to males and not their female counterparts is not yet known. For all children studied, however, the earlier that schizophrenia had developed in the mother, the greater the risk for her children.

While other investigators have as yet failed to confirm some of the specific findings of Mednick and Schulsinger, the team—among other achievements—has nevertheless documented heredity's role in schizophrenia, and uncovered evidence that factors associated with schizophrenia in one sex may not be associated with it in another. Moreover, the Mednick-Schulsinger team—and their counterparts around the world—have helped introduce a new and important mode for studying how and why children become mentally ill: longitudinal studies that track the fate of high-risk children over time rather than retrospective ones that merely look backward after the fact.

In one such longitudinal project, psychiatrist E. James Anthony and his associates at Washington University in St. Louis have been keeping tabs since 1968 on a number of children who have a psychotic parent.

Not long ago, Anthony described the case of a ten-year-old girl, here called Dora, the child of two schizophrenic parents who met in a mental hospital. They developed a relationship that flourished within the walls of the institution but rapidly deteriorated when both were discharged. Their own apartment became what Anthony describes as a "mini-institution," where they remained together in a chaotically crazy private world.

"Dora," Anthony reports, "was exposed from birth to almost every indignity conceivable in the human lexicon of sadism. She was neglected, battered, seduced, alternately over- and under-stimulated and even tortured at times when dragged screaming across a room by her hair. The grossness of the attack was such that the child, when seen, could only be described as an undifferentiated zombie who imitated the behavior of a human child but in every other way seemed less than human."

Dora was born with little chance for psychological well-being. Her genetic legacy was poor, and she was reared in an environment that was, in Anthony's words, "complete anarchy." Although, as we show later, in Chapter 12, the developing child can often demonstrate immense capacity to overcome life filled with risks, there is for every child—as for every adult—a point beyond which emotional resources cannot be strained.

Anthony and his coworkers have now followed Dora for almost 10 years, providing her with all the tender, loving care they could offer and the benefits of her own private therapist. Their interventions have had no healing impact. Dora has remained like a "burnt out schizophrenic case," an empty shell stripped of humanity.

By comparing such children to two other groups—children of apparently normal parents and children with a parent having a serious physical ailment—Anthony has identified three main types of disorganization seen in families where a parent is psychotic.

The first is typically found where the parent is a victim of schizophrenia classified as *hebephrenic* (infantile behavior, senseless thought processes, and inappropriate emotions) or *catatonic* (negativism and withdrawal to the point of immobility). Children of such households suffer neglect from what often amounts to extreme degrees of laissez faire and permissiveness. They begin to lead separate lives of their own, unsupervised and undisciplined, and there is a high incidence of behavior problems among them. As an example:

The social investigator arrived at a derelict building, badly in need of repair and found two of the children, a boy aged 9 and a girl aged 7, squatting comfortably on a wall sharing a cigarette. . . . When asked the whereabouts of their mother, the boy said that "Old Annie" was where she always was, in the back room. "Take care you don't hurt her when you go in," he added, "she lies on the floor by the door." (There was a curious warmth in his voice and he might have been speaking of a favorite pet.)

The second type emerges when the schizophrenic parent is of the *paranoid* variety. The family lives in an environment of "organized disorganization" incorporated into the workings of the delusional system of the sick member. Its entire style of life is radically altered to the great bewilderment of the children. For example:

In a recent case, a father with paranoid schizophrenia turned his home into a beleaguered fortress in which the family mounted watches against the enemy, and weapon training was rigorously enforced. A great deal of secrecy prevailed, and no one was allowed to come and go without an examination of credentials. A child who went out shopping was closely interrogated on his return. One of the children complained bitterly that he even had to report before going to the bathroom.

A final type emerges when the psychotic parent is of the *reactive* type, in which contradictory communications, inconsistency, highly ambivalent but powerful emotions, chaotic management, and a disturbing degree of intrusiveness into the lives of the children are the rule. An "environment of irrationality envelops the family and makes for unpredictable storms and crises." At one moment the children are pulled into intimate closeness and at the very next rejected "with bitter and unjustified recriminations." For instance:

A 5-year-old girl was believed by her father to be a love child of the mother by some other man. At these times he would become furious and, without reason, suddenly seize upon the little girl and start beating her and dragging her across the room by her hair. At other times, he would observe that she was wearing clothes that he had bought her and a bracelet that he had given her and would be overcome by the conviction that she was his daughter and completely like him in every way. He would then proceed to caress her passionately, frightening the child by his vehemence.

The St. Louis group occasionally sends an observer to live with a family for a week—if the observer can stand it that long—and to record several times a day what goes on. In the following excerpt, the observer is talking about "Gary Steiner," the seven-year-old adopted son of a schizophrenic father, who is in his mid-thirties. It is evening.

Then everyone came on upstairs and we adults were going to play Scrabble. Gary demanded that he be given the game. There are apparently three Scrabble games in this household, but the other ones could not be found, so Gary threw a temper tantrum. He went into his room crying and yelling and screaming. He forced everyone, especially Mr. Steiner, away and out of his room . . . alternately shouting and yelling, "Go away" and "Leave me alone." This progressed. It started about 10:35 and got progressively worse from there. He yelled and sobbed convulsively and shook. He was actually shaking and tore shreds from his foam rubber pillows. There was a pile of shreds of pillow, approximately ½″ × ½″ × ¼″ shreds. Mrs. Steiner said that this was an example of his tantrums, and she commented that at least this time he wasn't violent. Very often he would kick and push away and literally throw things actively at anyone who tried to interrupt the tantrum or come into his room at all. She was talking to me about how she could not leave Gary with a sitter and therefore could not go out. She couldn't trust him with a sitter. . . . Mrs. Steiner would like very much to get Gary into a "controlled environment."

Such families had a marked effect on their temporary guests. Among the observers' reactions, Anthony reports, the following "stood out significantly":

"Cultural shock" resulting from class and ethnic differences; emotional disturbances of anxiety and depression; perplexity resulting from incongruous affects and communications; feelings of alienation on exposure to gross psychotic phenomena (hallucinations and delusions); cognitive dissonance in association with thought disorder (irrationality and illogicality); a dislocation of reality resulting from juxtaposition with unrealistic attitudes and ideas; a sense of confusion stemming from environmental disorganization; urges to fight back against aggressions or to escape from them out of the family; feelings of being trapped and of being picked upon and victimized; a withdrawal into oneself as a defense against the possibility of being overwhelmed; psychosomatic complaints (headaches, abdominal pain, GI disorders, and menstrual disturbances); the fear of becoming crazy (of acting or feeling unrealistically, irrationally, or confusedly); and, finally, disturbing dreams and nightmares.

On second and third assignments the observers became as interested in what they were observing in the family as in what they were observing in themselves. What surprised them most was their realization that many of their reactions were not dissimilar to those of family members. It was a common finding that families appeared less crazy toward the end of the week living in, which could mean either that the family was adjusting to the observer or that the observer, as one put it, was becoming "a little crazy" herself.

It is easy to imagine what living in such a family not for just a week but for years might do to a person's mental health.

Nevertheless, the majority of children with a psychotic parent—though they are at the greatest risk to serious mental illness—do not become psychotic themselves. Two questions arise: Can children headed toward a breakdown be detected? And what can be done to offset their vulnerability?

A number of studies provide evidence that the answer to the first question is yes. In one of the most recent, Harriet S. Lander and other members of Anthony's group examined 141 sons and daughters from families in which one parent was either schizophrenic or manic-depressive. The investigators hypothesized that highly vulnerable children could be identified on the basis of close involvement and identification with the psychotic parent and of personality traits of submissiveness and suggestibility. It was felt that these factors "would make the child more likely to internalize, at least in part, the distorted perceptual and cognitive world of the psychotic parent."

Earlier, psychiatrist Loren R. Mosher of the National Institute of Mental Health and two colleagues had studied 11 pairs of identical twins, one of whom was schizophrenic, and found that in 10 cases the psychotic twin identified with the sicker parent and tended to be the more submissive.

To pick out the children at greatest risk, the St. Louis investigators scored each of the 141 on a vulnerability rating scale. The items included: identification with the sick parent, credulity about parental delusions, influence of parental illness on the child, undue submissiveness, undue suggestibility, and involvement with the ill parent—as shown by the child's expressed desire to live with that parent and by the inclusion of that parent in the child's wishes and dreams.

The researchers then concentrated on the 19 "highly vulnerable" children, considered to be the ones who had scored 5 or more on an eight-point scale, and on their opposites, the 21 children who had scored 0 or 1. The two groups were designated the High Vulnerables and the Low Vulnerables. Three clinical psychologists, who did not know to which group the subjects belonged, assessed the psychological functioning of each child.

As had been hypothesized, the High Vulnerables did show significantly more disturbance. About a fourth of them, in contrast to none of the Low Vulnerables, were diagnosed either as borderline psychotic or psychotic. Thirty-seven percent, as against nine percent of the Low Vulnerables, showed serious or incapacitating disturbance. The number of well-adjusted children among the Low Vulnerables was "encouragingly high"—13, or sixty-two percent; among the High Vulnerables it was only 2, or ten percent.

Several factors were found to be of value in protecting the child from the impact of a parent's mental illness. These included the child's ability to stand away psychologically from the sick person and to defend against the kind of submissive involvement with him or her that could lead to the adoption of disturbed thought processes. Also important was confidence and "a kind of healthy skepticism."

Longitudinal studies such as those by Mednick-Schulsinger and Anthony should vastly increase our ability to pick out children most likely to become psychotic and perhaps show also how to ward off their apparent doom.

One factor that may influence the mental health of children at risk because they have a psychotic parent appears to be the age of the child. In an important phase of their work, Anthony and his fellow researchers have found not only that children of the mentally ill have an increased probability of becoming disturbed themselves but also that their vulnerability to stress increases during certain periods of their development.

The ages during which children appear to be most vulnerable to the strain of having a sick parent are the years that range from four to seven, from nine to eleven, and, in the teen years, from fourteen to sixteen. However, when the illness is severe, a child of any age can be affected.

Although all the data have not yet been analyzed, the St. Louis research has significant implications for the scientific community and the planning of mental health services. Anthony points out that new policies in mental hospitals—under which patients are treated with antipsychotic medicines and quickly returned to the community—are exposing an increasing number of children to the effects of parental psychosis. "Some mentally ill parents in apparent remission can cause serious family discord favorable to the development of mental illness in the children," he cautions.

Off and on for some 25 years, sociologist John Clausen and associates have been studying the impact of mental illness on the family. Their first sample, which they have recently followed up, was composed of 80 families having a psychotic mother or father and was studied at the National Institute of Mental Health in 1952–59; their second sample was made up of 40 families of patients entering treatment in 1973–74, half in the original study area and half on the West Coast.

"At very least," report Clausen and Carol L. Huffine, "the mental illness of a parent tends to introduce profound uncertainty into the lives of children. . . . Conflict and recrimination frequently pervaded the family life space. With no explanation from a trusted caretaker, those children fortunate enough to have siblings seem often to have clung to each other for support and hope."

Even so, "many children learned to cope with uncertainty and, indeed, to achieve a sense of competency and maturity far beyond what would normally be expected at their ages"—a subject discussed at greater length in Chapter 12. The Clausen-Huffine data "suggest that a supportive parent or other close relative was a prime ingredient in such achievements." However, where the supposedly well parent "leaned heavily on a child for support or where the child was made to bear the burden of the patient's condition, rebellion or despair were more likely outcomes than competent coping."

At least three of the children have so far been briefly hospitalized for schizophrenia, several others appear to be "extremely vulnerable," and most are just entering the period of greatest vulnerability to a schizophrenic break. "On the other hand, several of the children who had turbulent times in adolescence have as young adults shown considerable growth."

Fraiberg believes that some babies are hopelessly burdened by the past of their parents even before they enter the world. There are a sizable number of men and women, who, despite the most heroic interventions, will simply not "make it" as parents.

The failure is glaring, Fraiberg believes, among the children of paranoid schizophrenic mothers and fathers. "If the parent is in a mental state where he can't make connections with us, let alone with a child," Fraiberg asks, "who can help him? So we have a number of failures where we feel that the child's best interest lies in substitute care—possibly foster care. I don't think you are saving the children if you keep them at home in such cases. If indeed the parents are unable to function and are in and out of mental hospitals, and are still hallucinating when they are back home with the child, and the voices are beginning to come from the baby itself—we wouldn't even consider that we should risk the child's life in a situation like that. Under those rare circumstances we have recommended placement."

Clausen and Huffine are shocked at the paucity of measures to help the well spouse and the children of a mentally ill parent. "One finding," they write, "is particularly dismaying. . . . Neither in the 1950's . . . nor in the 1970's . . . have we found significant evidence of an awareness on the part of treatment personnel that the family and especially the children need help. It appears that no one now takes the time to meet with the well spouse and the children, to assess their needs for information and guidance. With all the lip service to community mental health, we find this a distressing state of affairs."

One answer is for hospitals to set up preventive clinics—as Anthony has done—to handle the problems of the family when a psychotic patient is admitted or discharged.

Children of Dissension and Divorce

When Alex was three years old, his father abruptly left home, and a divorce followed. Though an immature and unwilling husband, the father had developed a fairly close relationship with his son. Alex responded to the family's breakup with the loss of toilet training, increased irritability, and acute anxiety. His mother responded with anxiety and anger, followed by an immobilizing depression.

Alex is one of numerous children in a study of the effects of parental divorce being conducted by Judith S. Wallerstein, Joan B. Kelly, and their associates at a community mental health center near San Francisco. Thirty-four children are involved.

In the youngest preschool group, including children from 2½ to 3¼ years old, regressions occurred most precipitously in those who had been given no explanations of the father's departure. By the time the children were followed up, a year after the parents had separated, most of the symptoms had disappeared in six of them. But in general the children were too quickly seeking physical contact with strange adults, thus displaying "a general neediness in relationships."

The children in the middle preschool group—from 3¾ to 4¾ years old—followed a different pattern from those in the youngest group. Less than half of them regressed. Instead, they became frightened, confused, and sad. Some suffered from self-blame. Even though no overt family turmoil had accompanied the divorce, seven of the eleven children in this group deteriorated clinically during the first year.

Six of the fathers of these more troubled children had psychiatric disorders; moreover, all seven had used fairly harsh disciplinary measures and had set overly high expectations. So in each case the father's departure resulted not only in the loss of a parent but also in changes in the standards of conduct and methods of punishment.

And the mothers? One effect was often a "less supportive relationship with their children."

Like the younger children, those in the oldest preschool group—from five to six years of age—showed heightened anxiety and aggressiveness when their parents separated. But these children, unlike the younger ones, "seemed to have a reasonable understanding of the divorce-related changes."

Between the parents of the children in this group, there had been considerable fighting just before the separation and, indeed, throughout the marriage. So the children had been exposed to turmoil in addition to the divorce. Still, many of the children expressed sadness, longing for their fathers, and an intense wish to restore the family as it had been.

Five of the fourteen children in the oldest group showed troubled behavior when first seen and were worse a year later. All the more troubled girls—four out of the five vulnerable children—"were suffering with impaired self-esteem, poor peer relations, and moderate to severe learning inhibitions."

Wallerstein and Kelly were surprised to find that during the first year after the breakup twice as many parents changed their attitude toward their preschool child as remained the same. "Many of the more anxious, conflicted, uncaring, or actively rejecting parents became freer, happier, and closer to their children." Contrariwise, many of those who had been close and affectionate with the children at the time of separation moved "to a more estranged, more conflict-ridden, or neglectful parental role."

Close to half of the fathers developed a better relationship with their youngest child; about one-quarter, a worse relationship. With the mothers, this pattern was reversed: the relationship between mother and child improved only in about one-fourth of the cases, worsened in close to one-half. And the worsening of the mother-child relationship was strongly associated with deterioration of the child's psychological health. No connection was found between these changes and the mothers' employment, or lack of it, outside the home.

If other research is any indication, some of the children in this study may still have to face their worst troubles. Further, statistics suggest that the problems left in the wake of separation and divorce—at least in the wake of the emotional turmoil leading to family breakup—are certain to increase. Though the marriage rate in 1975 was only a little greater than it had been in 1900, the *divorce* rate had grown by almost seven times. The number of divorces over a recent 10-year period more than doubled; the number of marriages increased by less than 1.2 percent. Out of every six children under eighteen, one now lives with just a single parent—even though experts in family life suggest that under today's circumstances, with the older and more experienced members of a kinship often living far from the young people, even two parents have scarcely the information and the experience to bring up the child in the way he or she should go.

A number of researchers have been concerned with the effects of unstable family relationships on the child's social behavior. Research has generally shown that delinquent children are much more likely to come from homes broken by separation or divorce than from stable homes.

For example, psychiatrist John F. McDermott, Jr., examined the intake records of some 1,500 children up to the age of fourteen who had been evaluated at the University of Michigan's Children's Psychiatric Hospital. Those children whose parents were divorced were compared with those whose families were intact. McDermott found a significantly higher rate of delinquency in the divorce group and, apparently associated with it, a cluster of symptoms such as running away from home and poor behavior at home and in school.

In addition to finding that children in the divorce group were more prone than the others to "acting out"—that is, to expressing their unconscious emotional conflicts in rebellious behavior—the investigators judged that these children were significantly more often suffering from depression. More than a third were considered depressed, and virtually all the rest showed signs of hidden or mild depression.

The depression was manifested in various ways. One child, whose behavior was considered accident-prone, had had a series of bicycle accidents. Another child constructed hangman's nooses; a third often put sharp objects into his mouth and threatened to swallow them; still another daydreamed of killing himself. Other signs were fatigue and boredom and, particularly frequent, running away from home. Some runaways said they had wanted to visit the absent parent; others, that they had hoped to be reassured they were still wanted. Most often the psychiatrists viewed running away as an attempt to get away from depressive and hostile-aggressive feelings both in the child and as the child perceived them in others.

Psychological testing showed that children often "felt unable to fend for themselves and in dire danger of being injured, crushed, or stepped on by external forces." But they quickly turned from such a state to acting out—in order "to defend against the incipient depression." A sad fourteen-year-old girl said she was never happy except when she was tormenting and fighting with the boys at school. She hated all males, she said, except her real father.

McDermott substantiated earlier findings that a child often interprets separation and divorce as a kind of punishment for the child's own wrongdoing. One boy, for example, did not begin stealing until after the divorce; McDermott explains he was acting out feelings of deprivation. But the boy told the clinician that his parents had got divorced because he stole. Another child felt that his parents were shouting at each other one day because he had broken a dish, "even though the child intellectually knew that it was because of the mother's infidelity."

But in some cases, McDermott points out, "it appeared to be actually true at an unconscious family level that the divorce was indeed associated with the child in a very specific personal way. . . . In the more obvious cases, children with physical handicaps or serious illness seemed to be the focus."

There were many problems of identification. "Some children seemed almost forced into sexual acting out when they had had fathers who were described as 'no-good,' oversexed, and promiscuous. Many times the mother claimed that the onset of the child's symptoms followed a visit with the father sometime after the divorce. Eleven children were noted to have run away immediately after a visit with the father—a father who had quit the family and himself set a precedent."

Despite abundant clinical data like McDermott's, a number of investigators do not ascribe the child's mental health problems to the divorce itself. Studies by Michael Rutter and his associates in London, for example, strongly suggest that even though a child's delinquency often follows his parents' divorce, the divorce and the separation are not in themselves the cause of the delinquency.

Rutter cites three studies in which homes broken by death were compared with normal homes and with homes broken by divorce or separation. The homes in the first case, he points out, were likely to have been fairly normal before the break, whereas those broken by divorce or separation were likely to have been marked by discord. All three studies found that among boys from homes broken by divorce or separation the delinquency rate was twice as high as among boys from unbroken homes. But among boys from homes broken by death, the rate was not significantly higher than among boys from normal homes. Consequently, "it may be the discord and disharmony, rather than the breakup of the family as such, which lead to antisocial behavior."

The Rutter team undertook research to verify this suggestion. Where the marriage had been judged good, the team found, the rate of antisocial behavior among the sons was 0; where the marriage was only fair, the rate was 22 percent; where the marriage was very poor, the delinquency rate jumped to 39 percent. Plainly, says Rutter, "parental discord is associated with antisocial disorder in the children." In that case, he points out, the deviancy rate should be higher among children whose parents are unhappy in their marriage but have remained together than among children from broken but harmonious homes. Several studies have found that this is true.

Demonstration of a close relation between family discord on the one hand and conduct disorders or antisocial problems on the other—even when there had been neither separation nor divorce—has been confirmed during the last five years both by Rutter's group and those of other investigators. One group found "that among boys who had already made a court appearance for delinquency, those from intact homes with severe and persistent daily problems were more likely to become recidivist than those from intact homes without serious problems or those from broken homes." Rutter concludes: "It seems quite clear that family discord and disharmony are indeed the damaging factors, with separations largely incidental." As he points out, this "still leaves open the question of why and how disturbed interpersonal relationships lead to conduct disorders. Moreover, family discord is only one of the causes of delinquency."

This investigator has also found strong evidence that "the longer the family disharmony lasts, the greater the risk to the children." Among children who have first lived with one set of unhappily married parents and then, following divorce, a second set of the same sort, the rate of antisocial disorder is twice as high as among children experiencing their first set of unhappy parents.

Are the ill effects of bad family relationships in early childhood permanent?

On the basis of a study of 65 children who had been separated from their parents some time earlier because of family discord or deviance, Rutter answers *not necessarily*. The current situation of about half of these children was judged to be very poor; that of the rest of the children, at least fair. The rate of antisocial behavior among children in a very poor family situation for the second time was 60 percent; among the others, 30 percent. "Given a change for the better in the family situation," the investigator comments, "the outlook for the child's psychological development correspondingly improves." He adds: "How readily, how completely, and how often the adverse effects of disturbed relationships in early childhood may be reversed" cannot be answered without further research.

Some other findings of Rutter's group:

• Where there was little tension in the family, there was little antisocial behavior in the children; where there was much tension and also a lack of warmth between husband and wife and between parent and child, the rate of antisocial behavior was significantly higher.

• In families where the marriage was very poor, boys having a good relationship with at least one parent had a deviancy rate less than half that of boys having a poor relationship with both parents.

Could it be that it was the children's antisocial behavior which led to parental discord, rather than the other way around? Studies of foster parents, of nursing mothers, and of parents of children with congenital handicaps, Rutter notes, have all shown not only that parents influence children but also that children influence parents. However, Rutter's group found that even among children who had been separated from their parents in the earliest years of life because of family discord, antisocial disorders often developed later. And he observes that "in some of these cases the marital difficulties must have preceded the child's birth because older children had already been taken into care following some family crisis."

However, certain factors in the child *are* important. Large-scale studies by Rutter's team on the Isle of Wight found that two groups of children were more likely than other children to develop antisocial tendencies: children with organic brain disorders and children with severe reading difficulties.

Sex, too, has a major role. The rate of deviant behavior among boys, but not among girls, is associated with the state of the parents' marriage. As Rutter remarks, there seems to be "a tendency for the male to succumb more readily to psychological stresses, in parallel perhaps with the very well documented finding that the male is much more susceptible to biological stresses."

Temperamental characteristics—a subject discussed at length in Chapter 4—seem also to be highly important. "Children who lacked fastidiousness (that is, they did not mind messiness and disorder) were significantly more likely to show deviant behavior one year later" in school. The same was true of children whose behavior was difficult to change (or who were nonadaptable) and of children "who were markedly irregular in their eating and sleeping patterns."

People's lives as children often presage their later lives as adults. Several studies, Rutter notes, "have shown that people who are brought up in unhappy or disruptive homes are more likely to have illegitimate children, to become teenage mothers, to make an unhappy marriage, and to divorce. Furthermore, a variety of investigations have found that parents who batter their children tend to have seriously disturbed upbringing themselves, often associated with neglect, rejection, or violence."

A study by a Rutter associate compared the backgrounds of parents who for the second time had had a child removed from their care with those of parents undergoing other severe social stresses. The findings:

Far more of the fathers and mothers [whose children had been taken away] had had multiple chronic adverse experiences in childhood, often associated with overt psychiatric problems. However, it was not just a matter of stresses in childhood. The parents [of such children], unlike the controls, had failed to move out of the stress situations. Two factors seem crucial. They bore children in their teens, and they married or cohabited with someone from a similar disadvantaged background.

What influences parental behavior? Rutter ticks off five main variables discovered in recent research as of great cogency:

- The parent's own childhood experiences.
- The events of the post-natal period, with early physical contact between mother and newborn child apparently fostering closer physical relationships and increased communication later.
- The influence of the child himself. "Neonatal characteristics have. . . been found to influence parental responses, and so with the behaviors of older children."
- The very experience of bringing up children. "With their second child [parents] tend to be more relaxed, more consistent, and less punitive."
- The wider social environment. "In our studies of families of 10-year-old children, we have found that the marital discord and maternal depression are much more common among working-class women living in inner-city areas."

The Family: Changing but Enduring

The increased incidence of divorce is only one of the factors which appear to be changing the pattern of family life. "Profound changes are taking place in the lives of America's children and young people. The institution which is at the center of these changes and that itself shows the most rapid and radical transformation is the American family, the major context in which a person grows up." So wrote social psychologist Urie Bronfenbrenner in his paper entitled *The Origins of Aliena-*

tion in 1974. Nothing that has happened since has served to reverse that trend.

Bronfenbrenner has described census data that help define changes in the structure of the American family, and of the child's position in it during the last quarter century. The changes have been profound, and the "bottom line" is the depletion of the child's familial resources.

The number of adults left in the home who might care for the child has been decreasing steadily. One out of every six children under eighteen is now living in a single-parent family, almost always with the mother. Since divorce has increased and many divorced women with children do not remarry, this trend toward single-parent families has been sharply accelerating. Recent U.S. Census Bureau figures show that of the 66 million children under eighteen, more than 11 million currently reside in single-parent residences. A significant component in the growth of single-parent families has been a sharp rise in the number of unwed mothers; more young women are postponing the age of marriage, but some of them are having children nevertheless. Whatever the cause, two out of every five American children born in the 1970s can expect to reside for five years or more with a single parent.

Such changes in household patterns are occurring more rapidly among younger families with younger children and among those experiencing economic deprivation and urbanization. The changes reach their maximum among low-income families living in the central core of our largest cities. Significantly, however, in terms of such characteristics as the proportion of working mothers, number of adults in the home, single-parent families, or children born out of wedlock, the middle-class family of today increasingly resembles the low-income family of the early 1960s.

Kenneth Keniston points out that "not only parents but grandparents, aunts and uncles have disappeared. Kinship networks have been dispersed as parents relocate to follow jobs and promotions. Brothers and sisters are increasingly scarce, too. Sixteen years ago, the average child had almost three siblings; today, the statistically average child has less than one."

In sum, children today find considerably fewer sources of affection, guidance, and support in the family than ever before. For the typical child, it is either from parents or from no one that he or she will receive psychological nurture. Sally Provence of Yale's Child Study Center sees this as a critical problem. "I'm personally convinced that no two parents can rear a child entirely alone," she says. "Yet young parents have fewer supports for parenting than ever before. It's either drag the kids along or get a sitter." Says child education authority Ira J. Gordon:

"I think all of the families in this country are in trouble in some way. All need support of one kind or another."

Often today's children show their conflict and distress, their despair over having failed to achieve that precious feeling of place in the family, by cutting the tie. Every year at least one million children, more of them from middle-class families, run away from home.

In recent years, men and women have varied the nature and configuration of the family. Despite the stresses and pressures exerted on it, however, the family as a social institution has bravely survived.

Anthropologist Margaret Mead reminds us that "the human family—composed of mother, father, and dependent children—is as old as humanity itself. It certainly dates back to long before human beings understood the procreative role of the father—that the children of the woman for whom he cared and who cared for him were his biological children."

Traditions, styles, and patterns may differ today as in the past. Columbia professor Michael Novak has described the range. "The Jewish family is not quite like the Italian family; the families of the Scotch-Irish of Appalachia have emotional ties different from those of families from Eastern Europe. The communal families of the South Slavs are not like those of the Japanese. There is not *one* family pattern in America: there are many."

Those who are ready to write finish to the American family as a viable social system cite the spiraling statistics of dissent and divorce that characterize the American way of family life. Novak contends, however, that the figures hide as much as they reveal. "Some 66 percent of all husbands and wives stick together until death do them part. In addition, the death that parts a marriage comes far later now than it did in any previous era. Faithful spouses stay together for a longer span of years than ever. For centuries, the average age of death was, for a female, say, 32, and, for a male, 38. That so many modern marriages carry a far longer span of years with a certain grace is an unprecedented tribute to the institution." Novak adds: "It is the destiny of flesh and blood to be familial."

Mead, too, contends that the family is far from dead. "It is going through stormy times," she writes, "and millions of children are paying the penalty of current disorganization, experimentation and discontent. In the process, the adults who should never marry are sorting themselves out. Marriage and parenthood are being viewed as a vocation rather than as the duty of every human being."

Still, as the next chapter portrays, we are a long way from providing the family support systems each child desperately needs.

8

Growing Up Abused

At a conference on the roots of children's violence held at New York University in March of 1976, Henry J. Foster, professor of law at N.Y.U., told the story of Andre, a patient encountered by a young law student at Bellevue Hospital a few months earlier.

Andre had been found wandering the streets of the city, was picked up by police, and was taken to the station house. After some effort, the police learned the name of his mother, but when they called to tell her that they had Andre, she said simply: "*You* keep him. I don't want him."

The police noticed that Andre had a rash. They took him to Bellevue Hospital, where doctors found that he had chicken pox. That night, in the children's ward, a baby in the crib next to Andre started to cry. When the nurse left the ward for a moment, Andre got out of bed, took the baby from the crib, slammed it against the wall, and dashed it to the floor. The crying stopped.

The psychiatrist who worked with Andre for many years reports that Andre was psychotic immediately after the killing. She also learned that in Andre's home, to cry was "bad," and when he was bad, he suffered a beating, either from his mother or from one of her assortment of boyfriends who moved through the house, mauling the child at will.

Andre was *four years old*—in Professor Foster's view, perhaps the youngest known killer on record. While not every abused child will develop a violent personality, Andre's shattering case history does illustrate one of the recurring findings of child abuse research: Battered children often grow to batter their own, smaller victims. Researchers are beginning to identify other outcomes of child abuse as well, and this chapter is devoted to describing them, along with what we know about the characteristics of abusive parents, their young targets, and the environment in which parental crimes against children are committed daily in homes across our land.

History of an Endangered Species

The two-year-old child lies frail and immobile in her crib. Only her eyes move, as if fearfully searching the world for the next violent blow. Her body—shoulders, back, legs, arms, chin, cheekbones—is a mosaic of angry bruises and scars, and her shrunken buttocks are laced with cigarette burns. The child cannot or will not speak, and her response to a gesture of open-armed tenderness is panic—and an empty, tearless, and agonizing scream.

Another child, only seven, but appearing ancient, has become a grotesque satire of youth—the product of chronic abuse and mutilation by his elders. His feet are crushed, his shoulders bent out of shape, his head held at a tilt, the result of repeated insult to the brain. As he walks alone in the busy market, he excites the curious gaze and revulsion of passers-by.

The two cases are indistinguishable, both in their stark brutality, and in the scorn they portray for the destiny of an innocent child. They differ only in their origins. The first child was recently a patient at Children's Hospital, Washington, D.C. The second has been dead over 2,000 years, recalled only in archives of Roman times. Taken together, they portray a fact that shouts at us from the pages of history: Since the beginning of time, the world's children have constituted an endangered species—a yielding target for the frustrations, conflicts, projections, unresolved hates, and smoldering anger of the adults who so often tyrannically bestride their lives.

Although child abuse and neglect have only recently commanded a wave of national attention, the bleak outlook for so many contemporary children is no new phenomenon. As chronicled by child historian Lloyd deMause, the history of childhood is a panorama of incredible cruelty and exploitation.

The melancholy journey of children through time could have been foretold by the ancient tradition of child murder, first committed as ritual sacrifice to appease angry gods. When the young Isaac dutifully accompanied his father, Abraham, to the mountain to be slaughtered, he was collaborating in a test of Abraham's obedience to his Lord. With a knife already placed at his throat, Isaac was saved only because Abraham had proved his piety. The classic tale of the near slaughter of Isaac is hardly unique in the annals of human history. From biblical lore and mythology to the present day, it is children who, with surprising frequency, have become the sacrificial lambs used by adults in barter for a better fortune.

Although preached against by the early Hebrew prophets, the sacrifice of firstborn sons was common in ancient Palestine. The Book of Chronicles tells of the Moabite King Mesha, for example, who burned his eldest son for the god Chemosh, and of the Ammonites who offered their sons to their god Moloch. Ultimately, animals and other tokens were substituted, but the notion that a child's life is expendable has not yielded easily.

In the accounting of deMause, children have been discarded in the past as just so much waste matter. They have been thrown into rivers, onto dung-heaps, and into cess trenches, have been exposed on hills and roadsides, and have even been "potted" in jars to starve to death. They were, in Euripides' terms, "a prey for birds, food for wild beasts to rend."

The assumption that the murder of infants was an atypical aberration of epochs past is not supported by the facts. Nor is infanticide a unique cultural blemish restricted to Eastern peoples—as some Westerners may like to assume. In his detailed survey of the phenomenon over time, William L. Langer demonstrates that the slaughter of legitimate as well as illegitimate children was chronically in evidence not only in antiquity but also, though at a slower pace, during the Middle Ages. Moreover, child murder—especially of the illegitimate child—has continued into the modern era.

The abuse and neglect of children carry an equally long and sordid history. The child who will be transformed by an enraged mother into an emergency-room case tonight is actually one in a long line of violated children stretching over the centuries and soiling our past like a giant blood stain.

DeMause examined 200 statements of advice on child rearing offered by writers before the eighteenth century, and he found that most approved of child beatings. "Virtually every childrearing tract from antiquity to the 18th century recommended the beating of children," he concludes. The advice fell on willing ears. Over the centuries, children have been beaten and battered regularly, beginning even at birth.

DeMause believes that a very large percentage of the children born before the eighteenth century would be regarded as truly "battered" by today's standards.

The tradition of physical punishment administered freely to children gained acceptance over the centuries virtually as a way of adult life— and not only among the poor and uneducated. Venerable figures in history are embedded in the pattern—the poet Milton mercilessly beating his nephews; Beethoven abusing his pupils with a knitting needle, or even biting them; the father of Louis XIII, a whip at his side, teaching the two-year-old not to whimper when confronted by a flogging. John Calvin preached that a parent's duty to God and the child required breaking the will of the infant at the earliest possible age. And, consider one mother's testimony on child rearing, given in eighteenth-century England: "When turned a year old (and some before), they were taught to fear the rod, and to cry softly." The words are of Susannah Wesley, wife of John, the founder of Methodism.

While the act of abusing children is hardly new, current clinical and scientific interest in the subject is surprisingly still in its infancy.

The Act and Its Victims

In July of 1962, the *Journal of the American Medical Association* published an article by pediatrician C. Henry Kempe and four fellow physicians that quickly became a benchmark in pediatric medicine. Titled "The Battered-Child Syndrome," the article exposed for the first time as a medical phenomenon the brutal reality of countless children's lives over the ages. Here, in its medically impersonal yet chilling detail, are the essential conclusions reached by Kempe and his team, and the suggestions they gave to their fellow doctors for spotting a battered child among other suffering children in their care.

The battered-child syndrome may occur at any age, but, in general, the affected children are younger than 3 years. In some instances the clinical manifestations are limited to those resulting from a single episode of trauma, but more often the child's general health is below par, and he shows evidence of neglect including poor skin hygiene, multiple soft tissue injuries, and malnutrition. One often obtains a history of previous episodes suggestive of parental neglect or trauma. A marked discrepancy between clinical findings and historical data as supplied by the parents is a major diagnostic feature of the battered-child syndrome. The fact that no new lesions, either of the soft tissue or of the bone, occur while the child is in the hospital or in a protected environment lends added weight to the diagnosis. . . . Subdural hematoma [bleeding between the brain and skull], with or without fracture of the skull, is, in our experience, an extremely frequent finding even in the absence of fractures of the long bones. The characteristic distribution of these multiple fractures and the observation that the lesions are in different stages of healing are of additional value in making the diagnosis.

The publication of Kempe's article sparked a wave of interest in the phenomenon of child abuse; it was as if medical charts had suddenly verified the existence of an ancient crime. In the press, each day brought new essays of outrage. "The reports of injuries read like the case book of the concentration camp doctor," wrote one astonished reporter. As in the case of any behavioral phenomenon, statisticians quickly began their attempts to define the scope of the problem. How extensive is child abuse?

The answer is still unclear, primarily because a universally binding definition of child abuse is difficult to establish. The range of physical punishments endured by children—and the reasons for them given by adults—make the task of defining the act difficult. Moreover, the channels through which child abuse cases are reported are often blocked with defensiveness, denial, and rationalization by both physician and parent alike.

Still, for the researcher, a standard accepted definition of abuse is necessary to assess its prevalence and study the impact of prevention programs. After reviewing the various criteria used by researchers to define child abuse, psychologist Ross D. Parke, working in collaboration with Candace Whitmer Collmer, suggested that abuse be considered to exist when the children suffer nonaccidental physical injury as a result of acts—or omissions—on the part of their parents or guardians "that violate the community standards concerning the treatment of children."

Estimates of the number of American children abused in roughly such terms each year range from a half million to one and a half million. Moreover, 2 in every 1,000 abused children are estimated to die as a result of the trauma suffered at the hands of their tormentors.

Most researchers in the field have long believed that surveys of child abuse cases seriously underestimate the problem. Many parents never bring their battered children to medical attention, and others who are repeated abusers manage to shift from one doctor or hospital to another in the hope that the child's injuries will be regarded as accidents. Often, the types of injuries inflicted are not readily detected, and even if they are, the physician may fail to report many cases to a central registry, thus leaving behind no trace of the brutal reality.

Now, as a result of a recently completed national survey, the assumption that child abuse is more prevalent than shown by earlier statistics has been reinforced. A team of sociologists studying a nationally representative sample of 2,143 families has found that child abuse is a dramatic and visible aspect of a much broader pattern of violence that characterizes the American family today. In a 1977 report to the American Association for the Advancement of Science, University of New Hampshire sociologist Richard J. Gelles, a member of that team, reported some of the first results of the study dealing specifically with violence toward children.

Gelles's findings are based on a survey of over 1,100 couples who had at least one child between three and seventeen living at home. Among parents of children age three to nine, he found that over 80 percent use physical punishment, including acts which often go well beyond "routine" slaps. Moreover, the pattern applies to older as well as young children. The survey shows that over a third of all American children between fifteen and seventeen had been hit by their parents during the survey year. Although all of them are hardly victims of chronic battering, the statistics do portray a surprising readiness by adults to use physical force in dealing with the young.

The study reveals, moreover, a staggering range and severity of violence toward children by their parents, inflicted primarily on sons by their mothers. For example, 20 percent of the parents had hit the child with some object, and over 4 percent indicated they had "beaten up" the child. Even more astounding, according to Gelles, is the fact that nearly 3 percent of the parents used a knife or gun on their young targets. Applying this rate to the population of children aged three to seventeen, Gelles estimates a total of about 1.2 million children whose lives had been threatened by lethal weapons in the hands of their parents.

The types of violent acts most likely to lead to serious physical injury for the child include kicking, biting, hitting with a fist or object, beating up the child, threatening the child with a knife or gun, and actually using a knife or gun. Close to 4 percent of the parents admitted at least one of these acts in the previous twelve months. This suggests that each

year well over one and a half million American children of the ages
three to seventeen experience an attack by their parents which could
cause severe bodily harm or death.

Telling as these statistics are, they still do not capture the incredible
range of abuses to which children are subjected by their adult guardians. Psychologist David Bakan has summarized them:

Children have been brought into hospitals with skulls fractured and bodies
covered with lacerations. . . . Children have been whipped, beaten,
starved, drowned, smashed against walls and floors, held in ice water baths,
exposed to extremes of outdoor temperatures, burned with hot irons and
steam pipes. Children have been tied and kept in upright positions for long
periods. They have been systematically exposed to electric shock; forced to
swallow pepper, soil, feces, urine, vinegar, alcohol, and other odious
materials; buried alive; had scalding water poured over their genitals; had
their limbs held in open fire; placed in roadways where automobiles would
run over them; placed on roofs and fire escapes in such a manner as to fall
off; bitten, knifed, and shot; had their eyes gouged out.

The conclusion is inescapable: tens of thousands of children now
being conceived have in store not love and support but rage and
rejection—and savage batterings of their fragile bodies. Survey data,
however weighty, mask the true reality—the sight and sound of a child
being brutalized by an adult. In a country that purports to value all its
young, percentages are less telling than the pain of one soft bone
crushed beyond repair, and statistics less affecting than a single scream
of innocent agony.

What are the effects of abuse on young victims? What are the survivors like? The next section confronts these questions.

The Fate of Abused Children

It may reflect our lack of commitment to the young that only meager
scientific effort has been directed toward learning about the consequences later in life for abused children. Michael S. Wald, professor of
law at Stanford University, has made an exhaustive analysis of the legal
ramifications of child abuse. He has found, to his amazement, that until
only about 1970, no one studied the children at all—only the parents.
Moreover, as University of Pittsburgh social worker Elizabeth Elmer
points out, virtually all of the studies which do exist are weakened by

the absence of control groups, making it impossible to define exactly how abused children compare with comparable samples of unabused children.

Despite the paucity of solid scientific data, however, sufficient evidence already exists to begin outlining the impact of abuse on its victims: If they survive at all, abused children appear to have their intellectual functions impaired and to suffer from a range of physical, psychological, and social problems that scar not only them but, should they reproduce, the next generation as well.

Clinical observations, for example, have long suggested that abuse can seriously alter a child's physical resources—not only the ability but even the willingness to survive. In his paper entitled "The Unwelcome Child and His Death-Instinct," psychoanalyst Sandor Ferenczi concluded decades ago that "children who are received in a harsh and disagreeable way die easily and willingly. Either they use one of the many proffered organic possibilities for a quick exit, or if they escape this fate, they keep a streak of pessimism and of aversion to life." Pioneer child researcher Rene Spitz dramatically demonstrated the condition in studies of children placed in foundling homes. Those children who endured the rejection and neglect of their "caretakers" suffered physical deterioration and a dramatically higher death rate than would otherwise be expected. In extreme cases, total withdrawal to an apathetic, vegetablelike existence promptly led the child to its "quick exit."

Such early findings are now being reinforced by additional clinical data. At the 1976 meeting of the American Psychopathological Association, for example, psychologist John Money of the Johns Hopkins University School of Medicine described a relatively rare, yet telling condition known as *psychosocial dwarfism*—a direct outcome, he contends, of severe and malignant child abuse. The endocrine system of the victimized child may simply cease its usual production of growth hormones, Money reports, and in the environment of abuse, neglect, and starvation, the young body stops growing normally. The result is a dwarfed child, stunted in both physical and mental growth—a grotesque anomaly of normal child development. Such children, Money points out, can be readily misdiagnosed as psychotic or mentally retarded.

When finally seen by a physician, children suffering psychosocial dwarfism show evidence of the physical and psychic trauma they have endured. Their bodies are often laced with infected lesions, burns, and scars; an investigation of their families reveals that many of the children had been isolated, severely punished even while asleep, and chronically starved.

Like many mothers and fathers of abused children, the parents of Money's dwarfs frequently offered "righteous" reasons for abusing their young. In the name of discipline, for example, one boy was denied food and water and reduced to stealing them in his own home. He was sometimes allowed food on the condition that he crawl on his hands and knees to the dinner table; the other children, seated at the table, were required to throw food to him as if to a dog. Not surprisingly, when first seen, Money's child dwarfs had peculiar eating habits. They would starve themselves or eat until they vomited; others ate from a bowl of dog food or drank from the toilet bowl. Some engaged in night roaming activity—as if on the prowl for food.

When children with psychosocial dwarfism are removed from the family to a hospital or foster home, Money reports, their precipitous physical decline is reversed. Their body chemistry changes. They begin to produce growth hormones, and resume normal development. One child grew eight inches during the first year away from his family. In Money's study of 16 such patients, an improved living environment led also to a catch-up in mental growth—a rise in intelligence quotient and increased learning achievement.

For many abused children, lingering physical disabilities merge with intellectual and emotional ones in a pattern that invites lifelong problems. In 1974, for example, pioneer child abuse researcher Harold P. Martin reported the results of a five-year follow-up of 58 abused children. Although the injuries suffered by these children had not been especially severe, approximately a third showed poor physical growth, and over half suffered neurological abnormalities. More than 60 percent evidenced personality difficulties, including low self-esteem, inability to enjoy interpersonal relationships, learning disorders, and behavior problems. The children's average IQ was in the normal range, but nearly three times the expected number fell below 85.

The studies by Money and Martin—and many others like them— portray the dramatic impact of child abuse, but they are without the benefit of data from matched groups of children not suffering abuse. A rare study using such control subjects—in this case, children suffering comparable body injuries through accidents rather than abuse—has now been reported by Elmer. In her 1976 report to the American Psychological Association, she described the results of an eight-year follow-up designed to compare a small group of abused children with a matched group of accidentally injured children, utilizing measures of health, development, behavior, and school progress as gauges.

Infants—all of them from poor families—were selected for study from referrals to the X-ray department of Children's Hospital of Pittsburgh. All of the tiny patients were suffering from what the investigator calls an "impact event"—for example, a fall or a blow. Each injury was judged by a pediatrician, a family interviewer, and Elmer herself to be the result either of abuse or accident. To place a child in the abuse category, the three judges had to agree, using one or more of three specific criteria: an actual report of abuse, a conflicting history or one suspiciously inadequate to explain the patient's condition, or evidence of injuries incurred at more than one time. All children not judged to have been abused were placed in the accident category.

At the outset of the study, a number of differences between the two groups were apparent. The abused babies weighed significantly less, their heads—often beaten and bruised—were smaller, and they showed signs of neurological problems. They tended also to be slower in motor development and were significantly more variable and negative in their moods.

By the time the babies returned for a final outpatient evaluation one year later, five of the abused children had been placed in substitute care. Yet such children as a group still weighed less, were shorter in stature, and showed a smaller head circumference—although no longer significantly so. Health problems continued to be more severe among the abused children. Even some whose weight had been satisfactory at the beginning of the study, for example, were now significantly below the average for their ages. Mental, motor, and language development, however, had slackened in both groups, with more than half of each scoring below normal. Differences in personality had disappeared, also, largely because the accident children had become more negative and thus had begun to resemble the abused children more closely.

Now, eight years later, Elmer has matched 17 of the abused children with 17 from the accident group in age, race, and sex, comparing them not only with each other but with control groups of hospitalized children who had experienced neither abuse nor accidental injuries in infancy. After the intervening years, she finds that the earlier differences have disappeared. There are now no substantial differences among the children in their physical health, language development, intellectual status in school, self-concept, or behavior. What most surprised Elmer, however, was the extent of various problems across the *entire* sample. Seventy percent of all the children, for example, had speech problems, including poor articulation, chronic hoarseness, intermittent loss of speech, and stuttering, all of them often associated with tension and anxiety. Over half showed some degree of behavior disturbance, and nearly 40 percent were doing poorly in school. None of these disabilities, however, was significantly greater in one group than in either of the others.

Elmer's results suggest that the effects on children of poverty—and the family disorganization that often accompanies it—may be as powerful as abuse. All of her subjects, abused or not, grew up in impoverished homes that were chaotic, disorganized, and marked by an abiding threat of violence. Such an environment, whose effects on mental health are described in a later chapter, may be a powerful, overriding factor that masks even the special impact of abuse.

Elmer's results do not mean, however, that child abuse itself has no appreciable effect. It would take a great deal more controlled research with children across a broad range of age and economic levels to measure rigorously specific outcomes. Meanwhile, studies of many samples of children continue to remind us that the penalties paid by the victims may be enormous.

Brandt F. Steele, professor of psychiatry at the University of Colorado Medical Center and a staff member of Denver's National Center for the Prevention and Treatment of Child Abuse and Neglect, has recently detailed some of the effects of abuse on the psychological development of the child. Unlike Elmer's subjects, most of Steele's families were above the poverty level. Moreover, his concern is not alone with children who have suffered physical trauma—fractures, burns, bruises, and internal injuries—but with those experiencing emotional deprivation and degradation, nutritional neglect, sexual abuse, and life in an environment shorn of all stimulation as well. He is particularly concerned with children who suffer such conditions in the early months and years of life.

Steele's results are unequivocal. "Maltreatment during this period," he reports, "not only results in immediate damage, but can also lead to deficits which affect the entire course of the child's life and distort all of his later psychological, emotional and cognitive development."

Problems in an abused child's development can often be explained in brute physiological terms. Repeated blows to the head—and the resulting bleeding inside the skull—ultimately mean the destruction of brain tissue. Parents may succeed in producing the same outcome, however, without obvious head trauma. Steele finds that subtle hemorrhages, diffusely scattered through the brain substance, can take place when an infant is simply shaken, leaving no external signs of injury.

The net result of the brain damage endured in either case may range from a lowered IQ to profound mental retardation, defects in vision, and impairment of motor skills. Commonly, the baby suffers a delay in language development considerably greater than one might expect from the IQ score itself.

Steele is not surprised to find such disturbances resulting from injuries to the brain, but he is surprised—and disturbed—that many of the same impairments are suffered by children without head injuries and the accompanying neurological damage. They are the victims instead of a harsh, neglectful, and emotionally abusive environment. In approximately a third of the children without head injuries, for example, Martin reported borderline IQs or lower, and again, a large number suffering significant language deficits.

It is this inability to handle language that emerges as one of the most common characteristics among abused and neglected children. "Many of them" Steele has found, "show significant learning problems when they enter the educational system in pre-school, kindergarten or first grade." Steele contends further that a significant number of those living their young lives in our institutions for the mentally retarded are there as a result of abuse and neglect. "Many of the children who utilize the services of our overloaded special education programs in the public schools," Steele adds, "are there for the same unhappy reasons."

Steele reports also among abused and neglected children a "tragically low sense of self-esteem" which endures into adulthood. "It is a residue," he says, "of the many times the child was criticized, belittled and punished or injured when he failed to meet the excessively high parental expectations. Success, if it ever occurred, was not praised, and there was no way to develop a sense of worth." Steele is impressed also by the apathy and depressive mood, the lack of any spontaneity and joy among abuse victims.

Among the most poignant characteristics found by researchers is the abused child's *hypervigilance,* a tendency to be wary and watchful of the world—as if expecting the next unreasonable blow to fall at any moment. It is the same fearful attitude found among concentration camp survivors who, for years after they emerged from their long ordeal, were readily startled and panicked by even normal sounds—of footsteps or shouting—that reawakened old horrors. Steele finds that when abused children observe violent physical and verbal actions of others, even though not directed at them, the result is often terror that cannot be assuaged.

What happens ultimately to abused children? "Some with the help of fortunate circumstances, can lead fairly normal lives," Steele contends.

"Other children who are more severely damaged are never able to develop adequate skills of learning and living. They maintain precarious borderline adjustments, and are often in trouble. A small proportion become quite aggressive, [and are] repeatedly in trouble at home, in the neighborhood and at school. A larger number appear very well-adjusted, are extremely compliant, obedient, thoughtful and helpful. But this is a superficial adaptation to avoid disaster; underneath they are lonely, empty and emotionally disturbed."

Not surprisingly, such disturbance sometimes finds expression in the later sexual lives of abused children.

The Sexual Problems of Abuse Victims

A special problem found in dramatic evidence among abused children is embedded in their sexual attitudes and behavior. One of the most striking results of Elmer's study, for example, was the finding that so many of her sample of abused children grew later to develop significant difficulties in their sexual identification. Elmer herself was surprised. She did not set out to assess sexual problems, but comments from several of the examiners converged to suggest that this was a significant area for investigation. Seven of the abused children were spontaneously described by their examiners as confused in their sexual identification or unable to separate their sexual from their aggressive impulses. Only two of the children suffering accidental injuries were thought to have such problems, and even these were less severe.

One foster mother pictured her abused son as isolated from his peers and disinterested in the normal activities of typical boys; instead, he enjoyed making clothes for his Barbie dolls, with which he played for hours on end. In the laboratory he often folded his arms high on his chest, in an attempt, he said, to imitate breasts. Like many of the other abused children, he appeared anxious, forlorn, and frightened of outside attack—not in fantasy, as is the case among many children, but by real people. Under an early barrage of abuse from the outside world, he—and many of the other young victims—seemed to have lost his sense of identity and to have entered a prolonged and unresolved sexual crisis.

Can it be that while traumatic injuries suffered either through accident or abuse leave some psychological scars in common, it is the relentless and purposeful attack on a child by a significant adult "protector" that serves especially to disintegrate the young personality?

The findings of Elmer and her team agree with observations made centuries ago. Aristotle concluded that homosexuality becomes a way of life among "those who are abused from childhood." Moreover, the connection between abuse and sexual problems did not escape the sharp clinical observations of early psychoanalytic theorists. Ferenczi concluded that unwelcome, rejected children grow to be frigid and impotent, and from his vast clinical files, sex pathologist Richard von Krafft-Ebing deduced decades ago that traumatic experiences in childhood often produce adult sexual deviations.

In a paper he called "A Child Is Being Beaten," Freud reported that the fantasy of a child being beaten was present in a surprisingly large proportion of his patients. That fantasy, he contended, unconsciously involved beatings of the genitalia, no matter what part of the body was actually being violated. Moreover, in Freud's analytic terms, a child's physical punishment is always experienced—at a dark, subterranean unconscious level—as castration.

Such contentions might be dismissed as the idle fantasies of an esoteric genius were it not for supportive data now available from research such as Elmer's—and, even more dramatically, from animal studies. During their ground-breaking research on infant development, Harlow and his team of investigators at the University of Wisconsin amassed convincing data linking early abuse with later sexual pathology among primates.

Harlow's original purpose was to establish experimental neuroses in infant monkeys by arranging for them to be traumatized and abused by their mothers. Later, as the animals grew older, he and his fellow researchers were struck by some of the long-term and difficult-to-reverse effects of their early manipulation. Prominent among these were sexual difficulties and aberrations.

One experimental approach was to inflict on the young monkeys a "rejecting mother" who, on schedule or demand, violently separated her baby from further contact. A wire frame, embedded in the mother's spun-nylon covering, was displaced abruptly upward and backward, causing the infant to be relentlessly disconnected from its source of protection and love. Next, Harlow developed an "air blast mother" with a series of nozzles down the entire center of her body which released compressed air under high pressure—an extremely noxious stimulus to monkeys—and then a "shaking mother," which could be made to jerk her infant violently until its teeth chattered. Finally, he devised a "porcupine mother," extruding brass spikes over the front of its body and offering an abusive and painful response to the infant's attempts at nuzzling.

As the months and years passed, Harlow and his coworkers found the traumatized monkeys to deviate increasingly from the normal. They saw them sitting in their cages, strangely mute, staring into space, relatively indifferent to people and also monkey peers. Many clutched their heads in both hands, rocking back and forth in the manner of the typical autistic child; others engaged in violent frenzies of rage, grasping and tearing at their legs with such fury that they sometimes required medical care. Eventually, Harlow realized that he had, indeed, raised a laboratory filled with neurotic monkeys.

Because of housing pressures, some of the animals lived in pairs for several years while growing to sexual maturity. In the earliest reports of his classic studies, Harlow began to note the absence of normal sexual behavior among his abused breed. "When the older, wire-cage-raised males were paired with the females at the peak of estrus, the introduction led only to fighting, so violent and vicious that separation was essential to survival. In no case was there any indication of normal sex behavior. . . ."

At this point Harlow took the 17 oldest of his experimental female animals showing consistent estrus cycles and a similar number of obviously mature males, and he engaged them in an intensive reeducation program. He paired the females with "the most experienced, patient, and gentle males," and the males with his "most eager, amiable, and successful breeding females." The results were startling. "When the laboratory-bred females were smaller than the sophisticated males, the girls would back away and sit down facing the males, looking appealingly at these would-be consorts. Their hearts were in the right place, but nothing else. When the females were larger than the males . . . they would attack and maul the ill-fated male."

Harlow reported the training program for the males to be equally unsatisfactory.

They approached the females with a blind enthusiasm, but it was a misdirected enthusiasm. Frequently, the males would grasp the females by the side of the body and thrust laterally, leaving them working at cross purposes with reality. Even the most persistent attempts by these females to set the boys straight came to naught. Finally, these females either stared at the males with complete contempt or attacked them in utter frustration.

Harlow's whimsical prose does not soften the harsh results of his research. Monkeys abused in their infancy tended to grow into sexually incompetent and perverse adults, and their attempts to engage in normal sexual activity ended in frustration and failure.

Perhaps the most malignant outcome of child abuse, however, is the seed of violence so often sown in the heart and mind of the young victim. The biblical warning that foresaw the "sins of the fathers" visited on their children is nowhere more fully realized than in the ugly intergenerational chain of violence spawned in the home.

Planting the Seeds of Violence

Centuries ago, the sage Ben Sirach intoned: "The branch sprung from violence has no tender twig." His observation has now been confirmed repeatedly by investigators, who find an unusually high rate of violent behavior—including juvenile delinquency and crime— among children abused earlier by their adult parents and guardians.

The number of such untender twigs in American society is proliferating at an alarming rate. While violence in general has been steadily increasing in our society, there has been an especially remarkable spurt in the incidence of violent behavior among the young in recent years. Violent crimes committed by children of all ages have been increasing between three and four times faster than they have in the general population.

Data for Washington, D.C., are illustrative. Each day in the nation's capital, an increasing number of juveniles, usually youngsters fifteen years old or younger, go on trial for violent crimes, including a fast-rising number of murders and armed robberies. Homicide cases rose by two-thirds in 1975 from the previous year, armed robbery cases doubled in number, and a growing cohort of juveniles were tried for mugging, robbery, and aggravated assault. While such trends can be explained in part by the rising numbers of young people in the population in general—a function of the high fertility rates after World War II—the bulge in the lower end of the age curve hardly accounts for the phenomenon altogether. The young population, it would appear, is increasingly given to violent behavior.

No array of statistics can accurately portray the challenge posed by a violent child to those who share his world. For parents, siblings, peers, teachers—and, ultimately, law enforcement authorities—such children test the limits of adult compassion and caring, raise tides of guilt and self-doubt, and challenge the most sympathetic responses in our repertoire.

Perhaps out of a nagging discomfort with our own role in child violence, we have in recent years attempted to simplify the issue radically. Parents, pundits, and congressional committees alike have, for example, focused with remarkable intensity on violence as por-

trayed on television as the culprit—as if this was the prime stimulus for
violent behavior in our young. Granted, they have been well supported
by a host of studies, demonstrating that some children do, in fact, use
filmed models to learn aggressive behavior.

Conveniently overlooked in the single-minded emphasis on the
tube, however, is an even more pervasive and potent force: real-life
violence in the family. It may be comforting for some to project blame
onto the silent eye in the living room, yet television is hardly the prime
model for our children's violent behavior. What appears on the small
screen is actually a pale, two-dimensional representation of the violence that many children experience in depth each day—in kitchens,
living rooms, and bedrooms across the country. Based on their national
survey, sociologists Murray A. Straus, Suzanne K. Steinmetz, and
Gelles conclude that violence between members of the same family
occurs more often than it does between any other individuals or in any
other setting except wars and riots.

In the report of her follow-up study of abused children Elmer has
described families living in an environment in which violence is ever
present—neighborhood shoot-outs in which a mother and her children
are forced to take refuge under beds or in stairwells, fathers beating
mothers and pushing them down flights of stairs, women attacking their
children for minor misdeeds. "As part of many spontaneous stories told
to the examiners," reports Elmer, "great concern was shown by the
children that they might become victims of attack. Most children of this
age are involved with fantasies of witches, devils and monsters that will
eat up others or set fire to them. . . . These children, by contrast, linked
their fears of injury or mutilation to real persons, not fantasy figures."
One of Elmer's young subjects spent five minutes demonstrating with
materials at hand just how a child might be tied with a lamp cord so that
he could be beaten. The model did not come from television. It sprang
instead from real life—his own.

Steele reports studies in the Denver area showing that fully 80
percent of youngsters picked up as juvenile offenders have been
abused and neglected early in life. In one investigation of 100 youngsters picked up for the first time, 84 were found to have been physically
abused before school age, and 92 had been bruised or lacerated or had a
bone broken by a parent within a year and a half previous to confronting
the law. Follow-up studies cited by Steele tell the same story. In
California and New York, for example, children reported to be abused
and neglected were followed for a dozen years or more. Nearly two-
thirds of them emerged as delinquents.

No one will deny that other factors may be involved in the origins of violent behavior in the young. The importance of abuse as a springboard for the later abuse of society, however, cannot be swept away. "My mother must have thought I was a canoe, she paddled me so often." So wrote Arthur Bremer who, as a young adult, sought to even the score one summer day by gunning down presidential candidate George Wallace. "If we want to understand violence in general," concludes Steele, "we must pay attention to how we treat our infants and small children."

The seeds of violence, it seems clear, may be planted successfully among children who fall short of being defined clinically as "battered." It does not require fractures, burns, or bruises to learn the lessons of violence—only a pervasive acceptance of aggression as a style of life.

University of Pennsylvania sociologist Marvin E. Wolfgang has devoted his career in recent years to enlarging our understanding of the social roots of violence. He argues convincingly that the criminal violence among children that assaults us from the morning headlines is nurtured in generous measure by a society which unequivocally teaches our young to accept violence as a natural element of their lives.

To begin with, says Wolfgang, there is in every family an implicit acceptance of violence in some form. "The use of physical force by parents to restrain and punish children is permissible, tolerated, encouraged," he points out, "and is thereby part of the normative process by which our society regulates its childrearing." Wolfgang acknowledges that there are varying degrees of parental force used in different cultures and at different times and that some are defined, however vaguely, as excessive and brutal. Nevertheless, our norms do permit or even encourage parents to apply force with their own hands against the child. This "acceptable" form of violence may consciously be used to discipline the child, to set limits of permissible behavior, to reduce the domestic noise level, to express parental disapproval, and even to displace aggression actually meant for other targets.

The child who grows up among adult violence may logically wonder, says Wolfgang, why he should not use violence himself in order to make other people behave in accordance with his wishes. The answer, the child realizes, is simply that he does not have sufficient force—physical and social—to impose pain on others without suffering retaliation. All that he lacks is power. And as soon as he gets it, he may well take it as right that he should use it.

In the case of four-year-old Andre, the opportunity—and the superior power—came early.

The Personalities and Attitudes of Abusive Parents

"You've gotta be crazy to do something like that."

Those words, spoken recently by a friend in discussing a neighborhood case of child abuse, reflect a common view about parents who abuse their young. Research data, however, suggest otherwise. Diagnosable mental illness is rarely a characteristic of such parents. Abusive parents do not fall neatly into traditional psychiatric diagnostic categories such as schizophrenia or manic-depressive psychosis. Although some psychotic individuals are responsible for child abuse, Kempe estimates that less than 10 percent of abusive parents can actually be classified as mentally ill.

Are there instead certain personality characteristics that abusive parents share in common?

Various investigators have suggested a bewildering array of traits, describing such parents, for example, as immature, impulsive, rigid, domineering, self-centered, hypersensitive, and more. They have not succeeded, however, in constructing a coherent portrait. In 1972, after an extensive analysis of the existing research literature on the subject, John J. Spinetta and David Rigler were able to find general agreement only that the abusive parent allows aggressive impulses to be expressed too freely; there was little consensus, however, on the source of these impulses. In another review one year later, Gelles found that among the 19 traits identified by various investigators as typical of abusive parents, there was agreement by two or more authors on only 4; the remaining 15 traits were each unique to a single researcher's findings.

The most systematic study of personality attributes of child-abusing mothers was reported in 1969 by Barry Melnick and John R. Hurley. They compared two groups of ten mothers, largely poor and black, one made up of abusive mothers, the other serving as controls. The groups were matched in age, social class, and education. The abusing mothers revealed lower self-esteem, less family satisfaction, less need to give nurturance, higher frustration of their dependent needs, and a less openly rejecting stance toward children. Even these findings, however, are not necessarily generalizable—for example, to fathers, or to parents of either sex at higher socioeconomic levels. It is noteworthy, too, that on two-thirds of the personality dimensions studied, the two groups of mothers differed not at all.

But there do appear to be some qualitative differences between the two types of parents. Three characteristics of abusive parents stand out: an acceptance of abuse as a way of parental life, a tendency to harbor grossly unrealistic expectations of children and to view them as evil, and a background of abuse in their own childhood.

To begin with, parents given to child abuse appear to regard physical punishment as quite natural and appropriate in rearing their young. Elmer reports the experiences of a colleague during visits to the homes of families being studied. "Even though the parents knew they were under observation by outside professionals," says Elmer, "several reacted to their children's objectionable behavior by hitting them." The parents had been judged abusive by the court and *knew*, therefore, that they were in trouble, yet evidently it did not occur to them to curb their attacks.

Elmer found the same attitude toward punishment among parents in her own study. One mother, angry at her child for not bathing, looked about for a strap with which to beat the child. It was only by chance that the strap could not be found; otherwise the beating almost surely would have taken place—despite the presence of an interviewer. Such parents, in Elmer's view, simply do not see corporal punishment as related to abuse; instead they are "doing what comes naturally."

For the parent given to abuse, it is never too early to begin showing the child who is boss. Slaps, spankings, beatings—all these begin virtually at birth. Moreover, the attitude does not appear to depend on social class. Barbara M. Korsch and her colleagues interviewed 100 mothers of infants under eighteen months of age, all of whom ranged from low to middle class. One-quarter of the mothers had started to mete out physical punishment before their babies were six months of age. Almost half the women were spanking before the infants were twelve months of age, even though they believed it was preferable to defer such punishment until the age of one year. Elmer's study focused on families ranging from very low to very high socioeconomic classes, but the tendencies of the mothers were much the same as among those studied by Korsch. "Over 80 percent were using physical punishment by the time the children were 12 months old," reports Elmer. Few mothers distinguished between teaching and punishment.

With such a readiness to apply physical force, it is not surprising that the line between child discipline and child violation often becomes blurred. A father in suburban Washington said recently with self-righteous conviction: "I don't believe in injuring a child or doing him permanent harm, but I know that when I beat the hell out of my kid, it sure clears the air."

This father—and many more parents like him—enjoy broad support, even of Scriptures. Consider, for example, the injunction from Proverbs: "Withhold not chastisement from a boy; if you beat him with a rod, he will not die. Beat him with the rod, and you will save him from the nether world."

More significant, perhaps, professional groups often express their unqualified advocacy of physical punishment. In one 1974 survey, two-thirds of the educators, police, and clergy sampled condoned physical discipline in the form of spanking by hand, while over 10 percent of the police and clergy supported the use of belts, straps, and brushes. Armed with such support, millions of adults perceive their assaults on children—however severe—as falling far short of abuse.

In the view of Kempe and his staff, there appears to be an unbroken spectrum of parental acts toward children ranging from "reminder pats" on the bottom through severe spanking and bruising, to the breaking of bones and the fracturing of skulls. The readiness of parents to yell, scold, punch, hit and yank very small children is shocking, and the investigators feel, therefore, that in dealing with the abused child, they are not observing an isolated, unique phenomenon but only the extreme form of an attitude toward child rearing common among parents in our culture.

The abusive parent, already comfortable with physical force, appears also to harbor surprisingly unrealistic expectations of the child. From their direct observation of abusive parents and their children, Steele and Carl B. Pollock concluded not only that parental demands for performance are heavy, but that they are premature by far, "clearly beyond the ability of the infant to comprehend what is wanted and to respond appropriately." Such parents persistently deal with their children as if they were much older than they really are.

Broderick reports the experience of one physician who works with abusive parents. A mother brought her 2½-year-old to the interview because she could not secure a baby-sitter. She was there because her nine-month-old baby had suffered more than a half dozen fractures at her hand. As the doctor invited the mother in from the waiting room, she ordered her child to wait for her and not to move out of her chair for the next 15 minutes. The doctor insisted that the little girl come in also. When she did, the child immediately noticed that the ash tray was full, emptied it in the wastebasket, and took a Kleenex from a box on his desk to wipe it out with. When the doctor commented on how unusual a performance this was the mother said, "Oh, yes. She's Mommy's little helper. She does almost all the housework." The episode may not be very extreme. Abused children are often seen by their parents not for what children are—helpless, needy, and with still limited abilities—but rather as mature and capable in all respects.

Abusive parents tend also to view their victims as evil, harboring malevolent intentions that must be exorcised. Elmer has heard parents describe a baby weighing 15 pounds as "out to get me" or as "a little Communist." The abused child is seen somehow as purposely malicious and antagonistic.

For historian deMause, the roots of such attitudes lie deeply buried in the psyches of offending parents. Throughout history, he contends, adults have used their children as objects onto which they could project their own unconscious conflicts and struggles. In psychoanalytic terms, such parents "void" their feelings onto their young.

It is a background of abuse in their own childhoods, however, that emerges as the most overriding characteristic of adults who violate their children. "It is out of the pool of abused, neglected children that the next generation of abusive parents will come," says Steele. "These unfortunate people have carried into adult life their main psychological patterns of lack of trust, fear of social contact, inability to have pleasure, low self-esteem, mild depression, great neediness and inability to empathically love. . . . When they have children they repeat the behavior of their own parents; they expect their children to behave in ways to satisfy the excessive parental needs. Especially in times of crisis the parents turn to their babies for comfort; the children are bound to fail and are punished or neglected. The cycle repeats itself."

One battering mother, Steele reports, put it this way: "I have never felt loved all my life. When he cried, it meant he didn't love me. So I hit him." Or, consider this observation: "He's the boss—all the time trying to run things—but I showed him who is in charge around here!" Those are the words of a father describing his nine-month-old boy whose skull he has just split in a fit of anger, as if the innocent baby were, himself, a punitive father. Throughout history, according to deMause, adults have unleashed similar long-smoldering hate and anger against the defenseless child.

The chain of abusive and neglectful behavior thus created has emerged consistently in attempts by researchers to tap the psychological roots of abusive parents. Most dramatic, perhaps, is the evidence that surfaced from the work of Harlow, part of it described earlier. Harlow and his coworkers at the University of Wisconsin succeeded in producing child batterers among monkey mothers simply by depriving them, as children, of all signs of maternal or peer love.

Harlow admits his own surprise. "Frankly we never thought we could produce the battered child syndrome in the rhesus monkey," he says. Yet he did—by raising motherless monkey mothers, animals who had "never known mother love themselves and had never had the chance to express love to a mother nor to exchange affection in play with agemate monkeys." He has since concluded that mother love can be prevented almost perpetually by withholding such love from the mother-to-be, even if she isn't to be a mother for many years.

Two different behaviors characterized the unloved, motherless monkeys grown to be mothers themselves. One was to totally ignore the babies, to neglect them—a response that is totally foreign to the behavior of both human and monkey mothers, who, typically, "at the dimmest detection of distress, rush to the babies and clasp them to their breasts with tender love and care."

The second basic behavior was, in Harlow's words, "grim and ghastly." When the infant made contact with the mother's body, he reports, "the mother would disattach the infant. She would literally scrape it from her body and abuse the infant by various sadistic devices. The mother would put the baby's face against the floor and rub it back and forth. . . . In most cases our experimenters were able to stop sadism at this point, but some mothers were so violent and vicious that the baby was barely saved or even lost. Not infrequently the mother would encircle the infant's head with her paws and in one case the skull of the neonate was crushed before the mother and child could be separated, so little had we anticipated the severity of the events in the reproduction of the battered child syndrome."

"These motherless mothers," Harlow emphasizes, "had never known affection of any kind, in spite of being raised in a faultlessly, physically hygienic environment with bodily needs satisfied."

How comparable are the human adult's vestigial responses to early trauma?

"There are practically no exceptions," says Selma Fraiberg, whose evidence emerges from a long career as a clinician and researcher studying children born bereft of normal human bonds. "I do not think I have ever seen an abuser of a child or for that matter an abuser of his wife who had not experienced abuse in his own childhood."

Children Who "Ask for It"

Elmer has described an unfolding situation common to many young married couples:

They eagerly awaited the birth of their little bundle of joy and prepared the pink dress, the pink crib, the pink and white room. As it turns out, pink is not suitable, for the baby is a boy. Moreover, the dress is slobbered on, the crib is where the baby cries, not where he sleeps. In fact he rarely sleeps, eats sporadically, spits up much of his food, and is often smelly and dirty. He never listens; whatever his mother says, he does just the opposite. No matter what methods the parents try, the baby doesn't learn to become dry and clean, to eat neatly, to live on schedule. . . . Instead of living happily ever after, the couple becomes more and more fatigued, more irritable, less tolerant of normal baby behavior.

Such circumstances, Elmer believes, are often a prelude to physical punishment of the newborn and, ultimately, to abuse. The case highlights a fact of family life experienced by countless parents. The new arrival introduces a stress which often tests the limits of a parent's capacity to protect and care for a child, especially when no strong commitment to the newcomer exists from the start.

Certain characteristics of the newcomer—high among them excessive irritability and crying—can help push parents beyond their threshold of violence. Newborns who fret a great deal appear to run a greater risk of harm than those who are placid and easily soothed. Such a "difficult" temperament may be determined by constitutional factors, as described in Chapter 4. Or, as Martin and Patricia Beezley have pointed out, it may arise from subtle early malfunctions of the infant's central nervous system, rarely identified by medical or nursing staff. The result, in any case, is a child who is typically described by parents as irritable, colicky, fretful, and difficult to feed, satisfy, or diaper. Parents of such children, they report, develop feelings of inadequacy, guilt, and anger; nothing about the baby's behavior makes them feel good about being parents. For adults with a "high potential to abuse," such an infant can soon precipitate vicious attacks.

To compound the problem, the difficult baby who suffers abuse may quickly develop behavior patterns which, in turn, invite still more harm. Bakan concludes that abused children, unlovable to begin with, tend to take on characteristics which make them even more unlovable. "The child who is abused and neglected," he finds, "becomes ugly in appearance and behavior and invites further abuse and neglect. Abused children develop such traits as fear of being alone, continued whimpering, shyness, fear of novel situations of any kind, hypersensitiveness to pain, overreactiveness, fear of engaging in any action at all even to help themselves. . . ."

Even professional personnel sometimes find abused children difficult to manage and care for, and the result can be a surprising degree of aversion and outright neglect. In one hospital, investigators found that the child in the bed farthest from the nurse's station was not infrequently an abuse victim. Abused children were found to have fewer toys strewn on their beds and fewer pictures in their rooms. The responses they get from the nurse may lack the usual warmth. The victim, it would seem, begins early to contribute to his or her own disastrous fate.

Of all the infant's characteristics, the one that appears most likely to invite abuse is low birth weight. Supporting data have emerged from a host of studies. From hospital records between 1960 and 1969, for example, Michael Klein and Leo Stern retrieved the charts of children diagnosed as victims of "battered child syndrome," 51 in all. Nearly one-fourth of them had weighed below 6 pounds at birth—over three times as many as one would expect to find in the population at large. Since mothers of low-socioeconomic status are more likely to give birth to underweight children, the researchers reexamined their data, controlling for social class. Among poor families, the incidence of abuse was still over twice as high among low birth weight infants.

What is it about the frail infant, born prematurely, that invites violence? To begin with, Parke and Collmer point out, the underdeveloped newborn often violates the common parental expectations that the baby will be attractive and lovable. It is neither. Moreover, such infants impose greater demands on their parents than do normal children. Feeding disturbances are common, and the babies are more irritable and cry more. Progress in muscular development, speech, and socialization is often naggingly slow during the first two years. "Although research is badly needed to specify the exact characteristics of the low birth weight infant that elicit parental abuse," Parke and Collmer conclude, "it is clear that the burden, stress, and disappointment associated with the birth and care of a low birth weight infant could increase the probability of abuse."

Child development researchers Sarah Friedman and Blanche Jacobs, at the National Institute of Mental Health have observed how nurses help propagate or intensify negative attitudes toward especially high-risk infants. "We see how they talk about the children," says Friedman. "They often hate them. If they develop a hate for the child everyone begins to disown the child. You come in and ask 'how is this baby doing?' The answer is *I* don't know. *I'm* not taking care of this child." Jacobs adds that the dynamics of a nursery for premature infants is very different from the norm. The staff can often gang up on babies that they don't like. A baby that doesn't thrive is a symbol of failure, and they don't like it. If he or she is ugly to begin with and troublesome, the spiral of neglect can begin.

The researchers point out that the mother who comes to visit her premature child after leaving the hospital picks up a lot of cues from the attitudes of hospital staff. The cycle of neglect and isolation builds up.

The problem may be compounded by the impact on the mother of her separation from the premature infant at the very start of their relationship. A child born prematurely is typically not available to the mother for long periods precisely at the time when critical attachments are beginning to take hold. So, too, is the child born by caesarean section—whose risk of later abuse has been found to be nearly 10 times greater than that of children born normally. A host of studies of both animal and human mothers and infants, some of them reported earlier, have demonstrated that such early separation can have a significant effect on the mother's behavior and attitudes—her skills as a mother, her self-confidence, even her physical interactions with the child.

From their studies, John H. Kennell and his associates have reported subtle evidence with potentially explosive ramifications. Mothers who were permitted physical contact with their premature infants beginning in the first days of life, they found, spent significantly more time engaged in cuddling and other intimate behaviors during later feedings than did mothers who first handled their babies only after 20 days. Mothers enjoying early contact more often held their infants cradled close to their body or on their chest or shoulder; furthermore, they were more likely to look at and talk to the infant during feeding rather than to pay attention to others. Separated mothers, in contrast, often held their infants at some distance from their bodies and showed less evidence of attachment. The potential for abusive behavior is less in mothers who have enjoyed the opportunity to form strong emotional bonds with their infants. The premature newborn, removed from contact with the mother, is a likelier victim later, therefore, when encounters begin in earnest with a mother who has not made the critical early connections of love.

Help for Abusers and Their Victims

In November of America's bicentennial year, as many citizens prepared for their festive Thanksgiving, a three-year-old boy in Washington, D.C., died, unable to survive the batterings suffered at the hands of the adults entrusted with his care.

The young boy, named Raynard, was born to a woman, now twenty-three, who had left her son in the care of a young man in the apartment which the couple shared. She had gone to seek medical aid for her younger, eight-month-old son. About an hour later, a neighbor found Raynard on the living room sofa, dead from a beating so severe that it had ruptured most of his internal organs.

Raynard's ugly death, itself tragic, is not the most important aspect of his story. More significant is that during his young life, Raynard was repeatedly at the brink of doom, yet society could provide nothing to help stay the final execution. He had suffered at least three previous injuries—a skull fracture, a broken leg, and scald wounds on both feet—each reported as possible episodes of physical abuse. Raynard's case, different only in its grisly details from thousands of others taking place each day across the country, highlights the weakness of current efforts to prevent the abuse of children. It exposes the awesome need for programs that will effectively reduce the suffering of little children and break the chain of abuse that links the generations.

At some point during Raynard's short lifetime might preventive measures have been introduced to end the relentless attack on the child and offer him—and his family—a chance for normal existence? Not all cases of child abuse are comparable, of course, and no one preventive measure, therefore, can work in all cases. In the view of a number of experts in the field, however, a range of existing programs appears to offer hope for reversing the rising tide of child abuse. Parke and Collmer have described six categories of such programs:

- *Parent Groups,* which provide abusive parents with an opportunity for group discussion and emotional support. Group members—often isolated in their own individual lives—report that they profit from knowing that other people have problems and feelings similar to their own.
- *Home Support Programs,* which involve lay therapists functioning as family friends of abusive parents. In contrast to typical social workers, who carry a load of 15 to 30 cases, an aid is assigned to only one or two families, with the aim of providing advice and support over an extended period on a regular basis, usually in the parents' home; the aid is available by phone day and night, and the parent is encouraged to make contact during a crisis.
- *Hot Line Telephone Services,* organized along the lines of those successfully offered to suicidal persons. The public, made aware of these 24-hour emergency services through the media, is encouraged to call for support in a crisis situation, or to seek referral to an agency offering direct advice and therapy.

- *Crisis Nurseries and Drop-off Centers*, providing the stressed parent with 24-hour emergency short-term care for infants. Such facilities emerged from the frequent observation that when harassed parents are faced with the task of caring for their children without a break, abuse is more likely to occur. Elizabeth P. Rice and her co-workers have found even the occasional provision of substitute homemakers to be effective in relieving stress among overwhelmed mothers.
- *Child-Care Instruction*, based on the demonstrable fact that many abusive parents share common misunderstandings about child rearing. In some instances, the essentials of child care are taught in parent group meetings while in others, individual instruction is offered in the home. Emphasis is on the practical aspects of child care, including the troublesome area of child discipline.
- *Public Education*, aimed at increasing general awareness of the origins and nature of child abuse. Because many adolescents share only vague and unrealistic ideas about parental feelings and behavior, such educational efforts are especially useful to them.

Parke and Collmer offer an important reminder. Many claims have been made on behalf of various intervention efforts, but none has been sufficiently evaluated. Still, until systematic assessments are carried out, such programs must be regarded as vehicles of hope for both victim and abuser.

When Should Therapy End and the Law Take Over?

For those engaged in the helping process, a sharp and rending dilemma often presents itself—how to balance the therapeutic impulse with the feelings of revulsion, outrage, and censure evoked by the abusive parent. When is it appropriate for the psychiatrist, for example, to say: "This mother cannot be helped by me or anyone else. It is time to end our attempts at therapy and begin to take legal steps to protect the child from further harm." Child abuse experts Alvin A. Rosenfeld and Eli H. Newberger characterize the dilemma as one of "compassion versus control."

On the one hand, they point out, an increased understanding of the origins of child abuse has led practitioners to view abusing parents not as evil murderers "but as human beings caught in a complex web of personal and social deprivation which inhibits the normal loving relationships between parents and their children." Behavior which an outside observer might regard as destructive or even criminal is viewed by those involved in its treatment in terms of the patient's family dynamics, past and present. In effect, abusive parents are seen as victims and thus effectively relieved of responsibility for their actions. As a result, the clinician is expected to approach each case with "an abundance of human kindness" and without a punitive outlook.

While such an approach often yields good results, Rosenfeld and Newberger are quick to spot its limitations in many instances. "We have seen injuries and fatalities which are traceable to a physician's, nurse's, social worker's, or judge's inability to act on perceived danger, for fear of alienating the parents," they write. While the clinician proceeds with "utopian notions about the curative power of love and genuine concern," the child may suffer and die. Rosenfeld and Newberger quote typical comments by clinicians: "Perhaps one more week." "This time I'm sure she won't do it again. We had a really good talk." These, they say, are the familiar refrains of the professional who has become overly committed to the notion that it is the family as a whole that is the victim. Meanwhile, the baby suffers—or is destroyed.

Themselves seasoned in the diagnosis and treatment of child abuse, Rosenfeld and Newberger acknowledge that the compassionate stance must be tempered in many cases by a rational coming to terms with the risk to the child; an approach may be substituted that involves, for example, legal action to limit and contain abusive behavior. In this event, the clinician—or an administrator in the role of supervising treatment—proceeds on the conviction that individuals must take full responsibility for their actions, and that the State will hold them accountable. The helper in this case is not inhibited from taking the drastic step of signing a care and protection petition in the juvenile or family court. For the helping professional, it is difficult to take the role of the "not so friendly policeman who may blow the whistle on an intolerable situation." Hence, such a role may better be taken by the administrator of the case instead of by the actual therapist.

According to legal expert Wald, about 150,000 child "neglect" proceedings are heard each year by juvenile courts throughout the country. They are instituted to protect children who are inadequately cared for or victimized by their parents. If a child is found to be neglected, the court can order that the parents accept supervision and therapy as a condition of continued custody or that the child be removed from home and placed in a foster home, group home, residential treatment center, or institution. Available data, Wald concludes, indicate that as many as half of neglect proceedings result in removal of the child from the natural parents' home.

Rosenfeld and Newberger propose a number of criteria that clinicians might use to help decide whether an abusive parent should best be approached with compassion or control. If the child's injuries appear to be the result of an isolated experience triggered by stress, if the parent shows some concern or guilt, if the parent's behavior is not deviant in other ways—for example, alcoholic or criminal, if the child is seen by the parent as basically good and worthy of love, if the parent is able to view the child as a separate entity ultimately worthy of compassion and empathy, and if the parent appears to have sufficient strength of personality to be able to learn to control violent and aggressive impulses, then a compassionate stance appears appropriate. If, on the other hand, the child is the victim of severe and recurring injuries and if the parent seems unconcerned, displays other deviant behavior, sees the child as intrinsically "bad," cannot distinguish the child's needs from his or her own, and lacks the psychological health and adaptive strength to deflect harmful impulses, then an intervention approach weighted toward "control" may well be invoked.

Ultimately, the best hope for all lies in the development of techniques for anticipating child abuse, for preventing it before the pattern begins to take hold at all. The work of one seasoned research team is directed toward this end.

An Early Warning System

At the National Center for the Treatment and Prevention of Child Abuse and Neglect in Denver, Kempe and his coworkers have acted on the conviction that it may be possible to pick up signs of trouble between the newborn infant and its mother at birth. Children who are most likely to be battered later can often be identified from their mothers' reactions during labor, and during and after delivery, Kempe believes.

One of the important clues to future difficulties for the child, for example, is lack of direct eye contact between parents and newborn, says Kempe. Other parental reactions that might suggest future problems of child abuse and neglect include lack of an active interest in the baby, unreasonable levels of expectation toward newborns, disappointment over the child's sex, hostile reactions, and inappropriate comments.

Kempe believes that, as a result of his early identification techniques, prevention of major injuries is possible. "We can do nothing about how people are raised. We can do nothing about how they see their children. But we can from the very first do something about lifelines and rescues and about crisis management." Kempe believes that his approach can identify families who need extra help—that is, "outreach services" that all potential child abuse victims should have.

In the Colorado study (in which Kempe's collaborators were Jane D. Gray, Christy A. Cutler, and Janet G. Green), 100 mothers believed capable of "abnormal parenting practices" were evenly divided among a High-Risk Intervene (HRI) group and a High-Risk Nonintervene (HRN) group. Fifty mothers at low risk for abnormal parenting were selected as controls. The following methods were used in collecting information;

- A prenatal interview, with information being gathered on the parent's upbringing, feelings about this pregnancy, expectations for the unborn child, attitudes toward discipline, availability of support systems, and the present living situation
- A questionnaire administered to the mother during the prenatal or early postnatal period and covering the same ground as the prenatal interview
- Assessment of mother-infant interaction through forms completed by the labor and delivery room nurses or through videotapes
- Observations and/or interview during the postpartum period

As it turned out, "information gained from observers in the delivery room was most accurate in predicting potential for abnormal parenting practices." The investigators add: "If delivery room observation is not feasible and only one opportunity for evaluation exists, the early postpartum period affords the best opportunity. . . ."

Intervention was provided by a pediatrician, who examined the baby in the newborn nursery, talked with the parents, and scheduled the first pediatric visit when the infant was two weeks old. After that, the doctor saw the child bimonthly and at other times when the mother or the doctor felt it necessary. And this physician also telephoned the family two or three days after the child left the hospital and during the weeks when a clinic visit was not scheduled. The pediatrician also provided support whenever a medical or other crisis was present. The families were not told that this service was exceptional. Also included in intervention were weekly visits by public health nurses. Lay health visitors—persons who assess the child's general health status, offer emotional support to the family, and provide liaison with the health system—were used where indicated.

When the children were at least seventeen months old, home visits were made to 25 randomly selected families in each of the groups under study. Some of the findings:

• No child in the HRI group (high risk, intervention) and none in the low-risk group suffered an injury thought to be secondary to "abnormal parenting practices" that was serious enough to require hospitalization. However, five children in the HRN group (high risk, no intervention) required inpatient treatment for serious injuries, which included a fractured femur, a fractured skull, barbiturate ingestion, a subdural hematoma, and third-degree burns.

One of the five serious injuries [the burns] was preceded by relatively minor inflicted trauma, including cigarette burns, scratch marks and strap marks. These all received medical attention but were never reported, nor was an attempt made to involve other helping agencies in an effort to prevent further injuries. There is a possibility that the third-degree burns and the resulting contractures could have been prevented if intervention had been initiated promptly. In another case, a subdural hematoma and its resulting intellectual deficit and neurological handicap might have been prevented if intervention had been instituted during a "social admission" to a hospital just prior to the injury. If appropriate interventions to alleviate social pressure had been undertaken at this point, there is a possibility that the injury would not have occurred.

• Possible indicators of high risk had been considered to be the mother's race, age, and marital status, and the family's socioeconomic level. As it turned out, the mother's race was *not* a significant variable. However, single and young mothers were considered a higher risk for abnormal parenting practices; also "there was a trend toward 'financial difficulty' in mothers in the high-risk groups."

The Denver investigators arrived at a conclusion that is reported forcefully in their own words: "Families identified as being in need of extra services must have access to intensive, continuous intervention which is both positive and supportive. It makes little sense to provide excellent prenatal, obstetrical, and neonatal pediatric care in our hospitals, only to abandon the most needy young families at the hospital door and leave to chance, or to parent motivation, the needed access to helping professionals."

Such prediction efforts, Parke and Collmer believe, are among the most important recent innovations in the area of child abuse research. If they are successful in identifying potentially abusive caretakers, education programs for parents can begin immediately after the child is born—thus short-circuiting the developing patterns of interaction that portend later abuse. It is far easier to prevent the evolution of such patterns than modify them after they have taken hold.

The preventive approach is typified by a program initiated at the Cincinnati General Hospital and is described by Parke and Collmer. Teenage mothers are recruited during their hospital stay to attend weekly group discussion classes aimed at teaching them how to interact with their infants and stimulate them. The mothers are supplied with basic information about normal infant development, thus correcting unrealistic parental expectations. And, through direct instruction, role playing, and the imitation of models, the mothers learn to become more effective caretakers.

In thus providing parents with the capacity to deal well with their children, we may yet reverse the inexorable chain of violence that now binds the generations.

9

Schooling for Life

Fifteen years ago, when Teddy was seven, he encountered a brutish teacher to whom he scrawled the following note:

Dear Mrs. Hall:

I have many questions: First, why do you pick on me? And why do you think I am always asking stupid questions even before I have asked the question? And if you get an "F" in school citizenship do you fail the year?

Teddy Segal

That anguished message was undoubtedly written in desperation and dark foreboding. Its author is a creative and verbal young man who, from earliest infancy, has absorbed information and inspiration like a sponge, whose thirst to know and to understand was strong and insistent from the instant he drew breath. Teddy's encounter with a hostile and insensitive teacher temporarily thwarted his inquisitive nature and soured him for a time on one of the most delicious experiences of his life: the act of learning. More important, the encounter shook his developing self-concept to its roots.

Teddy was fortunate. The home to which he returned each evening was a place of support and stimulation. The scars inflicted by an inadequate teacher were compensated by the love and encouragement of his parents.

Not every child is so fortunate. For countless millions of children, school is the central feature of life—not only the source of friendships but the sole well of adult stimulation, leadership, and inspiration from which they can draw. Moreover, many of these children approach their school experience in a psychologically vulnerable state, already wounded in the war waged by millions of our young for emotional survival. When the school bell inexorably rings each Monday morning, they move into the classroom from an unstable and threatening world, bringing with them the emotional scars and psychic traumas suffered in their private worlds outside.

Applying national mental health statistics to a class of thirty elementary-school children, we may safely conclude that at least two of them will later spend some time in an institution for the treatment of a psychosis, five will suffer severe depression, and eight or more will enter marriages ending in discord and divorce. The teacher who looks out at the scrubbed faces of children each morning might well pause to consider not only the day's lesson plans but also the tides of psychological pain which threaten to engulf the children in his or her care. For many of them, the classroom is the last bastion of hope for emotional stability and well-being.

Molding a Child's Self-image

A child's emerging self-concept can dramatically affect the course of development, and the teacher's impact on it can be enormous. The seven-year-old, for example, who feels confident and masterful will mature along a track quite different from one who feels unsure and inadequate. Many of the child's self-doubts, it is true, arise from within, but they can either be reinforced or reduced by the outside world; still other childhood anxieties might never take root were it not for the ego-destroying message that key adult figures so cavalierly deliver to the young.

It is in the school especially that children's perceptions of their capacities and competence take hold; here they learn to recognize their self-image—and begin to behave accordingly. The power of a teacher to influence that image is awesome. All of the necessary psychological forces are in place. The insistent need to please authority figures, or at least to capture their attention, is already embedded in the mind and heart of the student; the teacher is in command, the student is in the subservient role; and a system of rewards and punishments is on display or strongly implied. It is just this confluence of factors that provides a fertile ground for subtle psychological control and manipulation of the self-concept, no less in the classroom than in the psychotherapist's office or the captor's brainwashing cell.

The power of a teacher over the young schoolchild arises in large part also from her similarity to mother. For the child newly introduced to school, teacher is often a psychological—and, sometimes, even physical—replica of the mother reluctantly left behind at home. Most often, the child's first teacher is a woman. Especially if they are both members of the same social class, her appearance, attitudes, and actions are similar to the mother's. The young child looks to the teacher as a source of support away from home and knows quickly that she will reward "good" behavior and punish "bad."

In a 1963 Columbia University doctoral dissertation, Daisy Franco found school beginners tended to have remarkably similar views of their mothers and teachers. Franco's study was based on the well-grounded psychoanalytic theory that childhood feelings and attitudes toward parents are readily transferred onto others. Evidence of such transference did, in fact, emerge. If the mother was perceived as a disciplinarian or as a helper, the teacher tended to be seen likewise. Moreover, this correlation persisted throughout the school year, even among those children whose perceptions of mother and teacher were unstable. A child's view of his or her mother might change, but it did so in tandem with that of the teacher.

Among the 75 kindergarten children tested by Franco at the beginning of the school year, 38 percent expected violent physical punishment from both teacher and mother; at the end of the year the percentage had changed hardly at all. Since there was no reason to believe that the teachers actually inflicted physical punishment, Franco concluded that the children's unrealistic expectations must have reflected a distortion of their perceptions of the teacher, transferred—at least in part—from their views of their mothers.

In the light of findings such as Franco's, it is clear that the teacher's impact on the student can be enormous—in fact, life making or life crippling—as was dramatically demonstrated a few years ago in a study by Robert Rosenthal and Lenore Jacobson. These researchers gave a battery of intelligence tests to a group of grade school students and told them that the results would be fed into a computer and then communicated to their teachers. When the teachers were informed who the brightest 20 percent in the class were, they were amazed; the great majority were very ordinary students. They felt, nevertheless, that the computer must be right and accepted the outcome of the tests.

The result was a dramatic change in the teacher's attitude toward the "brightest" students. It was now graced with respect and confident expectations of success. The impact on the children was remarkable. A follow-up study revealed that the average IQ test score of these children, formerly considered totally ordinary, was now significantly higher than that of their fellow students.

The experimenters then revealed the truth to the teachers. No computer had been used. The tests had never been scored. The "brightest" 20 percent had been chosen at random. The amazing transformation in the students' performance could only have resulted from the altered attitudes of the teachers.

The universality of the findings by Rosenthal and Jacobson has yet to be established in various school settings and for all children. Still, it is apparent that many teachers often transmit unambiguously their expectations to their young subjects, who, like the students in the experiment, then begin behaving in ways that validate those expectations. The children faithfully begin to play the role which the directors of their life's scenario have laid out for them, and a self-fulfilling prophecy is set in motion.

The actual mechanics by which teacher expectations are communicated are not altogether clear. Words are evidently not essential, however. Rosenthal and Jacobson believe that subtle features in the interaction between teacher and pupil may be enough—for example, the teacher's tone of voice, facial expression, or posture.

Psychologist Alan L. Chaikin and his associates used a number of such nonverbal cues to study how the teacher's expectations are actually transmitted. He found that teachers anticipating superior performance from their students engaged in more positive nonverbal behaviors—among them, smiling, leaning forward toward the student, making eye contact, and nodding the head—than teachers with either no expectations or with expectations of only inferior performance. Chaikin's results strongly suggest that the teacher need not tell the students outright what the world anticipates from them. The message is there in subtle yet potent ways.

The data from these studies carry an important message. The dynamic impact of the teacher's attitudes on children is clearly even greater than many have heretofore suspected. In our children's journey through school, they are likely as a result to develop images of themselves that will serve them either well or poorly later, in the real world outside the classroom.

How the Teacher's Personality
Can Affect the Child's Mental Health

Equally significant in its potential impact on the child is the personality of the teacher. It is remarkable that although we speak routinely of selecting our doctors, psychiatrists, or lawyers on the basis of their personalities, the pairing of teachers with our children is left altogether to chance.

Over three decades ago, psychologist Arthur T. Jersild surveyed a sample of schoolchildren to find out what kinds of teachers were typically liked and disliked. Pleasing physical characteristics such as good grooming, a nice voice, and attractive appearance were important, and so were such teaching qualities as being interesting and enthusiastic and giving children a role in class affairs. But the children also emphasized heavily a number of traits of personality—being kind, cheerful, natural, even-tempered, fair, consistent, and impartial. There is no reason to doubt that the same characteristics are equally important to the schoolchild today. They differ little from those traits which school administrators typically regard as the earmarks of the effective teacher.

Do children know what kinds of teachers are best for them? Do their preferences embody the kinds of traits that would significantly advance the child's intellectual and emotional growth, or are they essentially self-serving? The evidence from research is that children may, indeed, know best.

In a study by Louis M. Heil and Carleton Washburne of fourth, fifth, and sixth graders, three types of teachers were distinguished on the basis of psychological tests. One group was made up of *turbulent* teachers, whose underlying aggressive feelings are likely to be expressed both in words and actions. Such teachers do not appear to be too concerned about being accepted by others, nor are they particularly warm or emphathetic; to their charges, the turbulent teacher is likely to seem blunt, impulsive, unpredictable, and tense. A second group was made up of *self-controlled* teachers—methodical, self-disciplined, and intent on making things run smoothly. Such teachers are not likely to expose their thoughts and feelings freely or to search for the limelight; they tend to be sensitive to the reactions of others and responsive to their ideas. Standing in sharp contrast to the others was a third group of teachers identified as *fearful*—for example, over being alone or of their own sexual impulses. Such persons tend to feel helpless, dependent, and defensive; they are very conscientious and rigid, afraid of doing the wrong thing, and irritated by those who do not abide by the rules.

Heil and Washburne analyzed the relationship between teacher personality and the students' academic growth and social development. In general, children made the greatest academic progress under the self-controlled teacher and the least under the fearful teacher; children under self-controlled teachers averaged about half again as much academic progress as those under fearful ones. Similarly, growth in "friendliness" during the school year was significantly greater under self-controlled teachers than under either turbulent or fearful ones.

Subsequent studies appear to support these results. Students seem to prefer—and to profit most from—teachers who are warm, empathetic, poised, graced with self-assurance and enthusiasm, and interested in pursuing their link with parents and the community.

The private conversations of schoolchildren frequently reveal their strong feelings about the teachers who are so much a part of their lives. We tend too often to dismiss our childrens' observations as petulant and self-serving when, in fact, they may reflect startlingly accurate insights into the corrosive personalities of the teachers who influence them each day. When young elementary-school children say, "I hate my teacher because she's mean" or "I can't stand the way Miss Brooks talks to us," they may be conveying clearly how much impact the teacher is having on their own development.

In a series of revealing studies spanning over a decade, Hugh H. Anderson and his colleagues analyzed the contrasting effects on students of teachers who were either "dominative" or "integrative." The first group was overbearing, authoritarian, rigidly insistent on conformity and given to using force, commands, threats, shame, and blame as psychological weapons in the classroom management of children. The second was inclined to more democratic and humane approaches, extending invitations rather than commands to activity, questioning the children about their interests, showing sympathy, and participating with children in their tasks.

Anderson found that children assigned to a more integrative teacher tended to behave in a more mature manner than did children taught by the more dominating type. They showed significantly greater spontaneity and initiative and more constructive attitudes in social relationships. Children subjected to a dominating teacher, on the other hand, showed significantly more nonconforming behavior, paid less attention to their work, and engaged more in disruptive activities.

"If it is a pedagogical objective for a teacher to reduce the conflict and increase the harmony in her schoolroom," Anderson has written, "then the study showed that the dominating teacher was defeating her own purpose." Such teachers, lacking insight into the child's needs, frequently induce more frustration than affection; the result is aggression by the child—and, in many cases, counterattacks by the teacher.

School Authorities as a Socializing Force

Many parents view the school as the primary place where their children will learn to become law-abiding members of the community, and to live by the rules that society imposes on its citizens. It is in the classroom and playground, after all, that children become involved for the first time not only with their peers, but with forces of authority outside the home. The teacher, the principal, the pupil personnel worker—all of these represent potent vehicles for orienting the child's attitudes toward laws that govern us all. The nature of those attitudes may portend a great deal about the child's ultimate adaptation and adjustment to the world beyond the school gates.

How does a child learn best not to infringe on the rights of others or to thwart society's forces of authority and restraint? Although disobedience of children undoubtedly ranks among the major frustrations of parents and teachers alike, relatively little attention has been given to clarifying the role authority figures and law enforcers play in shaping the child's tendencies either to misbehave or to comply.

June L. Tapp, professor of child psychology and criminal justice studies at the University of Minnesota, working with social science researcher Felice J. Levine, has attempted to close some of the gap in our understanding of the subject. Their research efforts have been devoted to enlarging our awareness of the processes by which children learn to operate under the rules and regulations of society.

Tapp and Levine set out to develop a deeper understanding than we now have of just how children view authority, justice, and the role of law in society. They studied children, both black and white, in the United States, as well as in Denmark, Greece, Italy, India, and Japan. The researchers were surprisingly successful in getting the children, all of them between the fourth and sixth grades, to talk about some loaded issues: What is a fair rule? What would happen if there were no laws? Is it ever right to break a rule? Who can make you follow the law? What are the effects of punishment?

Tapp and Levine found with few exceptions that American children—black and white alike—were astoundingly similar in their views
about human nature and the need for rules. Like youngsters throughout
the world, American children recognize the role of laws in controlling
crime and violence, disorder and anarchy, and in establishing boundaries for human behavior.

The children voiced a surprisingly fearful, distrusting view of
humanity. They saw rules as essential to keeping people orderly;
without them, they believed, violence and crime would inevitably
erupt and engulf the world. There was a consuming sense that violence
lurks within us all—that anarchy, disorder, chaos, and the unbridled
search for personal pleasure would be rampant in a society without
rules. "There would probably be all kinds of different murders and stuff
like that," said one child. "People would be going crazy. There would
be all kinds of burglaries, stealing cars and stuff." Another child, a
fourth grader, believed that "it would be a lot of disorganizing in the
world. You know, people would be going around killing each other.
There wouldn't be any school or anything like that." One girl observed
simply that "everyone would do what they wanted."

Although children appear to seek rules to maintain an orderly world,
Tapp and Levine found that young people do not see the adherence to
compliance systems as unconditional. With good reason—for example,
to save a life—rules could legitimately be violated. Children appear to
require a fair and rational system, one that emphasizes equality and
stresses participatory consensus.

The children's perceptions of authority tell us a great deal about the
way the school environment affects the students' view of the world.
"Who can make you follow a rule?" the children were asked. From
their responses, it was clear that strong emotional attachment to authority is a more important feature than the power of punishment in
enforcing rules and in gaining compliance. Severe or hostile punishment meted out by teachers—or police officers or parents—is apparently not an effective technique for either obtaining compliance to
rules or inducing a devotion to the law. Instead, a sense of close
personal affiliation emerges as the key element in the socialization
process, and in encouraging what the investigators describe as "the
acceptance and internalization of social and legal norms."

That is the social scientist's way of saying that children will tend to
follow the injunctions of those whom they love, not those who engender fear or hate. It is, in the researcher's language, the power of

"persuasion to virtue" rather than coercion that induces compliance and that institutionalizes deterrence. A strong identification with a teacher charged with enforcing the rules will lead a young student not only to emulate adult standards but to absorb a commitment to the law as a positive force in life.

If children are to exhibit respect for law, Tapp and Levine contend, "teachers must also be persuaded that the law is respectable—and to behave as if they do." The credibility of our children's teachers and their role as models are probably no more quickly eroded than at the moment they themselves resort to arbitrariness, coercion, or, worse yet, physical abuse in the name of education.

Teaching Aggression and Violence in the Classroom

Like parental child abuse described earlier, corporal punishment by teachers carries a long history. Over the centuries, despite an occasional voice of enlightenment, the approach of educators has too often been punitive and harsh, and their treatment of the young abusive rather than compassionate. School personnel have traditionally assumed that their task of educating the young bestowed on them the option of applying physical force whenever they deemed necessary.

Whipping children has traditionally been defended by teachers and schoolmasters as a means for ensuring the child's moral and intellectual development. Five thousand years ago, in the schools of Sumer, "a man in charge of the whip" punished young boys for their errant ways. Philosophers of ancient times used the rod without mercy, and Roman schoolmasters used a tough stalk of the giant fennel plant to inflict their will on the young children. The teachers of England and colonial America of the eighteenth century are rarely pictured without the menacing birch in their hands, ready for flogging the young student. Not only were corporal punishments sanctioned by law in colonial America, but they were considered the avenue of choice for rearing the young in straight paths of learning and righteousness.

A measure of our progress is reflected in contemporary American legal history, circa 1975, when the basest authoritarian impulses of the nation's teachers were reinforced by no less than the highest court of the land. In October of that year, the United States Supreme Court upheld a lower court decision that under circumscribed conditions— the presence of a witness, a preliminary warning, and an explanation to parents on request—teachers may apply physical punishment in the schools. Less than two years later, in April of 1977, the Court reaffirmed that decision.

Equally significant, the ruling has been surprisingly well received across the country. With shocking frequency, parents *ask* school personnel to beat their children as deemed necessary. A 1969 National Educational Association poll showed that two-thirds of our elementary school teachers favored the "judicious use of physical punishment in the classroom." If research data on the origins of violence have any validity, the court, in effect, assented to the effective breeding of violence in our young by violence-prone teachers. As shown earlier, children who are exposed to physical abuse at home rarely learn either respect for the law or the impulse to help build an orderly world. Instead, they often become increasingly violent themselves.

Is the effect of abuse in the schools different?

According to evidence such as that provided by Tapp and Levine, abusive and arbitrary treatment engenders only anger, humiliation, and rage—and more violence. When children are "hit," they learn that arguments are readily solved by physical force, that might does indeed make "right." They learn that adults in our society respect physical force, not moral force. Children learn by example from schools using corporal punishment that to get what you want, you need only attack the weak. Their adult models are teaching them that the avenue for changing the opinions of others is violent coercion.

How prevalent is the use of teacher force?

Eighty percent of American schools permit the corporal punishment of children; only New Jersey, Massachusetts, and Maryland legally prohibit it. "In many states, a child has more legal protection if he is in a state institution than if he attends a public school," says St. Louis psychologist Gertrude J. Williams.

"If the suggestion were made that nonachieving, uncooperative school administrators, boards, and teachers should receive the corporal punishment applied to children it would be viewed as bizarre and demented," Williams argues. Yet the offenses for which children receive brutal treatment are not dramatically different—"talking out of turn," "not trying hard enough," or being "too aggressive."

Moreover, the contention that physical force can be selectively applied by teachers to those who "need" it is rarely supported by the facts. It is not the tall, menacing student, looming over the tiny, helpless teacher, who is the object of abuse. Younger children are actually more likely to be struck by school personnel than older children. In delivering such school "training," we are helping to add violence and aggression to the repertoire of coping strategies available to our young.

The Scars that Labels Leave

The welts left by the abusive teacher may be no more harmful in the long run than the psychological scars imposed by the psychological labels we affix to so many children in our schools.

What's in a name?

Since Shakespeare posed that question, it has been asked plaintively by millions of people who have felt unfairly victimized by a stigmatizing label. Few such victims of "naming" have as much reason to despair as America's schoolchildren. Armed with test scores and staff evaluations, contemporary psychometricians and educators have attempted to make our educational system more efficient by ascribing to our children a host of diagnostic labels that ostensibly will identify both their problems and potential. The results have often been disastrous—not only for the learning process but for the mental health of children as well.

In his book entitled *The Futures of Children,* Vanderbilt University provost and psychologist Nicholas Hobbs puts the issue squarely. Inappropriate classification, Dr. Hobbs contends, "can blight the life of a child, reducing opportunity, diminishing his competence and self-esteem, alienating him from others, nurturing a meanness of spirit, and making him less a person than he could become. Nothing less than the futures of children is at stake."

Hobbs's contention, well supported by research data, is hardly new. As early as 1905, Alfred Binet, the originator of the universally used Binet Intelligence Test for children, voiced his concern with the stigmata of labeling, and its effect on the growing institution of testing which he set in motion. "It will never be to one's credit to have attended a special school [for poorer students]," he wrote. "We should at least spare from this mark those who do not deserve it. Mistakes are excusable, especially at the beginning. But if they become too gross, they can injure the name of these new institutions." It is now 65 years later, and in the view of many, our mistakes are no longer excusable.

Retarded, hyperkinetic, delinquent, mentally ill, emotionally disturbed—a burgeoning list of such labels is being affixed to schoolchildren without our understanding their implications for the child's psychological well-being. Granted that diagnostic classifications can be useful in highlighting the need of a given child for specific services, the fact remains that, as currently used to classify our children, they are typically too broad and encompassing to describe the individual child in any meaningful way. Most often, such diagnostic nets simply imprison the child in a meaningless spiral of self-fulfilling psychopathology.

Jane Mercer, chairperson of the University of California Sociology Department at Riverside, is one of the leading figures now studying the deleterious consequences of labeling. She learned graphically of its hazards as a new Ph.D. just beginning her research career. Over 15 years ago, Mercer began work at California's Pacific State Hospital in Pomona with a group of senior investigators intent on assessing the problem of mental retardation. The aim of the research team was to determine the prevalence of mental retardation in the state of California. A simple task, it seemed—to count the number of mental retardates so that their prevalence would be known just as unequivocally as it is possible to know, for example, the prevalence of persons suffering from tuberculosis or diagnosed cancer.

The study focused on the city of Riverside—a medium-sized American city of approximately 100,000 and a self-contained community rather than a suburb of its neighboring metropolis, Los Angeles. Moreover, the city's social structure covers the full range, with an upper class that goes back to early settlement days as well as a middle and lower class. The population is about 8 percent black and 13 percent Mexican-American.

The researchers planned simply to locate persons with the "symptoms" of mental retardation, to count them, to describe who they were and where they lived, and to calculate prevalence rates for various subpopulations. During their study they communicated with 241 organizations in the community—for example, schools, clinics, hospitals, residential treatment centers, law enforcement agencies—and asked each one to provide information describing each mentally retarded person being served by that group. No standard definition was imposed; an organization could use whatever definition was customarily applied by its staff to label the retarded person as such.

The public schools clearly emerged as the leading source for labeling mentally retarded in the community. Not only had they named more persons as such than any other organization, but they shared their mental retardation labels more widely throughout the area. The register finally included 812 persons, of whom the public schools had contributed 429; of these, 340 were not identified by any other organization.

Mercer and her coworkers then compared the various kinds of information used by different agencies as a basis for labeling persons as mentally retarded. She found that the public schools rely primarily on IQ test scores but rarely consider any other aspects of the child's history such as medical status. Ninety-nine percent of their cases had been given such a test, but only thirteen percent had received a medical diagnosis. In contrast, California's Department of Mental Hygiene had gathered not only IQ test scores but also medical diagnoses for over 90 percent of its "retardates." The schools' labeling system, it appeared, was relatively loose. Nearly half of the persons nominated by them as retarded actually had IQs above 70, and 62 percent had no reported physical disabilities.

Considering their proportion of the community's population, it turned out, school-age children were clearly the most over-labeled group under study. Before children begin school, only those with the very lowest IQs and the most serious physical disabilities are identified. After graduation from school, too, only the most intellectually and physically subnormal adults continue to be labeled as retarded. It is while children are in school that they stand the greatest risk of being stigmatized with the "retarded" label.

The researchers found persuasive evidence of a tendency to label via stereotypes. Those in the lowest socioeconomic categories were greatly overrepresented on the register, while those from higher strata of society were underrepresented. Ethnic disproportions were especially marked among "retarded" public school children. There were four-and-a-half times more Mexican-American children and twice as many black children named as would be expected from their proportion in the population, and only half as many Anglo children. When the researchers compared Riverside school data with data from other school districts in the state of California, they found that this overrepresentation of Mexican-American and black children in classes for the mentally retarded was statewide rather than simply a local pattern. There is little reason to believe that the pattern is not national as well.

The Riverside study highlights how vulnerable schoolchildren are to the labels slapped on them by educational systems when they do not meet arbitrarily set criteria of IQ test performance—especially when they come to the testing room already bearing the twin stigma of poverty and minority status.

If the labeling process were to have no implications for the mental health and adjustment of the children involved, it would carry little significance. In real life, however, its impact is enormous. Behind the retarded label—and other brandings—inappropriately affixed by the school lies a significant threat to the child's well-being. Mercer's files are filled with illustrative case histories.

Bill, for example, is a black boy with an IQ of 66 and has been in "special education" classes for 6 years. Here is his mother's story:

They told me Bill needed help in reading and if he was put in special class he would be able to get better help because the class is smaller. . . . Bill is being retarded in special education. He doesn't like being labeled as retarded. It's affecting him. He begs us to have him removed from that class. His teacher told Bill she would see that he'll never get out of that class.

Mercer was motivated to turn her survey findings into constructive action and to see to it that the tens of thousands of children, like Bill, who are stigmatized by the school's labeling system, are given a fair chance to realize their potential. The result is a recently published testing technique designed to compensate for the "cultural bias" of standard IQ tests through which so many of our children are mislabeled.

The technique, known as the System of Multicultural Pluralistic Assessment (SOMPA) and designed for use with children five to eleven years old, compares a child's intellectual performance not with a fixed universal standard but with the scores of other children from a similar social and cultural background.

Mercer contends that when used in a school, the technique can enable teachers to distinguish between students who are generally retarded and those who—while still in need of special instruction—do poorly on existing tests because they are unfamiliar with the cultural content and values built into the test. "Many minority-group students are labeled retarded when they really have considerable potential," she argues. "They are put in slow classes when what they really need is something like an English-as-second-language program." Mercer's system is designed to help teachers make such judgments, and avoid the quick label.

The SOMPA approach was developed on the basis of studies of 2,100 children, five to eleven years old—a third of them Caucasian, a third Latin, and a third black—and consists of three separate scales. First, a child's medical history is obtained and scanned for biological conditions associated with learning problems, and tests are made of the child's physical coordination. Secondly, data are obtained from interviews with parents and others on how well the child is functioning not only academically—an area for which the traditional IQ test is used—but also in other areas, including, for example, relationships with other children, ability to get around town on his own, and spend money sensibly. Finally, data are accumulated on the child's family and cultural background.

Once all three sets of data are compiled, the scores on both academic and social performance are weighted through comparison with those of other children from a similar social and cultural background. When applied by schools, where the indicators of academic performance are of central importance, the corrected figure can be used in determining a child's "estimated learning potential," while the uncorrected scores are used to target immediate educational needs.

We might find that Bill, with an IQ score of 66 on the standard scale, is actually not unlike most children when he is compared with others from homes where the same amount of English is spoken and where the culture gap is equally great. "Or," says Mercer, "you might find a student with a standard IQ score of 110. When his background is taken into account and the score adjusted accordingly, he may have picked up enough of the dominant culture to score well above average for his own sociocultural group. His estimated potential may be 130, and he ought to be handled as a gifted child." Mercer sees many practical implications if the pluralistic assessment approach is adopted by schools. "It should help avoid situations in which normal, and even superior, students are misclassified as retarded," she points out. And, as a result, it will avoid also for many children the catastrophic impact of being arbitrarily removed from the mainstream of the educational process.

When a Schoolchild Is Removed from the Mainstream

One of the specially malignant effects of the labeling process is its frequent removal of the tagged children from normal contacts with their peers. Special classes can, of course, help fill the child's special needs. Too often, however, they are based on superficial criteria of intellectual performance, and serve not only to brand some children as inadequate but also to block mutually enriching relationships among children with complementary strengths and weaknesses.

The current trend toward removing atypical children from the mainstream of the school experience is often based not only on criteria of intellectual performance but other indices as well. In the American school system, there has been a triggerlike reaction to any child who appears different, who is scarred either by psychological circumstance or physical disability; such a child is quickly removed from the normal processes of education and cast into a setting in which he or she can no longer interact with the larger school society. Mercer is among those who see the process as disastrous not only for the labeled child but also for those children who remain in the mainstream. Special classes or schools may seem logical in the two-dimensional world of educational boards and committees but make little sense in the real lives of children, growing up in a universe of increasing diversity and change.

In building a school society containing pockets of children segregated by demonstrated intellectual capacities or by physical or psychological disability, we are actually removing from our young an important training ground in the continuing struggle we all wage for adaptation and adjustment. "We have come to recognize that those having learning problems can learn a great deal from being with normal peers," says Mercer, "and that those who are physically handicapped can profit from a normal environment as well. After all, children who are hurting either psychologically or physically are going to be dealing with normals all their lives, and they can hardly learn to do so if they are segregated during their entire childhood."

Mercer contends that we have also ignored the penalties for the "normal" child of segregating our children. "If you have no problems, how are you going to learn to work with, to be concerned about, to be tolerant of, to be kind and loving toward children who learn slowly, or are emotionally troubled, or are in wheelchairs? How can you learn to be a human being?"

The answer that Mercer and other proponents of "mainstreaming" typically are given is that only by removing atypical children can we protect them from cruel and abusive treatment by their peers. She sees the argument as weak. "The solution," she contends, "is not to isolate children for fear that they will be treated unkindly. It is rather to train children in acts of kindness. We have been working on the wrong side of the equation, and thus depriving the majority of children from an opportunity to practice the skills of compassion and concern for others."

One teacher recently described what transpired when a girl with a visual handicap became a member of her third grade class. The children worked hard at the challenge. They had to rearrange the furniture, for example, so that it was easier for her to get around, and they made accommodations in the playground, on the school bus—and in their hearts. The experience helped the children counter the natural tendency we have to set apart those who are disabled in some way, or who do not behave exactly as we would like, so that we do not have to think about them.

In expecting the least from our children, in assuming that they are incapable of adapting to the needs of the special child, we are, in effect, adding still another damaging tag to the long list they already carry. Labels of "meanness" or "selfishness" are hardly valid for all children, especially before we have even begun to test their capacities for compassion and caring.

The impetus to remove atypical children from the mainstream has led in a shocking number of instances to the exclusion of some children from the educational process altogether. The national controversy over the makeup of American classrooms so prominent in recent years has been waged mainly in terms of race. Slowly and painfully, the rights of children to be educated among their peers regardless of racial characteristics are being granted. Virtually overlooked in the racial desegregation controversy, however, has been the unwillingness of many school systems to accept children who are different in ways other than skin pigmentation.

Marian Wright Edelman, as founder of the Children's Defense Fund in Cambridge, Massachusetts, has highlighted the dilemma. In the Fund's report, *Children Out of School in America,* she and a team of researchers draw a profile of those children who are chronically excluded from the mainstream of the American educational process.

Specific case histories are telling. Dale, for example, is a bed wetter whose school requires every eighth-grade boy to spend a long weekend in the country to learn how to live outdoors. Because of his problem, Dale dreaded the trip. On the second night away from home, he wet his sleeping bag. His tentmates discovered his accident, told the counselors, who in turn lectured Dale. The child was mortified. When he returned home he pretended he was sick, and for two days refused to attend school. Several days later, the school principal asked Dale's parents to report for a meeting. He told them that Dale could not attend school unless he could control himself. Dale's mother explained that he lost control only at night, but the principal stood his ground, saying, "I can't stop him from going to school, but I can stop him from going to *this* school." He suspended Dale, ruling that he could not return until he could prove he was able to control himself.

Is Dale's case an exception? Edelman's group believes not. There are thousands of children with special needs whose education is aborted in triggerlike suspensions or expulsions. Problem children, she contends, are "pushed out," and in the process, their capacities for adjustment are significantly weakened.

Edelman and her team are convinced that only a fraction of the deeds for which children are cast out of school are serious. Their survey reveals that if a child is not white, doesn't speak English, needs help seeing, hearing, walking, reading, learning, adjusting, is pregnant or married, is not smart enough or is too smart, then the school officials are more likely to decide they don't want the student. A Japanese boy who pushed his teacher because he called him a "Jap" was suspended for three months. An Italian epileptic boy who suffered a seizure in school because his mother could not afford to buy his medicine until payday was threatened with expulsion unless his mother consented to have him placed in a special class for children with "learning disabilities." Edelman contends that some school officials have forgotten the reason they are there. "Expediency and efficiency in administration," she concludes, "have somehow become more important than educating children."

The capriciousness of the American school system in dealing with the atypical child is certain to erode rather than enhance the child's chances for good mental health. Edelman believes that the two million such children found out of school in her census data are only a portion of the problem. The figure ignores truants, children cast out for disciplinary reasons, non-English-speaking children who never enroll, and all the children in jail and other institutions who receive no education. While it is true that there are growing legal restraints against violating the rights of children in this way, the impulse continues strong to isolate from the rest of youthful society those children who, because they are "different," challenge our best instincts for compassion and caring.

Becoming What Your School Label Says You Are

Unfairly labeled children who are cast out of the mainstream of the educational process are inevitably perceived differently by their teachers, their peers—and, when the circle is complete—by themselves. Sociologists such as Mercer emphasize the difference between being victimized by a label and finally accepting it. In sociological terms, it is the difference between *primary* and *secondary deviance*. Primary deviance occurs when someone labels another person—for whatever reason—as "dumb" or "stupid" or "stranger" or "outsider" or as a mental retardate in the public schools; secondary deviance occurs at the point when the labeled individual accepts the tag, incorporates it into his or her own self-concept, and begins to play the role into which he or she has been typecast.

As part of Mercer's dissertation research, she studied a group of persons who had been placed in hospitals for the mentally retarded. Some of them had gone home to their parents, and some of them still remained in the hospital.

What distinguished these two groups?

Mercer found that those who went back to the family had not fully accepted the negative label; they had not made it part of their very being. They believed from the very beginning that the whole episode was a mistake—that they didn't belong in a hospital, that they were not mentally retarded.

Most important in the process, their families had backed them in their view that hospitalization was a mistake. Family members were intent on seeing to it that the victims were released from the hospital and reentered the mainstream as normal human beings. Primary deviance had occurred, and there is no doubt, says Mercer, that it was damaging; it put a dent on a school career and was stigmatizing. But it never became secondary deviance because neither the "retardate" nor the family ever accepted the label as legitimate.

In contrast was the group who stagnated in the hospital—a group with similar IQs, comparable on most vital statistics save one: *their* families *had* accepted the label. When Mercer and her team visited such families, they would find the mothers saying, "Oh, yes, it's too bad, he's mentally retarded. We know he'll have to live here with us all his life, he won't ever be able to earn a living." Secondary deviance had malignantly taken over in the life of the victim.

Often it is the mother, Mercer believes, who stops the process. "Hey, wait a minute," she says to the school, "you're wrong. My child is not what you said he is. He is not a delinquent, or retarded. He is going to make it."

Children frequently have a critical need for such a defender on the homefront against the onslaught of the school-induced erosion of their emerging sense of competence; to save themselves from the school's unfair portraits, children need to find at home an advocate, someone who will persistently rebuild their resources depleted by a society that has labeled them unfairly.

I recall how important this factor was in my own life. As a Jewish child growing up in the 1930s in a town rife with anti-Semitism, I was never allowed to forget that I was a member of a minority group. Many of my classmates and even some of my teachers were quick to point out how atypical I was, how strange my eating preferences, how peculiar it was to run home at sundown on Friday evening to begin the Sabbath, and how out of tune I was with the realities of society.

My father was a typical old-world Jew—bearded, scholarly, and strange to the mainstream of the community. I remember vividly walking along the streets of my city and becoming the object of pranks and jokes and slanderous jibes among those for whom "kikes" and "Jew-boys" were the scum of the earth. I sensed myself as an outcast and a deviant, labeled with what seemed to me to be an incurable disease called "Jewishness."

I had, however, a port in the storm to which I could return each night. It was my mother who reversed the damage begun by the school society. It was she who, in subtle or brazenly overt ways, would keep driving home to me that no matter what "they" say, I was the greatest—that I had brains undreamed of by my tormenters, and potential that would one day be unleashed in more benign settings. When I was taunted at school by cruel peers or unhappy teachers, I did not fall victim to secondary deviance. I returned home to my advocate and strength. Had I lacked that support, I may well have become bitter and defenseless against the erosions in my self-concept imposed by the world outside.

My own mental health was protected by a sensitive parent who evidently knew the distinction between academic achievement and personal growth, and who recognized that no amount of learning could compensate for pyschological blemishes that would threaten my sense of competence and well-being. Unfortunately, the same wisdom is not always found in the repertoires of those in the schools to whom we entrust our children.

Parents as Teachers

Often the emotional and intellectual growth of the child are advanced best by the combined efforts of adults who figure heavily in both of the child's worlds—school *and* home.

Since a child's first teacher is generally the mother, much research effort has gone into learning how she can make the most of her pedagogical opportunities to prevent academic failure and emotional problems in her children.

A good example of how mothers-as-teachers can beneficially influence their children's lives is provided by the research of Ira J. Gordon and his associates at the University of Florida. The families involved were all at the lowest socioeconomic level, where the children are more likely than other children to fail at school, develop personality disorders, display antisocial behavior, and become mentally ill. If the simple methods developed by Gordon's team and used by the Florida mothers can prevent or reduce the occurrence of dire outcomes in families at the lowest rung, they should be effective, also, when used in families higher up.

The Florida investigators worked with 150 families that had a baby three months old—the time at which a child begins to be particularly susceptible to the environment. They centered their attention on the mother rather than the baby because, when efforts are centered on the child, other researchers had found, substantial benefits accrue but tend to disappear soon after the efforts stop.

If mothers could be taught how to help a child develop his or her potential, Gordon reasoned, the effects should last considerably longer. They might even, in fact, be permanent. For the typical disadvantaged child, given no special help, lags a year or more behind most other children when school begins and never catches up.

Moreover, a relationship has been found between self-concept, a person's view of himself or herself, on the one hand, and mental health on the other. There is a relationship, too, between competence and self-concept. So the child who becomes competent in some school-related skill, such as reading, has a better self-concept and, therefore, a stronger foundation for mental health. The Florida project was aimed at developing not only cognitive skills, which would be needed for progress in school, but also favorable attitudes toward education and life in general. The mothers as well as the children were expected to be affected.

Gordon decided also to work with the mothers through a group of specially trained paraprofessionals—women from eighteen to fifty-five years old who had graduated from high school, had had some experience with children, could record what they did and observed in the homes, and displayed a warm personality. These were called *parent-educators,* or PEs. All were at the same socioeconomic level as the mothers they were to teach.

Scattered over 12 counties, the research population included representatives of both the urban and the rural poor. Some of the latter lived in unpainted cabins two miles from a water supply. Eighty percent were black; the others, white. In keeping with this racial distribution, 15 of the parent educators were black, and 3 were white. During the second two years, though, blacks sometimes visited white families, and whites sometimes visited black families. Gordon found that the PEs color did not influence either their reception or the project's outcome.

Weekly visits to the homes were built around the paraprofessionals' demonstration of an activity or task that had grown out of studies of how children develop and sharpen their skills and senses. The parent-educators had learned a great variety of these during a six-week training program. In the beginning, the tasks had been suggested by the child development authorities on the staff; later the PEs themselves contributed about half of them. Here is an example of one play task introduced during the child's first year.

With the baby lying on his back, hold a rattle about 12 inches above his or her stomach. Shake it until the baby looks at the rattle; then say, "See the rattle." Move the rattle slowly toward the baby's hand until he or she looks at hand and rattle simultaneously. Then say, "Get the rattle." When the baby grasps the rattle, smile, speak to him or her by name, and say, for example, "Johnny has the rattle." Purpose: To help the baby connect grasping with seeing, and action with action words.

During their visits, which lasted less than an hour, the PEs also checked on how well the mother and child were working on the task introduced the previous week, answered questions, and listened to the mother's problems. In middle-class homes, Gordon has found, these problems usually pertain to child rearing. But in the lower-class homes of this project, most of them grew out of the families' poverty; they concerned basic survival. Because the project was unable to handle such problems itself, it helped the parent-educators become referral agents to the available social services.

The Florida project used two control groups of 30 families each. The families in one of these received no services; those in the other received monthly visits by a nurse, who expressed interest in the family and took photographs. The nurse's activities were an effort to control for a spurious effect found in studies of environmental changes introduced among industrial workers—the so-called Hawthorne effect. In other words, the investigators wished to learn if a simple show of interest by the nurse would produce effects comparable to those that might occur among those served by purposeful changes—in this case, by the introduction of parent-educators.

The answer, by the time the children were a year old, was clearly no, so the two groups were merged. Half of the controls were then randomly assigned to the home visit program, and half of the children in that program were assigned to the control group. This was done so that at the end of three years, Gordon could make comparisons among groups that had been in the program for varying lengths of time and at varying ages.

For the last year of the project, Gordon established seven "home learning centers" to enable children in their third year to benefit from contact with peers. The centers were the homes and backyards of some of the project families. Three were set up in low-income housing projects in Gainesville and one in each of four Florida towns. A parent-educator directed each center. Assisting her was the home's mother. For advice, the PE could go to a university faculty member or graduate student.

Groups of five children would meet at the centers for two hours twice a week to engage in group and individual activity and to interact with the adults. The program was like an abbreviated nursery school experience. Weekly visits to the homes continued.

Except to administer tests and conduct interviews, the project has not been in touch with the children and their families since the former were three years old, but it is following them.

Major findings to date:

• When the children were six, those in four of the experimental groups scored significantly higher than the controls on the Stanford-Binet intelligence test. The groups were composed of the children who had been in the program all three years, or the first two years only, or the last two years only, or only the last year, when the program included both the home learning centers and the parent-educators' visits. The average IQ scores of the groups ran from 94 to 98 and placed them within the range of normal intelligence; the controls' average was 89 which placed them below that range. (The average IQ of black children, five or six years old, in five southeastern states is 80.) The white and black children in the program scored approximately the same. Although no significant differences appeared among the four groups, Gordon reports indications that the three-year program was the most effective.

• In third grade, 28 of the 30 children who had stayed in the program more than a year were in regular classes; only 2 were in special education classes—those for children who have fallen decidedly below grade level. However, 6 out of 20 control children were in such classes. This difference could be expected to occur by chance only 5 times in 100.

- In teaching the child mental and motor skills, the mother was also providing evidence of her love, interest, and expectations. Prominent among other family practices found to be important was the extent to which the family recognized the effect of the environment upon the child. To measure this factor, the investigators asked a number of questions, such as the following: Are there books in the home? Is the child taken to the library, the zoo, the museum, other places? Does the family know how the child is doing in school? When the child uses incorrect language, is he or she corrected? The answers to the questions were grouped into seven variables. For every one of these, when the children were six, there were differences between the mothers whose children were in the program and the mothers of the controls.

- The extent to which the family took advantage of community opportunities for learning was found to be particularly important.

- The stronger the mother's belief, when the child was three, that she had some control over events, the more likely her child would score well on the intelligence test at six. (This is the *locus of control* factor. Many people—those who are mentally more healthy—believe that they have some control over what happens to them; others believe that they are purely at the mercy of circumstances.)

- Nice things happened to the mothers, too. When the children were six, significantly more of the mothers in the project, as compared with mothers of controls, were married, had gone back to school or taken adult education courses, were holding a better job and had moved into better housing, and were involving their children in neighborhood or community activities. Moreover, significantly more of the project mothers wanted their child to finish high school at least, thought that their child should make his or her own occupational choice, and said their six-year-old was teaching other children in the family what had been learned in school. Such findings held particularly true of mothers who had been in the project all three years.

In other research, Gordon and his associates videotaped mother-child interaction beginning when the baby was three months old; then, nine months later, they administered tests of infant development. The families were all from below the poverty level. The study showed that the children who were most likely to score well on the tests were those whose mothers had talked *with* them rather than *at* them, had given them interesting things to do, and had encouraged them to continue an activity once they had begun it.

Also associated with high scores on developmental tests at the end of the child's first year—particularly in the case of girls—was a behavior Gordon calls *ping-pong.* He describes this as "a you-do-something, I-do-something, you-do-something, back-and-forth activity between mother and child. The mother elicits, the child responds, the mother elicits or corrects, the child responds, the mother elicits, and so on."

Also found to be important was a characteristic labeled *persistence.* The mother or the parent-educator would start the child on some activity and then step back. On the average, the longer the child continued with the activity—that is, the higher his or her score on persistence—the greater his or her developmental score at the age of one.

Eye-to-eye contact between mother and child—or *mutual gazing,* as the project termed it—turned out to be related to developmental scores, too.

Gordon points out that his research results, which emphasize the importance of the mother-child interaction, are similar to those of other child development authorities here and abroad. "The role of the caring adult—I don't want to limit this to the mother—in providing intellectual stimulation, security, and a loving relationship," he says, "seems to make a fundamental difference." He believes that such a person's influence early in a child's life, or the lack of such influence, helps determine—to a greater extent than any other single factor—not only intellectual competence but also emotional strength and mental health.

The Anti–Mental Health Bias of the Educational System

Because its emphasis is on achievement and performance rather than on personality growth and development, it is not surprising that the school often overlooks the child's long-range mental health needs. Kenneth Keniston, chairman of the Carnegie Council on Children, believes that, as a result, we are creating in our children the "computer terminals of tomorrow." He is convinced that we are victims of a growing emphasis on the child as a brain. We are nurturing, in his view, "a breed of children whose value and progress are judged almost exclusively by their capacity to do well on tests of IQ, reading level or school achievement."

Virtually forgotten, Keniston believes, is that "children, like adults are whole people, full of fantasies, imagination, artistic capacities, physical grace, social relationships, cooperation, initiative, industry, love and joy."

Keniston blames neither teachers nor parents but rather the pressures of an advanced industrial economy. Because of that pressure, he believes, we measure the effectiveness of education by whether it produces income increments, not by whether it improves the quality of life of those who are educated. Similarly, he contends, "we measure the success of schools not by the kinds of human beings they promote but by whatever increases in reading scores they chalk up. We have allowed quantitative standards, so central to our adult economic system, to become the principal yardstick for our definition of our children's worth." Our professed devotion to other human qualities we say we value more—for example, vitality, caring, imagination, resourcefulness, cooperation, and moral commitment—remains, in Keniston's view, just that.

Keniston is not alone in bemoaning the weak mental health orientation of the American school system. Cornell developmental psychologist Urie Bronfenbrenner sees our children's academic experiences as reinforcing rather than reducing their growing sense of alienation. In Bronfenbrenner's view, "the institution which has probably done the most to keep children isolated from challenging social tasks is the American school system."

American education, Bronfenbrenner believes, seems peculiarly one-sided in its emphasis on learning subject matter rather than the skills of living as a productive member of society. The result, in his view, is that "the schools have become one of the most potent breeding grounds of alienation in American society."

Bronfenbrenner sees it as significant that we have no accepted term in our vocabulary for education in its broadest sense—terms such as the German *erziehung*, the Russian *vospitanie*, and the French *education*. In many countries of Western and Eastern Europe, these are regarded as the core of the educational process; they take in not only "education" in the American sense but the development of the child's qualities as a person, including his or her values, motives, and patterns of social response.

Bronfenbrenner believes it is crucial for the healthy development of children that schools be reintegrated into the life of the community. To accomplish the task, he suggests the establishment in the school, beginning even at the elementary level, of what might be called *functional courses in human development.* These would be distinguished from courses or units on family life as they are now taught in the junior high school, in which the material is typically presented vicariously through reading or discussion, not through actual role taking. In contrast, the approach proposed by Bronfenbrenner would have as its core a responsible and active concern for the lives of young children and their families.

Such an experience could be facilitated by locating day care centers . . . in or near schools, so that they could be utilized as an integral part of the curriculum. The older children would be working with the younger ones on a regular basis. In addition, they would escort the little ones to and from school or center, and spend some time with them out of school. In this way, they would have an opportunity to become acquainted with the younger children's families, and the circumstances in which they live. This in turn would provide a vitalizing context for the study of services and facilities available to children and families in the community, such as health care, social services, recreation facilities, and of course, the schools themselves. Obviously, the scope of responsibility would increase with the age of the child, but throughout there would have to be adequate supervision and clear delineation of the limits of responsibility carried by older children in relation to the young. The same pattern of responsible involvement could also be applied in relation to other groups such as the aged, the sick, the disadvantaged, and those living alone.

A sense of community and commitment to others can be practiced and learned also within the school itself, Bronfenbrenner asserts. He cites as an example the Russian pattern of "group adoption" through which each class takes on responsibility for the care of a group of children at a lower grade level. For example, a third-grade class "adopts" a first-grade class in the same school or a kindergarten in the immediate neighborhood. The older children escort the younger ones to school, play with them on the playground, teach them new games, read to them, help them learn. Moreover, the manner in which they fulfill this civic responsibility enters into the evaluation of their school performance.

Some of these elements, Bronfenbrenner points out, are already present in the cross-age tutoring programs which have developed around the country. Here again, however, the focus tends to be on the development of skills and subject matter knowledge rather than concern for the total child as an individual and as a member of the larger community. Our emphasis, in short, has been too much on the child's gray matter and too little on matters of the heart and soul.

The Teacher as a Charismatic Figure

While it is clear that philosophies of education can affect the psychological development of the schoolchild, in day-to-day terms it is the individual teacher who remains the key influence. "The teacher himself," writes education expert Harold W. Bernard, "even more than the techniques he uses, is a key factor in the mental health of pupils—just as parent personality transcends child-rearing techniques."

Bernard is among many educational experts who is convinced that the central person in a child's school life can counterbalance a host of negative mental health factors outside. To be sure, much of this evidence is in the form of personal anecdotes related by adults who recall the remarkable influence of one or two of their teachers. Still, the evidence is persuasive. As Bernard puts it: "A mentally healthy teacher—one with confidence in himself and his pupils, who expects much and gets much, one who is concerned and recognizes that the time is now and the place is here—is a dynamic influence for mental health in the classroom."

In the lives of many children, it has been just such a teacher who has managed to turn the tide from self-depreciation and defeat to self-confidence and achievement. For example, sociologist Mercer has found a number of instances among young Southern California Chicanos who have bucked a tide of adversity and succeeded. "There is one thing that seems to be a common factor in their background," Mercer observes. "Almost inevitably, when you begin to talk to them about their own early life, they will mention that there was a teacher at some point who convinced them that they were competent even though the system was saying 'no.' It appears as a recurring theme. At some critical juncture—about the fourth or fifth grade—there was a teacher who made a real difference."

The case of Uvaldo Palomares is typical. Uvaldo had struggled through the early grades of impoverished schools. He was a thoroughly overlooked member of a large and desperately poor migrant worker family. Uvaldo's was the kind of deprived background that so often produces nonachievers, and in fact, at one time, consideration was given to putting him in a class for the mentally retarded. Only his mother's insistent protests reversed that decision despite the fact Uvaldo could not read.

Then, during his third year of repeating the second grade, as Uvaldo remembers it, he was on the playground one day playing marbles with a group of children. A teacher had apparently been watching him as he won all of the marbles from his playmates. After the game was over, she moved in and sat down beside him. "You know, Uvaldo," she said, "any kid who is smart enough to play marbles as well as you do is smart enough to learn to read. Now *you are going to learn to read.*" And so she began to teach him to read, convincing him all the while that he could "make it." Uvaldo's feelings about himself changed. He remembers vividly the enormous excitement he felt at having a teacher who was really convinced he could learn, who took hold, who was determined that he would succeed. She wasn't going to let him off the hook until he realized her expectations.

Uvaldo is now a successful California psychologist, saved from a lifetime of wasted potential by a teacher who really cared—and acted on her convictions. His case history highlights Bernard's view of the teacher's enormously powerful role in dealing with people who are still very much in the process of "becoming." "We must stop 'passing the buck'—blaming parents, society, and material conditions—and act on the assumption that what each teacher does will make a difference. We cannot wait for psychiatrists and psychologists to solve all of the problems for us. We cannot wait for the local or Federal funding that will supply better housing and equipment. The boys and girls are here and they will grow in some direction, whether or not there is guidance, intervention, correction, and concerned interest."

A rousing charge, but there is good reason to wonder if the audience is altogether equal to the challenge. Too many teachers fail to see themselves as a potent force in the lives of the young. The bland view they hold of their calling mimics that held by society. As an illustration, although we blithely entrust our children to their teachers, we pay these teachers—and evidently value them—less than we do plumbers, electricians, or orthodontists. Thus we continue to recruit into our children's lives adults who are unmotivated for the awesome task at hand. Only an inversion of such national priorities —and the attitudes they engender—can reverse the tides of frustration and stress that threaten to engulf so many children as they enter their schoolrooms each day.

10

The Power of Peers

The biblical scene is the Palestinian desert over 5,000 years ago. Abraham and Sarah have been blessed miraculously in their latter years with a son, Isaac. Living in their household is the bondwoman, Hagar, and her son, Ishmael, fathered earlier by the same Abraham.

In what may be the earliest recorded recognition by a mother of the power of peers, Sarah orders her husband to "cast out this bondwoman and her son." Ishmael, she fears, is an unwholesome influence, and despite Abraham's protestations, Sarah insists that he be removed from the environment of young Isaac. In the confrontation, God supports Sarah: "In all that Sarah saith unto thee, hearken unto her voice. . . ."

The resolution is a poignant and dramatic one: "And Abraham rose up early in the morning, and took bread and a bottle of water, and gave it unto Hagar, putting it on her shoulder and the child, and sent her away."

Sarah was acting out of the kinds of instincts of caring and concern that have always characterized great mothers really committed to their young. Since then, thousands of parents have similarly observed— either with satisfaction or alarm—the influence of friends and associates on the lives of their children. In the last quarter century, the hypotheses and inner convictions of parents have been refined and validated by a host of child development researchers. Their data are convincing. Sarah was right. Peers do, indeed, exert a considerable

232

force—positive as well as negative—on the destiny of the child. Put another way, children affect children more than many of us may have heretofore imagined.

The Need for Peer Associations

The urge to socialize, to relate to others, is apparent from the earliest stages of the child's existence. At the start, it is the mother who is the key "other person." In short order, however, the young infant becomes aware that there is a world of people alongside the main road that leads from sucking mouth to mother's milk.

The need to relate to other human beings is basic. We are all born with an "appetite" for human contact; a hunger for companionship, emotional support, and a sense of connectedness to society appears to be insistent in children from the beginning.

Even the youngest infant demands not only to be changed or fed but also to be raised up, held, hugged, fondled, made noises to. When you were six months old, you could already discern "friends" from "strangers"—people who really figured in your life from those who were just passing through, superficial and essentially unconnected. In terms relevant much later, you already knew the difference between the human contact demonstrated by a caring, sharing friend and the flat and empty stare of the "person" across the subway aisle.

The baby's first attachment, to the mother who fills needs and nurtures, is usually solid. Father may be special, and there is an awareness of brothers and sisters and other persons, but the baby does not yet differentiate among them or recognize their unique existence as independent beings outside himself. Differentiation emerges slowly, as he grows to form distinct relationships with them. Soon enough, the baby becomes involved in "parallel play." Starting at about age two, and for about a year and a half thereafter, he plays and talks alongside, rather than with, other children. He enjoys their company, but he does not yet recognize that they have something unique to offer.

The change is gradual. Usually sometime between the age of three and four, a child is likely to find himself with a pal, a peer who has stumbled into his life in the yard, in the nursery, in the park. Now it is only a short psychological step to group play, group friendships, and a purposeful selection process by which each of us relates especially to those friends who are most meaningful. From this point onward, the child's destiny will be determined in part by the power of peers.

Significantly, it is in the quality of children's early interactions with friends that we may see reflected best the outlines of their later adjustment.

What Faulty Peer Relationships Portend

"He just doesn't seem to get along with his friends."

The comment is often made by both parents and teachers about children who seem chronically unable to form satisfying or enduring relationships with their peers. A growing body of evidence—from both clinical observations and systematic research—suggests that this weakness may be one of the most potent early indices of later psychological difficulties.

Willard W. Hartup, director of the University of Minnesota's Institute of Child Development, is among those who view the quality of a child's interactions with friends as a powerful diagnostic index. "Among the most sensitive indicators of faulty development," he observes, "are failure by the child to engage in the activities of the peer culture, and to occupy a relatively comfortable place within it." Put another way, if you were to survey all of the facets of a child's life, the one which might be the clearest "tip-off" of the quality of the child's adjustment is his or her ability to enjoy rewarding friendships.

The view is based in part on the work of Merrill Roff, now enjoying the warmth of a California retirement, who was for years a professor and a leading figure at the University of Minnesota Institute for Child Development. In his research, he painstakingly tracked the factors operating during childhood that presaged mental health problems in later life. Roff was drawn repeatedly in his studies to highlight the role of peer adjustments, a factor which proved to be predictive with surprising efficiency of later psychological problems of various kinds. He has expressed his findings a number of ways, but their theme is constant: "Childhood behavior that is antagonizing to peers," says Roff, "precedes various types of adult maladjustment."

Roff's evidence stems from a series of follow-up studies in which children with problems in adjusting to peers were found many years later to suffer more than the usual range of mental health difficulties, including poor adaptation in the military service, disabling neuroses, or even psychotic states in young adulthood.

In one study, for example, Roff focused on 164 young men who had been discharged from the military service. While in the service, half of these subjects had compiled a record of conduct problems serious enough to lead either to dishonorable discharge or at least 60 days of confinement; their violations included, for example, theft or robbery, disobedience, assault on a superior, drunkenness, forgery, escape from detention, and breaches of regulation governing the possession or use of firearms. In the other group, serving as a control, Roff chose subjects of equal intelligence who showed no evidence of similar "acting out" or antisocial behavior. They had reached and kept a grade of sergeant or higher without any indications of disciplinary or behavioral difficulties in the military.

Both groups were made up of young men seen many years earlier in child guidance clinics. Roff went back to their case files to glean whatever indicators he could about the quality of their childhood peer relationships. The data culled from the files included observations by teachers of the children as they interacted among their peers, comments about the children recorded by visiting teachers or case workers, observations by psychologists during testing, diagnostic statements about children's social adjustment by psychiatrists, and statements made by family members.

Roff then carefully constructed a guide for evaluating each item of information as a positive, a negative, or a neutral reflection of peer-group adjustment. Among the positive items were signs of liking by the child's peer group, freedom from problems in class or on the playground, successful play with older children, and indications that the child was liked by girls, especially at adolescence. Typical neutral items included evidence of a shortage of friends or the tendency to play primarily with younger children. Items evaluated as negative were, for example, any sign of active dislike by the general peer group, inability to keep any friends, and being regarded as "odd," "peculiar," or "queer" by other children.

When Roff compared the two groups, the results were unequivocal. Those young men whose childhood records of peer interactions had been characterized by negative items typically encountered a host of behavioral problems in their military careers. The control group, made up of young men with good adjustment in the military, had no such pattern of poor peer relations embedded in their clinical files compiled years earlier.

Roff found that early peer-group difficulties tended to characterize also those suffering neurotic complaints in the military service later on. Youngsters who habitually antagonized their friends to an unusual degree were those whose lives some years later were scarred by anxiety reactions, conversion hysteria, obsessive-compulsive behavior, depression, and other neurotic symptoms.

Similar data emerged from Roff's studies where more serious and disabling mental illnesses were concerned. He examined 166 former child guidance clinic cases, of whom 83 were diagnosed as psychotic (primarily schizophrenic) in the young adult period, the remaining 83 serving as control cases. Again, the statistics told a consistent story. Those children who grew to be victims of severe mental illness had a more prominent history of childhood peer problems than those who did not.

Here is a description of one child, from his early clinic records:

Stubborn, aggressive, does not get along with other children, quarreling continually, resents authority and discipline, surly and shows disrespect for rights of others. Third grade teacher is a pleasant person who spoke of him with a great deal of heat and emotion. She said he is very peculiar. He comes to school with a chip on his shoulder frequently, and then anything you say annoys him. He hates being told to do anything. He is very resentful of authority. The only thing he likes to do is draw and he could sit and draw all day long . . . a slow learner and very mean. In a game, he will not take part as the other children do. He hates monitors, and they are always complaining about him.

And here is the same child, described in clinical terms, many years later:

Psychosis with psychopathic personality, paranoid trends. He was admitted to the hospital following an assault. On examination, he showed inappropriate emotional reactions, especially discussing his assault charge. When questioned regarding his resistive and destructive behavior on the ward, he merely passed it off as if he were justified. On the ward, he has been very noisy, assaultive, and aggressive at times. His statements often assumed a disconnected, disorganized, and illogical character. One month later he assaulted another patient and was abusive.

Roff's results are now buttressed by more recent studies which also portray a distinctively poor mental health future for the child with a history of difficulties in social adjustment. The prognostic power of peer interactions has been highlighted, for example, in the research of

Emory L. Cowen and his colleagues at the University of Minnesota, and more recently, at the University of Rochester. From their poor peer relations, a number of first-grade children had been "red-tagged" as being at greater risk for mental health problems later on. Now, after 13 years, these very children do, in fact, appear with a disproportionately high frequency on the Psychiatric Register of Monroe County, New York, a roster of patients receiving care in psychiatric facilities in that area.

Moreover, Cowen found that assessments of children's social competence by their own peers were by far more powerful predictors of later behavior disorders and the need for future psychiatric treatment than the views of parents, teachers, or even clinicians. The Rochester investigators concluded that while 8- to 10-year-old peers may not do as well as adults in identifying all forms of maladjustment, they are more sensitive in picking out "the real McCoy"—the peer who is destined to become more seriously and chronically disturbed as an adolescent and young adult.

Because peer relationships convey so much about a child's potential for emotional difficulties, it is hardly surprising that there is embedded in them, too, the seeds of healthy development as well. "There are some necessities in children's development," says Hartup, "that require interaction with coequals—that is, individuals who have the same kind of developmental status and competencies in the cognitive and social areas as they do. The relations between adults and children have evolved to serve a very special set of functions—to ensure basic survival, to help keep the child safe from physical danger and harm, and to help build relations with authority figures. But in some very critical areas of adjustment, relations with coequals are the key."

Many contemporary child development experts would agree. The imprint of peers on the child's personality is second only in importance to that of parents, and in some areas it is actually predominant. It is largely through the child's interaction with peers that many of life's most important attitudes and behaviors are shaped in the young—for example, learning to find sexual expression, to display and modulate aggressive instincts, to live by ethical standards, even to overcome disabling fears and anxieties and gain a sense of emotional security. All of these, and more, emerge largely from the give-and-take of peer relationships. Young friends, it would seem, are more than passive playmates. They are key instruments in the symphony of human development.

Learning Sexual Attitudes and Behaviors

When we were children, our parents viewed the task of teaching us "the facts of life" as a sacred responsibility. It was inevitably one of the awkward and poignant moments of family life when father or mother took a deep breath and attempted to discuss the unmentionable with their young. Our parents could hardly have known that in their children's sexual orientation, rather than playing the lead role, the parents must inevitably be only bit players at best.

Pioneer sex researcher Alfred C. Kinsey left little doubt that the child's sexual attitudes and basic sexual repertoire are shaped primarily by contacts with peers rather than adults. "Children," he wrote, "are the most frequent agents for the transmission of sexual mores. Adults serve in that capacity only to a smaller extent. Even before there has been any attempt at overt sex play, the child may have acquired a considerable schooling on matters of sex. Much of this comes so early that the adult has no memory of where his attitudes were acquired."

In the view of Hartup, it is peers rather than parents who wield the most natural influence in sexual matters. "If parents were given sole responsibility for the socialization of sexuality," he feels, "*Homo sapiens* would not survive." Hartup does not discount the well-intentioned efforts at sex education by contemporary mothers and fathers, but he reminds us that the parent-child relationship is hardly well suited to the task of helping the child adapt to the world of sex. One factor at work is considered to be the incest taboo, which creates a psychological chasm between the generations that is difficult to breach. Unquestionably important also are parental modesty, discomfort, and lack of information and explanatory ability. In consequence, it is often *only* through peers that children can engage in the information gathering and role modeling that help produce their sexual life-style.

The powerful modeling process among peers also accelerates the child's development of a sexual identity. Psychologists have devoted considerable efforts to studying how a child first learns to identify as a female or male and to assume society's norms for a particular sex. While it is true that *sex-typing*, as the process is called, first arises from the child's interactions with parents, there is strong evidence that it is the peer culture which powerfully supports and extends the process begun in the earliest preschool years.

A vivid demonstration of the power of the peer culture in early sex-typing is contained, for example, in a series of experiments by Skira Kobasigawa in 1968. He found that when kindergarten children are exposed to peer models who inhibit themselves from playing with toys generally considered inappropriate for children of their sex—such as dolls in the case of boys and guns in the case of girls—they more readily learn to exert self-control over inappropriate responses; in contrast, when the child is exposed to peer models who freely display behavior usually considered inappropriate to their sex, inhibitions are weakened, especially if the model is of the same sex. In the decade since Kobasigawa's study, differences in playthings between boys and girls have begun to disappear somewhat, but the findings still suggest what an important role peers can play in the development of the child's sexual identity.

It is a long step between children's play with peers and later sexual behavior, but do such findings imply nevertheless that deviant sexual behaviors arise from atypical or impoverished early contacts with friends? Hartup believes that many deviations—including homosexuality—are accelerated by a combination of early "hang-ups" with parents and later ones with peers. While peer modeling seldom fully explains either atypical or criminal sexual behavior, it may clearly be a contributing factor. Roff showed in 1966 that a history of poor peer relations is more characteristic of homosexual males than of a comparison group of heterosexual males, and individual case studies show with considerable frequency that persons committing crimes of sexual assault have long histories of peer rejection and social isolation.

Finding Out How to Behave Aggressively

As in the case of sex, children typically learn to deal with their instincts of aggression via their friends rather than their family. Some of the evidence comes from animal research. In his classic studies of primates (described later in this chapter and elsewhere in this book), Harry F. Harlow showed that it is through peer contacts that young animals build a repertoire of effective and acceptable aggressive behaviors and the capacity to cope with disturbing tides of aggressive feelings. Field studies of primates by psychiatrist David A. Hamburg and animal behavior expert Jane van Lawick-Goodall demonstrated also that socialization requires the kind of "rough-and-tumble" experiences with peers in which play alternately escalates into aggression and subsides into more benign and frolicsome interactions.

Parents can hardly provide a comparably natural environment for the normal development of aggressive behavior. The sometimes rough, give-and-take play experiences necessary for learning how to handle aggression are incompatible with the nature of the child's bond with the mother. Among all primate species, children maintain an abiding link to their mothers long after the time when their aggressive feelings begin to be tested, and a child can hardly experiment with "letting it all hang out" toward someone to whom he or she is still securely tied. While extreme case histories never prove a law of behavior, it is noteworthy how many cruel murders reported in the newspaper are committed by men who are described later as having been "loners" in childhood, dominated by their mothers.

Fathers, it is true, may contribute more significantly to the child's learning about aggression, not only because they more frequently model aggressive behavior for their children, but because emotional ties to the father appear to be less emotionally constraining than they are to the mother. Nevertheless, it is doubtful whether fathers alone can effectively socialize even their male children's aggression; the father's role in Western culture requires him to spend most of his time outside the family and, even in close-knit families, paternal contacts with the young child are insufficient to produce all of the learning required for the successful modulation of aggressive behavior.

Nature, it seems, has dictated that the child's relations with other children contribute more to the successful control of aggressive behavior than parent-child relations. "How can a child effectively learn everything he has to know about handling aggression," Hartup asks, "in a relationship where somebody is always bigger and more capable than you are?" Children who are constantly hostile or, at the other extreme, children who are unusually timid in the presence of aggressive attack, may very well have lacked exposure to the kinds of interactions with peers that teach a youngster how to express—and control—aggressive urges. Hartup believes that peer contacts which never allow for displays of aggression, or which counter aggression unreasonably when it occurs, may set the stage for difficulties in handling aggressive instincts later in life.

The child learns about aggression not only through direct interaction with peers but, as in the case of sex, by imitation. Years of research on the nature of peer interactions have convinced Hartup that peer modeling is "among the most powerful social influences to which children are exposed," and not only during late childhood and early adolescence but during the earlier years of childhood as well.

Nursery-school children, for example, learn quickly to behave aggressively when they are exposed to displays of aggression by their peers. California State University psychologist David J. Hicks showed this to be the case even when the tiny-tot models are observed on film rather than in the flesh. In one experiment, celluloid models were shown banging an inflated plastic doll with a bat, throwing plastic balls at the doll, striking it with a mallet, or punching it in the nose. Afterward, the little viewers were subjected to a mildly frustrating experience and then studied in an experimental room containing a variety of play materials like the ones used as instruments of aggression in the film. The frequency and form of aggression displayed by the children were significantly related to those absorbed during the earlier exposure to aggressive models. Moreover, Hicks's data suggest that emulation of peer models is even more frequent than that of adults.

It is hardly surprising that large-scale investigations support the contention by many parents that their children become more assertive and aggressive only *after* they attend nursery school. In two such schools in Eugene, Oregon, details of over 2,500 aggressive acts (including bodily attack, attack with an object, and invasion of "territory") and their consequences were recorded and analyzed by Gerald R. Patterson and his coworkers. The results showed that aggressive behavior was often strongly reinforced by other children who either yielded to the aggressor's wishes, withdrew from conflict, or surrendered something—for example, a toy or a favored place in line.

The nursery school often provides a surprisingly efficient setting for training young children in assertive behavior. Children who were passive or only moderately aggressive when they entered nursery school became more aggressive during the period of their attendance if they interacted frequently with their peers. When they began to participate in social activities, for example, some passive children quickly became frequent victims of aggression; eventually, however, they counterattacked, and it was not long before they began to initiate frequent assertive actions on their own.

As in any area of child development, however, the impact of the environment was a function of the child's own resources. Children, for example, who were socially passive (the "wallflower" type), did not show significant increases in aggressive behavior. Nor did some other passive children who did interact but were unsuccessful in their counterattacks against their more aggressive peers. Experiences with peers, it would seem, may result in substantial changes in aggression, but the extent of the changes is clearly influenced by the child's past history and personality.

Developing Moral Standards from Within

The very young child typically behaves as if she or he believes that society's rules are eternal and unchanging and that the power of adults to dictate standards of behavior is inviolate and total. In order to grow into true maturity and independence, however, each child must turn from what the great Swiss psychologist, Jean Piaget, described as "this objective moral orientation" to a subjective one, from living by standards of behavior which arise not from the outside but from within. According to the widely respected theory of psychologist Lawrence Kohlberg, we reach our most advanced stage of moral development when we can judge our actions by our own principles rather than by what will please others.

For that orientation to develop, the child needs opportunities to see moral rules not as dictates from a supreme and forbidding authority but as products that emerge from group agreement. Such opportunities are provided through the social give-and-take among peers. A child cannot learn to develop moral standards only from his family and teachers, because he sees these primarily in authoritarian terms; a peer group, on the other hand, inherently contains the dynamic checks and balances that alone can nurture moral development.

Piaget saw clearly that moral understanding arises in large part from the degree and quality of a child's social interaction. He described the very young child as being locked into a period of *egocentrism*— meaning not selfishness or preoccupation with self but rather the inability to put one's self in the position of another person and to see life through another's eyes. Young children are prisoners of their own perspective. Only later, as these same children interact with their peers, do they lose their egocentric orientation and begin to learn their role in society.

Experiments by Piaget and his coworkers showed that this early rigidity of viewpoint applied even to the child's perception of the physical world. Children were shown a large picture of mountains and asked how the mountains would look to a person far to the left in the picture, and to another person far to the right. The younger children were unable to entertain the idea that the mountains would look different when seen from different positions. Similar cognitive shortcomings surfaced when children were asked to think about the members of their family circle. Asked if he had a brother, a small boy said that he had one, named Paul. Asked then if Paul had a brother, he replied in the negative. Piaget interpreted this sort of mix-up as a sign that the child was unable to transcend his own perspective, to imagine himself in Paul's position, and therefore to realize that he himself was a brother to Paul. No commands to see things differently would alter the child's perspective. Only further growth and experiences with the physical and social world would accomplish the task.

Learning social perspective—to put ourselves in another's psychological position and to share a mutual responsibility for each other's well-being—also requires experience more than preachments and directives from the child's elders. It is the peer experience that helps transform the egocentric child into a person with the kind of social consciousness and moral sensitivity that spring from within.

Some of that experience is gained by copying, or modeling the behavior of peers. Although studies of aggressive behavior dominate the modeling research literature, this should not be taken to mean that children learn to imitate only negative traits. Positive and wholesome behavior is also readily transmitted from one child to another. When a child is exposed to an altruistic model, for example, altruistic tendencies are very likely to be strengthened.

In one experiment by Hartup and Brian Coates, preschool children watched a model attempting to solve simple maze puzzles, receiving as a reward six trinkets for each correct solution. The trinkets could then be placed for safekeeping in either of two nearby bowls, one of them designated as the subject's, and the other as belonging to a classmate. Acting on instructions from the investigator, the model consistently put five of the trinkets in the bowl belonging to the other child.

Having been exposed to a model of altruism, the subject then played the game himself, after his peer had finished his turn and left the room. The results were quite clear. Those who observed the model shared more of their trinket winnings than control subjects not exposed to altruistic models. The effects took place even though the model was not seen to be under any unusual pressure to share, or rewarded in any way—even with praise—for his generosity. Apparently, observation of the simple act of sharing awakens similar behavior among even very young children.

Peer models, it appears, can also induce in children the tendency to function either within or outside the rules of society. In an experiment conducted over 25 years ago, researchers Daniel Grosser, Norman Polansky, and Ronald Lippitt asked grade-school boys to complete a series of block designs and to enjoy an interval of relaxation between trials. The subjects were told that they could relax in whatever way they wished, but that in case they decided to play with the available toys, they ought to know that some of them were "forbidden." Some of the boys worked in the presence of a confederate who had been planted by the experimenter to remain at his desk and simply to relax during the break; other subjects watched a model who got up and played with the forbidden toys; still others, given the same instructions, completed the task with no one else present.

The subjects were clearly affected by what they observed. Those who saw other children playing with the forbidden toys broke the prohibition themselves most frequently, and those who saw models who remained passive throughout played with the toys least—less even than those who had no model to go by. Similar results have since been obtained by other investigators. They suggest that peer modeling is, as Hartup believes, an extraordinarily powerful tool in the child's development.

Finding Emotional Security

Many parents, committed to the happiness and well-being of their children, are frustrated at times over their inability to provide the emotional support, encouragement, or healing that a child appears to need at moments of stress. It might be well to acknowledge at such times the key role that peers, rather than parents, must play in meeting the insistent emotional needs of the child. Again, it is often friends rather than family who are critical and who are best able to lend the psychological support a child desperately seeks.

If they were to relate only to their family and other adults, children might easily conclude that they are unique in facing a particular anxiety or wrestling with a specific issue. It is in the peer group that children find others functioning at their own level of intellectual and emotional development, human beings with whom they can interact as equals, comparing perceptions of life and sharing stresses and conflicts. From their interactions with friends, children come to know that, psychologically, they are not alone—that their strange feelings of isolation or fear or aggression are shared by others. The memory of long, front-stoop conversations I had as a child with a neighbor friend will always live in my memory. It was from him that I learned, among other things, that other boys also bear unbearable anger toward their fathers, and that they, too, brood about such crushing issues as size of penis, or the smile of the girl across the school aisle.

Researchers have documented the capacity of peers, serving as models, to undo even disabling fears that beset a child. In 1967, a group of investigators headed by Albert Bandura studied 48 children between the ages of three and five who had been identified as fearful and avoidant of dogs. The children were exposed to either a "fearless" four-year-old model who demonstrated progressively stronger approach responses toward a dog, a dog with no model present, and a play period in which neither the model nor the dog was present.

Those subjects who observed the model interact with the dog showed a significant reduction in avoidance behavior, measured both immediately and one month later. These children were noticeably less avoidant than were the children in the other two groups.

The same effect takes place even when the peer models are on film. In a later study, Bandura compared the reduction of avoidance in children who had dog phobias when these children were exposed to films showing either one child or many children interacting with dogs. Both films produced reductions in avoidance behavior, as compared to the effects of watching a movie which did not include animals. The film with many models was the more effective, reducing fears sufficiently to enable the children to interact with dogs under potentially threatening circumstances.

Under extraordinary circumstances, peers may serve even more potent functions. In the very early years they can become the chief objects of the child's attachment and emotional dependence. This was dramatically illustrated in an unusual study conducted by Anna Freud of six German-Jewish orphans whose parents had been killed in the gas chambers during World War II. These children arrived at the same concentration camp when they were a few months old and were always together as a group thereafter. When they were all between three and four years old, they were taken to live together in a large country house in England, where they were systematically observed for a year. By this time, the dependence these children had on each other appeared to be similar to the kind of attachment normal children have toward their mothers. As Freud describes it:

The children's positive feelings were centered exclusively in their own group. It was evident that they cared greatly for each other and not at all for anybody or anything else. They had no other wish than to be together and became upset when they were separated from each other, even for short moments. No child would consent to remain upstairs while the others were downstairs, or vice versa, and no child would be taken for a walk or on an errand without the others. . . .

The children's unusual emotional dependence on each other was borne out further by the almost complete absence of jealousy, rivalry, and competition, such as normally develop between brothers and sisters or in a group of contemporaries who came from normal families. There was no occasion to urge the children to "take turns"; they did it spontaneously since they were eager that everybody should have his share. Since the adults played no part in their emotional lives at the time, they did not compete with each other for favors or for recognition. They did not tell on each other and they stood up for each other automatically whenever they felt that a member of the group was unjustly treated or otherwise threatened by an outsider. They were extremely considerate of each other's feelings. . . .

During a year's observation, the children never formed as close or strong ties with adults as they had with each other. It appears that the reward value of the other children continued to be higher than that of adults. In the author's words: "Their companions of the same age were their real love objects. . . . This explains why the feelings of the six children toward each other show a warmth and spontaneity which is unheard of in ordinary relations between young contemporaries."

It is a long step from the concentration camps of World War II Europe to the animal cages of a Midwestern university, yet Anna Freud's insights are mirrored in the results of primate studies by Harlow at the University of Wisconsin, some of which are described earlier in this book. On the basis of his extensive studies of the early affectional ties in young animals, Harlow has come to believe that among all the "love systems" to which we are heir—mother love, infant love for mother, heterosexual love, paternal love, and agemate or peer love—it is the last which is most important in the child's development.

In support of his thesis, Harlow cites the results of research in which young primates were first denied and then supplied with the company of their peers. Stephen J. Soumi, a Harlow student and now head of his former teacher's primate laboratory, raised pairs of infant monkeys together to establish strong peer relationships and then abruptly separated them for various periods. Each time, the result was a classic picture of *anaclitic* (from the Greek "leaning on") depression—the profound melancholy of the young typically seen among infants and young children who have suffered acute emotional starvation. Such depressive reactions have long been known to result from abrupt infant separation from the mother—for example, by being placed in an institution or a foster home. Now Soumi has shown that the deprivation of early affectional ties with peers can be equally disastrous for the infant's later development.

When the infants deprived of their peers were still only about ninety days old, they behaved as normal infant monkeys do, with all the infantile self-clasping and huddling that you would expect at that age. It soon became clear, however, that these animals had been reduced to a state of *permanent* infantilism. If they had been following a normal sequence, at 90 days they should have started to play, at 180 days play should have dominated their lives, and at 270 days even more so. The infantile responses of fright and withdrawal should have been dropping out steadily. Instead, they remained fixed at the 90-day level.

Harlow himself was surprised at the results of subsequent studies designed to find out whether these psychologically damaged monkey babies could be healed by exposure to friends. On the basis of earlier work, he had come to believe that isolated monkeys deprived of affectional ties for as long as six months had been destroyed emotionally forever. Soumi, however, took such animals and placed normal animals with them in pairs. The new friends were three months younger—a choice based on the fact that the depressed and by now terror-ridden animals were not as likely to be further terrorized by these younger peers. Furthermore, the younger animals were at the maturational stage where normal play was beginning, and this gave the previously isolated animals a normal developmental model to follow.

The no longer deprived primates were first tested in their normal living cages so that they would not have to contend with a new environment, and subsequently in more strange and complicated surroundings. "The results," Harlow found, "were good beyond all predictions." The animals rapidly learned to give up the abnormal self-clutching and huddling behavior; they gradually began to accept approaches from the normal, younger animals and even to initiate approaches themselves. Finally, they passed the critical test of free, uninhibited play—the earmark of the normally developing child.

Over 30 years before Soumi's ingenious experiments, Harry Stack Sullivan, the famous American analyst who focused on interpersonal relations in the origins of mental illness, perceived clearly the therapeutic power of peers. From clinical insights rather than laboratory data, he emphasized the importance of "chumships" on the child's development. In preadolescence, he wrote, a child develops "a real sensitivity to what matters to another person." The child is now guided by what can be done " 'to contribute to the happiness or to support the prestige and feeling of worth-whileness of my chum.' "

Soumi's studies and Sullivan's teachings should not be taken to mean that peers inevitably act as a healing force. In real life, peers—like any powerful force—can be destructive as well as restorative, and the emotional scars that a youngster may suffer at the hands of friends are not always quickly healed. For years, we have heard about the unerasable psychic stains left by unfeeling or unhappy parents on their children. In focusing so heavily on child-traumatizing mothers and fathers, we have failed somehow to give sufficient attention to the equally high potential of friends to place a psychological blight on each other.

Not long ago, a college junior came to see a psychologist for help with what she called her "social problems." Kathy was a bright and attractive twenty-one-year-old, who, if anything, underestimated the extent of her difficulties. She was, in effect, totally isolated from the outside world. Each day when she finished her classes, she returned to her room at home to begin the only activities that consumed her life—homework and television. During or after classes, she felt and behaved as if she were totally removed from classmates and acquaintances. "I just can't seem to get into a conversation with anyone," she complained, and even the thought of calling a friend for dinner or a movie caused Kathy acute episodes of anxiety. Kathy was neither schizophrenic nor pathologically depressed. She had simply grown isolated from the world outside, and the prospects of human interaction were even more painful than the loneliness and longing that were her daily companions. Like Soumi's psychologically injured monkeys, Kathy had turned inward altogether.

Kathy's problems were not spawned by abusive or rejecting parents, although her mother especially did nothing to discourage Kathy's growing sense of isolation. Instead, it was the aggression and cruelty of her peer group years earlier that Kathy correctly saw as the source of her difficulties.

As a young adolescent in the eighth and ninth grades, when Kathy was beginning her first serious attempts to win the affection and esteem of friends, she became the prime victim of a school "clique," both boys and girls, who set out to taunt and frighten her. She became the target of a constant barrage of pranks and cruel jokes. "Maybe it was my appearance of naivete or vulnerability that attracted them," Kathy now wonders, "but their sights were set on me especially because they could see me crumble before their very eyes. Each day I would have my books stolen or scribbled on, or the john locked while I was inside, or my locker painted with insults. I was even pushed and shoved in the hallways, and more than once chased down darkening winter streets after school. Worst of all, though, was the barrage of comments about my appearance. I had a fair case of acne then, and my breasts were late in flowering. Each morning I was greeted as 'pimple puss,' or 'tiny tits.' There was no way for me to stem the tide. This was a powerful and influential group that was attacking me, and I had no friends to take up my defense, or to whom I could turn. I was isolated. I still am."

Kathy will be a while learning the sense of trust in others that was demolished by her peers. Ultimately, like terrorized primates, she will come to understand that the world outside her own narrow orbit can offer warmth and security as well as pain and isolation.

Despite episodes such as Kathy's, more often than not, peers serve as a positive rather than destructive force—sometimes as the major or sole source of strength and support in the child's life. Beset by violence and discord at home, and without even a flicker of tenderness to warm their way, many children find solace and strength otherwise unavailable in the company of their peers. It is their friends who rescue them from psychological oblivion, who provide resources, and to whom, in the words of Francis Bacon, they "may impart griefs, joys, fears, hopes, suspicions, counsels, and whatever lieth on the heart to oppress it."

The healing power of friendship became tangible recently for Angela, a freckle-faced fourteen-year-old. "I was at the end of my rope," she said looking into the distance for a moment. "It was last year, and I just broke up with Mark. I had a falling out with my parents, too, and besides, they weren't getting on that well themselves. To make matters worse, my older sister left for college. So there I was, angry, depressed and alone. Except for Barbara. Right now, I think Barbara saved my life. She didn't give me advice on what to do next, and she didn't try to tell me everything was going to be great tomorrow when we both knew it wasn't going to be.

"What she did do was to listen for as long as I wanted to talk or cry, and she decided to stay over with me for a few weekends. Barbara was just there. She was available. And everything she said and did told me that she was sharing my pain, that she *really* cared."

It is doubtful whether any adult could have fulfilled the same role for Angela—or for all the Angelas who, each day, are sustained by the power of friendships.

Peers and Parents: Antagonists or Allies?

Despite their demonstrable value to the child, for many parents the child's peers represent a distinct threat. The power of peers is viewed by countless mothers and fathers with alarm and concern. Such parents approach child rearing very much as if it were a contest of influence:

who will most effectively control the destiny of my children—I, who gave them life and sustenance, or their friends who are likely to exploit and ruin?

It is rarely productive to state any child development issue in such contrasting terms, and the results of studies focusing on this issue demonstrate why. The data portray the complex interactions that exist between these two major forces—parents and peers—in the life of the child.

The susceptibility of children to peer group influences and to a turning away from parental influences is likely to be considerably greater for the children who grow up in a home which does not nurture their emotional needs. Such children are likely to be insecure and carry with them into the world a strong need for acceptance and nurturance by others. Moreover, such children need not be anxious about the prospects of letting their parents down, for they have not that much to lose; acceptance by the group is all there is for these children, and they are, therefore, quite willing to adopt its values at any cost.

Because the quality of a child's ties to the family are critical in determining how powerful peer influences will be, many authorities believe that the impact of the peer group is stronger in America today than it was years ago. As the influence of the nuclear family has grown thinner, American children have reached out more insistently to the apparently heartier and more "durable" society of peers. Although research data in support of this hypothesis are only suggestive, it is difficult to argue with the conclusion that the weaker the family unit, the more likely a child is to be influenced by peers.

An indicative pattern emerges, John D. Campbell notes, when American children are contrasted with those from other cultures. Mexican youngsters, for example, and Chinese young people living in Hawaii have been shown to be less influenced by their peers than American youth, presumably because they live with far more commitment within an extended family that includes such relatives as grandparents, aunts, and uncles. Their ties to peers are, therefore, less urgent. The same factors operate among many European young people.

In contrast, there are a number of societies—for example, within the Israeli Kibbutz society or the Soviet educational system—in which peers play a much stronger role, partly through conscious effort on the part of the leaders of the society to increase the contacts which the child has with his peers, and to reduce the role of the parent.

The parent-peer issue need not be seen as an inevitable conflict between the attitudes and values of adults and those of the child's

friends. Many parents have needlessly concluded that a major intergenerational conflict exists, and they feel threatened, therefore, by any
signs of identification of their young with the peer culture.

Hartup sees the two forces—parents and peers—as complementary
rather than antagonistic. "In any cultural situation that we know anything about, both forces carry considerable significance for the child's
development," he points out. "In some aspects of growing up, contact
with older and wiser persons—the ones the child is dependent on—
represents the primary force; in other instances, it is contact with
coequals that is critical. These are just not substitutes for one another.
Most of the influences are complementary."

No one would argue that the effects of peer modeling are always
benign, but the abiding suspicions that many parents have of their
children's friends are hardly warranted. There is no reason to assume
that peer influences work primarily at cross-purposes to the positive
influences of parents and teachers. From evidence provided by a host of
studies like those described earlier, Hartup argues that peer modeling
effects are largely constructive; many desirable effects are traceable to
the child's imitation of agemate behavior.

Hartup's conclusion runs counter to the popular assumption among
many parents that, except for their exertion of a strong counterforce,
their child will be dragged by peers into an abyss of ruin. It is a
reflection of our arrogance and paranoia, perhaps, that we assume the
best traits in our children are those *we* inculcate and the worst, those
which they have learned outside the home from their peers. That is
hardly true in every case—or perhaps in even most cases. The generous
spirit can be learned from a friend rather than from an adult, honesty in
dealings with others may come from the street, not the home, and fears
may be quieted through peer associations rather than an association
with an anxious mother or father.

Hartup believes that our society has virtually ignored the positive,
growth-inducing qualities of peer interactions. Too many parents see
the undesirable behavior of their children only as the result of faulty
associations. "I wouldn't want to take the position that exposure to
deviant social norms of the peer group never loses an individual child
in the direction of deviance," Hartup acknowledges. "It clearly does,
and I think some of the delinquency research literature supports that. A
really heavy involvement in a peer culture which espouses deeply
antisocial norms is something that is going to place the individual in
considerable risk for moving in that kind of direction. Still, I think such
findings have been exaggerated, and the public has been overexposed

to them in a variety of ways. There is a sensational sort of quality that accompanies this. For whatever reasons, TV, newspapers, and all the media really don't give a very accurate picture of childhood where peer relations are concerned."

Hartup feels that the popular culture tends to omit or overlook many ways in which contacts with peers are constructive in development and in which interactions with peers really don't basically modify the kinds of influences that parents continue to have. "For example," he points out, "if you look at the relation between a child's educational aspirations, vocational goals, and basic moral values, and those of his parents, you will find the concordance between the two to be markedly high. Contrary to popular assumption, there continues to be a high degree of family influence all throughout the course of development, and the peer culture just doesn't disturb that as much as the popular media tend to suggest."

Studies by William A. Westley and Frederick Elkin over 20 years ago showed, for example, that children actually tend to select their friends largely on the basis of values acquired from their parents. More recently, sociologist James S. Coleman found a large majority of the teen-agers he studied to be averse to joining a particular club in school if their parents disapproved of the group, and Matilda W. Riley and her associates found that when children try to imagine what they will be like as an adult, they typically project a portrait of their own parents' values as they see them.

Unlike Sarah in the biblical desert, today's urban parents cannot so easily control the peer relationships of their children or pick their friends for them. Nor should they. In Hartup's view, they ought instead to be sensitive and involved in this critical aspect of their children's lives. "I think that one can be too inquisitive and too curious about a child's friends," says Hartup. "Some parents begin to live vicariously in their youngsters' social worlds. But I do think that a comfortable involvement is something children not only enjoy, but really need as they struggle to acquire a sense of competency with peers."

Parents should not overlook the weight of evidence. Peer interaction is an essential element in the development of the child. "Experience with peers is not a superficial luxury to be enjoyed by some children and not by others," says Hartup, "but is a necessity in childhood socialization. Ensuring each child the opportunity for productive interaction with peers is not an easy task, but such experiences remain the child's inalienable right."

11

Cancers of the Social System

Poverty and Racism

"Oh, to recapture the joys of childhood!"

In one form or another, that refrain is often heard from those engulfed by stress. The truth is, however, that childhood as a period of undiluted pleasure is a fiction concocted by adults who have chosen to forget the melancholy themes that accompany our earliest years. The days and nights of all children are touched by pain and anxiety, fear and bewilderment, wants unfulfilled, needs unmet. Episodes apparently innocuous to the bystander may leave a wound in the soul of a child—a sudden and inexplicable leave-taking, the angry shouts of parents heard from an adjoining bedroom, the slight of a teacher, the forgetfulness of a friend. Such experiences are common to rich and poor alike, to children of all races and in all places—on farms and in cities, in the ghetto tenement, in the plastic high-rise, and the well-shrubbed suburb.

For millions of children, however, the everyday hurts of childhood, shared with all children, are the more benign of their experiences by far. These are the victims of society's twin cancers—poverty and racism—which invade young lives and blight their development with a cruel inexorability. One of every four American children is likely to be victimized. The results are frequently crippling, sometimes deadly.

Kenneth Keniston argues that the prevalence of America's social cancers exposes as a myth the nation's touted regard for its children. He cites the infant mortality rate in the United States, ranked fifteenth among developed nations maintaining comparable data. Childhood malnutrition, he reminds us, is on the increase; because the daily diets of millions of our children are deficient in essential nutrients, these children suffer setbacks in growth, coping abilities, and intellectual development, and must frequently endure illness. To be poor virtually ensures inadequate health care; poor health—with its erosion of normal development—is passed from parent to child, generation to generation. The ravages of racism are equally devastating—inflicting psychic scars that further reduce the child's capacities for normal development and mastery of the environment.

It is not only the children of the poor and of minorities who suffer. The cancers discussed in this chapter reflect the impoverishment of an entire culture; they result in lives and potentials unfulfilled—among not only the disadvantaged but also among those who exist beside them, and who, although often unaware, are themselves diminished. Like physical cancers, the action of those highlighted in this chapter is subtle, but the symptoms may ravage. No etiology has been agreed upon; no universal cure has been found—at least not at a price the society seems willing to pay.

If left untreated, what are the prospects for the mental health of children suffering the ravages of our social cancers? One approach to understanding the outlook begins with a consideration of the relationship between social class and psychological well-being.

Social Status and Mental Health

A universal feature of societies is that they are stratified; for a variety of reasons, individuals acquire differential wealth, status, honor, and power. The phenomenon has given rise among behavioral scientists to an important research question: What are the effects of an individual's social status on the quality of mental health?

Although research designed to answer the question is complex—requiring large numbers of subjects and long periods of time—scores of attempts have been made. The approaches and definitions of investigators have differed—and therefore the findings of one study have often tended to contradict those of another. Recently, however, a husband and wife team of social psychologists, Bruce and Barbara Dohrenwend, completed a comprehensive review of studies that, over the years, have sought the link between social status and psychological disorders.

Using sophisticated statistical techniques to compare data across studies, they have discerned an overall pattern.

Among some 25 studies, the Dohrenwends identified 20 that show a consistent trend. The highest rates of mental illness exist among those at the lowest end of the social ladder, and the lowest rates among those at the top.

The Dohrenwends remind us, however, that a fundamental question, first raised forty years ago, still stands: Do individuals who are predisposed to psychological disability "drift" downward in a society that places high value on achievement, or do environmental conditions among the lowest social classes induce psychological disorders?

It appears that both are true. Certainly the mental and emotional disabilities of the poor, however, can no longer be ascribed to a genetic "fault" or to a constitutional weakness, peculiar to the impoverished. In significant measure, the stresses of life among the lower classes appear to foster the development of psychological disorder.

Among the research supporting this explanation is a study by two Yale sociologists, Lloyd H. Rogler and August B. Hollingshead, of 40 lower-class families in the slums of San Juan, Puerto Rico. Twenty of the families were selected for the study because one of the parents had been reliably diagnosed as schizophrenic. The rest were chosen because they seemed like the others in every respect except for the absence of schizophrenia.

The only major difference the investigators detected in the backgrounds of the two groups lay in the amount of stress encountered during the year immediately preceding the onset of clinical symptoms. The schizophrenics and their families had suffered more economic difficulties, more severe physical deprivation, more conflicts between husband and wife, more frequent and severe difficulties with relatives outside the immediate family, more quarrels and fights with neighbors, and more physical illness. In short, the schizophrenics had become recognizably ill, and for the first time recognizably different from the others in attitude and behavior, only after a greater accumulation of adversities, some of them calamitous. The data argue convincingly that environmental stresses—no doubt often acting on genetic vulnerability—strongly influenced the onset of clinical symptoms.

But it is necessary still to question further why these individuals succumbed so dramatically to the stresses of their lives. One reason might be a paucity of community resources—or an unfamiliarity with facilities—intended to help individuals alleviate the effects of stress. Another might be that poor life conditions irreparably weaken an individual's resources for dealing with stress. If so, an important contributing factor would appear to be the manner in which a child is reared. Although genetic influences are not ruled out, a family's place in the social order clearly affects the child's developing thoughts, attitudes, and behavior patterns. Social position not only influences a family's income and educational opportunities but also—evidence continues to accumulate—it affects how children and adults both think and act.

How Social Class Influences Child Rearing

Harvard psychologist Jerome Kagan, on the basis of research by himself and others, finds that differences in social class make for differences in several important characteristics manifested during the first years of life.

One of these substantial features is *a sense of effectiveness,* or the belief that one's actions are instrumental in causing changes in the environment. The significance of this, even in infancy, has been demonstrated by John S. Watson in experiments at the University of California, Berkeley. Watson hangs a mobile above a baby's crib. If the action of the mobile depends upon something the baby does, such as moving his arms or turning his head, the baby quickly learns to do what is needed to make the mobile work. But if the mobile's action does not depend upon what the baby does, the outcome is different. When this baby is later placed in a situation where the mobile won't work unless he does something to make it work, he has a hard time learning what to do.

Kagan reports that the middle-class child at five seems to have a better sense of his or her potential effectiveness than the lower-class child. The difference probably can be explained by difference in parental behavior.

The middle-class mother who responds to her infant's smiling or vocalization by talking or smiling back is laying the foundation for the belief that the child is a causal agent. The mother who comes to her child when he cries is clearly contributing to the child's faith in his ability to ensure an effective response when he is distressed.

The lower-class mother is less likely to enter into such interactions, this investigator suggests, and consequently her child has a lower expectancy of success—for example, in school.

Social class makes a difference also in the child's *exposure to language* during the early years and, therefore, in the ability to comprehend it and use it effectively. Careful observations of infants and mothers in their homes showed that middle-class mothers were more likely than lower-class mothers to engage in face-to-face sequences in which the mother talked to the child without providing any distracting stimulation, such as tickling the baby or changing diapers. As early as two years of age, middle-class children have been found to show superior competence in language.

Finally, there are class differences in the *reward of mastery*. Middle-class mothers tend to notice and praise many infant accomplishments—such as smiling, coordinating eye and hand movements, standing, walking—that lower-class mothers tend to ignore. When a child can expect rewards for his victories, Kagan notes, his attempts to master new skills are strengthened.

In sum, the middle-class child's experiences during his first two years make him better prepared to master school tasks because he believes in his own potency, he possesses richer language resources, and he is more confident of success. Moreover, compared to the child of the lower class, the middle-class child is more highly motivated to gain the teacher's acceptance.

Research underway by Kagan and his associates is extending these findings of the effect upon children of their families' social class—or, rather, the effect of the attitudes and child-rearing practices typical of the parents in a given class. Preliminary results show that a ten-year-old's aspriations, motivations to work, IQ, problem-solving strategies, and expectations of success have all been heavily influenced by whether he has been brought up in a working-class or a middle-class family.

Another researcher, sociologist Melvin L. Kohn of the National Institute of Mental Health, analyzed data on a cross section of employed Americans and found that social class had a variety of psychological effects, both on the men and on their children. What was true of the father was later found to be generally true of the mothers as well. No matter what a man's race or religion or in what section of the country he lived, the higher his social class, the more likely he was:

- To value self-direction in his life rather than conformity to outside authority
- To express more self-confidence
- To feel more in control of forces affecting his life
- To be more open-minded in his views of others and of social institutions
- To feel more personally responsible in matters of morality

- To be more trustful
- To be more receptive to change
- To show greater intellectual flexibility

Social class turned out be more strongly related to parental values than any other major social factor—such as race, religion, geographical location, and national background. Indeed, it was almost as closely related as all the other factors combined.

As might be expected, Kohn found social class to be related to men's values not only for themselves but for their children in turn. Moreover, fathers in middle-class families were much more likely than those in working-class families to assume responsibility for providing emotional support for their children, particularly their sons. Fathers in working-class families tended to be content with imposing restrictions.

Differences in parental values were reflected in how parents viewed their children's misbehavior. When middle-class parents, who tended to value self-direction, considered punishing a child, they were more likely to take into account the reasons for the child's misbehavior. Working-class parents, who tended to value conformity, were more likely to punish because some rule set by themselves or society had been broken.

Interestingly, working-class mothers were more likely to punish daughters than sons for fighting with friends, smoking, petty stealing, or defying orders. Such mothers seemed to differentiate between qualities valued for their children: daughters were to be ladylike; sons, manly. Middle-class mothers, though, made little or no distinction between the sexes. They seemed to feel that "the conduct of both boys and girls should be judged by the same criterion: intent." They punished accordingly.

There was a difference, too, in the type of behavior that especially pleased parents. Middle-class parents were more likely to be pleased by their children's accomplishments; working-class parents, by their obedience.

Why do differences in social class affect parental attitudes and values? Because, Kohn answers, a social class embodies "systematically differentiated conditions of life that profoundly affect men's views." He and his associates have concentrated on examining one set of such conditions—those determining how much opportunity people have for self-direction in their work—meaning to what extent they are required, and are free, to use initiative, thought, and judgment in the performance of a variety of complex tasks.

Differences in this opportunity, the investigators conclude, account for a substantial part of the impact of social class. "The conformity of people at lower social class levels is in large measure a carry-over from the limitations of their occupational experiences. . . . The job does mold the man—it can either enlarge his horizons or narrow them."

Aren't some of the values held by lower-class families—for example, conformity to outside authority—found to some extent at least among families at higher levels? To be sure, Kohn answers. At the lowest levels, though, a larger proportion holds conformist values. And, in contrast, self-direction as a value is found almost exclusively at the higher levels. This is not surprising, Kohn points out, because if a person is to value self-direction and to act accordingly, the conditions of life must be fairly good. If they are not, he is faced with such problems that the most he can hope for, typically, is to conform and stay out of trouble.

The Realities of a Child's Poverty

The work of Kagan, Kohn, and others elegantly illustrates a simple fact of child rearing: parents draw on their own experiences to bring up children in ways that will help them meet the demands of society. But in some families—notably the poor and the minority—the demands and expectations of society at large may conflict with the realities of their lives. The result is often enormous stress, and children are likely to be among the most vulnerable victims.

Parents who are poor certainly do not care less for their children. But, as Bronfenbrenner, Keniston, and others have dramatically described, many parents are so overburdened by life conditions that they are severely limited in their ability to provide the warmth, caring, and nurturance that is every child's birthright. According to a seventeenth-century saying: "When poverty comes in at the door, love flies out the window." So, often, does parental capability.

The stresses of the poor, and their effects, were acknowledged by participants in a 1970 White House Conference on Children: "The frustrations are greatest for the family of poverty, where the capacity for human response is crippled by hunger, cold, filth, sickness, and despair. No parent who spends his days in search of menial work, and his nights in keeping rats away from the crib can be expected to find the time—let alone the heart—to engage in constructive activities with his children or serve as a stable source of love and discipline."

Who are these "families of poverty?" At a time when nearly all families are feeling the sharp pinch of inflation, the definition of poverty might appear to be a statistical game having few hard and fast rules. Despite frequent references by politicians, newspapers, and government agencies to "the poor," their final tally fluctuates. In America, in the late 1970s, on the basis of the formula employed, anywhere from 12 to 24 percent of the population may be defined as living in poverty. But for the child with an empty belly, the statisticians' dilemmas are not very critical.

Among adults, however, the statistical fluctuations can inspire either optimism and hope, or anger and cynicism. The second of these is the view imparted clearly by Michael Harrington, whose book entitled *The Other America* has often been credited with having launched the nation's "war on poverty" more than a decade and a half ago. Harrington has now concluded that this war was never won on the battlefield but stands a risk of being settled by forfeit, as new techniques for counting and accounting for the poor continue to evolve. "The poor are being made invisible again," Harrington warns.

In fact, of course, they are not invisible. And even in the statistical profiles of poverty, the major distinguishing characteristics of the poor stand out with clarity and consistency. Two that predominate are age and color.

At the Bicentennial Conference on Children, sponsored by the National Council of Organizations for Children and Youth, it was revealed that one of every four children—more than 17 million in this country—live under conditions of poverty. Regardless of the definitions used, the fact remains that approximately one-half of the persons defined as poor are children and youth. Together with their families, they constitute more than 70 percent of the nation's poor.

The bleakness of this picture is compounded for most minority children, though much of the data available from the United States census specifically reflects the black experience. The statistics may vary, but the message remains the same: roughly 33 percent of American blacks live in poverty as opposed to 10 percent of whites. Racism, not race, appears to provide the explanation. Psychologist Kenneth B. Clark made the point in his *Dark Ghetto:*

Some of the problems of the lower class Negro are similar to and identical with the problems of poor people and slums in general. But in America, the white poor and slum dweller have the advantage of the social and psychological reality which is an essential part of American racism; that is, the belief that they can rise economically and escape from the slums. The

Negro believes himself to be closely confined to the pervasive low status of the ghetto, and in fact usually is.

Statistical profiles further indicate that the risk of poverty is far greater among persons—regardless of race—living in rural areas, particularly in rural areas of the South. While less than a third of the United States population lives in the South, more than half of the nation's poor are concentrated there.

Endlessly, the figures are computed and analyzed and categorized. They may be weighed against other figures describing benefits available to the poor by virtue of their poverty and intended to compensate for the material deprivations they endure. Yet as Harrington notes, "... Poverty is not simply a statistical phenomenon describing certain characteristics of an aggregate of individuals; it is social reality as well. That is, the poor do not merely lack income. They also go to jail for their wrongdoing, which the middle class, in most cases, do not; they get sick more often; they suffer from greater emotional and mental stress; and so on." The social realities that Harrington describes touch millions daily.

A similar assessment was made by members of the Joint Commission on Mental Health of Children. The Commission's 1969 report, *Crisis in Child Mental Health,* links eight interacting factors that characterize poverty. Low income is only one. Others too frequently include inadequate education, poor physical environment, meager and disorganized life-styles, poor physical and mental health, large families, and broken families. That *these* factors, in turn, represent only the tip of other potent and pervasive threats to a child's development was underscored by anthropologist Oscar Lewis. From his observations of the barrio, Lewis derived a list of some 60 physically and psychologically debilitating traits of the culture of poverty—among them, for example, violence, political apathy, child labor, and the psychologically devastating realities of struggling, day after day after day, simply to exist.

Throughout the 1960s, the observations of Harrington and other social commentators inspired unprecedented activity intended to ameliorate the effects of the "culture of poverty" on "socially disadvantaged" children. But much of the effort, with every good intention, was directed toward correcting flaws in the children themselves. The impact of poverty and deprivation was most often thought to result in intellectual deficits—inabilities on the part of children to learn, to perform and achieve academically—that portended life-long social and economic disadvantages; the result was a series of massive efforts to enrich the early educational experience of poor children.

Keniston reminds us, however, that the most powerful results of exclusion from the mainstream may be social and psychological, not intellectual—results which, like their causes, may be well beyond the capacities of the individual child to correct.

The children of the poor live in a world more dangerous by far than that of the prosperous. The poor child's world is a world of broken windows, lead paint, and stairs without railings. Or it may be a rural world, where familities cannot maintain the minimal levels of public health considered necessary a century ago.

Urban or rural, it is a world of aching teeth without dentists to fill them, of untreated ear infections that result in permanent deafness. It is a world wherein a child easily learns to be ashamed of the way he or she lives. Such a world teaches many children to suppress any natural impulse to explore, to reach out. And it teaches others that the best defense against a hostile world is a constant offense—belligerent aggressiveness, sullen (and justified) anger, deep mistrust, and readiness for violence. Harsh as it is to say it, such children are systematically trained for failure.

Our social and political history sings with commitment to equality and fair play. Nothing in our constellation of basic values even hints that our society should impose special burdens on special children. How then can we understand the perpetuation of exclusion?

The "exclusion" that Keniston so poignantly illustrates is the first cause in a chain of events that ultimately devastates the potential opportunities of millions of children. Excluded by race, by geography, by income from having access to the tools and benefits available to others, the deprived are measured, nonetheless, by the yardstick of the norm. Found wanting, they may be labeled as a problem in need of a solution, rather than as individuals possessing needs unfulfilled—and strengths untapped. Unfortunately, the label may obscure the underlying pattern of an impoverished life as a whole in favor of some of its more prominent symptoms.

Treating a Piece of the Child

The dangers in emphasizing selected symptoms rather than the whole life panorama associated with poverty were illustrated recently in a series of evaluations of early intervention programs for deprived children.

Over the last decade, of the many such efforts directed at the culturally deprived children of low-income families, several have focused on training mothers in techniques that would improve the quality of their interactions with their children. One of these is described in Chapter 9. It was reasoned that enriching the children's home social settings would upgrade their readiness for school. In the course of separate assessments by Bronfenbrenner and psychologist Robert Hess, it was shown that the children of participating mothers did indeed gain in school readiness. In IQ, as well as other measures of school achievement, the children were significantly more advanced than were children coming from comparable homes but whose mothers did not receive training.

Yet the most significant conclusion of the evaluations was that the gains made by the children were larger and more enduring when, in addition to improvement in the mother and child's social interactions, changes were made in the physical aspects of the children's home environments. Explained another way, when adequate health care, nutrition, housing, and other forms of support were not made available to the families, the gains that the children showed in school tended to fade once the direct intervention was discontinued.

Consider the possibilities for comedian and social activist Dick Gregory if, when he was a child, efforts had been made to strengthen him by a six-month tour in a Headstart program. Here is Gregory's account of his childhood plight, as described in his autobiography, *nigger:*

The teacher thought I was stupid. Couldn't spell, couldn't read, couldn't do arithmetic. Just stupid. Teachers were never interested in finding out that you couldn't concentrate because you were so hungry, because you hadn't had any breakfast. All you could think about was noontime, would it ever come? Maybe you could sneak into the cloakroom and steal a bit of some kid's lunch out of a coat pocket. A bit of something. Paste. You can't really make a meal of paste, or put it on bread for a sandwich, but sometimes I'd scoop a few spoonfuls out of the paste jar in the back of the room. Pregnant people get strange tastes. I was pregnant with poverty. Pregnant with dirt and pregnant with smells that made people turn away, pregnant with cold and pregnant with shoes that were never bought for me, pregnant with five other people in my bed and no Daddy in the next room, and pregnant with hunger. Paste doesn't taste too bad when you're hungry.

Child psychiatrist E. James Anthony correctly concludes that mental health interventions of a traditional sort are meaningless in the faces of severe poverty. Without basic requirements—addressed by the General Assembly of the United Nations in 1959 in its Declaration of the Rights of the Child—children are at risk. "The child shall have the right to adequate nutrition, housing, recreation, and medical services." No amount of mental health intervention is meaningful if such requirements are unmet. Or, as Anthony has put it: "You have to fill stomachs before you practice psychiatry."

By conservative definition, basic requirements for living are absent for some 17 million children and youth. In the hollows of Appalachia, in the deserts of the Southwest, in the forests of the far North, and in the slums of any large city, there exist children on whom society has turned its back. Not all succumb to the effects that follow, but all are at risk.

Moreover, social scientists agree that the risk is cyclical, that unless a victim of poverty is able to catapult well beyond a marginal existence, the legacy somehow tends to be passed from one generation to the next. Though a fraction of poverty-reared children do manage to break the cycle, many of these are destined to return to poverty, defeated by an unyielding economy. Even if they struggle free for a time from the grinding forces of the ghetto, or the economic dead ends of the rural hamlet, many later become submerged once again as if by an invisible weight. It is a harvest of disadvantage and pain that is likely, therefore, to await the children of the poor.

The Hungry Child's Handicaps

In recent years, increasing numbers of scientists have begun to study the biological nature of that harvest in the same intensive fashion that their counterparts in behavioral science have analyzed its social, cultural, and psychological nature. A key area of investigation has been nutrition—specifically, the effects of malnourishment on growth and development.

The term *malnutrition* conjures images of famine in India and of starving young Biafrans. Indeed, the United Nations estimates that in developing nations, about 50 percent of all young children are inadequately nourished, with 30 percent of these populations victims of severe and chronic malnutrition. Yet malnutrition is not limited to the unseen, unfortunate children of far away countries; it exists in America as well, perhaps just down the highway, or even around the corner.

What, specifically, are the outcomes for children of an inadequate diet?

The late pediatrician, Herbert G. Birch, writing in the *American Journal of Public Health*, described the role of adequate nourishment in the life of the developing child: "It has long been recognized that the nutrition of the individual is perhaps the most ubiquitous factor affecting growth, health and development. Inadequate nutrition results in stunting, reduced resistance to infectious disease, apathy, and general behavioral unresponsiveness. In a fundamental sense, it occupies a central position in the multitude of factors affecting the child's development and functional capacity."

More common to this country than the killing forms of starvation seen in developing countries is a condition termed "subclinical malnutrition," which cripples millions of our children in many ways. Even more common is a condition familiar, if only fleetingly, to all of us: hunger. One portrait of the hungry child is offered by Merrill S. Read of the National Institute of Child Health and Human Development:

In considering the consequences of hunger, the social and cultural correlates are often overlooked. Hunger is part of the constellation of poverty. As such, it may signify personal inadequacy to the child to the point that his motivation to achieve is reduced. In turn, this might interfere with his relations with his peers and teachers. Similarly, the inability of parents to provide basic necessities such as food for their children may have deleterious effects on their own self-image, their attitudes toward their environment, their concepts of achievement, and their relationships with their children.

Psychiatrist Brandt Steele describes what malnutrition means in terms of a child's biological development:

The cellular structures of the brain may ... be affected by severe, prolonged malnutrition. No new cortical cells are added to the brain after birth; but in the first few years of postnatal life there is rapid brain growth due to formation of large amounts of glial supportive structure and the development of billions of intercellular neuronal connections. Serious malnutrition during this crucial postnatal period can result in deficient growth of necessary brain structure which can never be fully compensated for. Gross delay and deficits in skull size and brain growth are often seen in infants suffering from prolonged poor nutrition. ...

For millions of women and their newborn infants, a poor diet carries potentially life-crippling ramifications. At a recent meeting of the Society for Neuroscience, University of California medical researcher Robert B. Livingston reported that "more than two million pregnant women, infants, and children under four years of age in the United States as of 1970 were undernourished to such a degree that the brain development of the unborn and young child was in serious jeopardy."

These conclusions were based on data developed by the Department of Health, Education, and Welfare's Ten State Nutrition Survey and on a study of nutritional status of preschool children conducted through the University of Georgia and Ohio State University. The infants and young children of mothers undernourished during pregnancy were found to be well below standard averages on such measures as birth weight, height, estimated brain weight, and head circumference. Though Livingston and his colleagues caution that a link between head size and intelligence and achievement is not definitive, it is clear that undernourished children are unable to live up to their potential—a handicap, correctable in many cases through diet, that applies to nearly 60 percent of unborn children being carried by women living below the poverty line.

Unfortunately, however, an inadequate diet, which we know can affect a child's development, is only one of a lengthy array of corrosive factors contributing to a poor child's handicaps. In a study of 19 children hospitalized in Denver during the mid-1960s with a diagnosis of generalized undernutrition, researchers Peter Chase and Harold Martin found that the children, more often than their counterparts in control families, had to compete with brothers and sisters under the age of two for limited family resources, had been affected by parental separation or divorce during pregnancy or soon after birth, and were often the result of unwanted pregnancies. These and other conditions, including inadequate family finances, led the researchers to suggest that the children be diagnosed as experiencing "psychonutritional deprivation." They concluded: "It seems impossible to separate undernutrition completely from associated environmental influences."

Chase and Martin's conclusion offers a bridge back from one delimited, albeit complex, area of study—the effects of malnutrition—to a murky mainland of research on other dimensions of poverty and their relationships to a child's mental health and development. Among them, perhaps the ultimate determinant of the degree to which the cancer of poverty will ravage is the child's family.

The Family Environment of Poor Children

The family is the world of the infant and the center of life for the developing child. Within the family, infant and child alike learn what kind of a place the world is—a giving place or a depriving place, a caring and sharing place, or a place where children learn to fend for themselves. Writing in the *Washington Post* on America's bicentennial birthday, Margaret Mead described the child's "need for a place":

The first consideration is the care of infants who are totally dependent on the vigilance of older persons. Homes must be so constructed that it is always possible for someone to be nearby to hear the baby cry. We also know that the infant needs continuity of care—someone who can recognize the difference among cries of hunger, rage, and pain; someone who knows what happened yesterday.

Then there needs to be someone who is caring for that infant and its caretaker—someone who makes sure that there is food and water, health and light, sustenance for the mother before the baby is born, for the mother who is breastfeeding her baby, and for the home in which the child takes its first safe—or hazardous—steps.

There needs to be a place where children will know that they belong, where they have an unquestioned right to be, where there will always be responsible adults to welcome them and care for them. For teenagers there needs to be a place from which they can run away without going too far, and come home again, as they try out what it is like to be on their own. For adult men and women, there needs to be a place where someone will always know and care if they fail to return when they said they would, however far away the distance they have traveled.

Contrast Mead's lyrical picture of a child's needs with the following grim portrayal of patterns found in families who participated in a study conducted by child psychiatrist Eleanor Pavenstedt:

The youngest child was usually found in his crib in a back room. Diapers were changed infrequently. As often as not, a partially full bottle was somewhere in the crib beyond the baby's reach. During our visits, crying often remained unheeded while the mother discussed her own worries and needs, or she would hold the baby with little attention to his comfort. The outstanding characteristic in these homes was that activities were impulse-determined; consistency was totally absent. The mother might stay in bed until noon while the children also were kept in bed or ran around unsuper-vised. Although families sometimes ate breakfast or dinner together, there was no pattern for anything.

The parents often failed to discriminate between the children. A parent, incensed by the behavior of one child, was seen dealing a blow to another child who was closer. Communication by means of words hardly existed. Directions were indefinite or hung unfinished in mid-air. Reprimands were often high pitched and angry. . . . The parents' needs were as pressing and as often indulged as were those of the children. . . . Many of these

mothers seemed to think nothing of leaving the home for hours on end with
a four- or five-year-old in charge of the babies.

Pavenstedt came to characterize the children growing up in these
chaotic environments as "immature little drifters." Neither recognized
by their parents nor trusting of them, they soon became wary of adults
in general and manipulative in their dealings with brothers, sisters, and
other children. Lacking appreciation of verbal communication other
than grunts and shrieks, the children were denied both the ability and
the opportunity to discuss and explore the larger world that they would
meet, at a disadvantage, in school.

Pavenstedt's children of poverty did not appear to develop during the
early years as well as their first capabilities had suggested. Though she
did not measure IQ changes over time, other investigators have done
so—with the consistent finding that older children, regardless of color,
reared in impoverished and blighted environments have lower IQ
ratings than younger children. Low levels of intellectual stimulation
within the family—combined with poor health and nutrition and environmental handicaps—take their toll during the earliest years.

Perhaps the most poisonous of the effects of poverty on the child is its
impact on family stability. The child's family anchor is often weakened
or destroyed altogether by grinding economic tensions.

Daniel Patrick Moynihan, in his controversial report on the black
family, provided evidence indicating that, historically, separation rates
among black parents have closely shadowed drops in national employment rates. The scenario is readily depicted: a father loses a job and
means of support for his family; a wife and mother loses a husband and
a child loses a father; a family loses structure and stability.

While Moynihan, in 1965, focused on the black family, the scenario is
equally applicable to white families. In 1977, more than half of all
families receiving family assistance funds were white. And for 83
percent of all Aid to Families with Dependent Children cases, father
absence was the basis for eligibility. In economic terms, the national
expenditure for this single dimension of families in poverty topped
$10.3 billion. In human terms, one of every seven children in the
country grows up without a father, with all of the potential erosions of
mental health described in Chapter 6.

The importance of an individual family's strength and stability and its
capacity to sustain even the most economically impoverished children
has been documented in countless case histories. On New York's lower
East Side and in Brooklyn tenements a half century ago, dozens of

children, many of immigrant parents, survived years marked by chronic hunger and abject poverty. Their names included, among many more, entertainer Eddie Cantor, opera star Jan Peerce, politician Al Smith, Nobel prize-winning medical researcher Julius Axelrod, and hundreds more who grew to be blessings to themselves and to society. Their strength came from families who were supportive and strong, united in the quest for a better life. Such lives dramatically illustrate the findings of a number of investigators, who have shown that family disorganization is not an unconditional trait of the poor.

As part of her project that yielded such a sorry picture of the family life of poor children, Pavenstedt and her colleagues observed child-rearing patterns among a second group of families. Though these shared the same destitute environment and low income, they managed to retain a strong measure of stability and organization. In sharp contrast to their counterparts, these parents "assumed the parental role; children were cherished, cared for, and trained in an organized home with daily routines." The children were the "focus of their mothers' feelings"; they enjoyed frequent opportunities to play with and learn from their fathers, and were mutually involved with their brothers and sisters.

Differences, though subtle, were found between children of the stable versus the disorganized families. "Under superficial appraisal," Pavenstedt wrote, "it is not easy to distinguish between these two groups of children. They come from the same neighborhood and are equally well-dressed." But the children could be contrasted in terms of such characteristics as their willingness to learn, their ability to relate to and to trust adults, and their capacities to communicate with others. Though often subtle, such differences marked the children from better organized families as potentially better able to cope with an often hostile and unyielding world.

As a result of her study, Pavenstedt underscored the danger of lumping "poverty families" into one category. Measured against the values of the middle class, the poor are often set apart and viewed as somehow deviant. This, perhaps, is their cruelest burden.

Pavenstedt observed that the families in her study, particularly the disorganized families, were fully aware of their devaluation by the larger society. They were not permitted to forget it: "Not only are various important life opportunities deficient, but their second class citizenship even lacks certain human or civil rights. . . ." Close on the heels of social devaluation comes self-devaluation and life-crippling damage to self-esteem.

Pavenstedt found the parents of the disorganized families often to be hopelessly resigned, "revealing little capacity to achieve or produce or be something valuable in personal, childrearing, marital, learning, or work terms. Most damaging of all for the children's feelings is their own mothers' tendency to devalue them." The stable families, on the other hand, refused to submit to the insidious attack on self-worth. Never identifying themselves with the conditions surrounding them, they tirelessly maintained, and often achieved, the goal of bettering their living conditions.

Similar points have been made by another authority. The slum dwellers who suffer the greatest deprivation are those who succumb altogether to the distinctive life-styles of the slum. This is the judgment of Harvard sociologist Lee Rainwater in his analysis of how slum conditons affect black families. "Many Negro families live *in* the ghetto but are not *of* its culture," he points out, "even though they, and particularly their children, can be deeply affected by what happens there." Dick Gregory remembers his mother teaching that distinction: "'We ain't poor, we're just broke.'"

The impulse to protect the child from the cancerous onslaughts of poverty appears to be predominant among some parents. Psychiatrist Gloria Johnson Powell, now director of the Child Outpatient Department at the UCLA Neuropsychiatric Institute, recalls her early beginnings as one of five fatherless children of a black family living in poverty in Roxbury, Massachusetts. "Everything my mother did and said somehow got the message across that we would succeed—and that we deserved to. There was never any doubt that I would go on to college." For Gloria, herself, a self-concept as "poor" or "disadvantaged" never developed. "In fact," she says, "it wasn't until I went off to college that I realized that I was poor. When I filled out the forms required to apply for financial assistance, I suddenly realized that the cost of one year of tuition, room, and board was more than my mother's entire annual income."

The malignant effects of economic stress are hardly limited to urban centers—nor are the capacities of some families to ameliorate them. Child psychiatrist David Looff has observed the families of Appalachia over a number of years. There, many of the poor have succeeded "remarkably well" in providing for their children's emotional and physical needs, a success that Looff traces to the close mother-child relationships common among Appalachian families.

"Although in the years to follow, Appalachian children—particularly children of the lower class—encounter difficulties in development, that first year of life is, from the infant's standpoint, relatively free of conflict," Looff found. Drawing on their earliest experiences, through which they came to view the world as a pleasant and rewarding place, the children later are readily able to establish trusting relationships with their immediate and extended families. The kinship system ensures that helping resources, however limited, will be shared along with the stresses and hardships.

A poor mental health prognosis for poor children, as the next chapter makes clear, is not inevitable, but for many American children—especially in urban centers—the future is especially clouded. They face one additional barrier spared their young brethren: racism. Potentially as crushing in effect as poverty and pestilent neighborhoods, it can be even more ravaging of the child's self-concept and well-being. It is a cancer that can afflict any child whose ancestry differs from that of most of his neighbors, but the full force of its onslaught is directed, irrationally, against one diverse cluster of children: children of color.

How Racism Feels to the Child

A black child stands at an apartment window. It is his birthday, which happens to fall on Veterans Day. Looking through the window, he notices a celebration in the streets below him.

"Look. A parade! What they parading for today, Mama?"

"Why, they're celebrating your birthday down there, son. . . ."

The little boy is pleased, and, though he knows that his mother is joking, he begins to dream that this parade is really for him. Over the years he elaborates on the dream and sees himself as the honored guest, an important and respected person for whom people hold parades and throw confetti.

Then he begins to notice that most of the people in parades are usually white. Most of the people on television, most of the ones in the news, most of the ones running in elections are white. And his own daydream begins to deteriorate. Later, these are his words: "Though you might keep watching parades, as they move in the distance, a lot of the dreaming you once did simply slows down, and suddenly one day it is as if, though you know the bands still must be playing somewhere, you yourself can't really hear the music anymore. . . ."

What has happened to the little boy with the delightfully self-centered dream? He has learned that most of the people in parades are the ones that exemplify the American cultural ideal. They are the ones that fall into the mainstream of American life. And he may well always be an outsider. He is black.

Conditions have been getting a little better, true. More white children have black friends—and to at least some of these children, the black friends are as close as the others. Black boys play on traditionally all-white football teams. In professional sports, the best players and the most acclaimed are often black. Black faces and bodies have become increasingly common on TV screens and in newspaper ads. In most places, and even in many places in the South, there has been an increasing acceptance of desegregation. There is a rising and quite visible black middle class.

Yet economically and educationally, the black child—and hence the black adult—is still discriminated against. Pervasive and often subtle, racism is felt in the life of every American child. It has been termed "the number one public health problem facing America" and "the only contagious form of mental illness." Among nonminority children, whose well-meaning parents may be the "gentle people of prejudice," institutional racism brings guilt, confusion, and cynicism.

More often than not, the research on minority groups in this country reflects the black experience as interpreted by white observers. When the conclusions are valid, though, many of them apply to other minority groups as well.

The harsh realities of minority experience frequently begin before a child is born. The odds are that he or she will be born into an economically deprived family; already, the child is at risk to the effects of prenatal malnutrition, to premature birth, and to other delivery complications. Infant mortality rates among the poor are two to three times higher than among white Americans of the middle classes. The rates are even higher among the minority poor. Only when these risks are successfully passed, or survived, do such children go out into the world to confront the barriers obstructing the aspirations parents have for them, as well as those dreams they have constructed for themselves.

Tools for Living: Identity and Self-esteem

Whether the minority child will succeed in meeting parental, social, and self-imposed goals depends in large part on the tools he or she has to work with. The first and most critical tool, forged in and by the family but wielded by the children, is their sense of knowing who—and how valuable—they are.

A child develops a sense of self-identity gradually. As Harold Proshansky and Peggy Newton point out, the preschool and early elementary school years are generally recognized as the crucial period of growth and differentiation of the child's feelings about self. And it is during this period that a child becomes increasingly aware of racial differences. One of the pioneering studies in the area of racial awareness was conducted in 1939, when Kenneth and Mamie Clark asked three-, four-, and five-year-old Negro children to point out "themselves" in a series of line drawings that portrayed black and white boys, a clown, and various animals. By the time they were four, the children were making no irrelevant choices of the clown or animal figures: the tendency to identify themselves as the black boys was well established by age five.

As children become aware of racial differences, researchers traditionally have reported that they also learn the labels and emotional responses associated with ethnic groups. Explain Proshansky and Newton: "Like any other attitudinal object or referent, the individual both 'identifies' and evaluates himself. Thus, he learns 'who he is' on dimensions such as appearance, group membership, achievement, and aspirations. This learning is never a neutral process, for the process of learning 'who one is' invariably carries with it value judgments. . . ." Researchers have held that when children learn they are black, they incorporate all the connotated meanings of blackness into their self-concept.

This is likely to mean acceptance of inferiority, passivity, and servility—characteristics all derived from rejection by society. If he accepts this image, say Proshansky and Newton, the black child "inherits a legacy of self-doubt, ambivalence, and low self-esteem." Uniquely black characteristics such as hair texture, facial features, and skin color may become a source of shame rather than pride.

However, other social scientists have questioned not only these explanations but even the existence of low self-esteem among blacks. One rebuttal is offered by sociologists Morris Rosenberg and Roberta Simmons on the basis of interviews conducted with more than 1,900 third- to twelfth-grade pupils in the Baltimore public schools. Interested in more than a simple comparison of self-esteem among black and white students, the researchers also aimed to measure the effects of social environments on self-attitudes and to learn how children of each race reacted to environmental influences.

The answer to the first question was straightforward: "In sharp contrast to most assumptions about the self-esteem of black children, the blacks in our Baltimore sample do not have lower self-esteem than whites; in fact, their self-esteem seems higher."

Rosenberg and Simmons attributed the black children's sense of self-worth, in part, to patterns of racial insulation that enabled them to view the world through a black perspective. Among 93 percent of the black children interviewed, their three closest friends were also black; among the white children in the study, 95 percent of their friends were white, too—figures that the researchers described as "probably typical of most 'integrated' cities of the Northern and border States."

But insulation was obviously not the only explanation. A large number of the older black students, since they attended junior and senior high schools where the majority of the students were white, were fully aware of their own race. Nonetheless, the interviews indicated that even among those students who perceived "most people's" ranking of blacks as very low in American society, the perception appeared to have little effect on the students' personal feelings of self-worth. "What the child may correctly conclude is that he lives in a bigoted, irrational society," the researchers comment. "But it is the white who is bigoted and irrational, not the black race in general, nor himself in particular, who is at fault."

Certainly, says child psychiatrist Jeanne Spurlock, the theme "black is beautiful," has provided many children "with a positive feeling of unity, peer acceptance, and protection against the onslaught of a hostile world." Because many aspects of the larger world are indeed hostile, other child experts urge that black parents go further than instilling pride, and actively acquaint their children with the realities of being black in a racist society. Among these experts is Frances Welsing, a child psychiatrist formerly affiliated with Howard University. "We abuse children very early on by lying to them," she told parents in an interview in the *Washington Post*. "Black parents are most guilty of this. We say everything's fine. We try to move to a nice quiet neighborhood. And we surprisingly don't have any problem battering the brain and the thought processes of children with that kind of stuff." If black children get consistent information, they stand in a better position to deal with racism and "white supremacy" as they grow older, Welsing says.

The white child, too, pays a developmental toll for racism. Spurlock has found that the child who learns bigotry and hatred of a class or group is being psychologically flawed, his sense of identity and self-esteem weakened. Kenneth B. Clark has put the case well:

Those children who learn the prejudices of our society are also being taught to gain personal status in an unrealistic and non-adaptive way. When comparing themselves to members of the minority group, they are not required to evaluate themselves in terms of actual personal ability and achievement. The culture permits, and at times encourages, them to direct their feelings of hostility and aggression toward whole groups of people, the members of which are perceived as weaker than themselves. They often develop patterns of guilt feelings, rationalization, and other mechanisms which they must use in an attempt to protect themselves from recognizing the essential injustice of their unrealistic fears and hatreds of minority groups.

The cancerous impact of racism, it is clear, may be felt by children who learn to hate as well as by those who come to be hated.

Accentuating the Positives of Children

Ironically, while many parents and educators fail to see the corrupting effects of institutional racism on white, majority children, they fail to see also the considerable coping skills exhibited by many minority children. In a study of New York City schoolchildren, Barry Silverstein and Ronald Krate observed the behavior of children coming from many different social and economic backgrounds. "Compared to typical middle-class children, black and white, the elementary school children we observed in Harlem generally appeared to be remarkably self-reliant and independent. Low income children in inner cities generally grow up fast; they develop characteristics that are functional and help them adapt to a life of hardship."

It may well be, however, that the children who successfully adapt to unique conditions of hardship are unable, as a result, to mesh their life-style with the American majority ideal. The special needs of those children were described to columnist William Raspberry by a young school teacher in Washington, D.C.: "Too many times, teachers in ghetto schools forget that their children have come to school with skills they have had to learn in order to survive, in order to cope. Instead of treating these skills as positive, they treat them as something that has to be overcome. So what happens, is they miss out on a chance to build on what the children already know. Not only that, but they leave the child with the feeling that maybe he doesn't know anything worth knowing, and maybe he's not worth anything himself."

While most teachers and other adults recognize the importance of positive self-concept, it may be difficult for them to move from theory to practice when the impulse is often to reshape the child's entire repertoire of coping skills. Observed Raspberry: "The teacher's job is to impart alternative skills and behavior patterns. But carefully. For the things that may one day be handicaps are, for the time being, assets, and not to be destroyed. The trick is to teach the new without condemning the old. You have to see value in what the child has already, and see the child himself as valuable—not just potentially valuable. . . ."

The insight offered by Raspberry and the young school teacher is borne out by Rosenberg and Simmons' interview data with the Baltimore pupils. "What [has] an unequivocal impact on their self-esteem in these environments is *what they believe their significant others think of them.*" The greatest proportion of the child's daily interpersonal interactions were seen to occur with parents, friends, and teachers. If these people "hold favorable opinions of him, respect him, and like him, then a firm foundation for healthy self-esteem may be established."

The message was reiterated, to cite only one instance, in a report by the U.S. Commission on Civil Rights—on the school needs of Chicano children. The underachievement of Chicano youths is perpetuated, the report suggested, because the children "are confronted with a school which either ignores their culture or regards it as an undesirable obstacle to success. This exclusion very often fosters in Chicano children feelings of inadequacy and inferiority." Small wonder. How can schools impart a sense of respect for these valuable children if no attempt is made to recognize their biculturalism, much less their bilingualism?

The IQs of Blacks and Whites

The major conceptual battleground for questions of cultural deprivation versus cultural difference, over the effects of schooling and the potentials of children, has been neither the classroom nor the school-board meeting but instead the field of genetics. For years, one of the stormiest issues in genetics has been: Why do black people in the United States score lower on IQ tests, on the average, than white people? When the people being compared are members of the same socioeconomic class, the difference amounts to 11 IQ points. The controversy grew furious in 1969 when an educational psychologist, Arthur Jensen, published a monograph on the subject. Jensen suggested that possibly the difference in IQ scores could be ascribed to a fundamental difference in the endowments of the two races, meaning that one race was perhaps naturally smarter than the other in matters measured by IQ tests. Though Jensen called for further study of the problem, he was bitterly and widely attacked as a racist.

One measure of the heat that Jensen's views have generated was seen recently, nearly a decade after publication of his monograph.

Many of Jensen's colleagues, members of the American Association for the Advancement of Science, erupted in protest over his election as a fellow of the association.

Two steps toward clarifying the issue are proposed by Kimble, Garmezy, and Zigler. The first is to realize that "there is considerable overlap in the scores of the two races. The normal variations in IQs found for white children range approximately from a rare 40 to a rare 200. Exactly the same range exists for black children. In terms of gross statistics, 15 percent of blacks receive higher IQ scores than 50 percent of whites. Thus, there are currently 3.5 million American blacks whose scores are higher than 83 million American whites."

The second step urged by these investigators "is to be skeptical of any position that views this difference as the inexorable reflection of genetic differences." Among the environmental factors that must be considered are:

• Differences between whites and blacks in health care, family life, and educational opportunity—*even within the same social class.* As evidence of these differences: the infant mortality rate is higher among black children, which suggests that "black children often have a poorer prenatal and early postnatal environment than white children of the same class"; black children, regardless of social class, come from broken homes at least three times as often as white children; blacks in northern States, which spend more for education than southern States, have been found to score higher on intelligence tests than either blacks or whites in southern States (though within States, whites scored higher than blacks).

• Shortcomings in IQ tests. One of these is cultural bias, which remains despite efforts toward "culture-free" tests. The biases appear particularly in the vocabulary sections, which use many words that are more familiar to white children than to black. But the biases appear elsewhere, too.

Kimble, Garmezy, and Zigler pose a more basic problem: Do intelligence tests really measure intelligence? "Intelligence is all the processes that assist the individual in adapting to his environment. Our standard intelligence tests sample just a few of the abilities known to belong in any comprehensive evaluation of intelligence." They give this example: "Standard tests thought to assess intelligence are not highly related to tests thought to assess creativity. This often leads to the conclusion that the creative person is not necessarily the 'intelligent' one. However, it makes just as much sense to argue that creativity *is* intelligence broadly defined, and our standard measures of intelligence do not include enough items that assess creative intellectual ability."

• Differences in motivation and in behavior while taking tests. "A variety of factors has been found to depress the test scores of black children, such as less motivation to score highly on tests due to lower aspiration levels . . . , greater anxiety in the test situation . . . , and the possibly inhibiting effects of being tested by an adult member of a different race. . . ."

• The effects of prejudice. "Until our society divests itself of the view that blacks are second-class citizens, and the destructive behaviors that emanate from such a view, we will never know exactly how much white racism has itself attenuated the scores of black children."

A recent report by black economist Thomas Sowell, of the Center for Advanced Study in the Behavioral Sciences, Stanford, California, has given the issue a new dimension. Using extensive data on white minorities during World War I and the 1920s, Sowell announced in *The New York Times Magazine* that the IQs of European immigrants then "were virtually identical to black IQs now." After years of exposure to American culture, however, these immigrant groups now have IQs at or above the United States average. The low-IQ immigrants included Italians, Poles, Greeks, and Jews. Northern and western Europeans, including the Germans and the Irish, had arrived generations earlier and by the 1920s had reached the national average. The IQ differences between the older and the newer immigrant groups were then also attributed to genetic differences. On the basis of such findings, Sowell asks, "Is there anything peculiar about either the level or the pattern of black IQs?"

An indication of the malleability of IQ test performance is given by psychologists Sandra Scarr and Richard A. Weinberg, who studied 130 black and interracial children adopted by white families when the children were two years old on the average. Several years later these children had IQs averaging 106—significantly higher than would have been predicted given their earlier family and economic backgrounds.

Prognoses and Prescriptions

For millions of children in this country, the doors to normal growth and development appear closed. Many of the everyday events that other millions take for granted—regular and nourishing meals, safe playgrounds, receptive teachers, family outings—are unknown. As youngsters preoccupied with the business of growing up, these millions of children may be unaware that they have been excluded from the mainstreams of society, that they are victims of society's cancers. But the lessons inevitably come. As if exclusion weren't enough, they are most likely to be thrust into a developmental track that promises a stressful rather than supportive family experience, poor health, inferior educational opportunities, and early introductions to delinquent and criminal behavior.

Is a disastrous mental health outcome foreordained for such children?

The harmful impact of poverty and racism on a child's development has been documented by social scientists of all ideological stripes, by physicians, educators, politicians, parents, and journalists. The existing literature is enormous, and this chapter has provided only glimpses of the directions and scope of pertinent research.

Still, because of the unpredictability of human potential, along with factors in the environment, all victims of society's cancers clearly do not suffer the same fate. There is among some children a built-in strength and resiliency allowing them to resist psychological ruin. Authors of the report of The Joint Commission on Mental Health of Children, *Crisis in Child Mental Health*, acknowledged this ability to resist:

> The wonder is not that poor people have higher rates of emotional disturbance, school failure, poor health, unemployment, family breakdown, and crime than other people do, but that many do manage to "develop normally," get jobs, stay married, and fail to rise up in revolt against a society that has so much, shares so little, and condemns the poor for their "shiftless ways.". . .

Garmezy goes further, concluding that the "hypothesized powerful negative effect of slum life on personal adaptation remains an assumption and not a given. Slums, like other environments, seem to produce individuals who vary markedly in their ability to cope. It is demeaning to suggest that for those reared in our festering slums, the prognosis for successful adaptation is inevitably bleak. Such a position ignores the history of an urbanized nation that has been built by a succession of ethnic groups each of which, in turn, has cast off disadvantaged economic status and pestilent neighborhoods without assuming burdens of psychopathology."

A poor prognosis is not inevitable. Despite such hopeful observations, however, the weight of the evidence is clear: the prognosis for the mental health of children who are poor and who suffer discrimination is blurred at best and often bleak.

In 1968, the National Advisory Commission on Civil Disorders, concerned with the cancers of poverty and racism, pointed out some national trends that run counter to optimism based on individual cases. The Commission reported that in the late 1960s, the odds were stacked against escaping the bonds of poverty. First, the report stated, a changing national economy had decreased the demand for blue-collar workers, the traditional stepping-stone for newly arrived immigrants seeking socioeconomic advancement. Secondly, racial discrimination was found to exert a crippling effect, creating "a bar to advancement unlike any other," in the words of the report. "Above all, Negroes suffered from segregation, which denied them access to the good jobs and the right unions, and which deprived them of the opportunity to buy real estate or obtain business loans, or move out of the ghetto and bring up their children in middle-class neighborhoods. Immigrants were able to leave their ghettos as soon as they had money; segregation has denied Negroes the opportunity to live elsewhere."

What can be done?

Social science has shown that it can make important contributions to the treatment of society's cancers. Nutritional programs for pregnant mothers and infants can effect subsequent development and learning. Headstart programs work, if they are sustained. Valuing a child's cultural heritage effectively bolsters that child's sense of value about himself or herself. But these contributions will not of themselves treat and prevent society's cancers. If children are apathetic in school simply because they are undernourished or cannot sleep at night for the noise in a crowded home, no amount of ingeniously devised, multi-media learning enhancement programs will make them the sparkling, vital students they have the potential to become.

When Rainwater observed ghetto family life, he wrote: "It is tempting to see the family as the main villain of the piece, and to seek to develop programs which attack directly this family pathology. Should we not have extensive programs of family therapy, family counseling, family life education, and the like? Is this not the prerequisite to enabling slum Negro families to take advantage of other opportunities? Yet how pale such efforts seem compared to the deep-seated problems of self-image and family process. . . . Can an army of social workers undo the damage of 300 years by talking and listening, without massive changes in the social and economic situations of the families with whom they are to deal? And, if such changes take place, will the social worker army be needed?"

Says child psychiatrist Leon Eisenberg: "When systems in the social organism go awry, it is absurd to attempt their correction by medicating the individuals whose aberrations are second and third order consequences of the basic lesion as it would be to treat the white count in meningitis rather than to eradicate the offending meningococci."

This remains an unfinished chapter. Social science can make a contribution that in the final analysis will be of little avail in the absence of political advocacy of children's needs and in the lack of widely held and fought-for human values that will make such advocacy possible. Until those forces—political advocacy and human values—are joined and dedicated to eradicating the cancer at its roots, the 17 million or more children living in poverty and, often, beset by discrimination, will remain among the excluded, most of them condemned to harsh, often painful, and perhaps wasted lives.

Meanwhile—today, tonight, tomorrow—the young victims of society's cancers must be strengthened in their quest for growth and survival. To guide us in that task, it helps to turn to those victims who do manage somehow to conquer their cancerous worlds and to flower and flourish despite lives of deprivation and trauma: the invulnerables.

12

Children Who
Will Not Break

Sandra is sixteen, born in poverty and raised in violence and deprivation. In her short lifetime, she has endured the death of two older sisters, the bitter separation and divorce of her parents, and a series of illnesses that seriously threatened her life. In one of the foster homes which sheltered Sandra, physical abuse and neglect were her daily portion.

By all known criteria, Sandra should be a psychological casualty, engulfed by symptoms or outright disabilities reflecting her young career of trauma and stress. In fact, the opposite is true. Sandra is an apparently well-adjusted adolescent, living now with a benevolent aunt newly arrived in this country, enjoying the rewards of close friends, and zestfully planning a college career.

How did Sandra get that way? How did she avoid the penalties we have learned to expect as sequels to deprivation and trauma? What is it that allowed her—and countless other children like her—not only to escape the ravages of pathology that so often follow prolonged and crushing stresses but to grow to maturity graced with a sense of optimism and an aura of well-being?

Answers to this enigma are only now beginning to emerge, primarily because psychologists focused much more heavily in the past on finding the roots of pathology rather than of mental health.

At the forefront of those working to reverse the trend is Norman Garmezy, professor of psychology at the University of Minnesota. Garmezy and his coworkers have been devoting their efforts to studies aimed at identifying not only factors which place children at risk for the development of mental illness and emotional disorders, but perhaps more important, those which seem to "innoculate" the child against the ravages of adversity.

Children from Poor and Pathological Homes

Children of the poor have long been regarded as especially vulnerable to mental health problems—and, as the preceding chapter portrays, for good reason. Even as he searches out the invulnerables, Garmezy acknowledges that the stresses of the poor "layer their lives with burdens far in excess of those any responsible society should allow," among them social disorganization, unstable and broken families, poor prenatal care, and birth defects. The impact of such burdens is reflected in the relatively heavy incidence of mental illness among young members of the lowest social classes. In one study, for example, sociologist Leo Srole and his colleagues surveyed a large sample of New York City families and then divided them, according to the fathers' socioeconomic status, into six groups. Those in the lowest group had the poorest mental health. Only one-tenth of the people at this level were rated as well. In explanation, Srole suggested that poverty and the conditions associated with it, "create a 'sick' slum community that often carries its own pathogenic 'contagion,' in particular for the children in its midst." The life setting of the slum-level child, he pointed out, is "heavily weighted with deprivations of body, mind and spirit. . . ."

Earlier in this book studies are reported showing that children of the mentally ill also carry with them through life an increased probability of becoming ill themselves, and of succumbing to stresses throughout their development. To be born to a schizophrenic parent is to run a higher risk than other children either of developing a psychosis or, at least, of leading a troubled life.

Despite the increased risks to their mental health, however, the fact is that many children both from disadvantaged and from psychologically diseased families not only survive but even triumph over the hazards strewn before them. America's young population includes untold numbers destined to soar above their limiting environment and to develop into productive children and young adults. Somehow, such children manage to pick their way safely among the psychological land mines all about them and to grow into wholesome, competent, human beings.

Garmezy has forcefully challenged the inevitability of a poor mental outcome for all disadvantaged children. Instead of an image of despair, degradation, and deficit, he invites us to focus on children who, despite their membership in the lowest social and economic classes, not only remain unscarred but function at a remarkably high level.

The fate of "high-risk" children growing up among schizophrenic parents is also far from uniform. Given both a poor genetic track record and an environment that has aptly been described as "crazy-making," clearly not all such children break down. Some emerge relatively unscathed, while still others actually learn from their experience how to overcome obstacles and to cope with problems. For them, the environment becomes not an overwhelming threat but a challenge to be met and mastered.

Among those born into schizophrenic households, Washington University psychiatrist E. James Anthony estimates that 16 percent will develop to be "odd, queer, peculiar, strange or crazy children and adults," and 31 percent will grow to be shy, seclusive, oversensitive, or apathetic. Another 32 percent, however, will be only mildly maladjusted and neurotic, and 12 percent will become average, well-adjusted persons. Moreover, 9 percent will not only escape psychological blight but develop into outstanding, creative people. Anthony calls the last group the *superphrenics.* These are "supernormal" children who have developed remarkable capacities to adapt to the corrosive presence of mental illness among their parents.

As an example, Anthony tells of a woman, suffering from schizophrenia of the paranoid type, who insisted on eating at restaurants because she thought someone was poisoning the food at home. Her twelve-year-old daughter adopted the same phobic attitude. Another daughter, ten, would eat at home when the father was there; he was normal. Otherwise she would go along to a restaurant. But a seven-year-old son always ate at home, and when the psychiatrist asked how he could do so, the boy simply shrugged and said, "Well, I'm not dead yet."

The older girl eventually developed an illness like her mother's. The younger went to college and did reasonably well. The boy—the invulnerable—performed brilliantly all through school and afterward. His mother's illness apparently had given him both a tremendous need and a tremendous ability to overcome all sorts of problems.

To describe a central characteristic of children blessed with apparently unusual capacities for normal development, investigators in the "risk research" field with increasing frequency use *competence*. The invulnerables achieve success in their academic school tasks. They are able to sustain friendships, are valued by their peers, and assume responsibility for others. They model themselves after constructive figures, absorb constructive values, and live in the anticipation of success rather than failure. In the words of psychiatrist J. C. Whitehorn, as he defined people of good mental health, they "work well, play well, love well, and expect well."

To date, most researchers studying invulnerable children have focused on the first of these criteria—specifically, school achievement—as the major index for competence. In doing so, they have admittedly highlighted only one of the social roles society requires children to play—that of a student. Although Garmezy agrees that the ideal definition of competence is considerably broader, he does not dismiss the importance of school achievement as an earmark of invulnerability. School, after all, is the child's factory, his place of work, and it is a considerable feat, he believes, for a child to "work well" despite enormous stress. These children of defeated and sick families are clearly resisting hardship, and are adapting, sometimes miraculously, to a threatening and hostile world.

Portrait of the Invulnerables

Garmezy and his research colleague, Keith Nuechterlein, reviewed all existing studies bearing on disadvantaged children who somehow display a high degree of competence in spite of the stressful environments in which they are mired. Other investigators—among them Anthony—have focused their attention on the surprisingly resilient children among the offspring of psychotic parents. Out of their combined findings there begins to emerge a profile of the "invulnerables."

• To begin with, these children are socially skillful, bringing a tone of warmth and ease to their relationships with both peers and adults. They are open, easygoing youngsters, popular and well liked, standing in sharp contrast to more fragile children of comparable background, who are often lethargic, tense, sullen, restless—and considerably less well accepted by their peers.

• Competent children are well regarded not only by their peers but also, and perhaps more important, by *themselves*. Such children operate out of a sense of power rather than impotence and of self-regard rather than self-derogation; the emphasis is on their pluses rather than their minuses. They feel capable of exerting control over their environment—of influencing events, rather than becoming the passive victims of fate. Sociologist James Coleman's extensive 1966 study of 645,000 students drawn from the third, sixth, and twelfth grades of 4,000 American public schools provides strong evidence of the power of this attitude in the achievements of disadvantaged youth. It was a sense of "personal control" that was more closely related to achievement than a variety of wide school or family characteristics measured in his survey. A 1969 survey by sociologist Edgar Epps describing 2,800 black and white children from inner-city schools in Atlanta and Detroit showed similarly that the best predictor of academic achievement was the child's sense of control over the environment.

• Competent children reveal also a reflective rather than an impulsive approach to life. They seem to operate with a sense of caution and self-regulation, keeping a sensible rein on their impulses. Rather than "shooting from the hip," such children will reflect a while when challenged—not only in their academic work but in their social relationships as well. They manage, in effect, to keep their "gut" reactions under control. For example, when confronted by children who want to fight, they can ignore them or simply walk away; there is no insistent need to "act out" every impulse that bubbles to the surface.

• The child who survives adversity is motivated from within to perform well. Contrary to the stereotype of disadvantaged children as lacking in drive, many emerge from studies as quite the opposite. Their reactions to school success and failure appear much like those shown by highly motivated, middle-class schoolchildren. Teachers rate these youngsters as goal-directed, eager to learn, doing more than is required of them, and participating fully in class discussion. Moreover, the children themselves express a preference for educational pursuits, and aspire to high vocational goals; they take responsibility for learning, accept blame for failure, and display a willingness to defer immediate gratification for the sake of long-range achievement.

• The families of disadvantaged but achieving youngsters show more concern for education—reflected in the parents' aspirations for their children's educational achievement and their willingness to assist actively with homework and to participate in school-related organizations. Even the physical aspects of the homes of achieving, lower-class children are different—less crowded, for example, and neater and cleaner; and there are more books.

• Parents of disadvantaged but competent children appear to permit them considerable self-direction in everyday tasks and to recognize the validity of their personal interests and goals, thus helping them in their struggle for growth and autonomy. In spite of omnipresent parental interest, support, and encouragement, the roles of parent and competent child remain well differentiated. Mothers of underachieving youngsters, in contrast, appear to behave more as siblings; they are more heavily involved in fulfilling their own needs, and expect their children to assume responsibilities far beyond their age and capabilities.

• A significant factor emerging from the life histories of competent children from disadvantaged families appears to be the presence in the environment of a charismatic, inspirational person. These children seem to be "turned on" by an identification with at least one figure among the adults who touch their lives. Often this is a parent. Consider a boy named James, born and raised on the Upper East Side among desperate living conditions. He was one of seven children, two of whom died in infancy. He was surrounded by trouble and illness. His father was an alcoholic. James early began working at odd jobs and had a regular one at fourteen. He and his brothers brought every cent home so that the family would have enough to eat; sometimes, even so, it did not. A number of his schoolmates and street companions wound up in the penitentiary; one died in the electric chair. What saved him and his brothers? Here are the words of James himself: "We had a mother to answer to. . . . We loved her profoundly, and our driving force was to do what she wanted because we knew how much it meant to her." The speaker? James Cagney.

The inspirational person is not necessarily a member of the family. He or she may be a playmate's parent, an older friend, a teacher, a member of the clergy, a physician—anyone who can help a child acquire self-assurance and a vision of what can be achieved.

• Resistance to the stress of living with a psychotic parent appears to require in a child a well-developed sense of personal identity. At the Washington University School of Medicine in St. Louis, Harriet S. Lander has found that such children are less submissive and less suggestible than others. They are able to maintain a safe psychological distance from the psychotic parent, and are thus not drawn into the preoccupations and delusions of the abnormal adult world about them. Anthony regards this loss of closeness in relationships as the price such children must pay for their invulnerability. Invulnerables seem to develop an objective, dispassionate, and remote relationship to people, thus allowing them to maintain their own integrity and to fend off disturbing influences.

• Finally, children who appear invulnerable in spite of a psychotic parent are able somehow to find the silver lining in the heavy emotional clouds hanging over them. Swiss psychiatrist Manfred Bleuler reminds us that some psychotics can be incredibly good parents, and that some children can see beyond a schizophrenic mother's pathology to her true parental qualities. They learn to distinguish what is strange or sick in a parent from what is good and lovable. Moreover, a nonschizophrenic parent can make up for the devastating impact of the one who is ill. "Sometimes," Bleuler observes, "gifted, warmhearted marriage partners are able to nullify all the evil influences of the other, schizophrenic partner."

The foregoing portrait of invulnerable children is beginning to serve as a base for significant research explorations. It has sparked a number of investigators in their attempts to find, early in the lives of children, the signposts of competence and psychological strength. If they are successful, their results may enable us to build into the lives of all high-risk children the capacities to conquer the psychological Everests strewn in their developmental path.

The Search for Healthy Markers

The boy, now a senior in secondary school, has been given a doctor's certificate stating that a "nervous breakdown" forces him to leave school for six months. As a young child, he spoke late, and he has never been a good student; he has no friends, and his teachers regard him as a problem. The father is ashamed not only of his son's poor adjustment to school but of his lack of athletic ability as well. The boy's parents simply regard him as "different." Why else would he have such odd mannerisms, make up his own religion, and constantly chant hymns to himself?

This case history—described by Victor and Mildred Goertzel—is of a young child growing into a life not of neurosis and suffering but of triumph and achievement. His name: Albert Einstein.

Despite young Albert's apparently poor prognosis, could anyone have sensed the underlying bedrock of competence in this super scientist? Who could have seen beyond the apparent web of pathology and maladjustment to the positive signs of creativity and well-being that lay beneath the surface? The task for researchers is to find the signs of psychological health that may lie dormant in the apparently vulnerable child. These are likely to be the traits that need to be nurtured, the psychological keys that need to be turned to open doors otherwise shut forever.

The usual way of studying how the circumstances of childhood affect characteristics in a later period is to start with the grown person and try to work back. In contrast, so-called longitudinal studies *begin* with the child. Typical of these have been studies by the Institute of Human Development of the University of California, Berkeley, begun half a century ago, and probably offering the richest collection of data ever assembled on human beings over a long period.

One of these, the Guidance Study, was primarily interested in personality development. It began studying its subjects as infants. There were 248 of them, every third child born in Berkeley over an 18-month period beginning January 1928. The children were weighed, measured, tested, interviewed, and observed at numerous times through their fortieth year. Special attention was given to their life at home during the preschool years. Information about them was also obtained from their parents, teachers, classmates, and themselves.

The project's original director was Jean Walker Macfarlane, who was succeeded by Marjorie P. Honzik.

When the children in the Guidance Study were teen-agers, Macfarlane and her associates made predictions about them as adults—their personalities, their success in marriage and work, their ability to cope with the problems of life: in short, their mental health. Though the investigators had had few scientific guides, they were surprised by the results of the analysis after the subjects had been followed up at the age of thirty. In many cases, the predictions turned out to have been wrong. The reasons ought to be helpful for parents, teachers, doctors, and everyone else associated with children.

Many of the most mature adults—integrated, competent, clear about their values, and accepting of themselves and others—were found to have been those who as youngsters had been faced with difficult situations and whose characteristic responses had seemed to compound their problems. They included chronic rebels who had been expelled from school, highly intelligent students who were nevertheless academic failures, children filled with hostility, and unhappy, withdrawn, oversensitive schizoids. But the behavior regarded by the investigators as disruptive to growth and maturity seemed in these cases to have led directly or indirectly to adult strength. One of the former rebels recalled that he had desperately needed approval "even if it was from kids as maladjusted as I was." To maintain his rebel status, he said, he had had to commit all of his intelligence and stamina, a circumstance he believed had contributed to his adult strength in tackling difficult problems. "I hope my children find less wasteful ways to mature," he remarked, "—but who knows?"

Close to half of the subjects fell into the group for whom crippled or inadequate personalities had been predicted. But as adults almost all of them were better than had been expected, and some of them far better.

One man, for example, held back several times in elementary school, had not graduated from high school until he was almost nineteen. His IQ over the years had averaged less than the group's. He had shown little interest in studies, school activities, or people. His school had not recommended that he go to college. The research staff thought he'd always be a misfit, a sideliner. But 12 years later he was a talented environmental designer, a good father, and an active worker in community affairs. "Obviously," says Macfarlane, "his tested IQs were no measure of his true ability."

One girl, who early was suspicious of and even hostile to members of the study staff, lived with a rejecting mother and a poorly adjusted aunt. She hated home and she hated school, partly because of her poor clothes. To escape, she married while still in high school a boy as erratic and immature as she. They soon separated. At thirty, with the investigators dreading the impending interview, in came a personable, well-groomed, gracious woman with two buoyant but well-mannered children. She had married again and was living a stable, contented life.

Why were the predictions wrong in such cases?

For one thing, Macfarlane answers, the investigators gave too much weight to the troublesome and pathogenic elements in a child's life— quite naturally, in view of the studies that have traced neuroses and psychoses to such elements—and too little weight to the healthful, maturity-inducing elements. (The latter were present even in the case of the girl who sought escape through marriage at seventeen. She always remembered that another aunt had given her affection and happiness—had helped her plant seeds that grew into flowers, had given her a kitten to love, had taught her to bake, and one year had been able to help her buy clothes "so I could finally risk being friendly.")

The investigators also overestimated the durability of certain "undesirable" behaviors and attitudes shown habitually over a long period. Sometimes the undesirable but long-continued patterns were converted, to the investigators' surprise, into almost the opposite characteristics. For example, it was predicted that overdependent boys with energetic and dominant mothers would pick wives like the mothers and continue the pattern of overdependence. Instead, nearly all such boys chose girls who were lacking in confidence. The boys thus won themselves a role as the proud male protector and giver of support, and in this role, say the investigators, they thrived.

Along the same line, a number of those in the study who were socially inept and insecure as children and adolescents became, again to everyone's surprise, highly successful salesmen. Looking back, MacFarlane sees this as a quite natural transformation. The boys did not have easy, intimate relationships growing up because they did not have them at home. As adults they still fear intimate relationships but have an unconscious desire for social intercourse. Selling gives them the needed contacts without the feared intimacy. (She could be wrong, she adds. The director of sales training for a large firm told her he deliberately picked shy people because they would concentrate on selling the product instead of themselves.)

One man who is remembered with special pride is the highly successful manager of a large business concern. Years ago he had been a shy little boy without friends. Though he had dropped in from time to time to see members of the Guidance Study staff, his communications had often been limited to hello and good-bye. After high school he enlisted in the Army and, since he had taken some shop courses, was asked to help with the building and repair work at his post. First he was flattered that anyone should think he could do anything; then he was proud that he could actually do it. After his service, he went to business school, where he got all A's, as compared to C's in high school. Now he says the most interesting part of his job is to give people "something to do that is a little harder than what they have done or think they can do—but not something they would fail at—and then to watch them expand. Nothing is more exciting to me than to see people get confidence"—which he himself had lacked for so long.

A number of other subjects had had similar experiences. They did not achieve "ego identity"—did not find themselves—until they had been forced into or been given an opportunity to take on a responsible role that gave them the sense of worth they had missed at home. Often these people did not find this new and satisfying role until they had left both their childhood homes and their hometowns.

In recently reviewing research by herself and others in the Guidance Study, Honzik does find some interesting examples of consistency lasting from the early to at least the middle years. Perhaps the most enduring one is that of intellectual functioning. Members of the Guidance Study group, for example, were tested 16 times between the ages of twenty-one months and forty years. Though the correlations between the scores at twenty-one months and forty years are negligible, they become significant for girls at 2½ years and for boys a year later. The best predictions could have been made about the age of eight.

Despite such data, Honzik points out that "change rather than consistency often appears to be an individual's salient characteristic." She and Macfarlane recall that when the study began in 1928, it was "the accepted 'fact' . . . that your IQ was your IQ and you had reached it by age 18." We now know that "intellectual and personal growth may go on, with new dimensions added over many decades."

Honzik reports a remarkable finding. "The closeness of the family's affectional relationships during the second year of life correlates significantly with intelligence test scores . . . even at middle age." In the case of girls, the important variable appears to have been the closeness of the mother-father relationship; with boys, the closeness of the mother-son relationship. What is really at work in both cases, the research indicates, is the "warmth of the language-learning situation in very early childhood."

The Macfarlane-Honzik study focused on children at various social and economic levels, and without the stigmata of mental illness among their parents. The good outcome for many of these subjects, whose prospects at various points in childhood or adolescence had looked bleak, can be expected also for many of those children who are surrounded by apparently hopeless poverty or are growing up among adults riddled by pathology. Such children clearly do not all remain illiterate, defeated, dependent, or confined to a life of mental illness. Several examples have already been given: the boy with the paranoid mother, and the boy raised in East Side poverty. Here is another, told by Anthony:

She was a child of the "poor whites" living in a two-roomed dilapidated and dirty apartment in the inner city. She had been the seventh of nine children, born prematurely with a congenital dislocation of the hip that was so inadequately treated at the city hospital that she developed a permanent limp. She was hospitalized several times in the first two years of life for "chest trouble" from which she almost died. Between two and five years, she was placed in a home with three of her siblings because the family living quarters had been condemned as overcrowded and unsanitary. The health visitor reported that the children were constantly exposed to crude sexual behavior of the father when he was drunk which was fairly frequent. His unemployment also made him irritable and he was brought before the court several times for physically abusing the children. The mother, not surprisingly, was chronically depressed and appeared to have little feeling left inside her for her husband, her children, or herself. A social worker wrote to say that she felt depressed every time she paid a visit.

When Mary was referred to me as a vulnerable child at high risk, I was struck by her immediate friendliness. She settled down at the interview in a warm, comfortable, trustful way that utterly took me by surprise since I was expecting almost the reverse. She was only nine years old and yet she had experienced, by all accounts, the dark and seamy side of life. She almost immediately put me at my ease and I soon found myself talking to her with much less guardedness than I usually use in a first interview. She talked of her home and said that sometimes "everyone got in the way" and "I have to keep an eye on the little ones because someone might stamp on them and not know they were there." Her dad was "grumpy" but this was because he didn't have a job. "If he hits us, it hurts a little but then we do something else and we don't feel it anymore."

I asked her about her mother and she replied indirectly: "We haven't got much money and all of us to eat. I try not to eat too much. Sometimes your stomach hurts and you want to eat more. We don't have too much clothes and some of them have big holes." I asked her if this made her feel sad and she said in a very matter-of-fact way: "It doesn't make me feel sad because I'm used to it. It makes my mom feel sad and she cries sometimes."

I wondered how she spent her time. "I'm collecting money for the poor children in India. They are starving. They haven't anything to eat and they go to bed hungry. They are always sick." I asked her what she would want if some kind fairy gave her three wishes for anything in the world.

She said: "First, I want to grow up soon. Then, I want to become a nurse. Then, I want to go and help look after the poor children in India." What did she want for herself? Her answer was characteristic for her and yet so uncharacteristic for this age of child. "I think I've got everything I want but (and her eyes sparkled) I'll have a good wish for you if you like. How would you like to go to Disneyland?" . . . it turned out that she had never actually left the neighborhood except to visit her mother in the hospital and to come to the clinic.

Many other examples and a hopeful conclusion appear in the reports of the noted Swiss psychiatrist quoted earlier, Manfred Bleuler. After studying the careers of 208 schizophrenics and their families for three decades, Bleuler finds that "most offspring of schizophrenics manage to lead productive lives." Indeed, he says, "one is left with the impression that pain and suffering can have a steeling—a hardening—effect on some children, rendering them capable of mastering life with all its obstacles, just to spite their inherent disadvantages."

Garmezy is optimistic about the potential for children growing up mentally healthy—even children who would appear to be relatively high risks for the development of mental illness. "Whatever model we choose for the etiology of schizophrenia," he says, "it is clear that the probabilities \stand on the side of the child escaping this ravaging disorder." The chances that schizophrenia will occur in randomly chosen groups of children in our country are estimated at from 1 to 3 percent—no higher. If we focus on more vulnerable children—those of families in which one parent is a victim of schizophrenia—the probability rises at least fourfold to, say, about 10 to 12 percent. In the case of children *both* of whose parents are schizophrenic, the percentage rises still more, to 35 to 45 percent.

Garmezy likes those odds. As an "optimist" in the risk field, he emphasizes the healthy side of the statistics. He bids us look on the positive side of the coin: among children growing up in a household marked even by the malignant presence of a schizophrenic parent, about 9 out of 10 will escape schizophrenia itself. Many of these will have lesser troubles, but some will know lives of creative accomplishment.

No one suggests, of course, that children subjected to early stress and trauma will inevitably be the stronger for their experience. But a few investigators have bid us to consider the possibility that a childhood without stress altogether may not be the best preparation for life later on either, at least for some children.

Stress and Adversity as a "Training Ground"

As Americans have become more affluent, increasing numbers of financially secure and devoted parents have been striving to protect their offspring from some of the nastier realities and stresses that they themselves encountered in early life. Are such maneuvers justified? Is a childhood hermetically sealed from the jarrings and vicissitudes of life really a good beginning toward psychological strength and emotional resilience?

Evidence has accumulated that it is not. Consider a case described by Thomas Meehan: He was born in Mount Vernon, New York, in 1925, the youngest of four children and the only son of an Austrian-American curtainmaker and his hardworking wife. Not long after he was born, the child's mother died, and his father, who was going through hard times, was forced to place his children in a series of foster homes around New York City. For a while, too, as one foster family after another rejected him, his father had to put him in the Hebrew Orphan Asylum at West 135th Street and Amsterdam Avenue.

When he was sixteen, his father had finally gotten together enough money to reassemble the family, and the five of them moved into an apartment in Forest Hills, where he started his first year of high school. After so many years of having been more or less on his own, however, he couldn't stand the mothering given to him by his three sisters, and so, dropping out of school in the spring of 1942, he ran away from home and joined the Marines.

Unlike most recruits who find themselves going through basic training at Parris Island, he loved the Marines ("I felt that the Marines were the only ones I had ever cared about or who had ever cared about me," he has told his interviewer), and serving mainly on Eniwetok, in the Pacific, he remained in the Marines until the fall of 1945, when he was discharged in Los Angeles with the rank of sergeant. Having no desire to go back home to New York, he enrolled as a freshman in the University of Southern California, where, as thousands of returning servicemen were swarming into the college, the admissions people at first failed to notice that he hadn't gone through high school.

When they discovered their mistake, they were going to kick him out but then relented to let him remain as a special student not eligible to receive a degree. So, though he stayed on for three years at Southern Cal, where he was the managing editor of the college humor magazine, to this day he has neither a high school diploma nor a college degree.

His name? Art Buchwald.

According to most prevailing theories of human development, a youngster like Buchwald should have struggled through life in a losing battle. An influential child-rearing theory warns that trauma and stress in infancy and childhood may be the source of later neurosis and instability. Yet Buchwald—and many more like him—have fashioned illustrious careers.

Data reported elsewhere in this book demonstrate, of course, that children subjected to traumatic experiences often do struggle through school, career, and marriage with little capacity to cope with the realities of life. But some investigators have begun to wonder whether a degree of adversity is not a prerequisite training ground—at least for some children—for sturdy psychological development.

Research evidence has admittedly come from the studies of animals rather than children, but the results are provocative.

For example, Seymour Levine and his colleagues at the Stanford University Medical School began during the 1950s to compare groups of rats. One group would be subjected to handling, shock, and other manipulations, such as being shaken in bottles or vibrated in their cages, while the control group was not. The investigators expected that the manhandled infants would mature less rapidly than the controls and become over-emotional adults, showing neurosislike behavior. They were wrong. For example, when rats that had been handled roughly as infants were placed in a large open container, they rummaged about and showed little timidity—while the controls cowered in corners.

An early experiment divided the infant rats into three groups. One group was shocked, one group was put through all the motions preparatory to shock but not the shock itself, and the third group—not handled at all—was left to rest quietly in isolated cages. When the rats matured, they underwent avoidance conditioning, a procedure in which they had to learn to take some action, such as pressing a bar in the cage, in order to avoid a painful shock. The animals that had been traumatized during infancy learned their lesson fastest. The rats that had been handled but not shocked learned almost as fast. But the animals that had not been stimulated in any way acted as though paralyzed by fear. Evidently the other rats' stressful experience in infancy had somehow prepared them to meet stress in adulthood. Other experiments produced similar results.

How could such differences in behavior be explained? Could they spring from physical differences? The investigators found that they could, indeed. Two interconnected glandular systems were involved—the pituitary and the adrenal. In a stressful situation, the pituitary—which in humans is a tiny oval gland located at the base of the brain, just above the nasal passages—releases a substance called ACTH (standing for *adrenocorticotropic hormone,* or a hormone that acts upon the adrenal cortex). Under the influence of ACTH, the adrenals—small glands above the kidneys—release several hormones. The best known of these is adrenaline, which tones up the body for either fighting the stressful situation or fleeing from it.

Rats that had been handled and stressed in infancy were found to be producing ACTH at a significantly earlier age than their unstressed fellows. Also, during the first 15 minutes after a shock, they produced more adrenal hormones, which meant that they were responding faster to the emergency. But their hormone level quickly dropped to normal. In contrast, the unhandled rats reacted slowly and kept releasing adrenaline and other hormones long after the need had passed.

During infancy, moreover, the stimulated rats grew faster, opened their eyes earlier, moved in a coordinated fashion earlier, gained weight more rapidly, and developed a good coat of fur sooner. Finally, these rats lived longer. The results strongly indicate that a degree of stimulation early in life, even though unpleasant and painful, aids an animal's development and prepares it to handle problems that arise later.

Though it is a long leap from rats to children, it is useful to recall what was reported earlier in this chapter about research at the Human Development Institute in Berkeley, California: the children who did best as adults often had experienced the most difficult childhoods.

Perhaps a certain degree of vicissitude and "handling" by life prepares some children, like the experimental rats, for the years ahead. "After all," explains Los Angeles analyst Rudolph Ekstein, of the Reiss-Davis Child Study Center, "each of us must overcome trauma to achieve adulthood. Birth is a trauma. So is toilet training, learning to crawl, to walk, entering school, the first date, and so on. The question is whether trauma can be turned into an opportunity or whether it will remain an obstacle. It should be viewed as something to build on."

Manfred Bleuler, in working with the families of schizophrenic parents, has described how he became aware of the "good and normal" aspects of many young people who, as children, had endured the stress of growing up with psychotic parents. "I saw how they worried about their parents," he writes, "how they struggled when their parents were to be transferred to other clinics which would be more difficult to visit. I saw how many of these children made economic sacrifices or interrupted their professional training in order to help their parents, or how they undertook to manage the family household and care for younger siblings in place of a hospitalized parent. Such children seem not only immune to pathological influences in the environment, but seem almost to thrive on them."

Again the invulnerable children! They may be our best research hope.

Turning Vulnerable Children Around

If we could find early clues to sources of strength, it might be possible to help youngsters develop these sources and thus turn children—even those who are apparently most vulnerable—from mental illness to mental health. Certainly it is possible to "accentuate the positive"—possible, though not easy, for patience and devotion in abundance are required if parents and professionals are to look beyond present difficulties to a rewarding future.

Children, we may be sure, are quick to sense whether the adults around them view their future with despair or hope. Macfarlane recorded the comments made by her adult subjects as they reminisced about their earlier troubled years and about the approach taken to them by the staff of the Berkeley Guidance Study. Here are two examples:

I sensed your respect for me, even when I knew I wasn't acting very sensibly and knew you wouldn't have had respect for me if there wasn't something there to respect. . . .

You asked questions, you listened, but you were the only grown-ups who didn't give advice. You helped me to ferret things out for myself, to make my own decisions. I try to carry this on in the raising of my children.

Macfarlane urges all adults who touch the lives of the young to take their cue from such insights and to look for strengths in children rather than for pathology. The challenge is critical not only for parents but for teachers as well. Garmezy points out that Alfred Binet himself, the grandfather of contemporary intelligence testing, saw it clearly. At the turn of the century, he moved into the Paris school system to identify those children who appeared unable to profit from instruction, and to help them build on their strengths. Today, Garmezy reminds us, there is a considerably larger number of children in our schools whose emotional burdens prevent them from profiting from the one major institution of society that can liberate them from incompetence. Through the creative collaboration of child development researchers and educational personnel, it should be possible to identify these children and capitalize on their hidden resources.

One example of what can be done has been demonstrated by researchers studying children who appear unable to learn. This condition, which is a significant cause of emotional distress and behavior disorders among children and adolescents, is variously known as learning disorder or learning disability, dyslexia, and reading failure. By whatever name, it is the greatest single reason children drop out of school. It characterizes 75 percent of the children who end up in juvenile detention centers. Among children referred to psychiatric clinics because of disturbed or disturbing behavior, it is one of the commonest signs. Because they fail to read adequately, many thousands of otherwise normal children are subjected to years of frustration, humiliation, self-depreciation, and torment. Many become shy and troubled adolescents who turn away from the world and fight themselves; others turn away from themselves and fight society. Some, judged retarded because they cannot read, are tragically assigned to classes, and even institutions, for mentally retarded children.

Reading failure, with its attendant emotional crises, is most prevalent among children who have been culturally disadvantaged. Out of several hundred New York City pupils studied by Jeanette Jansky and Katrina De Hirsch, for example, 33 percent had failed to learn to read by the end of the second grade. Among those who failed were 69 percent of the children from families low on the socioeconomic scale. However, 30 percent of the children from "comfortable" backgrounds were also among the failures; so were 33 percent of the bright children as measured by IQ tests. Learning disorder occurs at every economic level.

Clearly, the detection and prevention of learning disability would be a giant step toward armoring youngsters against psychiatric disability. Among the many investigators who are making it possible for society to take that step are a New York clinical and research team headed by Archie A. Silver, a psychiatrist, and Rosa A. Hagin, a psychologist. They are director and co-director, respectively, of the Learning Disorders Unit of New York University–Bellevue Medical Center.

Silver first became interested in the problem one day some 25 years ago when, as director of Bellevue's recently opened psychiatric clinic for children, he came face to face with a troubled and frightened ten-year-old named Lennie. Lennie could not read, would not do his school work, had no friends, and fought with his younger brother. He was neurologically sound and of normal intelligence. But he performed poorly on tests that required him to copy geometrical figures. When he tried to copy a diamond, for instance, the corners were distorted "in a peculiar dog-eared way, as though he could not decide on the direction to take when he had to draw an angle."

Lennie wasn't alone. Out of every ten children referred to Silver's clinic because of behavior disorders, it soon developed that eight were reading poorly and that many of them, like Lennie, had a defect of visual-motor function: either they could not perceive geometrical figures correctly or could not put on paper what they saw. Testing revealed many other deficits. There were children who could not distinguish between right and left, for example, or could not remember the correct spacing of sounds or could not pick out a certain pattern from a background of patterns. All such children—sent to the psychiatric clinic for treatment of problem behavior—had the same basic trouble: they lacked one or more of the skills essential to identifying words.

In addition to the usual psychotherapeutic treatment, the N.Y.U. investigators enrolled Lennie and 40 other psychiatric clinic patients in a remedial reading program. Ten years later, the great majority of the former patients seemed reasonably well adjusted emotionally, socially, and vocationally. But close to 40 percent were still reading at a level far below their general intelligence and still showed some evidence of the perceptual defects found earlier. Lennie, who was working full-time in a factory and part-time in a bar, proved to be excellent in arithmetic but only at ninth-grade level in reading.

Concluding that traditional remedial reading methods were clearly insufficient, the investigators began developing and testing a method that would attack the deficits directly and try to train them out. The teaching of reading usually starts with the recognition and comprehension of words. But in many cases, Silver and Hagin were convinced, it was necessary first of all to build visual and auditory perception, left-to-right progression, and related skills. Instead of teaching the child to read, they aimed to develop the skills essential to reading.

The resulting program was used first in an N.Y.U.-Bellevue clinic and then in a New York public school. One-third of all the first graders in this school had evidence of perceptual immaturity sufficient to require specific training if they were not to become reading failures. Virtually all of these children also had some degree of psychiatric impairment.

For 20 minutes a day, in the school's "resource room," each child received perceptual training built around his or her particular deficits. For example, if a child could not easily recognize and copy geometric forms and other patterns, and therefore had trouble discriminating letters and recognizing words, he or she was drilled in the recognition and copying of designs—simple ones first and then more complex. A child with normal hearing acuity but an inability to remember a series of sounds in proper order or to discriminate between words that sounded much alike was drilled in auditory sequencing and in the aural recognition of words.

When the training began, the reading scores of these children clustered in the lowest segment of the total first-grade scores. The following spring, the distribution of scores resembled in a general way that of the total group. A year later, toward the end of the second grade, the resemblance was closer.

Beyond this, mental health improved markedly. The percentage of those rated as severely impaired dropped from 23 in the first grade to 5 in the fifth. During the same time, the proportion of those with moderate impairment was halved, while the proportion of those without psychiatric impairment of any degree soared from almost zero to better than one-quarter.

At least in most cases, the investigators are certain that the improvement did not occur spontaneously but reflected the special training. "Success in learning," they conclude, "provided a strong point around which the developing personality could rally."

Silver and Hagin, as well as other investigators, have also developed a short battery of scanning tests for predicting which children are vulnerable to learning disorders. The battery has also been used to pick out which among these children seem also to be at neurological or psychiatric risk. Tragic outcomes for the children vulnerable to learning disorders are clearly not preordained. The children who are strongly motivated to learn in spite of their handicap can succeed, particularly if they have the encouragement and understanding of parents and teachers, and access to tutoring in needed skills—all of them attuned to the child's special requirements.

The needs for strengthening of children with other vulnerabilities are equally urgent, and the problem for the researcher is to identify precursor conditions and traits that might indicate in which direction a child is moving—toward either distinction or disaster. It is to find the resources which, in Srole's words, are "fortifying and immunizing against the potentially shattering impact of extreme . . . adversity; and to build them into the lives of our young."

The task is not the researcher's alone. All adults who touch the lives of children share a comparable responsibility. Not every child, of course, will encounter trauma and adversity. But all of them—poor and rich, black and white, weak and strong—need the caring and concern of adult protectors during the precious years that are a child's beginnings.

13

Protecting Your Child's Mental Health

Work on this book began with the expectation that there
would emerge no single answer to the riddle of the child's development. The sweeping generalizations and bland platitudes common in
the past were not expected to be sustained.

A study of the panorama of research findings in the field strengthened
rather than weakened our expectation. If there is a major theme that
appears from the network of studies of children under way around the
world, it is that our young are the product not of one force but of many.

The Mosaic of a Child's Development

Much as we might seek it, there is no simple answer to the question:
How do they get that way? The evidence against easy explanations is
overwhelming, and it may be found throughout the book.

Genetics can explain some, but by no means all, of a child's destiny; a
stable environment can protect the well-being of even a child considered to be at high genetic risk for mental illness. Constitutional forces
help fix a child's behavioral patterns and temperament beginning at
birth, but how the child fares in the real world will depend in turn on
the manner in which adults around the child react and adapt to his or
her unique style. Hidden physical problems can upset a child's emo-

302

tional equilibrium, but at the same time the stresses of family life can induce serious medical crises. A caring mother's abiding presence early in the life of her child is clearly a source of strength and stability, yet her absence need not have a deleterious effect if the father or another substitute caretaker act out of an equally strong commitment to the child's well-being. Erosions in the child's mental health induced by one wildly psychotic parent can be ameliorated by the other stable and healthy one. An eagerly anticipated child who enjoys warm and rewarding attachments during the first months of life may be protected against emotional problems—but not certainly; the benefits of early bonds can quickly come unglued in a harsh world of hunger and hate. And, as one more example, the flickering sense of self-confidence in a poor and persecuted child may be rekindled by a dedicated teacher who expects much and inspires greatly.

It is rarely mother alone, father alone, schools alone, friends alone— any one factor alone—that shapes the destiny of the child. From birth onward, children are affected by a mosaic of forces. While one or another element may stand out in the case of a particular child, it is typically a combination of them that ultimately leaves its mark.

Strategies for Protecting Our Children's Future

Because no single factor alone can explain a child's future, no single prescription holds the key to protecting the mental health of our children. The chances of stability and self-fulfillment among the young may be increased significantly only if we hear—and act on—*all* the messages embedded in the studies described in this book. None of them may be slighted if we are to safeguard the child's tomorrows.

What follows is neither a manual of child rearing nor an inventory of specific maneuvers adults may use in dealing with the young. For the most part, such prepackaged, how-to-raise-your-child guides cannot be applied universally. No child ought to be viewed as an excerpt from a statistical table whose minute-to-minute behavior can be planned in advance. More relevant by far than such isolated tactics are the broad strategies that, in the light of carefully developed research findings, apply to children everywhere.

Such strategies are provided on the pages that follow. The reader should be aware that these in no way comprise an exhaustive summary of the detailed findings and discussions embedded in the earlier chapters. They are presented instead to highlight some of the major insights into our children's development to which researchers have led us, and the implications these insights contain for helping us protect the mental health of the young.

- When a child is planned for and wanted, anticipated and made room for, its chances for psychological well-being are significantly improved. Children should be conceived, therefore, only if their existence is likely to be graced by parental commitment and devotion. The unbridled passions of sex must be matched by disciplined compassion for the resulting child.
- Parents must learn to recognize and accept the child's stamp of individuality. Children show strong temperamental differences virtually from birth, and it is clear that not every child can be handled in the same way. Despite the programmed advice of many experts on "parenting," no mother or father can give up working at the task of listening for, understanding, and dealing with the individual characteristics of *this* child.
- Whatever its basis, the attachment of infant to mother is an indisputable fact of human existence. Beginning in its earliest hours, the newborn establishes bonds with its mother that lay the foundation for many of life's relationships. The early roots of children, therefore, need to be nourished, their bonds of attachment strengthened from the start. The mother's right to an independent life outside the home cannot be denied, but her search for that life without at the same time assuring her baby's security can be costly beyond measure.
- Children who grow in an environment barren of stimulation and affection are at greater risk than others to deficits in their emotional and intellectual development. A growing child should be enriched by the committed presence of parents or guardians, not diminished by their psychological distance or physical absence.
- The father's impact, long sorely underestimated, is at least as important as the mother's. His inadequacy or unavailability can erode the child's emotional well-being, whereas his wholesome presence can promote it. In families shorn of the father's positive influences, adult male surrogates are needed to enrich the child's emotional resources. Warm and supportive masculine figures—whether stepfathers, members of the extended family, leaders of social organizations, or teachers—can substitute as male models and become beacons of security in the often uncertain world of the growing child.
- The stresses endured by adults cannot be hidden from the child's view altogether—nor should they. But neither ought children become the chronic targets for parental conflicts and passions. Parental discord often leaves its painful mark on the child. In the face of family tensions,

some children, already vulnerable to psychosomatic ailments, suffer acute illnesses, and children of divorce are more likely than others to engage in antisocial behavior and to endure depression. It is not so much the actual physical split between parents that appears to give rise to mental health problems in the young but rather the psychological distance and dissension that mark so many households. In resolving their discord, parents owe it to their children to protect them from becoming innocent casualties of the emotional warfare waged daily in so many homes.

• The influence of a living example on the child's behavior is even greater than many have believed. It is clear that children pattern much of their behavior after models encountered during their early years. As parents, we may safely act on the long held—but poorly practiced—assumption that our children will be affected more by what we do than what we say.

• The effects of a teacher's personality and attitudes can be enormous, helping lead the child down paths of either self-confidence and success or self-depreciation and defeat. Teachers, for example, who are warm, enthusiastic and compassionate are not only preferred by students but are the ones most likely to advance their emotional maturation and intellectual development. Moreover, a teacher's even unspoken expectations can help determine the quality of a student's performance and the viability of her or his self-concept. In the light of the teacher's awesome power, it is critical that the schools to which we entrust our children be staffed by men and women likely to help rather than to hurt their charges. Feelings of competence and well-being among our young are commodities too precious to be squandered in the schoolroom.

• Children are the members of society most likely to become victimized by labels. In the schools especially, our young are too readily branded as "retarded," "disturbed," "delinquent," or worse. Such labels are often stigmatizing to the child, closing off avenues of potential help when it is needed, and beginning a process by which the child may be removed unfairly from normal social contacts with other children. Worse yet, labeled children may ultimately incorporate into their self-concepts the brandings affixed to them and may come so to believe in their validity that life becomes a self-fulfilling prophecy. The task for schools is to deal democratically with each child as an individual, not as an item in a textbook category. For parents, the task is to counter the impact of unfairly affixed labels and to offer the child esteem and confidence when the messages of the world outside speak only of rejection and uncertainty.

- Though it may be hard for many mothers and fathers to accept, some of the child's basic attitudes and capacities will be shaped as much by peers as by parents. It is typically from friends that a child develops sexual information and patterns of behavior, learns how to modulate aggressive feelings, develops moral and ethical standards, and even finds precious reserves of emotional security in time of emotional travail. Parents may help guide their children in the selection of friends, but having done so, they must recognize that peer interaction is an essential ingredient in the mosaic of child development. Mothers and fathers will serve children best if they accept the power of their children's friends, recognize their presence, and work with rather than against them.

- The assumption among many parents that, except for their influence, children will be "ruined" is not borne out by research findings. Evidence suggests instead that children's imitation of peers is, in the main, constructive; children are less likely than many parents fear to align themselves with peers who do not share parental values and standards.

- The child's indiscriminate choice of friends is most likely when family ties are weak and when the child's sense of belonging is fragmented. Feelings of alienation and isolation within the home are not calculated to safeguard the child's identity or to prevent his or her seeking a new and often contradictory identity outside. Parents who offer their children only morsels of companionship and support, therefore, should have little complaint if these children look to peers as their sole reference point. The need for friends—whatever their orientation—may be particularly strong, for example, for a child whose home is bereft of parental presence, whose mother and father are motivated only by self-fulfillment rather than selflessness. Needing emotional sustenance, such a child may well find it in a group—any group— and be willing, in return, to adopt even antisocial values. What children look for in their friends in such cases is often what they have failed to find at home.

- An environment that is harsh and abusive—emotionally as well as physically—can produce an array of problems ranging from brain damage and speech impairment to sexual malfunctions and violence. Moreover, the victims of such an environment may grow to inflict similar pain on their own children. The application of abuse and neglect as instruments of child rearing must be viewed as a plague whose eradication would protect the mental health of generations of children yet unborn.

- For parents just a generation or so ago, "spoiling" the child was virtually the cardinal sin of child rearing. A mother—any caretaker—who responded quickly or consistently to a baby's call or cry was thought to be running the risk of rearing a child who would manipulate and exploit his or her elders from crib to grave. The result was a tendency among parents to hold back on such tangible demonstrations of their love and caring as picking babies up and holding them when they could not sleep, feeding them when they appeared hungry, and providing contact and comfort when they cried. We know now that the tendency to suppress such behavior is wrong. The more empathically and accurately parents read their children's signals, and the more sensitively they respond to them from the heart, the more likely the child will be protected from erosions in mental health. Children who know that they are operating from a firm base do not "spoil"; instead they are able to draw on a well of security lasting a lifetime. Don't hold back on the instincts of love and caring.

- Malnutrition can produce a host of physical and behavioral changes that deface both the body and the mind of the child—destroying brain cells along with the self-concept, inducing disease and depressing the child's capacities to cope with the environment. For millions of American children, the goals of mental health are as far as the nearest nourishing meal, and no psychological interventions will avail for them until the corrosive environment of poverty is altered.

- The poisons of racism threaten the well-being of both the hated and the hating child and create a milieu in which precious feelings of identity and self-esteem are threatened for life. The responsibility for protecting children from the erosions of mental health induced by racial prejudice—and, often, by poverty as well—lies not only with the family but also with a government truly concerned about the impact of social policy on individual lives.

The implications of child development research, it is clear, are relevant to all. No one dare project responsibility for the mental health of our children onto others. Anyone who touches the lives of the young is clearly responsible for their destiny. Each of us has both a healing and a hurting power.

That power is especially awesome when held by those who govern. The efforts and hopes of even the most highly motivated and nurturing parents may be destroyed quickly by the absence of adequate family supports and resources in the community, by a society that is uncaring and uncommitted.

What Our Government Must Do

For large numbers of parents, many responsibilities toward their children cannot be fulfilled without support from the government. In their recent report entitled *All Our Children,* Kenneth Keniston and the Carnegie Council on Education have for good reason attacked the notion, inculcated in many parents, that mothers and fathers alone are responsible for what becomes of their children and that they alone must be held accountable if things go awry. "Most children's problems are also social problems," Keniston insists, and the implication is clear: "Change must not be just personal but also political."

No matter how highly motivated, a destitute mother cannot alone protect her child against the psychological ravages of hunger and intellectual impoverishment; an anguished father, unable to find work and his self-concept eroded, can hardly be expected to be sensitive to the emotional needs of his young children; and even a community of parents cannot alone raise the personal and professional standards among the teachers to whom they entrust their children. The messages of child development research must be heard as clearly by our nation's social and political leaders as by individual parents.

The failure thus far to do so by those in power can be ascribed neither to ignorance nor malice. Instead, our children have been the victims of passive and passionless attitudes among those who govern—of a lack of deep commitment to the child. The symptoms are not difficult to find. As described by political scientist Gilbert Y. Steiner, a broad and well-defined national policy on children has never been clearly formulated; few tested ideas have been translated from researchers' journals to legal statutes; the nation's child advocates have failed to join in common cause; and the awesome responsibilities for children's programs have been scattered haphazardly throughout the Congress and federal bureaucracy.

During the presidency of Lyndon B. Johnson, a willing Congress helped create the Office of Child Development, intended to ensure that the children's cause did not go unattended. The uncertain role of that Office—and of our government's continuing uncoordinated efforts in behalf of children—tells its own story. "I have been particularly troubled by a myth . . . that we are a child-oriented society and we do all that needs to be done for our nation's children," says Edward F. Zigler, now Yale professor of psychology and formerly head of the Office of Child Development. The realities, Zigler believes, belie this myth.

Editorial writer Colman McCarthy of the *Washington Post* raises serious doubts whether America really values its young. "A case is easily made that America, far from doting on its children, actually hates them. Much of this loathing has been institutionalized, so that only the occasionally deranged molester on the street or the child abuser is seen as dangerous. The term 'child abuse' has a narrow legal definition, but for the victimized child it matters little whether he is brutalized directly by a crazed adult or obliquely by a political system that treats him as worthless."

Though such opinions may seem extreme, it is clear enough that the needs of children have not figured prominently in the priority-setting processes of our government. Federal programs continue to be weighed for their impact on the nation's budget, on foreign policy, on energy supplies, and on the quality of the environment—but not on the lives of children. "Today," reports the Carnegie Council on Children, "virtually the last question we ask of any public policy is how it will affect children. It should become the first question."

- If it is true that adequate substitute care for children of working mothers is critical to the child's well-being, why is it that a coherent day-care program is still unavailable to needy parents?
- If the father's presence is, in fact, an important ingredient in the child's development, why is it that welfare laws penalize families in which an unemployed father is present but not earning enough to support his children?
- If the continuity of family life does improve a young child's chances for good mental health, why do our tax laws make it more attractive to seek care for children outside the family than at home? (In the words of President Carter, "Quite often the actions of government have been an obstacle instead of an asset in holding families together.")
- If early contacts with the mother and father do establish critical bonds of emotional strength for life, why do our laws insist that Social Security credits toward later retirement may be earned only by working *outside* the home but not by staying home and caring for one's children?
- If members of the extended family can serve as emotional lifelines for troubled children, why do our laws permit the tax-deductible payment of costs for care for the elderly only outside, in a nursing home—not if they live in their own homes with their own children and grandchildren?

One answer suffices for all the questions asked. It lies in the collective priorities of our citizens. In the final analysis, it is the values of the people that are reflected in what our leaders buy with our tax dollars— better day-care facilities or bigger bombs, an improved network of mental health centers or a smoother web of highways. Consider this anomaly in national priorities: We know that a child's sense of competence can ultimately make or break him or her as a person, yet our nation spends over 33 million budget dollars every year for the control of outdoor advertising and junkyards, but only a third as much for the National Right to Read Program—designed to give all children a basic skill needed to function in our society.

If the prevention of mental health problems in succeeding generations of children required only the development of a serum, progress might have been achieved long ago. Given sufficient resources, this nation does not lack the technological and intellectual prowess to defeat polio, measles, and even, one day, cancer.

Progress in behalf of our children, however, rests more heavily on ideals than on ideas, on principles rather than pragmatics. Much of the knowledge we need to protect our children's mental health is already known; the challenge, alas, is not to develop a psychological serum but to deliver a suffering society. It will require a social conscience, a sense of caring for *all* children, to translate what we know into what we do. Only so can we collectively induce the social changes required to protect the mental health of our young and to prevent still more cohorts of disturbed and disturbing children in the years beyond our own.

Lobbying for Children

Orville Brim, president of the Foundation for Child Development, has depicted the low status of children in America: "When the going gets tough, children are the first to go. They don't vote. They have no clout. The economic value of children in society has declined over the past 100 years. Their perceived value in the family has deteriorated and the wish to have children has declined."

Few will doubt the validity of Brim's diagnosis. Unlike other special interest groups, the nation's children have no effective voice, and as a result, most of the governmental lobbying efforts in their behalf have been tangled and ineffective.

Lacking has been the child's potentially most powerful lobby— ourselves. Government programs in behalf of children are not likely to take shape without the demands of an informed citizenry, acting out of deep conviction. Each of us must ultimately act by speaking out for the young—not only for those in our own families and communities but for children everywhere. Keniston has described the ideal: "The devotion that individual parents now feel to their own children would be broadened to include everyone's children. The next generation's strength and well-being would become everyone's responsibility."

In tangible terms, what can each of us do?

We can begin, Keniston suggests, by voicing questions rarely posed about children. Whether in dinner-table discussions or national policy debates, we should be asking "not only about how to change—or help—individual families, but about measures to modify economic and social factors that affect families." In addition to worrying about report cards and pediatricians and growing pains, he contends, our concerns should broaden to encompass all aspects of life that affect children, including "jobs, the structure of the labor market, and the degree of social justice in the nation. . . . Public advocates have to ask about tax reform, about reorganizing health care, about racism, about sexism, about energy—all for the sake of children."

As guardians of our young, we fall short if we remain unconcerned, for example, about the attitudes of our local school board members, about the policies the principal of the local school will follow, and about the quality of the school's teachers. We need to become more adept, Keniston believes, at taking political action "through community service councils and community health agencies . . . by encouraging organizations that are concerned with children, such as the local and national PTA or the Junior League, to keep pushing political issues that touch children. Writing letters to Congress, supporting lobbying efforts, and preparing tough questions for campaigning political candidates about their views on children should be as much a part of childrearing as changing diapers or drying tears."

No one can deny that pressures mount on the public treasury for a bewildering array of high priority efforts that significantly affect the lives of the American people—from national defense to the protection of our environment. Our nation does not have unlimited resources—for supporting either its children or other assets in our national inventory. As lobbyists for the young, therefore, we may well have to confront the inevitable managerial question: Would programs instituted by our government in behalf of the children turn out to be economically sound? In modern jargon, would they be "cost-effective"?

A shift in priorities in behalf of children undoubtedly would be advantageous in fiscal as well as human terms. An estimated 10 million of our youth under age twenty-five require mental health services. In the state hospitals of our nation, where the number of first admissions of adult patients has been declining steadily, admission rates for children have increased at an accelerated pace. For children under fifteen, for example, the rate more than doubled between 1962 and 1975. The loss to this nation of these children's economic productivity is incalculable. When added to the cost of actually caring for them in mental health facilities, the drain begins to make preventive programs look like acts of good management as well as of compassion.

No matter how successful, however, an investment in public debates over child programs does not absolve any one of us of our private responsibilities toward the children who are part of our own lives. Even were we to succeed in elevating child concerns to the highest levels of government, the futures of our children would continue to be hazardous without our giving them an equally high priority in our own hearts and minds. The destiny of our young will be determined not only in the corridors of political power but in the kitchens and living rooms across the land.

The Bottom Line: Commitment and Caring

In the end, none of the paths for protecting the mental health of children explored in this book can be followed without an abiding sense of commitment to the child.

Such a commitment does not involve unequivocal approval of the child's behavior. There are many occasions when adults are disappointed, angered, or hurt by their young, and it is in the best interests of neither child nor adult to deny such feelings. Nor does it entail a constant readiness to satisfy every childish whim and wish. No authority on child rearing has ever seriously suggested that our young must be supplied only with rewards and gratifications; firmness, consistency, setting limits—all of these have an important place in the day-to-day interactions between parent and child, and they have been shown to enhance rather than diminish the child's psychological growth.

Instead, a true commitment means an abiding concern for the child's welfare—one that is not conditional, that does not depend on the child's temperament, attractiveness, or intelligence, that does not wax and wane in response to the child's day-to-day behavior. We cannot raise our children with reservations in mind.

An unswerving commitment to our young means also an abiding belief in each child's potential, a deeply rooted conviction that *this* child—like all children—has the right and the power to grow and mature, to achieve emotional and intellectual fulfillment.

A generation ago most experts believed in the continuity of personality and mental ability from infancy onward. Now, however, long-term studies, some of them begun in the 1920s and 1930s, have called into question the idea that children remain essentially the same from the beginning. It is clear today that the young have a magnificent capacity to recover from early exposure even to a sickening environment. Moreover, poor outcomes—from even constitutional or genetic deficits—are *not* preordained.

Harvard professor of human development Jerome Kagan likens the characteristics of a developing young child to sand on a beach. A wave appears and moves the sand. Days later, another wave comes up and moves it again. "Child development is more fluid and dynamic than is generally realized," he has concluded. "There is much more change than has been thought; the child is much more resilient."

To realize their power of resiliency, however, our children need support. We are the waves that move the sand. In the course of writing this book, we talked to dozens of children in an attempt to elicit their views about their own development. What were the factors that most affected their own personalities, and what would *they* do one day to strengthen the mental health of their own children?

In words that differed in style and mood, a common theme emerged. Give us a sense of being wanted and cherished, a sense of importance and uniqueness, say these children, and you will have offered us the psychological armor with which to cope, no matter what the stresses that life offers.

"I think devotion and understanding does it. With that you can solve all kinds of problems. . . ."

"What hurts most is the lack of interest and guidance . . . What helps is the conviction that someone really cares."

"A lot of my capacities and strengths, I have to think, came from my home—from being given the feeling that I was important, that my future really counted."

Children do not receive such messages of strength from adults whose commitment is equivocal; they do so from those who are ready always to make the child a first priority. Protecting the mental health of children takes time and energy, pain, and self-sacrifice—for it demands the kinds of caring that often places the child's future interests above our own present ones.

In the final reckoning, all of the day-to-day variations in mood we spontaneously bring to the lives of children are of little significance if, beneath them all, there lies an abiding devotion to the child. Our young know well when we cherish them and when we do not. They can feel, shining through even our intermittent storms of temper and outrage, the unquenchable strength that exudes from the adult who really cares.

No book can teach us that kind of passionate commitment. With it we can safely shed the burdens of guilt and anxiety that so often mar the joys of rearing our young.

The word is old and casually used. Yet it defines the one force that binds all the healthy forces in a child's journey. The word is love.

References

CHAPTER 2

Anderson, J.: "Child Development: An Historical Perspective," *Child Development*, vol. 27, pp. 181–196, 1956.

Anderson, R. H., and H. G. Shane (eds.): *As the Twig Is Bent: Readings in Early Childhood Education* (New York: Houghton Mifflin, 1971).

Aries, P.: *Centuries of Childhood* (London: Cape, 1962).

Cable, M.: *The Little Darlings: A History of Childrearing in America* (New York: Scribner, 1975).

Coveney, P.: *Poor Monkey: The Child in Literature* (London: Dufour, 1957).

DeMause, L.: "The Evolution of Childhood," *History of Childhood Quarterly*, vol. 1, pp. 503–575, 1973.

Despert, J. L.: *The Emotionally Disturbed Child—Then and Now* (New York: Robert Brunner, 1965).

Kanner, L.: *Child Psychiatry*, 3d ed. (Springfield, Ill.: Charles C Thomas, 1957).

Kern, S.: "Explosive Intimacy: Psychodynamics of the Victorian Family," *History of Childhood Quarterly*, vol. 1, pp. 437–461, 1973.

Kessen, W.: *The Child* (New York: Wiley, 1965).

Langer, W. L.: "Infanticide: A Historical Survey," *History of Childhood Quarterly*, vol. 1, pp. 353–366, 1973.

Locke, J.: *Some Thoughts Concerning Education* (London: Cambridge University Press, 1892).

McGrath, N.: "By the Book," *New York Times Magazine*, June 27, 1976.

Mussen, P. H., J. J. Conger, and J. Kagan: *Child Development and Personality*, 3d ed. (New York: Harper & Row, 1969).

Sears, R. R.: "Your Ancients Revisited: A History of Child Development," in E. M. Hetherington (ed.), *Review of Research in Child Development*, vol. 5 (Chicago: The University of Chicago Press, 1975).

Senn, M. J. E.: "Insights on the Child Development Movement in the United States," *Monographs of the Society for Research in Child Development*, vol. 40, 1975.

Skinner, B. F.: *Walden Two* (New York: Macmillan, 1948).

Spock, B.: *Common Sense Book of Baby and Child Care* (New York: Pocket Books, 1946).

Sunley, R.: "Early Nineteenth Century American Literature on Child-rearing," in M. Mead and M. Wolfenstein (eds.), *Childhood in Contemporary Cultures* (Chicago: The University of Chicago Press, 1955).

Wishy, B.: *The Child and the Republic: The Dawn of Modern American Child Nurture* (Philadelphia: University of Pennsylvania Press, 1967).

CHAPTER 3

Åmark, C.: "A Study in Alcoholism: Clinical, Social-Psychiatric and Genetic Investigations," *Acta Psychiatrica et Neurologica Scandinavica*, supplement 70, 1951, cited by G. E. McClearn and J. C. DeFries, *Introduction to Behavioral Genetics* (San Francisco: Freeman, 1973).

Anthony, E. J.: "The Developmental Precursors of Adult Schizophrenia," in S. Kety and D. Rosenthal (eds.), *Transmissions of Schizophrenia* (Oxford, England: Pergamon Press, Ltd., copyright 1968).

Belmaker, R., W. Pollin, R. J. Wyatt, and S. Cohen: "A Follow-up of Monozygotic Twins Discordant for Schizophrenia," *Archives of General Psychology*, vol. 30, pp. 219–222, 1974.

Cytryn, L., and D. H. McKnew, Jr.: "Proposed Classification of Childhood Depression," *American Journal of Psychiatry*, vol. 129, no. 2, pp. 149–154, 1972.

Goldfarb, W.: "The Mutual Impact of Mother and Child in Childhood Schizophrenia," *American Journal of Orthopsychiatry*, vol. 3, no. 4, 1961.

———: "Families of Schizophrenic Children," *Mental Retardation*, vol. 39, 1962.

———: *Growth and Change of Schizophrenic Children: A Longitudinal Study* (Washington, D.C.: V. H. Winston and Sons, 1974).

———: N. Goldfarb, and R. C. Pollack: "Treatment of Childhood Schizophrenia: A 3-Year Comparison of Residential and Day Treatment," *Archives of General Psychiatry*, vol. 14, 1966.

Goodwin, D. W., F. Schulsinger, L. Hermanson, S. B. Guze, and G. Winokur: "Alcohol Problems in Adoptees Raised Apart from Alcoholic Biological Parents," *Archives of General Psychology*, vol. 28, pp. 238–243, 1973. (Cited by G. E. McClearn and J. C. DeFries, *Introduction to Behavioral Genetics* [San Francisco: Freeman, 1973].)

Gottesman, I. I., and J. Shields: *Schizophrenia and Genetics* (New York: Academic, 1972). (Cited by G. A. Kimble, N. Garmezy, and E. Zigler, *Principles of General Psychology*, 4th ed. [New York: Ronald, 1974].)

Heston, L. L.: "The Genetics of Schizophrenic and Schizoid Disease," *Science*, vol. 167, pp. 249–256, 1970. (Cited by G. E. McClearn and J. C. DeFries, *Introduction to Behavioral Genetics* [San Francisco: Freeman, 1973].)

Kety, S. S., D. Rosenthal, P. H. Wender, and F. Schulsinger: "Mental Illness in the Biological and Adoptive Families of Adopted Schizophrenics," *American Journal of Psychiatry*, vol. 128, pp. 302–306, 1971.

McClearn, G. E., and J. C. DeFries: *Introduction to Behavioral Genetics* (San Francisco: Freeman, 1973).

McKnew, D. H., Jr., and L. Cytryn: "Historical Background in Children with Affective Disorders," *American Journal of Psychiatry*, vol. 130, no. 11, pp. 1278–1279, 1973.

———, L. Cytryn, A. M. Effron, E. S. Gershon, and W. E. Bunney, Jr.: "Offspring of

Manic-Depressive Patients," paper presented to American Psychiatric Association, Miami Beach, Fla., May 1976.

Meyers, D. I., and W. Goldfarb: "Psychiatric Appraisals of Parents and Siblings of Schizophrenic Children," *American Journal of Psychiatry,* vol. 118, no. 10, 1962.

Pollin, W., J. Stabenau, and J. Tupin: "Family Studies with Identical Twins Discordant for Schizophrenia," *Psychiatry,* vol. 28, no. 1, pp. 60–78, 1965.

————, J. Stabenau, L. Mosher, and J. Tupin: "Life History Differences in Identical Twins Discordant for Schizophrenia," *American Journal of Orthopsychiatry,* vol. 36, no. 3., pp. 492–509, 1966.

Rosenthal, D.: *Genetic Theory and Abnormal Behavior* (New York: McGraw-Hill, 1970).

————: *Genetics of Psychopathology* (New York: McGraw-Hill, 1971).

————: (ed.). *The Genain Quadruplets: A Case Study and Theoretical Analysis of Heredity and Environment in Schizophrenia,* "Possible Inherited Factors: Patterns of Behavioral Disturbance, Premorbid Personality, and Test Performance," by D. Rosenthal and "Anamnesis" by D. Rosenthal (New York: Basic Books, 1963).

————, P. H. Wender, S. S. Kety, J. Welner, and F. Schulsinger: "The Adopted-Away Offspring of Schizophrenics," *American Journal of Psychiatry,* vol. 128, pp. 307–311, 1971. (Cited by G. E. McClearn and J. C. DeFries, *Introduction to Behavioral Genetics* [San Francisco: Freeman, 1973].)

————, P. H. Wender, S. S. Kety, F. Schulsinger, J. Welner, and R. O. Rieder: "Parent-Child Relationships and Psychopathological Disorder in the Child," *Archives of General Psychiatry,* vol. 32, 1975.

Schuckit, M., D. W. Goodwin, and G. Winokur: "The Half-Sibling Approach in a Genetic Study of Alcoholism," in M. Roff, L. N. Robins, and M. Pollack (eds.), *Life History Research in Psychopathology,* vol. 2 (Minneapolis: University of Minnesota Press, 1972), pp. 120–127. (Cited by G. E. McClearn and J. C. DeFries, *Introduction to Behavioral Genetics* [San Francisco: Freeman, 1973].)

Segal, J. (ed.): *Research in the Service of Mental Health,* National Institute of Mental Health, DHEW Publication (ADM) 75-236, Rockville, Md., 1975.

Slater, E., and V. Cowie: *The Genetics of Mental Disorders* (London: Oxford University Press, 1971). (Cited by G. E. McClearn and J. C. DeFries, *Introduction to Behavioral Genetics* [San Francisco: Freeman, 1973].)

Taft, L. T., and W. Goldfarb: "Prenatal and Perinatal Factors in Childhood Schizophrenia," *Developmental Medicine and Child Neurology,* vol. 6, 1964.

Yahraes, H.: "The Causes of Childhood Schizophrenia," in *Mental Health Program Reports,* National Institute of Mental Health, PHS Publication 1568, Rockville, Md., 1967.

CHAPTER 4

Bakwin, H., and R. M. Bakwin: *Behavior Disorders in Children,* 4th ed. (Philadelphia: Saunders, 1972), pp. 462–463.

Bernabeau, E. P.: "The Effects of Severe Crippling on the Development of a Group of Children," *Psychiatry,* vol. 21, pp. 169–194, 1958.

Bridger, W. H.: "Individual Differences in Behavior and Autonomic Activity in Newborn Infants," *American Journal of Public Health,* vol. 55, pp. 1899–1901, 1965.

Chess, S., and A. Thomas: "Temperamental Individuality from Childhood to Adolescence," *Journal of the American Academy of Child Psychiatry,* vol. 16, pp. 218–225, Spring 1977.

David, H. P.: "Children Born to Women Denied Abortion: Studies from Prague, Czechoslovakia," paper presented to American Psychological Association, Chicago, Ill., August 1975.

Forssman, H., and I. Thuwe: "One Hundred and Twenty Children Born after Application for Therapeutic Abortion Refused," *Acta Psychiatrica Scandinavica*, vol. 42, pp. 71–88, 1966.

Freud, A.: "The Role of Bodily Illness in the Mental Life of Children," in S. Harrison (ed.), *Childhood Psychopathology* (New York: International Universities Press, 1972), pp. 572–584.

Goldfarb, W., and A. Botstein: unpublished manuscript. (Cited in M. F. Waldrop, F. A. Pederson, and R. Q. Bell, "Minor Physical Anomalies and Behavior in Preschool Children," *Child Development*, vol. 39, no. 2, 1968.)

Gorman, C. K.: "Hypoglycemia: A Brief Review," *Medical Clinics of North America*, vol. 49, no. 4, pp. 947–959, 1965.

Harlow, H. F.: *Speaking of Love: Theory and Therapy*, a two-cassette album and manual (New York: McGraw-Hill, 1974).

——: "The Cause and Control of Aggression," Kittay Scientific Foundation International Kittay Award Lecture presented to New York Academy of Medicine, New York, October 1975.

James, F. E.: "Behavior Reactions of Normal Children to Common Illnesses Treated at Home," *The Practitioner*, vol. 188, pp. 670–674, 1962.

Klein, A. H., S. Meltzer, and F. M. Kenny: "Improved Prognosis in Congenital Hypothyroidism Treated before Age Three Months," *The Journal of Pediatrics*, vol. 81, no. 5, pp. 912–915, 1972.

Korner, A. F.: "The Effect of the Infant's State, Level of Arousal, Sex, and Ontogenetic Stage on the Caregiver," in M. Lewis and L. A. Rosenblum (eds.), *The Effect of the Infant on Its Caregiver* (New York: Wiley, 1974).

Lewis, M., and L. A. Rosenblum (eds.): *The Effect of the Infant on Its Caregiver* (New York: Wiley, 1974).

Quinn, P. O., and J. L. Rapoport: "Minor Physical Anomalies and Neurologic Status in Hyperactive Boys," *Pediatrics*, vol. 53, pp. 742–747, 1974.

——, M. Renfield, C. Burg, and J. L. Rapoport: "Minor Physical Anomalies: A Newborn Screening and One-Year Follow-up," *Journal of American Academy of Child Psychiatry*, Vol. 16, no. 4, pp. 662–670, 1977.

Rapoport, J. L., and P. O. Quinn: "Minor Physical Anomalies (stigmata) and Early Developmental Deviation: A Major Biologic Subgroup of 'Hyperactive Children,'" *International Journal of Mental Health*, vol. 4, pp. 29–44, 1975.

——, P. O. Quinn, and F. Lampbrecht: "Minor Physical Anomalies and Plasma Dopamine-Beta-Hydroxylase," *American Journal of Psychiatry*, vol. 131, no. 4, pp. 386–390, April 1974.

——, C. Pandoni, M. Renfield, C. R. Lake, and M. G. Ziegler: "Newborn Dopamine-B Hydroxylase, Minor Physical Anomalies, and Infant Temperament," *American Journal of Psychiatry*, vol. 134, no. 6, pp. 676–681, June 1977.

Richardson, S. A.: "Some Social Psychological Consequences of Handicapping," *Pediatrics*, vol. 32, no. 2, pp. 291–297, August 1963.

Rutter, M: "Maternal Deprivation 1972–1977: New Findings, New Concepts, New Approaches," paper presented to the Society for Research in Child Development, New Orleans, La., March 1977.

Sameroff, A. J.: "Concepts of Humanity in Primary Prevention," paper presented at the Vermont Conference on the Primary Prevention of Psychopathology, June 1975.

———: "Early Influences on Development: Fact or Fancy?" *Merrill-Palmer Quarterly,* vol. 21, no. 4, pp. 267–294, 1974.

———, and M. J. Chandler: "Reproductive Risk and the Continuum of Caretaking Casualty," in F. D. Horowitz et al. (eds.), *Review of Child Development Research* (Chicago: The University of Chicago Press, 1975), vol. 4, pp. 187–244.

Saxena, K. M., J. D. Crawford, and N. B. Talbot: "Childhood Thyrotoxicosis: A Long-Term Perspective," *British Medical Journal,* vol. 2, pp. 1153–1158, 1964.

Seidel, U. P., O. F. D. Chadwick, and M. Rutter: "Psychological Disorders in Crippled Children: A Comparative Study of Children with and without Brain Damage," *Developmental Medicine and Child Neurology,* vol. 17, pp. 563–573, 1975.

Shaw, C. R., and A. R. Lucas: *The Psychiatric Disorders of Childhood* (New York: Meredith Corporation, 1970), pp. 284–297.

Smith, D. W., R. M. Blizzard, and L. Wilkins: "The Mental Prognosis in Hypothyroidism of Infancy and Childhood: A Review of 128 Cases," *Pediatrics,* vol. 19, no. 6, pp. 1011–1022, 1957.

Steg, J. P., and J. L. Rapoport: "Minor Physical Anomalies in Normal, Neurotic, Learning Disabled, and Severely Disturbed Children," *Journal of Autism and Childhood Schizophrenia,* vol. 5, no. 4, pp. 299–307, 1975.

Tanner, J. M.: "Variability of Growth and Maturity in Newborn Infants," in M. Lewis and L. A. Rosenblum (eds.), *The Effect of the Infant on Its Caregivers* (New York: Wiley, 1974).

Thomas, A., and S. Chess: "Evolution of Behavior Disorders into Adolescence," *American Journal of Psychiatry,* vol. 133, pp. 539–542, May 1976.

———, and ———: *Temperament and Development* (New York: Brunner/Mazel, 1977).

———, and ———(investigators): research reported in H. Yahraes, "Styles in Temperament and Their Effect on Behavior," National Institute of Mental Health, DHEW Publication (ADM) 77-462, Rockville, Md., 1977.

———, ———, and H. G. Birch: "The Origin of Personality," *Scientific American,* vol. 223, no. 2, pp. 102–109, August 1970.

———, ———, and H. G. Birch: *Temperament and Behavior Disorders in Children* (New York: New York University Press, 1968).

Waldrop, M. F.: *Manual for Assessing Minor Physical Anomalies,* National Institute of Mental Health, Laboratory of Developmental Psychology, Bethesda, Md.

———, R. Q. Bell, and J. D. Goering: "Minor Physical Anomalies and Inhibited Behavior in Elementary School Girls," *Journal of Child Psychology and Psychiatry,* vol. 17, pp. 113–122, 1976.

———, and J. D. Goering: "Hyperactivity and Minor Physical Anomalies in Elementary School Children," *American Journal of Orthopsychiatry,* vol. 4, pp. 602–607, 1971.

———, and C. F. Halverson Jr.: "Minor Physical Anomalies and Hyperactive Behavior in Young Children," in J. Hellmuth (ed.), *Exceptional Infant* (New York: Brunner/Mazel, 1971), vol. 2, pp. 343–380.

———, and C. F. Halverson, Jr.: "Minor Physical Anomalies: Their Incidence and Relation to Behavior in a Normal and a Deviant Sample," in R. C. Smart and M. S. Smart (eds.), *Readings in Child Development and Relationships* (New York: Macmillan, 1972), pp. 146–155.

——, F. A. Pederson, and R. Q. Bell: "Minor Physical Anomalies and Behavior in Preschool Children," *Child Development*, vol. 39, no. 2, pp. 391–400, 1968.

Wasserstein, J., and H. Yahraes: "The Child's Emotions: How Physical Illness Can Affect Them," National Institute of Mental Health, DHEW Publication (ADM) 77-479, Rockville, Md., 1977.

Werkman, S. L., L. Shifman, and T. Skelly: "Psychosocial Correlates of Iron Deficiency Anemia in Early Childhood," *Psychosomatic Medicine*, vol. 26, no. 2, pp. 125–134, March–April 1964.

Yahraes, H.: "The Tie between Physical and Behavioral Irregularities of Children," National Institute of Mental Health, DHEW Publication (ADM) 78-605, Rockville, Md., 1978.

Yarrow, M. R., C. Z. Waxler, and P. M. Scott: "Child Effects on Adult Behavior," *Developmental Psychology*, vol. 5, no. 2, pp. 300–311, 1971.

CHAPTER 5

Ainsworth, M. D. S.: "Social Development in the First Year of Life: Maternal Influences on Infant-Mother Attachment," in J. M. Tanner (ed.), *Developments in Psychiatric Research Viewpoints in Review: Essays Based on the Sir Geoffrey Vickers' Lectures of the Mental Health Trust and Research Fund* (London: Hodder, 1977).

——, S. M. Bell, and D. J. Stayton: "Infant-Mother Attachment and Social Development: Socialization as a Product of Reciprocal Responsiveness to Signals," in M. P. Richards (ed.), *The Integration of the Child into a Social World* (London: Cambridge University Press, 1974).

Barbero, G.: "Failure to Thrive," in M. H. Klaus, T. Leger, and M. A. Trause (eds.), *Maternal Attachment and Mothering Disorders: A Round Table* (New Brunswick, N.J.: Johnson & Johnson Baby Products, 1975).

Bee, H. L.: "The Effect of Maternal Employment on the Development of the Child," in H. L. Bee (ed.), *Social Issues in Developmental Psychology* (New York: Harper & Row, 1974).

Bell, S. M., and M. D. S. Ainsworth: "Infant Crying and Maternal Responsiveness," *Child Development*, vol. 43, no. 4, 1972.

Boocock, S.: "The Social Context of Childhood," *Proceedings of American Philosophical Society*, vol. 119, December 1975.

Bowlby, J.: *Attachment and Loss*, vol. 1, *Attachment* (New York: Basic Books, 1969).

——: "Childhood Mourning and Its Implications for Psychiatry," *American Journal of Psychiatry*, vol. 118, pp. 481–498, 1961

Brazelton, T. B.: "Mother-Infant Reciprocity," in M. H. Klaus, T. Leger, and M. A. Trause (eds.), *Maternal Attachment and Mothering Disorders: A Round Table* (New Brunswick, N.J.: Johnson & Johnson Baby Products, 1975).

Bronfenbrenner, U.: quoted in "The Parent Gap," *Newsweek*, Sept. 22, 1975.

Broussard, E.: "How a Mother Views Her Child—and Herself," from summary of oral presentation at Pilot Conference on Primary Prevention, Philadelphia, Penn., April 1976.

——: "Maternal Perception of the Neonate as Related to Development," *Child Psychiatry and Human Development*, vol. 1, no. 1, 1970.

——: "The Neonatal Prediction and Outcome at 10 and 11 Years," *Child Psychiatry and Human Development*, vol. 7, no. 2, Winter 1976.

DeMause, L.: *The History of Childhood* (New York: Psychohistory Press, 1974).

Erikson, E.: *Childhood and Society* (New York: Norton, 1963).

Fraiberg, S.: "Billy: Psychological Intervention for a Failure-to-Thrive Infant," in M. H. Klaus, T. Leger, and M. A. Trause (eds.), *Maternal Attachment and Mothering Disorders: A Round Table* (New Brunswick, N.J.: Johnson & Johnson Baby Products, 1975).

————: "The Origin of Human Bonds," *Commentary*, vol. 44, no. 6, pp. 47–57, December 1967.

————: E. Adelson and V. Shapiro. "Ghosts in the Nursery," *Journal of Child Psychology*, vol. 14, no. 3, pp. 387–421, Summer 1975.

Kagan, J., R. B. Kearsley, and P. R. Zelazo: "The Effects of Infant Day Care on Psychological Development," *Evaluation Quarterly*, vol. 1, no. 1, pp. 143–158.

Kennell, J. H.: "Evidence for a Maternal Sensitive Period," paper presented to Society for Research in Child Development, New Orleans, La., March 1977.

Kimble, G. A., N. Garmezy, and E. Zigler: *Principles of General Psychology*, 4th ed. (New York: Ronald Press, 1974).

Klaus, M. H., and J. Kennell: "Mothers Separated from Their Newborn Infants," *Pediatric Clinics of North America*, vol. 17, pp. 1015–1037, 1970.

————, R. Jerauld, N. C. Kreger, W. McAlpine, M. Steffa, and J. H. Kennell: "Maternal Attachment: Importance of the First Post-partum Days," *New England Journal of Medicine*, vol. 286, no. 9, pp. 460–463, 1972.

Leiderman, P. H.: "Mother-Infant Separation: Delayed Consequences," in M. H. Klaus, T. Leger, and M. A. Trause (eds.), *Maternal Attachment and Mothering Disorders: A Round Table* (New Brunswick, N.J.: Johnson & Johnson Baby Products, 1975).

Mahler, M. S.: "On Early Infantile Psychosis: The Symbiotic and Autistic Syndromes," *Journal of the American Academy of Child Psychiatry*, vol. 4, no. 4, 1965.

————: "On the Significance of the Normal Separation-Individuation Phase," *Drives, Affects, Behavior*, vol. 2, 1965.

————: "Thoughts about Development and Individuation," *Psychoanalytic Study of the Child*, vol. 18, 1963.

Mahler, M. S. (investigator): research reported in H. Yahraes, "How the Child Separates from the Mother," National Institute of Mental Health, PHS Publication 1568, Rockville, Md., 1967, pp. 113–123.

————, and K. La Perriere: "Mother-Child Interaction during Separation-Individuation," *Psychoanalytic Quarterly*, vol. 34, pp. 483–498, 1965.

————, F. Pine, and A. Bergman: *The Psychological Birth of the Human Infant* (New York: Basic Books, 1975).

Mead, M.: quoted in "The Parent Gap," *Newsweek*, Sept. 22, 1975.

Rothchild, J., and S. Wolf: *The Children of the Counterculture* (New York: Doubleday, 1976).

Shapiro, V., S. Fraiberg, and E. Adelson: "Infant-Parent Psychotherapy on Behalf of a Child in a Critical Nutritional State," in R. Eissler, A. Freud, M. Kris, and A. J. Solnit (eds.), *The Psychoanalytic Study of the Child*, 1976, vol. 31.

von Hoffman, N.: "'Bureaucratizing' Childhood through Government-Run Day Care," *The Washington Post*, Dec. 27, 1976. © King Features Syndicate, Inc., 1976.

Wolff, P. H.: "Current Concepts: Mother-Infant Interactions in the First Year," *New England Journal of Medicine*, vol. 295, no. 18, 1976.

Yarrow, M. R., P. Scott, L. de Leeuw, and C. Heinig: "Childrearing in Families of Working and Nonworking Mothers," *Sociometry*, vol. 25, no. 2, 1962.

CHAPTER 6

Anderson, R. E.: "Where's Dad? Paternal Deprivation and Delinquency," *Archives of General Psychiatry*, vol. 18, pp. 641–649, 1968.

Appley (Applezweig), D. (chairman and ed.): "Childhood and Mental Health: The Influence of the Father in the Family Setting—A Symposium," *Merrill-Palmer Quarterly of Behavior and Development*, vol. 7, no. 2, pp. 71–144, 1961.

Bach, G. R.: "Father-Fantasies and Father-Typing in Father-Separated Children," *Child Development*, vol. 17, pp. 63–68, 1946.

Bacon, M. K., I. L. Child, and H. Barry, III: "A Cross-Cultural Study of Correlates of Crime," *Journal of Abnormal Social Psychology*, vol. 66, pp. 291–300, 1963.

Bartemeier, L.: "The Contribution of the Father to the Mental Health of the Family," *Child and Family*, vol. 9, no. 3, pp. 202–208, 1970.

Bee, H. L.: "On the Importance of Fathers," in H. L. Bee (ed.), *Social Issues in Developmental Psychology* (New York: Harper & Row, pp. 367–377, 1974).

Beels, C. C.: "Whatever Happened to Father?" *New York Times Magazine*, Aug. 25, 1974.

Biller, H. B.: "The Father and Personality Development: Paternal Deprivation and Sex-Role Development," in M. E. Lamb (ed.), *The Role of the Father in Child Development* (New York: Wiley, pp. 89–156, 1976).

———: *Father, Child and Sex Role: Paternal Determinants of Personality Development* (Lexington, Mass.: Heath, 1971).

———: *Paternal Deprivation* (Lexington, Mass.: Heath, 1974).

———, and A. Davids: "Parent-Child Relations, Personality Development, and Psychopathology," in A. Davids (ed.), *Issues in Abnormal Psychology* (Monterey, Calif.: Brooks-Cole, 1973).

Bohannan, P. J.: "Stepfathers and the Mental Health of Their Children," final report, NIMH Grant MH21146, Western Behavioral Sciences Institute, La Jolla, Calif., 1975.

Bowlby, J.: *Maternal Care and Mental Health*, Monograph Series, no. 2, World Health Organization, Geneva, 1951.

Broderick, C. B.: "Fathers," *The Family Coordinator*, vol. 26, no. 3, pp. 269–275, July 1977.

Bronfenbrenner, U.: "Some Familial Antecedents of Responsibility and Leadership in Adolescents," in L. Petrullo and B. M. Bass (eds.), *Leadership and Interpersonal Behavior* (New York: Holt, Rinehart, and Winston, 1961), pp. 239–272.

Burton, R., and J. Whiting: "The Absent Father and Cross-Sex Identity," *Merrill-Palmer Quarterly of Behavioral Development*, vol. 4, no. 2, 1961. (Reprinted as A-277, "The Bobbs-Merrill Reprint in the Social Sciences" [Indianapolis: Bobbs-Merrill Sept. 1967].)

Carlsmith, L.: "Effect of Early Father Absence on Scholastic Aptitude," *Harvard Educational Review*, vol. 34, pp. 3–21, 1964.

Cohen, L. J., and J. J. Campos: "Father, Mother and Stranger as Elicitors of Attachment Behaviors in Infancy," *Developmental Psychology*, vol. 10, no. 1, pp. 146–154, 1974.

Dahl, B. B., and H. McCubbin: "Prolonged Family Separation in the Military: A Longitudinal Study," in H. McCubbin, B. B. Dahl, E. Hunter (eds.), *Families in the Military System* (Beverly Hills, Calif.: Sage Publications, 1976), pp. 112–144.

———, H. McCubbin, and K. Ross: "Second Generational Effects of War-Induced Separations: Comparing the Adjustment of Children in Reunited and Non-Reunited Families," *Military Medicine*, vol. 141, no. 2, pp. 146–151, January 1977.

Despert, L.: *Children of Divorce* (New York: Doubleday, 1953).

Emanuelson, M. S.: "Parental Personality Variables as Predictors of Specific Behavioral

Disorders in Children," Ed.D. dissertation (Ann Arbor, Mich.: University Microfilms, Publication 72-7305, February 1972).

Fish, K. D. and H. B. Biller: "Perceived Childhood Paternal Relationships and College Females' Personal Adjustment," *Adolescence,* vol. 8, pp. 415–420, 1973.

Glueck, S., and E. Glueck: *Unraveling Juvenile Delinquency* (New York: Commonwealth Fund, 1950).

Goodman, E.: "Life without Father," *The Washington Post,* Jan. 8, 1977.

Harlow, H. F.: "The Nature of Love," *American Psychologist,* vol. 13, pp. 673–685, 1958.

———, M. K. Harlow, R. O. Dodsworth, and G. L. Arling: "Maternal Behavior of Rhesus Monkeys Deprived of Mothering and Peer Associations in Infancy," in *Proceedings of the American Philosophical Society,* vol. 110, no. 1, pp. 58–66, 1966.

———, M. K. Harlow, and E. W. Hansen: "The Maternal Affectional System in Rhesus Monkeys," in H. L. Rheingold (ed.), *Maternal Behavior in Mammals* (New York: Wiley, 1963).

Herzog, E. and H. Lewis: "Children in Poor Families: Myths and Realities," *American Journal of Orthopsychiatry,* vol. 40, pp. 375–387, 1970.

Hetherington, M. E.: "The Effects of Father Absence on Personality Development in Adolescent Daughters," *Developmental Psychology,* vol. 7, pp. 313–326, 1972.

———, and J. L. Deur: "The Effects of Father Absence on Child Development," in W. W. Hartup (ed.), *The Young Child* (Washington, D.C.: National Association for the Education of Young Children, 1972), pp. 303–319.

Kimble, G. A., N. Garmezy, and E. Zigler: *Principles of General Psychology,* 4th ed. (New York: Ronald Press, 1974).

Lamb, M. E.: "Fathers: Forgotten Contributors to Child Development," *Human Development,* vol. 18, no. 4, pp. 245–266, 1975.

——— (ed.): *The Role of the Father in Child Development* (New York: Wiley, 1976).

———, and J. E. Lamb: "The Nature and Importance of the Father-Infant Relationship," *The Family Coordinator,* vol. 25, no. 4, pp. 379–385, October 1976.

Leifer, A. D., P. H. Leiderman, C. R. Barnett, and J. A. Williams: "Effects of Mother-Infant Separation on Maternal Attachment Behavior," *Child Development,* vol. 43, pp. 1203–1218, 1972.

Lynn, D. B.: *The Father: His Role in Child Development* (Belmont, Calif.: Brooks-Cole, 1974).

Malinowski, B.: "Parenthood—The Basis of Social Structure," in R. Coser (ed.), *The Family: Its Structure and Functions* (New York: St. Martin's, 1964).

Mead, M.: "A Cultural Anthropologist's Approach to Maternal Deprivation," in *Deprivation of Maternal Care: A Reassessment of Its Effects* (Geneva: World Health Organization, 1962).

Mendes, H. A.: "Single Fathers," *The Family Coordinator,* vol. 25, no. 4, pp. 439–444, October 1976.

Mitchell, G. D.: "Paternal Behavior in Non-Human Primates," in J. Money and H. Musaph (eds.), *Handbook of Sexology* (Amsterdam: Elsevier, 1975).

———: "Paternalistic Behavior in Primates," *Psychological Bulletin,* vol. 71, pp. 399–417, 1969.

———, W. K. Redican, and J. Gomber: "Males Can Raise Babies," *Psychology Today,* pp. 63–68, April 1974.

Munroe, R. H.: "Pregnancy Symptoms among Expectant American Fathers, An Inquiry into Their Psychological Meaning," unpublished Ph.D. thesis, Harvard University, Department of Human Relations, 1964.

Munroe, R. L., R. H. Munroe, and J. W. M. Whiting: "Structure and Sentiment: Evidence from Recent Studies of the Couvade," paper presented to the American Anthropological Association, Denver, Colo., November, 1965.

Mussen, P. H., H. B. Young, R. Gaddini, and L. Morante: "The Influence of Father-Son Relationships on Adolescent Personality and Attitudes." *Journal of Child Psychology and Psychiatry,* vol. 4, pp. 3–16, 1963.

Novak, M.: "The Family Out of Favor," *Harper's,* pp. 37–46, April 1976.

Orthner, D. K., T. Brown, and D. Fergusen: "Single-Parent Fatherhood: An Emerging Family Life Style," *The Family Coordinator,* vol. 25, no. 4, pp. 439–444, October 1976.

Parke, R. D. and D. B. Sawin: "Father-Infant Interaction in the Newborn Period: A Reevaluation of Some Current Myths," in M. E. Hetherington and R. D. Parke (eds.), *Contemporary Readings in Child Psychology* (New York: McGraw-Hill, 1977), pp. 290–295.

———, and D. B. Sawin: "The Father's Role in Infancy: A Re-evaluation," *The Family Coordinator,* vol. 25, no. 4, pp. 365–370, October 1976.

Pederson, F. A.: "Relationships between Father-Absence and Emotional Disturbance in Male Military Dependents," *Merrill-Palmer Quarterly of Behavior and Development,* vol. 12, pp. 321–331, 1966.

Peterson, D. R., W. C. Becker, L. A. Heller, D. J. Shoemaker, and H. C. Quay: "Parental Attitudes and Child Adjustment," *Child Development,* vol. 30, pp. 119–130, 1959.

Reuter, M. W., and H. B. Biller: "Perceived Paternal Nurturance—Availability and Personality Adjustment among College Males," *Journal of Consulting and Clinical Psychology,* vol. 40, pp. 339–342, 1973.

Rohrer, J. H., and M. S. Edmonson: *The Eighth Generation* (New York: Harper & Brothers, 1960).

Sears, P. S.: "Doll Play Aggression in Normal Young Children: Influence of Sex, Age, Sibling Status, Father's Absence," *Psychological Monographs,* vol. 65(6): 1–42 (Whole No. 323), 1951.

Siegman, A. W.: "Father Absence during Childhood and Antisocial Behavior," *Journal of Abnormal Psychology,* vol. 71, pp. 71–74, 1966.

Spock, B.: "What a Child Needs from a Father," *Redbook,* pp. 24–28, September 1974.

Stolz, L. M.: *Father Relations of Warborn Children* (Stanford, Calif.: Stanford University Press, 1954).

White, B. L.: *The First Three Years of Life* (Englewood Cliffs, N.J.: Prentice-Hall, 1975).

Wolfgang, M., and F. Ferracuti: *Subculture of Violence: Towards an Integrated Theory in Criminology* (New York: Barnes & Noble, 1967).

Yogman, M. W.: "The Goals and Structure of Face-to-Face Interaction between Infants and Fathers," paper presented to Society for Research in Child Development, New Orleans, La., March 1977.

———, S. Dixon, E. Tronick, L. Adamson, H. Als, and T. B. Brazelton: "Development of Infant Social Interaction with Fathers," paper presented to Eastern Psychological Association, New York, April 1976.

CHAPTER 7

America's Children: 1976, National Council of Organizations for Children and Youth, Washington, D.C., June 1976.

Anthony, E. J.: "The Behavior Disorders of Childhood," in P. Mussen (ed.), *Carmichael's Manual of Child Psychology,* vol. 2 (New York: Wiley, 1970).

———: "Developmental Precursors of Adult Schizophrenia," in S. Kety and D. Rosenthal (eds.), *Transmissions of Schizophrenia* (London: Pergamon, 1969).

————: "Naturalistic Studies of Disturbed Families," in E. J. Anthony (ed.),*Explorations in Child Psychiatry* (New York: Plenum, 1975).

————: "A New Scientific Region to Explore," in E. J. Anthony and C. Koupernik (eds.), *The Child in His Family: The Vulnerable Child* (New York: Wiley, 1978).

————: "The Vulnerable Child as Seen by the Child Psychiatrist," paper presented to the International Association for Child Psychiatry and Allied Professions," Philadelphia, Pa., July 1974.

Baumrind, D.: "The Contributions of the Family to the Development of Competence in Children," *Schizophrenia Bulletin*, vol. 1, no. 14, pp. 12–37, Fall 1975.

————: "The Development of Instrumental Competence through Socialization," in A. Pick (ed.), *Minnesota Symposia on Child Psychology*, Vol. 7, Minneapolis: U. of Minnesota Press, 1973, pp. 3–46.

Becker, W. C.: "Consequences of Different Kinds of Parental Discipline," in M. L. Hoffman, and L. W. Hoffman (eds.), *Review of Child Development Research* (New York: Russell Sage, 1964), vol. 1, pp. 169–208.

Bronfenbrenner, U.: "The Calamitous Decline of the American Family," *Washington Post*, Jan. 2, 1977.

————: "The Origins of Alienation," *Scientific American*, vol. 231, no. 2, pp. 53–61, August 1974.

————: "The Roots of Alienation," paper presented at the Dale Richmond Memorial Lecture to American Academy of Pediatrics, Chicago, Ill., October 1973.

Clausen, J. A., and C. L. Huffine: "Sociocultural and Social-Psychological Factors Affecting Social Responses to Mental Disorder," *Journal of Health and Social Behavior*, vol. 16, pp. 405–20, 1975.

Cushna, B.: "Agency and Birth Order Differences in Very Early Childhood," paper presented at meeting of the American Psychological Association, New York, 1966. (Cited in B. Sutton-Smith and B. G. Rosenberg, *The Sibling* [New York: Holt, 1970].)

Garmezy, N.: "Children at Risk: The Search for the Antecedents of Schizophrenia," part II, "Ongoing Research Programs, Issues, and Intervention," *Schizophrenia Bulletin*, no. 9, pp. 55–125, Summer 1974. (A report on longitudinal research by the Mednick-Schulsinger and many other teams.)

Gordon, I. J. (investigator) research reported in H. Yahraes. *Teaching Mothers Mothering*, Rockville, Md., National Institute of Mental Health, DHEW Publication (ADM) 77-520, 1977.

Keniston, K.: "The Emptying Family," *The New York Times*, Feb. 18, 1976.

Lander, H. S., E. J. Anthony, L. Cass, L. Franklin, and L. Bass: "A Measure of Vulnerability to the Risk of Parental Psychosis," in E. J. Anthony and C. Koupernik (eds.), *The Child in His Family: The Vulnerable Child* (New York: Wiley, in press).

Lasko, J. K.: "Parent Behavior towards First and Second Children," *Genetic Psychological Monographs*, vol. 49, pp. 96–137, 1954. (Cited by B. Sutton-Smith and B. G. Rosenberg, *The Sibling* [New York: Holt, 1970].)

Liem, J. H.: "Effects of Verbal Communications of Parents and Children: A Comparison of Normal and Schizophrenic Families," *Journal of Consulting and Clinical Psychology*, vol. 42, no. 3, pp. 438–450, 1974.

McDermott, J. F., Jr.: "Divorce and Its Psychiatric Sequelae in Children," *Archives of General Psychiatry*, vol. 23, November 1970.

Mead, M.: "The Once and Future Home," *Washington Post*, July 4, 1976.

Mednick, S. A., F. Schulsinger, T. W. Teasdale, H. Schulsinger, P. H. Venables, and D. R. Rock: "Schizophrenia in High-Risk Children: Sex Differences in Predisposing Factors," undated manuscript.

Miller, N., and G. Maruyama: "Ordinal Position and Peer Popularity," *Journal of Personality and Social Psychology,* vol. 33, no. 2, pp. 123–131, 1976.

Minuchin, S.: *Families and Family Therapy* (Cambridge, Mass.: Harvard University Press, 1974).

——— (investigator): research reported in J. Segal, *Psychosomatic Diabetic Children and Their Families,* National Institute of Mental Health, DHEW Publication (ADM) 77-477, Rockville, Md., 1977.

———, L. Baker, B. Rosman, R. Liebman, L. Milman, T. Todd: "A Conceptual Model of Psychosomatic Illness in Children: Family Organization and Family Therapy," *Archives of General Psychiatry,* vol. 32, pp. 1031–1038, 1975.

Mishler, E. G. and N. E. Waxler: "Family Interaction and Schizophrenia: Alternative Frameworks of Interpretation," *Journal of Psychiatric Research,* vol. 6 (supplement 1), pp. 213–222, 1968.

Morris, G. O., and L. C. Wynne: "Schizophrenic Offspring and Parental Styles of Communication," *Psychiatry,* vol. 28, no. 1, 1965.

Mosher, L. R., W. Pollin, and J. Stabenau: "Families with Identical Twins Discordant for Schizophrenia: Some Relationships between Identification, Thinking Styles, Psychopathology, and Dominance-Submissiveness," *British Journal of Psychiatry,* vol. 118, pp. 29–42, 1971.

Novak, Michael: "The Family Out of Favor," *Harper's,* pp. 37–46, April 1976.

Parke, R. D.: "Some Effects of Punishment on Children's Behavior—Revisited," in M. E. Hetherington and R. D. Parke (eds.), *Contemporary Readings in Child Psychology* (New York: McGraw-Hill, 1977), pp. 208–220.

Rutter, M.: "Maternal Deprivation 1972–1977: New Findings, New Concepts, New Approaches," paper presented to the Society for Research in Child Development, New Orleans, La., March 1977.

———: "Parent-Child Separation: Psychological Effects on the Children," *Journal of Child Psychology and Psychiatry,* vol. 12, no. 233–260, 1971.

Schaffer, L., L. C. Wynne, J. Day, I. M. Ryckoff, and A. Halperin: "On the Nature and Sources of the Psychiatrist's Experience with the Family of the Schizophrenic," *Psychiatry,* vol. 25, no. 11, 1962.

Schulsinger, H.: "A Ten-Year Follow-Up of Children of Schizophrenic Mothers: Clinical Assessment," *Acta Psychiatrica Scandinavica,* vol. 53, FASC. 5, pp. 371–386, May 1976.

Singer, M. T., and L. C. Wynne: "Thought Disorder and Family Relations of Schizophrenics," part 3, Methodology Using Projective Techniques," and part 4, "Results and Implications," *Archives of General Psychiatry,* vol. 12, pp. 187–212, February 1965.

Sutton-Smith, B., and B. G. Rosenberg: *The Sibling* (New York: Holt, 1970).

Wallerstein, J. S. and J. B. Kelly: "The Effects of Parental Divorce: Experiences of the Preschool Child," *Journal of Child Psychiatry,* vol. 14, no. 4, pp. 600–616, 1975.

Waxler, N. E.: "Parent and Child Effects on Cognitive Performance: An Experimental Approach to the Etiological and Responsive Theories of Schizophrenia," *Family Process,* vol. 13, no. 1, March 1974.

Wynne, L. C.: "Methodologic and Conceptual Issues in the Study of Schizophrenics and Their Families," *Journal of Psychiatric Research,* vol. 6 (Supplement 1), pp. 185–199, 1968.

CHAPTER 8

Bakan, D.: *Slaughter of the Innocents* (San Francisco: Jossey-Bass, 1971).

———: "Slaughter of the Innocents," *Journal of Clinical Child Psychology,* vol. II, no. 3, pp. 10–12, Fall 1973.

Broderick, C. B.: "Fathers," *The Family Coordinator,* vol. 26, no. 3, pp. 269–275, July 1977.

DeMause, L. (ed.): *The History of Childhood* (New York: Psychohistory Press, 1974).

Elmer, E.: "Child Abuse and Family Stress," paper presented to the American Association for the Advancement of Science, Denver, Colo., February 1977.

——: *Children in Jeopardy: A Study of Abused Minors and Their Families* (Pittsburgh: The Univeristy of Pittsburgh Press, 1967).

——: "Effects of Early Neglect and Abuse on Latency Age Children," paper presented to the American Psychological Association, Washington, D.C., September 1976.

——: "A Follow-up Study of Traumatized Children," *Pediatrics,* vol. 59, no. 2, pp. 273–314, February 1977.

——, and G. S. Gregg: "Developmental Characteristics of Abused Children," *Pediatrics,* vol. 40, pp. 596–602, 1967.

Ferenczi, S.: "The Unwelcome Child and His Death-Instinct," *International Journal of Psychoanalysis,* vol. 10, no. 127, 1929. (Cited by D. Bakan, *Slaughter of the Innocents* [San Francisco, Jossey-Bass, 1971].)

Foster, H. J.: opening remarks presented to the conference on *The Violent Child,* The Center of Forensic Psychiatry, New York University, New York, March 1976.

Freud, S.: *Collected Papers,* vol. 2, J. Riviere (trans.) (London: Hogarth, 1950). (Cited by D. Bakan, *Slaughter of the Innocents* [San Francisco, Jossey-Bass, 1971], p. 13.

Gelles, R. J.: "Child Abuse as Psychopathology: A Sociological Critique and Reformulation," *American Journal of Orthopsychiatry,* vol. 43, pp. 611–621, 1973. (Cited by R. D. Parke and C. W. Collmer, "Child Abuse: An Interdisciplinary Analysis," in M. E. Hetherington (ed.), *Review of Child Development Research,* vol. 5 [Chicago: The University of Chicago Press, 1975].)

——: "Violence toward Children in the United States," paper presented to the American Association for the Advancement of Science, Denver, Colo., February 1977.

Gray, J., C. Cutler, J. Dean, and C. H. Kempe: "Prediction and Prevention of Child Abuse and Neglect," paper presented to the Society for Research in Child Development, New Orleans, La., March 1977.

Harlow, H. F.: "The Cause and Control of Aggression," Kittay Scientific Foundation, International Kittay Award Lecture, presented to New York Academy of Medicine, October 1975.

——: "The Heterosexual Affectional System in Monkeys," *American Psychologist,* vol. 17, pp. 1–9, 1962.

——: *Speaking of Love: Theory and Therapy,* a two-cassette album and manual (New York: McGraw-Hill, 1974).

——, M. K. Harlow, R. O. Dodsworth, and G. L. Arling: "Maternal Behavior of Rhesus Monkeys Deprived of Mothering and Peer Associations in Infancy," *Proceedings of the American Philosophical Society,* vol. 110, no. 1, pp. 58–66, 1966.

——, ——, and S. J. Suomi: "From Thought to Therapy: Lessons from a Primate Laboratory," *American Scientist,* vol. 59, pp. 538–548, 1971.

Helfer, R. E., and C. H. Kempe, (eds.): *The Battered Child,* 2d ed. (Chicago: The University of Chicago Press, 1974).

——, and ——: *Child Abuse Is a Family Affair* (Cambridge, Mass.: Ballinger, 1976).

Kempe, C. H., F. N. Silverman, B. F. Steele, W. Droegemueller, and H. K. Silver: "The Battered-Child Syndrome," *Journal of the American Medical Association,* vol. 181, no. 17, 1962.

Kennell, J. H.: "Evidence for a Maternal Sensitive Period," paper presented to the Society for Research in Child Development, New Orleans, La., March 1977.

————, D. Gordon, and M. H. Klaus: "The Effect of Early Mother-Infant Separation on Later Maternal Performance," *Pediatric Research*, vol. 4, no. 5, pp. 473–474, September 1970.

Korsch, B. M., J. B. Christian, E. K. Gozzi, and P. V. Carlson: "Infant Care and Punishment: A Pilot Study," *American Journal of Public Health*, vol. 55, pp. 1880–1888, 1965.

Langer, W. L.: "Infanticide: A Historical Survey," *History of Childhood Quarterly*, vol. 1, no. 3, pp. 353–366, 1973.

Martin, H. P.: *The Abused Child: A Multidisciplinary Approach to Developmental Issues and Treatment* (Cambridge, Mass.: Ballinger, 1976).

————, and P. Beezley: "Prevention and the Consequences of Child Abuse," from the symposium *Early Intervention in a Child's Life*, sponsored by the Section of Child Psychiatry, University of Missouri-Columbia, November 1974.

————, P. Beezley, E. F. Conway, and C. H. Kempe: "The Development of Abused Children," in I. Schulman (ed.), *Advances in Pediatrics* (Chicago: Year Book, 1974), vol. 21, pp. 25–73.

Melnick, B., and J. Hurley: "Distinctive Personality Attributes of Child-Abusing Mothers," *Journal of Consulting and Clinical Psychology*, vol. 33, pp. 746–749, 1969.

Money, J.: "The Syndrome of Abuse Dwarfism (Psychosocial Dwarfism or Reversible Hyposomatotropism)," *American Journal of Diseases of Childhood*, vol. 131, pp. 508–513, May 1977.

Parke, R. D., and C. W. Collmer: "Child Abuse: An Interdisciplinary Analysis," in M. E. Hetherington (ed.), *Review of Child Development Research*, vol. 5 (Chicago: The University of Chicago Press, 1975).

Radbill, S. X.: "A History of Child Abuse and Infanticide," in R. E. Helfer and C. H. Kempe (eds.), *The Battered Child* (Chicago: The University of Chicago Press, 1968), pp. 3–17.

Rice, E. P., M. C. Ekdahl, and L. Miller: *Children of Mentally Ill Parents: Problems in Child Care* (New York, Behavioral Publications, 1971).

Rosenfeld, A. A., and E. H. Newberger: "Compassion Versus Control: Conceptual and Practical Pitfalls in the Broadened Definitions of Child Abuse," *Journal of the American Medical Association* vol. 237, pp. 2086–2088, May 9, 1977.

Spinetta, J. J., and D. Rigler: "The Child-Abusing Parent: Psychological Review," *Psychological Bulletin*, vol. 77, pp. 296–304, 1972.

Spitz, R.: *The First Year of Life* (New York: International Universities, 1965). (Cited by D. Bakan, *Slaughter of the Innocents* [San Francisco, Jossey-Bass, 1971].)

Steele, B. F.: "Psychological Dimensions of Child Abuse," paper presented to the American Association for the Advancement of Science, Denver, Colo., February 1977.

————, and C. B. Pollock: "A Psychiatric Study of Parents Who Abuse Infants and Small Children," in R. E. Helfer and C. H. Kempe (eds.), *The Battered Child* (Chicago: The University of Chicago Press, 1968).

Von Krafft-Ebing, R.: *Psychopathia Sexualis: A Medico-Forensic Study* (New York: Putnam, 1969).

Wald, M. S.: "State Intervention on Behalf of Neglected Children," in *Stanford Law Review*, vol. 27, no. 4, pp. 985–1041, April 1975.

————: "State Intervention on Behalf of 'Neglected' Children: Standards for Removal of Children from Their Homes, Monitoring the Status of Children in Foster Care, and Termination of Parental Rights." *Stanford Law Review*, vol. 28, no. 4, pp. 625–706 April 1976.

Wolfgang, M. E.: "Child and Youth Violence," paper presented to the conference on *The Violent Child,* The Center for Forensic Psychiatry, New York University, New York, March 1976.

———, and F. Ferracuti: *Subculture of Violence: Towards an Integrated Theory in Criminology* (New York: Barnes & Noble, 1967).

CHAPTER 9

Anderson, H. H., and J. E. Brewer: "Studies of Teachers' Classroom Personalities, II, Effects of Teachers' Dominative and Integrative Contacts on Children's Classroom Behavior," *Applied Psychology Monographs,* no. 8, 1946.

———, ———, and M. F. Reed: "Studies of Teachers' Classroom Personalities, III, Follow-up Studies of the Effects of Dominative and Integrative Contacts on Children's Behavior," *Applied Psychology Monographs,* no. 11, 1946.

Bernard, H. W.: *Mental Health in the Classroom* (New York: McGraw-Hill, 1970).

Binet, A., and T. Simon: "Sur la nécessite d'établir un diagnostic scientifique des'états inférieurs de l'intelligence," *L'Annee Psychologique,* vol. 11, pp. 1–28, 1905.

Bronfenbrenner, U.: "The Origins of Alienation," *Scientific American,* vol. 231, no. 2, pp. 53–61, August 1974.

———: "The Roots of Alienation," paper presented as the Dale Richmond Memorial Lecture to the American Academy of Pediatrics, Chicago, Ill., October 1973.

———: *Two Worlds of Childhood: U.S. and U.S.S.R.* (New York: Russell Sage Foundation, 1970), pp. 95–124.

Chaikin, A., E. Sigler, and V. Derlega: "Non-Verbal Mediators of Teacher Expectancy Effects," *Journal of Personality and Social Psychology,* vol. 30, pp. 144–149, 1974.

Edelman, M. W.: quoted in M. Casady, "Society's Pushed Out Children," *Psychology Today,* pp. 63–68, June 1975.

———, M. Allen, C. Brown, and A. Rosewater (project directors): *Children Out of School in America,* a report of the Children's Defense Fund, Washington Research Project, Inc., Cambridge, Mass., 1974.

Franco, D.: "The Child's Perception of 'The Teacher' as Compared to His Perception of 'The Mother,'" *Dissertation Abstracts,* vol. 24, pp. 3414–3415, 1964.

Gordon, I. J.: *The Florida Parent Education Early Intervention Projects: A Longitudinal Look* (Gainesville, Fla.: University of Florida, Institute for Development of Human Resources, 1973).

———(investigator): research described in H. Yahraes, *Teaching Mothers Mothering,* Rockville, Md., National Institute of Mental Health, DHEW Publication (ADM) 77-520, 1977.

———, and B. J. Guinagh: *A Home Learning Center Approach to Early Stimulation* (Gainesville, Fla.: University of Florida, Institute for Development of Human Resources, 1974).

———, M. Hanes, L. Lamme, P. Schlenker, and H. Barnett: *Research Report of Parent Oriented Home-Based Early Childhood Education Program* (Gainesville, Fla.: University of Florida, Institute for Development of Human Resources, 1975).

Heil, L. M., and C. Washburne: "Characteristics of Teachers Related to Children's Progress," *Journal of Teacher Education,* vol. 12, pp. 401–406, 1961.

Hobbs, N.: *The Futures of Children* (San Francisco: Jossey-Bass, 1975).

Jersild, A. T.: "Characteristics of Teachers Who Are 'Liked Best' and 'Disliked Most,'" *Journal of Experimental Education,* vol. 9, pp. 139–151, 1940.

Keniston, K.: "The 11-Year-Olds of Today Are the Computer Terminals of Tomorrow," *New York Times,* Feb. 19, 1976.

Mercer, J. R.: "Institutionalized Anglocentrism: Labeling Mental Retardates in the Public Schools," in P. Orleans, W. Russell, Jr. (eds.), *Race, Change, and Urban Society,* Urban Affairs Annual Review, vol. 5 (Los Angeles: Sage Publications, 1971).

———: *Labeling the Mentally Retarded* (Berkeley: University of California Press, 1973).

———: "Pluralistic Diagnosis in the Evaluation of Black and Chicano Children: A Procedure for Taking Sociocultural Variables into Account in Clinical Assessment," *California School Psychology,* vol. 19, no. 1, pp. 23–28, 1971. Reprinted in N. N. Wagner et al. (eds.), *Chicanos: Social and Psychological Perspectives,* 2d ed. (St. Louis: Mosby, 1975).

———: "Psychological Assessment and the Rights of Children," in N. Hobbs (ed.), *The Classification of Children,* vol. 1 (San Francisco: Jossey-Bass, 1975).

———: "Sociocultural Factors in Educational Labeling," in M. J. Begab and S. A. Richardson (eds.), *The Mentally Retarded and Society: A Social Science Perspective* (Baltimore: University Park Press, 1975).

Mussen, P. H., J. J. Conger, and J. Kagan: *Child Development and Personality* (New York: Harper & Row, 1969).

Rosenthal, R., and L. Jacobson: *Pygmalion in the Classroom* (New York: Holt, 1968).

———, ———: "Teacher's Expectancies: Determinants of Pupils' IQ Gains," *Psychological Reports,* vol. 19, pp. 115–118, 1966.

Tapp, J. L., and F. J. Levine: "Persuasion to Virtue: A Preliminary Statement," *Law and Society Review,* vol. 4, pp. 565–582, May 1970.

Williams, G. J.: "Violence against Children," *Journal of Clinical Child Psychology,* vol. 2, no. 3, p. 2, Fall 1973.

CHAPTER 10

Bandura, A., J. E. Grusec, and F. L. Menlove: "Vicarious Extinction of Avoidance Behavior," *Journal of Personality and Social Psychology,* vol. 5, pp. 16–23, 1967.

———, and F. L. Menlove: "Factors in Symbolic Modeling," *Journal of Personality and Social Psychology,* vol. 8, pp. 81–84, 1968.

Coleman, J. S.: *The Adolescent Society* (New York: Free Press, 1961).

Cowen, E. L., A. Pederson, H. Babigian, L. D. Izzo, and M. A. Trost: "Long-Term Follow-up of Early Detected Vulnerable Children," *Journal of Consulting and Clinical Psychology,* vol. 41, no. 3, pp. 438–446, 1973.

Freud, A., and S. Dann: "An Experiment in Group Upbringing," in R. Eisler et al. (eds.), *The Psychoanalytic Study of the Child,* vol. 6 (New York: International Universities Press, 1951), pp. 127–163.

Grosser, D., N. Polansky, and R. Lippitt: "A Laboratory Study of Behavioral Contagion," *Human Relations,* vol. 4, pp. 115–142, 1951.

Hamburg, D. A., J. van Lawick-Goodall: "Factors Facilitating Development of Aggressive Behavior in Chimpanzees and Humans," in W. W. Hartup and J. de Wit (eds.), *Determinants and Origins of Aggressive Behavior* (The Hague: Mouton, 1974).

Harlow, H. F.: "Age-mate or Peer Affectional System," in D. S. Lehrman, R. A. Hinde, and E. Shaw (eds.), *Advances in the Study of Behavior,* vol. 2 (New York: Academic, 1969), pp. 333–383.

———: "The Nature of Love," *American Psychologist,* vol. 13, pp. 673–685, 1958.

———: "Speaking of Love: Theory and Therapy," a two-cassette album and manual (New York: McGraw-Hill, 1974).

Hartup, W. W.: "Patterns of Imitative Behavior in Young Children," *Child Development*, vol. 35, 1964), pp. 183–191.

———: "Peer Interaction and the Behavioral Development of the Individual Child," in E. Schopler (ed.), *Proceedings of the First International Leo Kanner Colloquium on Child Development, Deviations and Treatment*, Plenum, New York, 1975.

———: "Peer Interaction and the Behavioral Development of the Individual Child," in E. Schopler and R. J. Reichler (eds.), *Psychopathology and Child Development* (New York: Plenum, 1976), pp. 203–218.

———: "Peer Interaction and Social Organization," in P. H. Mussen (ed.), *Carmichael's Manual of Child Psychology*, vol. 2 (New York: Wiley, 1970), pp. 361–456.

———: "Peers as Agents of Social Reinforcement," in W. W. Hartup and N. L. Smothergill (eds.), *The Young Child: Reviews of Research* (Washington, D.C.: National Association for the Education of Young Children, 1967), pp. 214–228.

———, and B. Coates: "Imitation of a Peer as a Function of Reinforcement from the Peer Group and Rewardingness of the Model," *Child Development*, vol. 38, pp. 1003–1016, 1967.

———, and M. D. Lougee: "Peer Interactions," *School Psychologist*, vol. 4, pp. 11–21, 1975.

Hicks, D. J.: "Imitation and Retention of Film-Mediated Aggressive Peer and Adult Models," *Journal of Personality and Social Psychology*, vol. 2, pp. 97–100, 1965.

Kinsey, A. C., W. B. Pomeroy, and C. W. Martin: *Sexual Behavior in the Human Male* (Philadelphia: Saunders, 1948).

Kobasigawa, A.: "Observationally Induced Disinhibition of Inappropriately Sex-Typed Responses in Young Children," *Japanese Journal of Educational Psychology*, vol. 14, pp. 9–14, 1966.

Kohlberg, L.: "The Development of Children's Orientations toward a Moral Order: I, Sequence in the Development of Moral Thought," *Vita Humana*, vol. 6, pp. 11–33, 1963.

———: "Development of Moral Character and Moral Ideology," in M. L. Hoffman and L. W. Hoffman (eds.), *Review of Child Development Research*, vol. 1 (New York: Russell Sage, 1964), pp. 383–431.

Mussen, P. H., J. J. Conger, and J. Kagan: *Child Development and Personality* (New York: Harper & Row, 1969).

Patterson, G. R., R. A. Littman, and W. Bricker: "Assertive Behavior in Children: A Step toward a Theory of Aggression," *Monographs of the Society for Research in Child Development*, vol. 32, no. 5, pp. 1–43, 1967.

Piaget, J.: *The Moral Judgment of the Child* (New York: The Free Press, 1965).

Riley, M. W., J. W. Riley, and M. W. Moore: "Adolescent Values and the Riesman Typology: An Empirical Analysis," in S. M. Lipset and L. Lowenthal (eds.), *Culture and Social Character, the Work of David Riesman Reviewed* (New York: Free Press, 1961), pp. 370–385.

Roff, M.: "Childhood Social Interactions and Young Adult Bad Conduct," *Journal of Abnormal and Social Psychology*, vol. 63, pp. 333–337, 1961.

———: "Childhood Social Interaction and Young Adult Psychosis," *Journal of Clinical Psychology*, vol. 19, pp. 152–157, 1963.

———: "Some Childhood and Adolescent Characteristics of Adult Homosexuals," *U.S. Army Medical Research and Development Command*, Report 66-5, May 1966.

————, and S. B. Sells: "Juvenile Delinquency in Relation to Peer Acceptance-Rejection and Socioeconomic Status," *Psychology in the Schools*, vol. 5, pp. 3–18, 1968.

Soumi, S. J., and H. F. Harlow: "Social Rehabilitation of Isolate-reared Monkeys," *Developmental Psychology*, vol. 6, pp. 487–496, 1972.

Sullivan, H. S.: *The Interpersonal Theory of Psychiatry* (New York: Norton, 1953).

Westley, W. A., and F. Elkin: "The Protective Environment and Adolescent Socialization," *Social Forces*, vol. 35, pp. 243–249, 1956.

CHAPTER 11

Anthony, E. J.: "The Vulnerable Child as Seen by the Child Psychiatrist," paper presented to the International Association for Child Psychiatry and Allied Professions, Philadelphia, Pa., July 1974.

Birch, H. G.: "Malnutrition, Learning, and Intelligence," *American Journal of Public Health*, vol. 62, no. 6, pp. 773–784, June 1972.

Bronfenbrenner, U., B. D. Goodson, and R. D. Hess: "A Report on Longitudinal Evaluations of Preschool Programs, Vol. 2, Is Early Intervention Effective?" Washington, D.C.: Department of Health, Education, and Welfare, Publication No. (OHD) 74-25, 1974.

Chase, H. P., and H. P. Martin: "Undernutrition and Child Development," *The New England Journal of Medicine*, vol. 282, no. 17, pp. 933–939, April 23, 1970.

Clark, K. B., and M. K. Clark: "The Development of Consciousness of Self and Emergence of Racial Identification in Negro Preschool Children," in R. Wilcox (ed.), *The Psychological Consequences of Being a Black American: A Sourcebook of Research by Black Psychologists* (New York: Wiley, 1971), pp. 323–331.

Clark, K. B.: *Dark Ghetto: Dilemmas of Social Power* (New York: Harper & Row, 1965).

————: "The Social Scientist, the Brown Decision, and Contemporary Confusion," *Foreword* (pp. xxxi–xlix), in L. Freidman (ed.), *Argument: The Oral Argument Before the Supreme Court in Brown vs. Board of Education, Topeka 1952–55* (New York: Chelsea House, 1969).

Dohrenwend, B. P., and B. S. Dohrenwend: *Social Status and Psychological Disorder: A Causal Inquiry* (New York: Wiley Interscience, 1969).

Eisenberg, L.: "If Not Now, When?" *The American Journal of Orthopsychiatry*, vol. 32, no. 5, pp. 781–783, October 1962.

Forum 15, "Children and Parents: Together in the World," *Report to the President of the White House Conference on Children, 1970* (Washington, D.C.: U.S. Government Printing Office, 1970), pp. 241–242.

Garmezy, N., "Vulnerability Research and the Issue of Primary Prevention," *American Journal of Orthopsychiatry*. vol. 41, pp. 101–116, 1971.

Gregory, D.: *nigger: An Autobiography* © 1964 by Dick Gregory Enterprises, Inc., reprinted by permission of the publisher E. P. Dutton.

Harrington, M.: *The Other America: Poverty in the United States* (Baltimore: Penguin 1963).

Hess, R. D.: "The Effects of Parent Training Programs on Child Performance and Parent Behavior," paper presented to the American Association for the Advancement of Science, Denver, February 1977.

Jensen, A.: "How Much Can We Boost IQ and Scholastic Achievement?" *Harvard Educational Review*, vol. 39, pp. 1–23, 1969.

Joint Commission on the Mental Health of Children, Inc.: *Crisis in Child Mental Health* (New York: Harper & Row, 1969).

Keniston, K.: "Do Americans Really Like Children?" *Childhood Education*, vol. 52, no. 1, pp. 4–12, October 1975.

————: "For Him, There is no Exit from the Cellar," *New York Times*, February 20, 1976.

Kimble, G. A., N. Garmezy, and E. Zigler: *Principles of General Psychology*, 4th ed. (New York: Ronald Press, 1974).

Kohn, M. L. *Class and Conformity: A Study in Values* (Homewood, Ill., Dorsey, 1969).

Kagan, J., R. B. Kearsley, and P. R. Zelazo: *Infancy: Its Place in Human Development* (Cambridge, Mass.: Harvard University Press, 1978).

Lewis, O.: "A Puerto Rican Boy," in J. C. Finney (ed.), *Culture Change, Mental Health, and Poverty* (Lexington: University of Kentucky Press, 1969), pp. 149–154.

Livingston, R. B., J. S. MacGregor, G. J. Fisher, D. H. Calloway, and A. B. Hastings: "Probabilities of Underdevelopment of the Human Brain as a Consequence of Undernutrition in the United States," paper presented to the Society for Neuroscience, New York, November 1975.

Looff, D.: "Assisting Appalachian Families," *Psychiatric Annals*, vol. 6, no. 5, pp. 15–35, May 1976.

Mead, M.: "The Once and Future Home," *The Washington Post*, July 4, 1976.

Moynihan, D. P.: "The Negro Family: The Case for National Action," in L. Rainwater and W. L. Yancy (eds.), *The Moynihan Report and the Politics of Controversy* (Cambridge, Mass.: The M.I.T. Press, 1967).

Pavenstedt, E.: "A Comparison of the Child-Rearing Environment of Upper-Lower and Very Low-Lower Class Families," *American Journal of Orthopsychiatry*, vol. 35, no. 1, pp. 89–98, 1965.

Proshansky, H., and P. Newton: "The Development of Negro Self-Identity," in M. Deutsch, A. Jensen, and I. Katz, *Race and Social Class in Psychological Development* (New York: Holt, 1968).

Rainwater, L.: "Crucible of Identity: The Negro Lower Class Family," *Daedalus*, vol. 95, no. 1, pp. 172–216, Winter 1966.

Raspberry, W.: "The Coping Skills of Ghetto Children," *The Washington Post*, March 24, 1973.

Read, M. S.: "The Biological Bases: Malnutrition and Behavioral Development," *Early Childhood Education*, The National Society for the Study of Education, pp. 55–59, (Chicago: University of Chicago Press, 1972).

Report of the National Advisory Commission on Civil Disorders (New York: Bantam Books, 1968).

Rogler, L. H., and A. B. Hollingshead: *Trapped: Families and Schizophrenia* (New York: Wiley, 1965).

Rosenberg, M., and R. Simmons: *Black and White Self-Esteem: The Urban School Child* (Washington, D.C.: American Sociological Association, 160 pp., 1971).

Scarr, S., and Weinberg, R. A.: "IQ Test Performance of Black Children Adopted by White Families," *American Psychologist*, vol. 31, no. 10, pp. 726–739, October 1976.

Silverstein, B., and R. Krate: *Children of the Dark Ghetto: A Developmental Psychology* (New York: Praeger, 1975).

Sowell, T.: "New Light on Black IQ," *New York Times Magazine*, March 27, 1977.

Spurlock, J.: "Some Consequences of Racism for Children," in C. V. Willie, B. M. Kramer, and B. S. Brown (eds.), *Racism and Mental Health* (Pittsburgh: University of Pittsburgh Press, 1973).

Steele, B.: "Psychological Dimensions of Child Abuse," paper presented to American Association for the Advancement of Science, Denver, February 1977.

Toward Quality Education for Mexican Americans (Report VI: Mexican American Education Study) (Washington, D.C.: U.S. Commission on Civil Rights, 98 pp., 1974).

Watson, J. S.: "Cognitive-Perceptual Development in Infancy: Setting for the Seventies," *Merrill-Palmer Quarterly*, vol. 17, pp. 139–152, 1971.

Welsing, F.: "Telling a Black Child About Racism," *The Washington Post*, September 9, 1973.

CHAPTER 12

Anthony, E. J.: "A Clinical and Experimental Study of High Risk Children and Their Schizophrenic Parents," in A. Kaplan (ed.), *Genetic Factors in Schizophrenia* (Springfield, Ill.: Charles C Thomas, 1971).

———: "A Risk-Vulnerability Intervention Model for Children of Psychotic Parents," in E. J. Anthony and C. Koupernik (eds.), *The Child in His Family: Children at Psychiatric Risk*, vol. 3, (New York: Wiley, 1974).

———: "A New Scientific Region to Explore," in E. J. Anthony and C. Koupernik (eds.), *The Child in His Family: The Vulnerable Child* (New York: Wiley, in press).

Bleuler, M.: "The Offspring of Schizophrenics." *Schizophrenia Bulletin*, no. 8, pp. 93–107, Spring 1974.

Cagney, J.: *Cagney by Cagney* (New York: Doubleday, 1976).

Coleman, J. S., E. Campbell, C. Hobson, J. McPartland, A. Mood, F. Weinfeld, and R. York.: *Equality of Educational Opportunity* (Washington, D.C.: Government Printing Office, 1966).

Ekstein, R.: "Residual Trauma-Variations on or About a Theme." *Issues in Child Mental Health: A Journal of Psychosocial Process.* in press.

Epps, E. G.: *Family and Achievement: A Study of the Relation of Family Background to Achievement Orientation and Performance Among Urban Negro High School Students*, Final Report of Contract No. OE-6-85-017, Survey Research Center, University of Michigan, Ann Arbor, Michigan, 1969.

Garmezy, N.: "Competence and Adaptation in Adult Schizophrenic Patients and Children at Risk," in S. R. Dean (ed.), *Schizophrenia: The First Ten Dean Award Lectures* (New York: MSS Publications, 1973), pp. 163–204.

———, and K. Nuechterlein: "Invulnerable Children: The Fact and Fiction of Competence and Disadvantage," paper presented to American Orthopsychiatric Association, Detroit, Michigan, April 1972.

———: "Intervention with Children at Risk for Behavior Pathology," *The Clinical Psychologist*, vol. 28, no. 2, pp. 12–13, 1975.

———: "Vulnerability Research and the Issue of Primary Prevention," *American Journal of Orthopsychiatry*, vol. 41, pp. 101–116, 1971.

———: "Vulnerable Children: Implications Derived from Studies of an Internalizing-Externalizing Symptom Dimension," in J. Zubin and A. M. Freedman (eds.), *Psychopathology of Adolescence* (New York: Grune and Stratton, 1970), pp. 212–239.

———, with the collaboration of S. Streitman, "Children at Risk: The Search for the Antecedents of Schizophrenia. Part 1. Conceptual Models and Research Methods," *Schizophrenia Bulletin*, no. 8, pp. 14–90, National Institute of Mental Health, DHEW Publication No. (ADM) 77-145, Rockville, Md., Spring 1974.

———: "The Study of Competence in Children at Risk for Severe Psychopathology," in E. J. Anthony and C. Koupernik (eds.), *Children at Psychiatric Risk* (New York: Wiley, in press).

—— and K. H. Nuechterlein: "Invulnerable Children: The Fact and Fiction of Competence and Disadvantage." (abstract) *American Journal of Orthopsychiatry*, vol. 77, pp. 328–329, 1972.

——: "Children at Risk: The Search for the Antecedents of Schizophrenia. Part II: Ongoing Research Programs, Issues, and Intervention," *Schizophrenia Bulletin*, vol. 9, pp. 55–125, National Institute of Mental Health, DHEW Publication (ADM) 75-145, Rockville, Md., Summer 1974.

Goertzel, V., and Goertzel, M. G.: *Cradles of Eminence* (Boston: Little, Brown, 1962).

Hagin, R. A., A. A. Silver, and C. G. Corwin: "Scanning School Samples for Vulnerable Children," paper presented to American Psychological Association, New Orleans, La., August/September 1974.

Honzik, M. P.: "Consistency and Change in Intellectual Functioning and Personality Characteristics During the Life Span," *Abstract Guide of XXth International Congress of Psychology*, Tokyo, 1972.

——: "Environmental Correlates of Mental Growth: Prediction From the Family Setting at 21 Months," *Child Development*, vol. 38, pp. 337–363, 1967.

——, and J. W. Macfarlane: "Personality Development and Intellectual Functioning From 21 Months to 40 Years," in L. F. Jarvik, C. Eisdorfer, and J. E. Blum (eds.), *Intellectual Functioning in Adults: Psychological and Biological Influences* (New York: Springer, 1973), pp. 45–58.

Jansky, J., and K. DeHirsch: *Preventing Reading Failure: Prediction, Diagnosis, Intervention* (New York: Harper & Row, 1972).

Lander, H. S., E. J. Anthony, L. Cass, L. Franklin, and L. Bass: "A Measure of Vulnerability to the Risk of Parental Psychosis," in E. J. Anthony and C. Koupernik (eds.), *The Child in His Family: The Vulnerable Child* (New York: Wiley, in press).

Levine, S., et al. (investigators): Research reported in G. Luce, "Hormones in the Development of Behavior," in *Program Reports No. 1*, National Institute of Mental Health, Public Health Service Publication 1568, pp. 37–58, Rockville, Md., 1967.

Macfarlane, J. W. "From Infancy to Adulthood." *Childhood Education*. vol. 39, pp. 336–342, 1963.

——: "Perspectives on Personality Consistency and Change from the Guidance Study," *Vita Humana*, vol. 7, no. 115, 1964.

——: "The Psychological Dilemmas of Adolescents," paper presented to American Academy of Pediatrics, New York City, April, 1967.

——, and M. P. Honzik (investigators): Research reported in H. Yahraes, "The Effect of Childhood Influences Upon Intelligence, Personality, and Mental Health," National Institute of Mental Health, *Mental Health Program Reports No. 3*, Public Health Service Publication 1876, Rockville, Md., 1969.

Meehan, T.: "Cruise Director on the Titanic." *New York Times Magazine*. pp. 10–26, Jan. 2, 1972.

Silver, A. A.: "The Learning Disorders Unit: A Review of Progress," *New York University Medical Quarterly*, vol. 30, no. 2, 1974.

——: "Early Signs of Delay in Learning," in I. N. Berlin (ed.), *Basic Handbook of Child Psychiatry*, in press.

——, and R. A. Hagin: "Developmental Language Disability Simulating Mental Retardation," *Journal of the American Academy of Child Psychology*, vol. 4, pp. 485–495, 1965.

——: "Profile of a First Grade: A Basis for Preventive Psychiatry," *Journal of the American Academy of Child Psychiatry*, vol. 11, no. 4, pp. 645–674, 1972.

————: "Fascinating Journey: Paths to the Prediction and Prevention of Reading Disability," *Bulletin of the Orton Society*, vol. 25, pp. 24–36, 1975.

———— and R. A. Hagin (investigators): Research reported in H. Yahraes and S. Prestwich, *Detection and Prevention of Learning Disorders*, National Institute of Mental Health, DHEW Publication (ADM) 77-337, Rockville, Md., 1976.

————, E. DeVito, H. Kreeger, and E. Scully. "A Search Battery for Scanning Kindergarten Children for Potential Learning Disability," *Journal of the American Academy of Child Psychiatry*, vol. 15, pp. 224–239, 1976.

Srole, L., T. S. Langner, S. T. Michael, M. K. Opler, and T. A. C. Rennie: *Mental Health in the Metropolis, the Midtown Manhattan Study*, (New York: McGraw-Hill, 1962).

CHAPTER 13

Brim, O. G.: "Macro-Structural Influences on Child Development and the Need for Childhood Social Indicators," *American Journal of Orthopsychiatry*, vol. 45, no. 4, pp. 516–524, July 1975.

Keniston, K., and the Carnegie Council on Children: *All Our Children* (New York: Harcourt Brace Jovanovich, 1977).

Steiner, G. Y.: *The Children's Cause* (Washington, D.C.: The Brookings Institution, 1976).

Toward a National Policy for Children and Families: National Research Council, National Academy of Sciences, Washington, D.C. 1976.

Zigler, E.: "The Future of Social Policy for Children," in *Notes from the Center* (#5), The Center on Human Policy, Syracuse, N.Y., November 1973.

Index

337

About the Authors

DR. JULIUS SEGAL is a psychologist and writer. He is director of the scientific and public information programs of the National Institute of Mental Health. Dr. Segal's articles on mental health have appeared in major national magazines for the past 25 years. His books and research reports have earned him The Science Writer's Award of the American Psychological Association, and the Superior Service Award of the U.S. government.

HERBERT YAHRAES is a free-lance writer who has been describing mental health research and other scientific efforts for over 30 years, many of them concerning children. His early work with the Associated Press and the newspaper *PM* won him a Nieman Fellowship at Harvard. He has received numerous citations for science writing and, with his wife, Dixie Yahraes, the Lasker Award for medical writing in magazines.